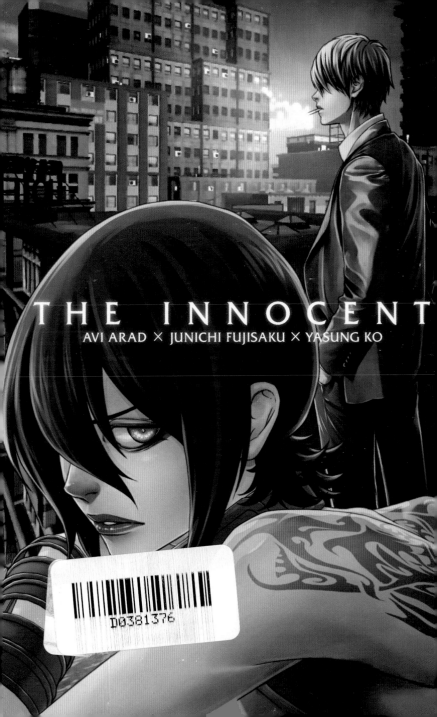

THE INNOCENT

AVI ARAD × JUNICHI FUJISAKU × YASUNG KO

CONTENTS

THE INNOCENT

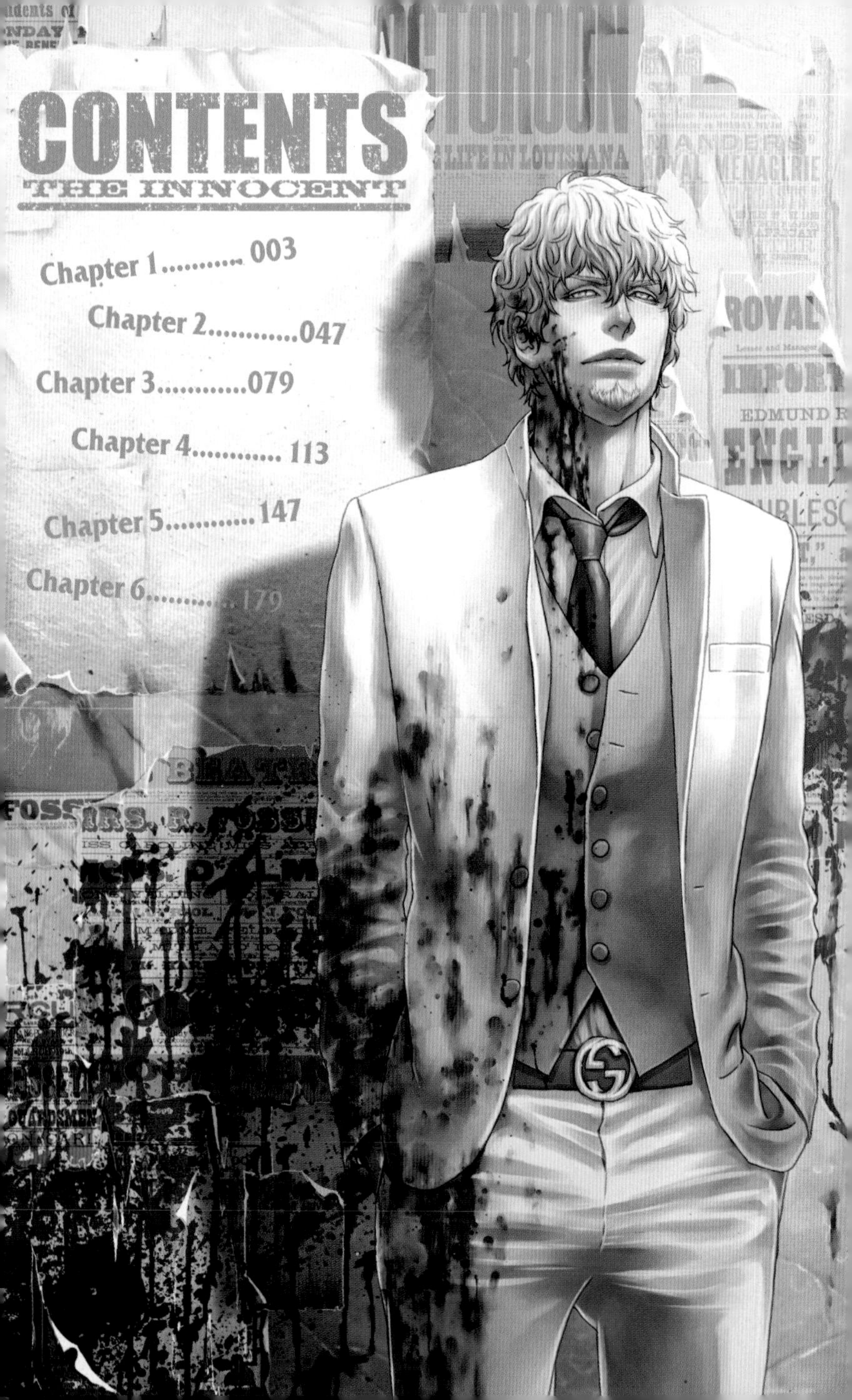

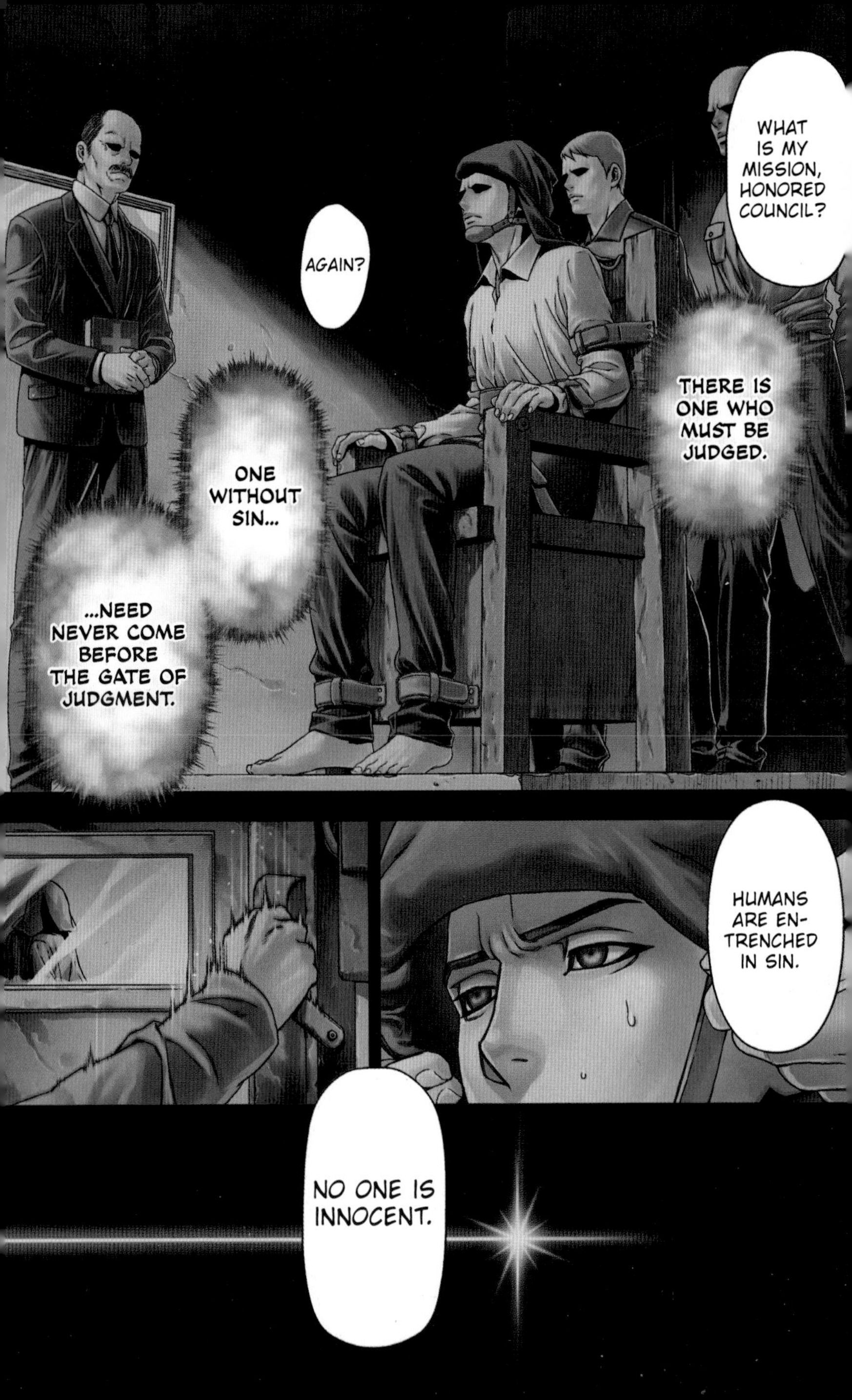
WHAT IS MY MISSION, HONORED COUNCIL?
AGAIN?
THERE IS ONE WHO MUST BE JUDGED.
ONE WITHOUT SIN...
...NEED NEVER COME BEFORE THE GATE OF JUDGMENT.
HUMANS ARE EN-TRENCHED IN SIN.
NO ONE IS INNOCENT.

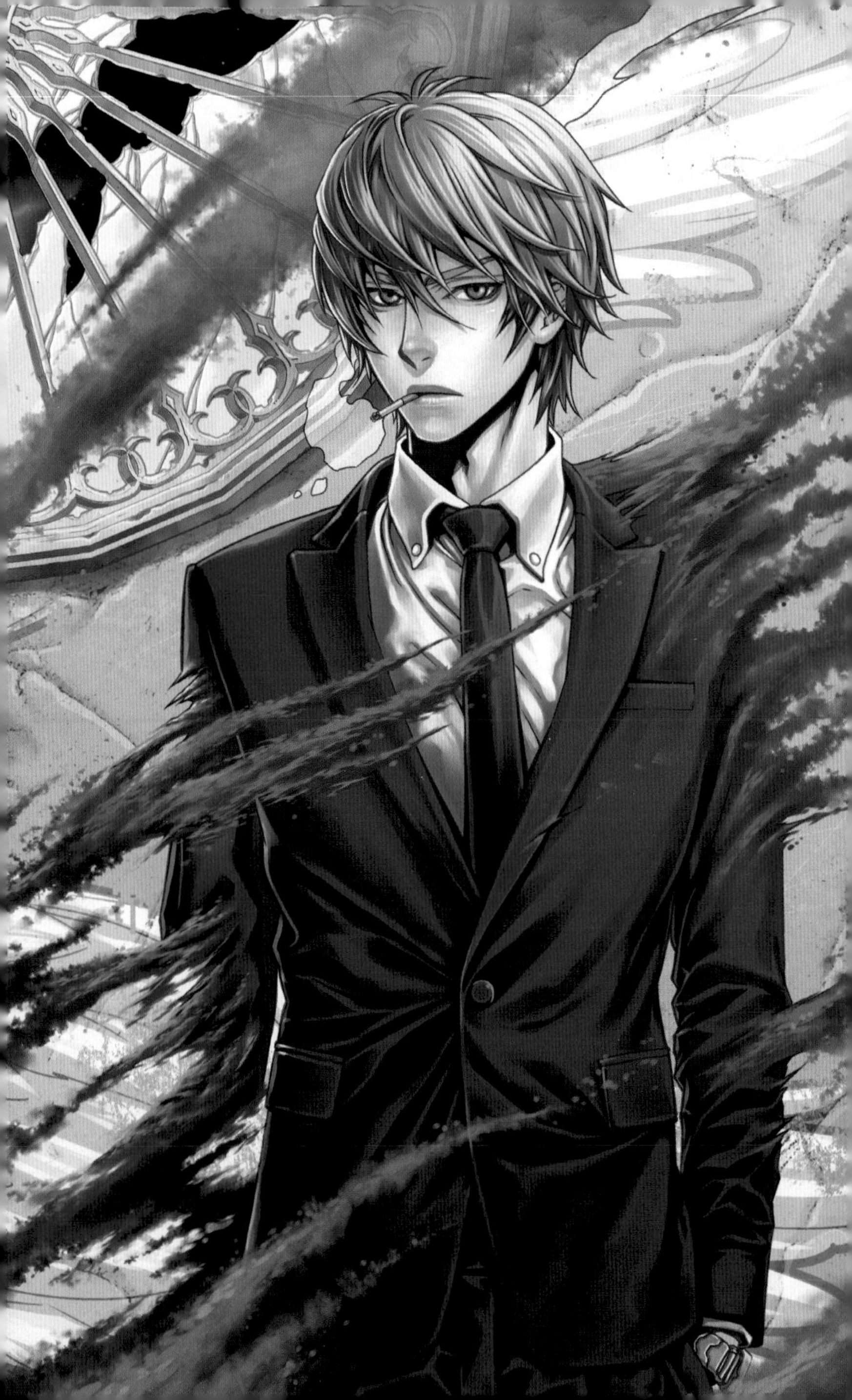

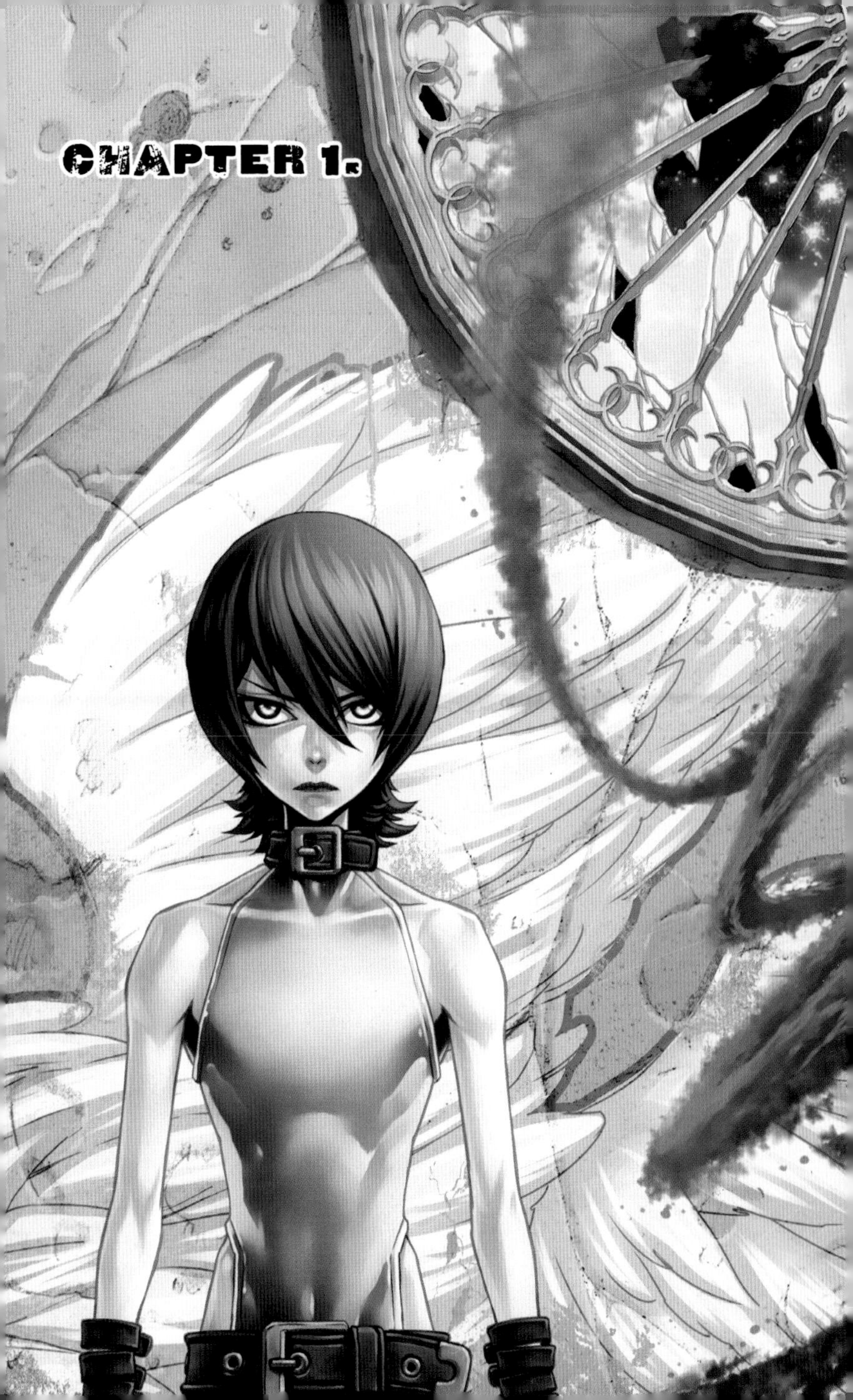
CHAPTER 1.

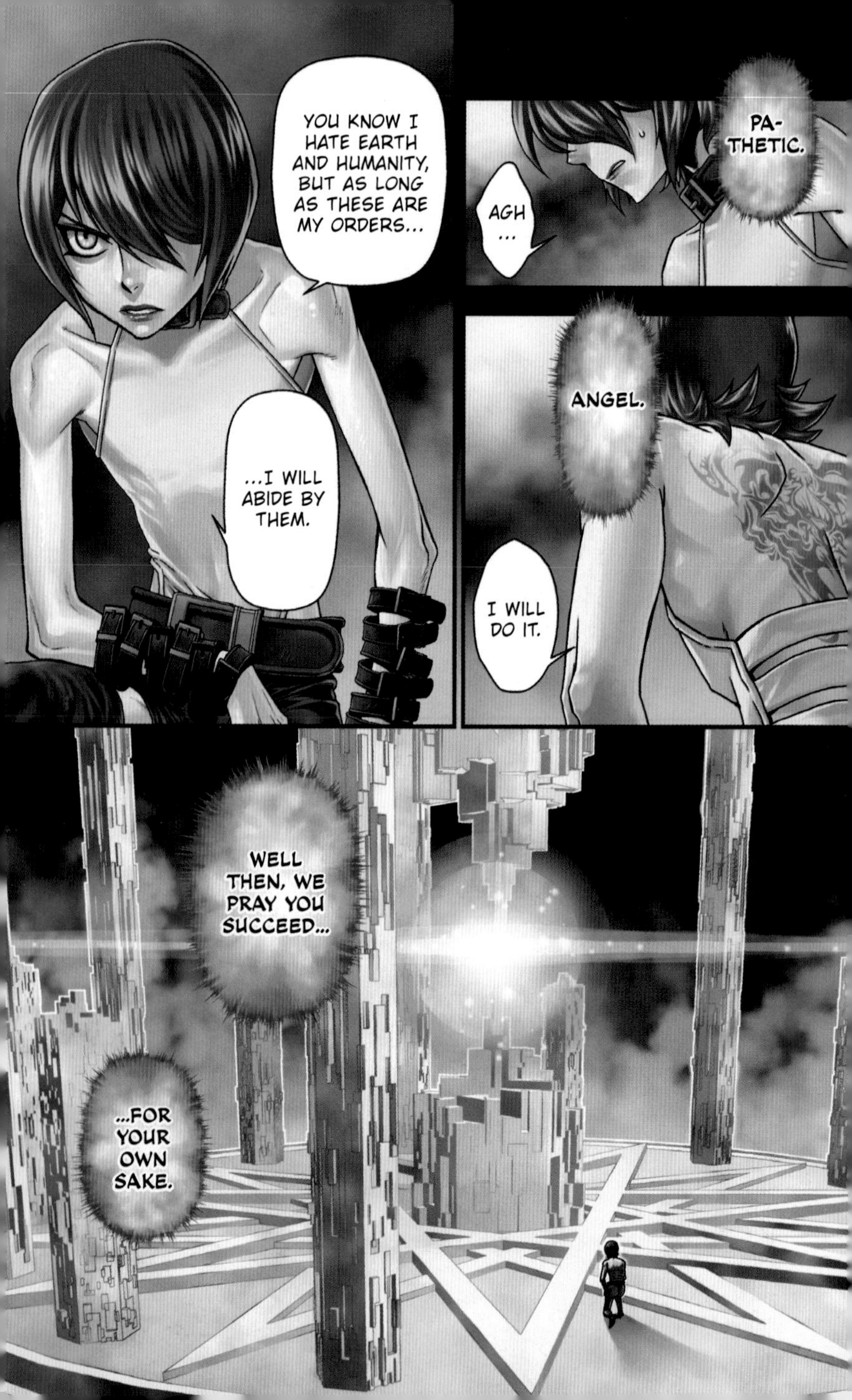
PA-THETIC.
AGH...
ANGEL.
I WILL DO IT.
YOU KNOW I HATE EARTH AND HUMANITY, BUT AS LONG AS THESE ARE MY ORDERS...
...I WILL ABIDE BY THEM.
WELL THEN, WE PRAY YOU SUCCEED...
...FOR YOUR OWN SAKE.

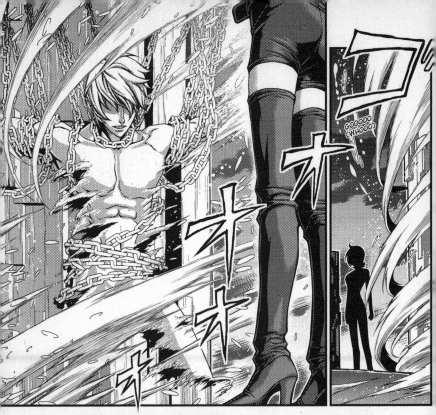

ゴ
ゴゴ

GOOOOO
(WHOOO)

ザ

ザ

ザ

ザ

...WHAT
IS
THIS?

HEY YOU!
PUT SOME-
THING ON,
WOULD
YOU?

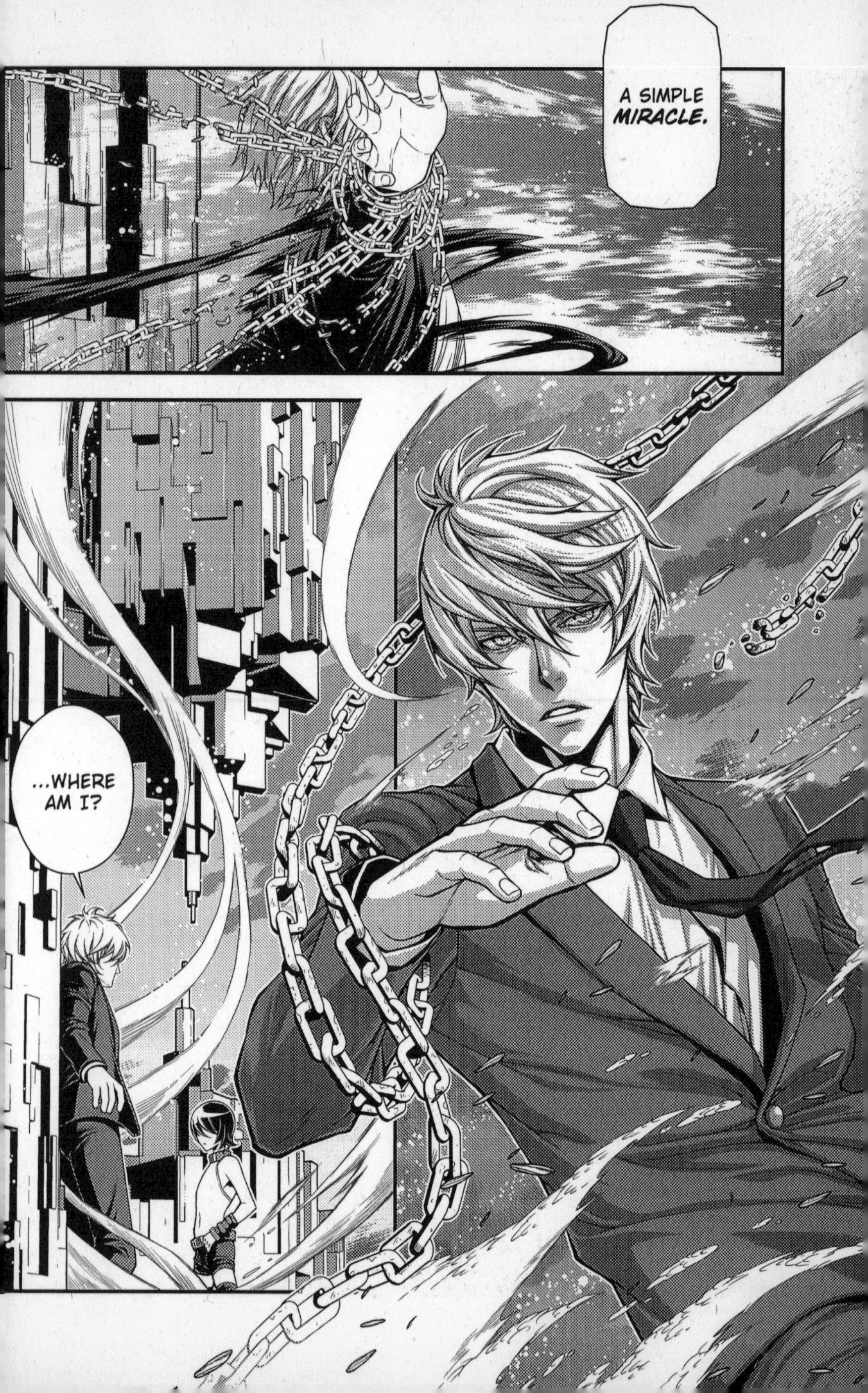
A SIMPLE MIRACLE.
...WHERE AM I?

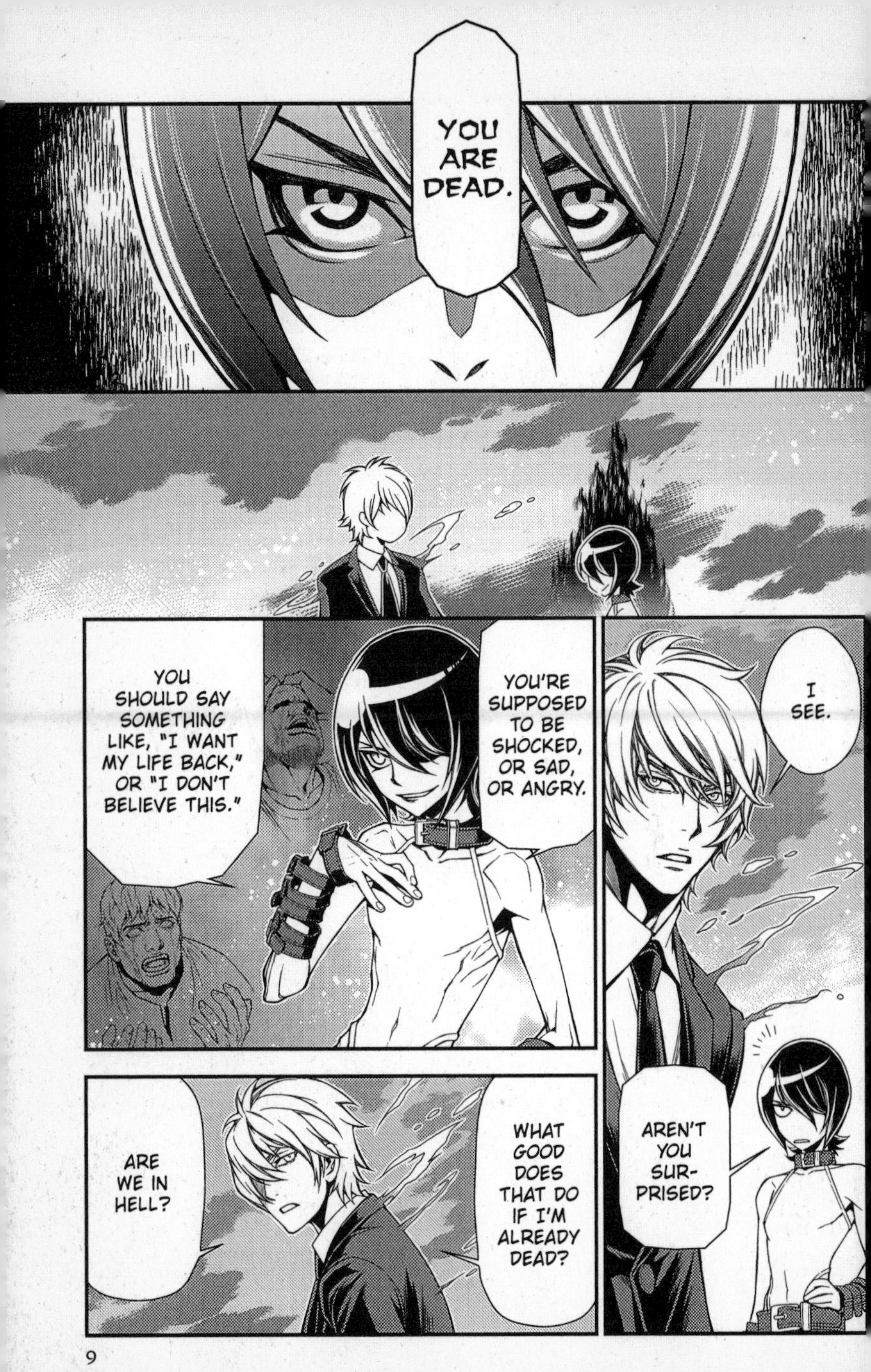
YOU ARE DEAD.
I SEE.
AREN'T YOU SURPRISED?
YOU'RE SUPPOSED TO BE SHOCKED, OR SAD, OR ANGRY.
YOU SHOULD SAY SOMETHING LIKE, "I WANT MY LIFE BACK," OR "I DON'T BELIEVE THIS."
WHAT GOOD DOES THAT DO IF I'M ALREADY DEAD?
ARE WE IN HELL?

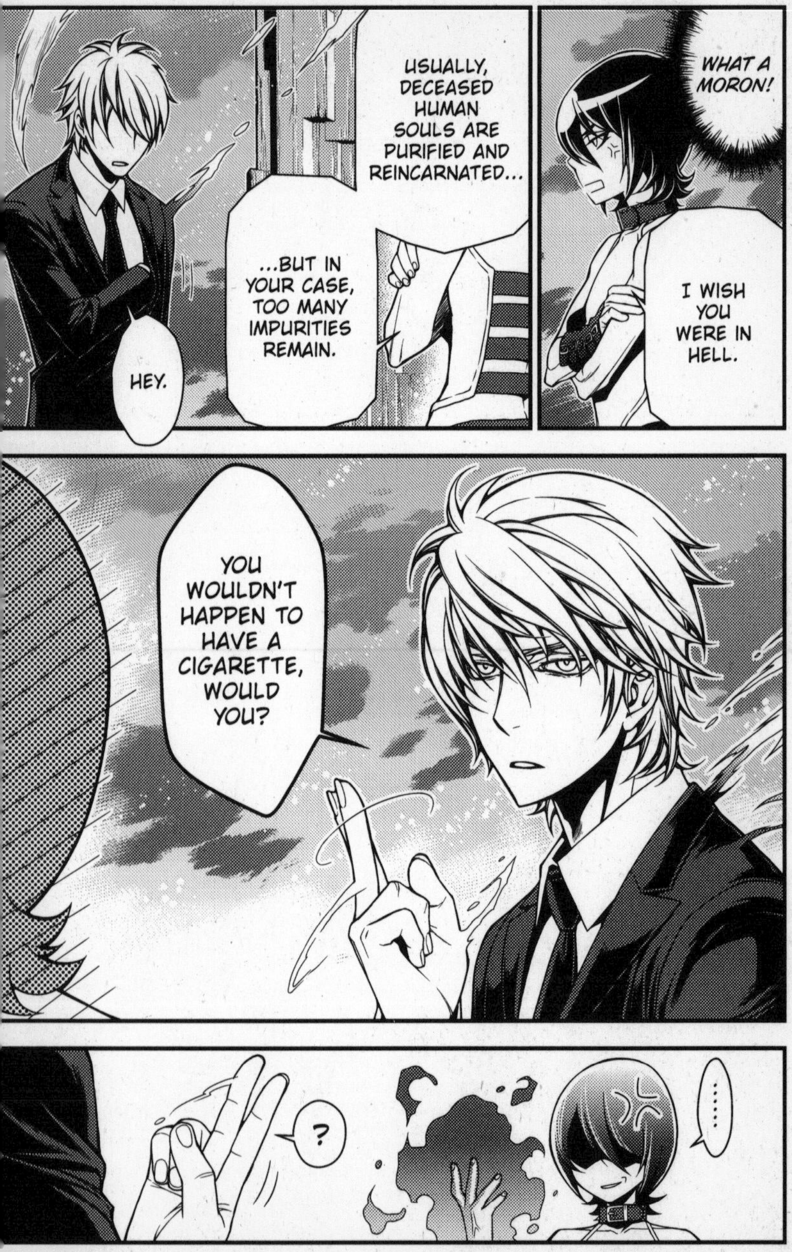
WHAT A MORON!
I WISH YOU WERE IN HELL.
USUALLY, DECEASED HUMAN SOULS ARE PURIFIED AND REINCARNATED...
...BUT IN YOUR CASE, TOO MANY IMPURITIES REMAIN.
HEY.
YOU WOULDN'T HAPPEN TO HAVE A CIGARETTE, WOULD YOU?
......
?

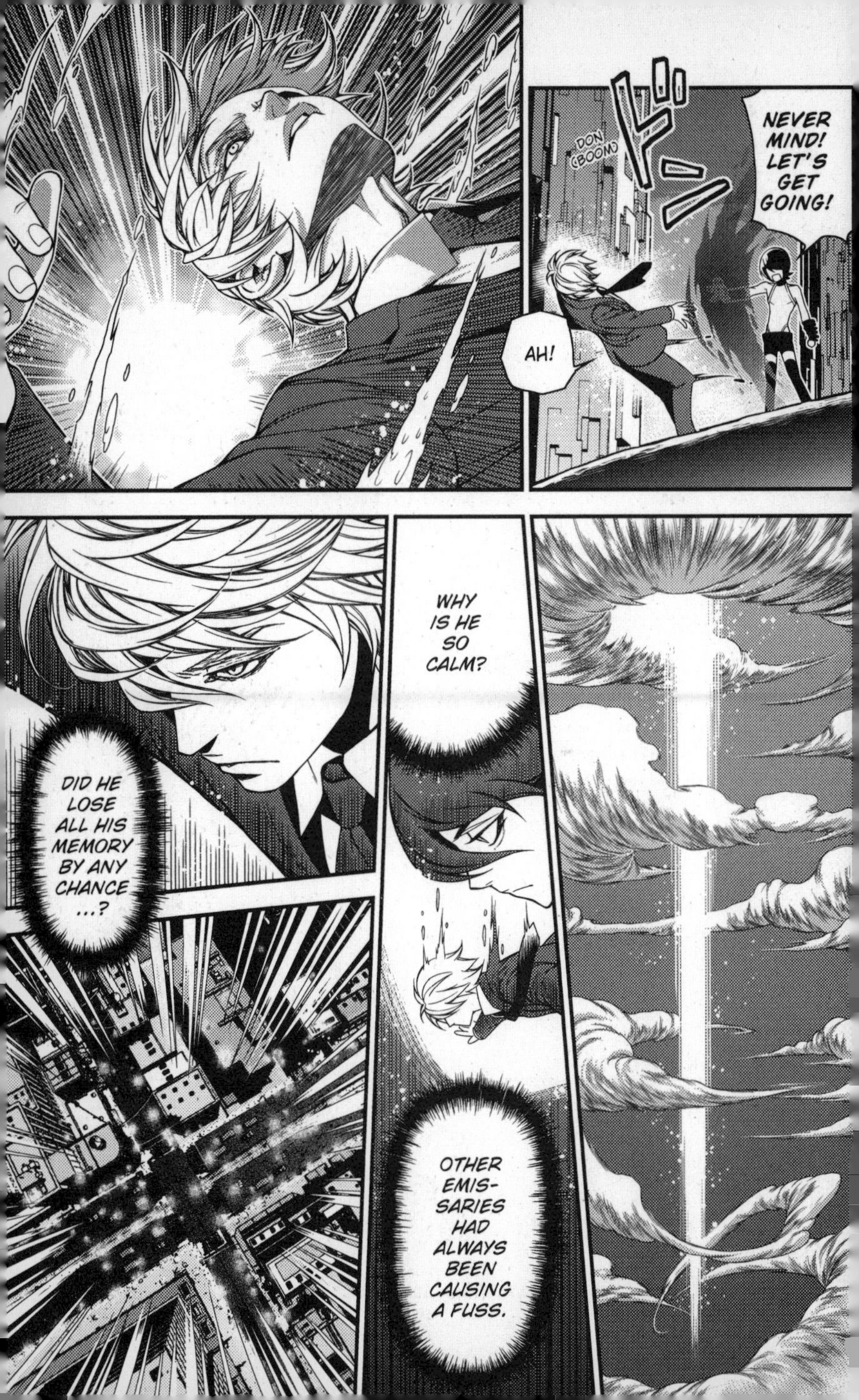
NEVER MIND! LET'S GET GOING!
DON (BOOM)
AH!
WHY IS HE SO CALM?
DID HE LOSE ALL HIS MEMORY BY ANY CHANCE ...?
OTHER EMIS-SARIES HAD ALWAYS BEEN CAUSING A FUSS.

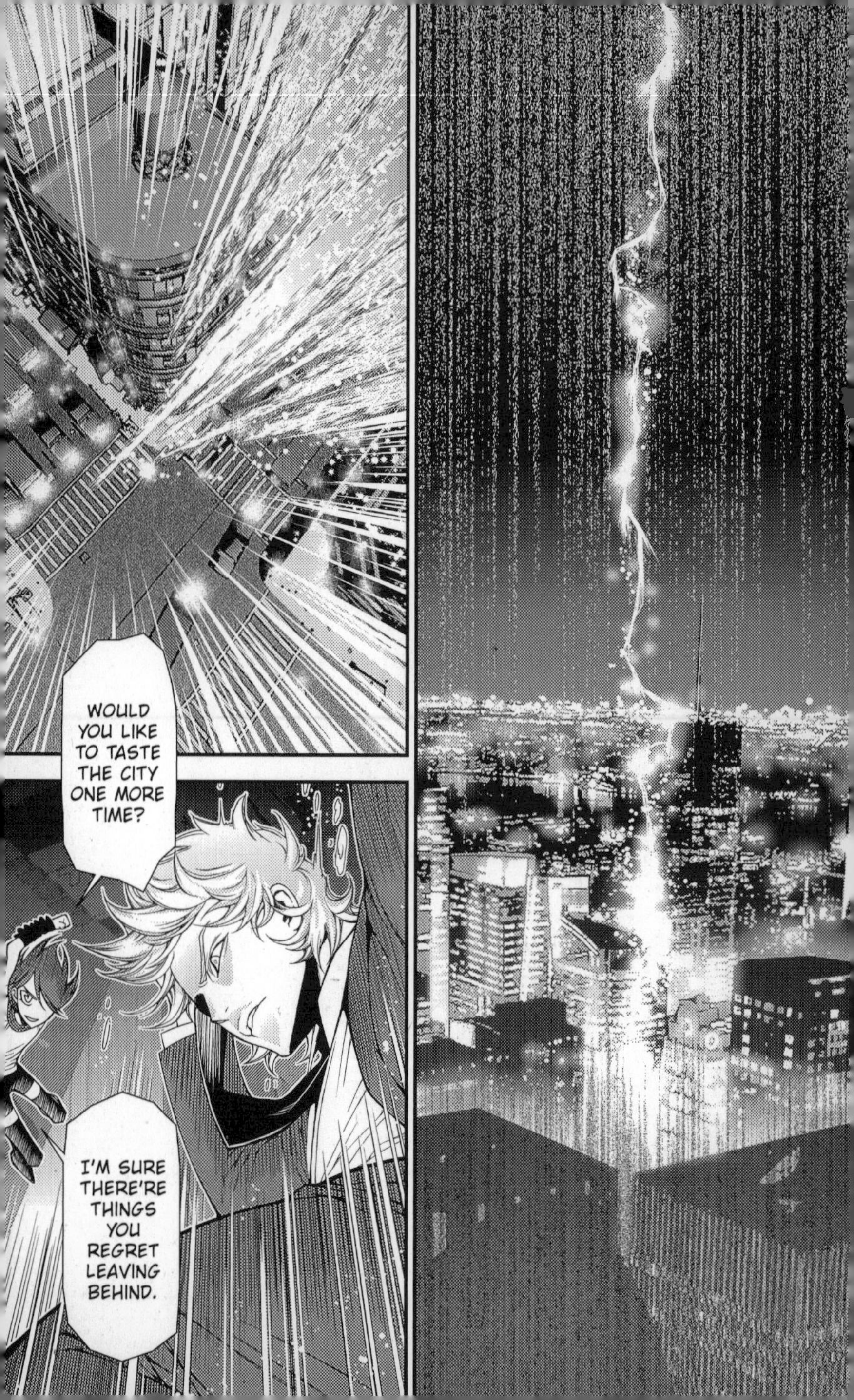

WOULD YOU LIKE TO TASTE THE CITY ONE MORE TIME?
I'M SURE THERE'RE THINGS YOU REGRET LEAVING BEHIND.

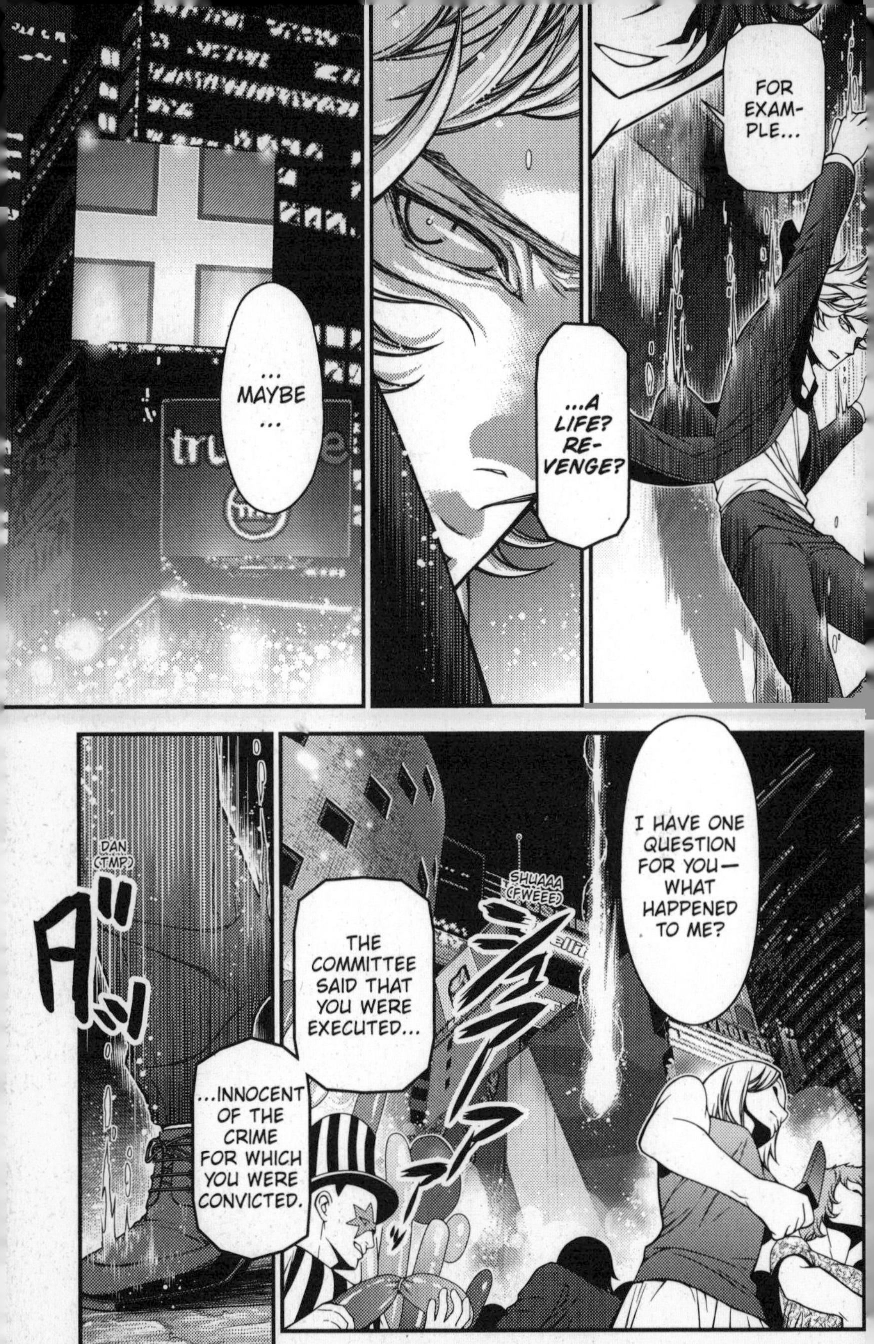
FOR EXAM-PLE...
...A LIFE? RE-VENGE?
...MAYBE...
I HAVE ONE QUESTION FOR YOU—WHAT HAPPENED TO ME?
SHUAAA (FWEEE)
THE COMMITTEE SAID THAT YOU WERE EXECUTED...
...INNOCENT OF THE CRIME FOR WHICH YOU WERE CONVICTED.
DAN (TMP)

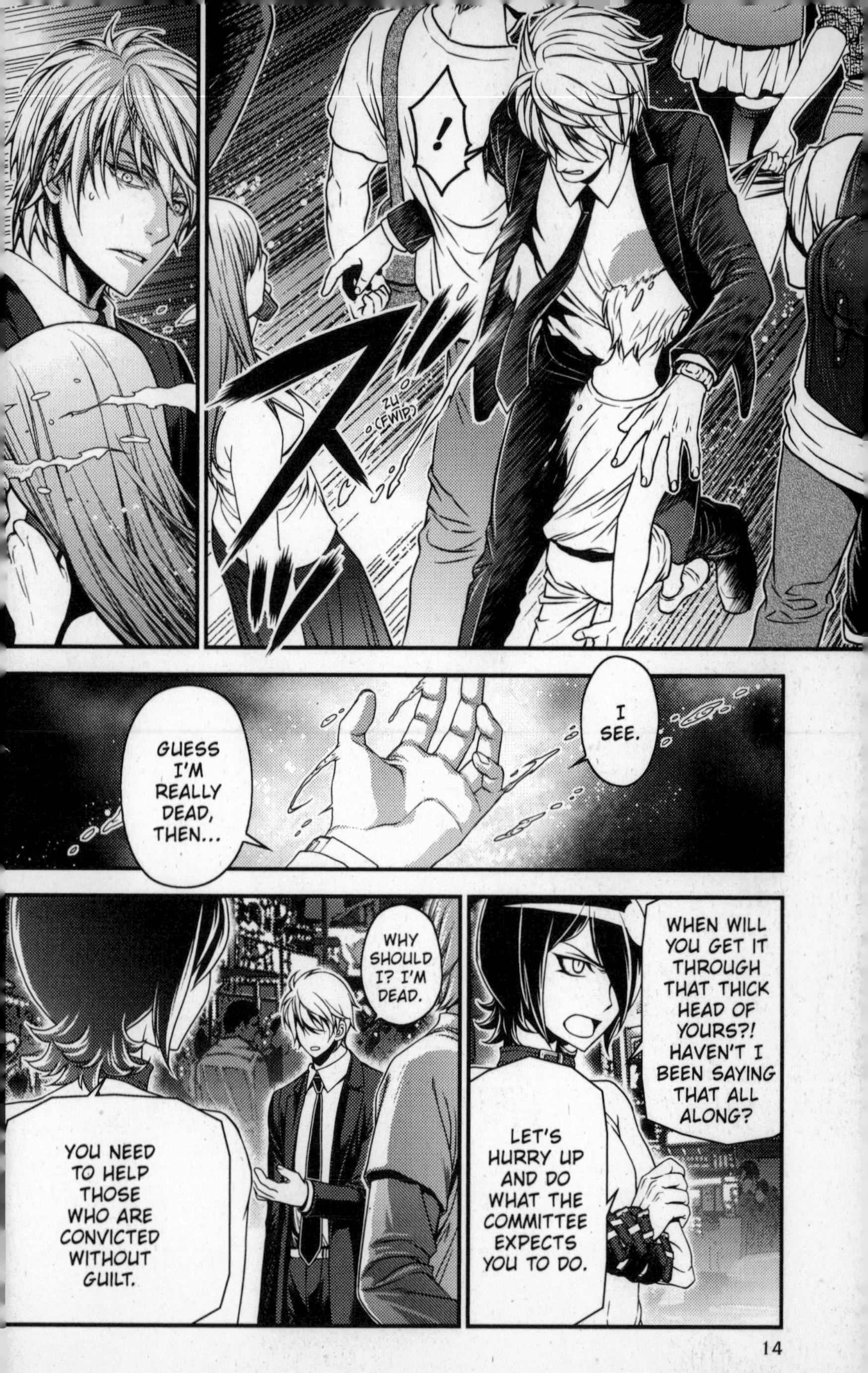
ZU (FWIP)
I SEE.
GUESS I'M REALLY DEAD, THEN...
WHEN WILL YOU GET IT THROUGH THAT THICK HEAD OF YOURS?! HAVEN'T I BEEN SAYING THAT ALL ALONG?
LET'S HURRY UP AND DO WHAT THE COMMITTEE EXPECTS YOU TO DO.
WHY SHOULD I? I'M DEAD.
YOU NEED TO HELP THOSE WHO ARE CONVICTED WITHOUT GUILT.

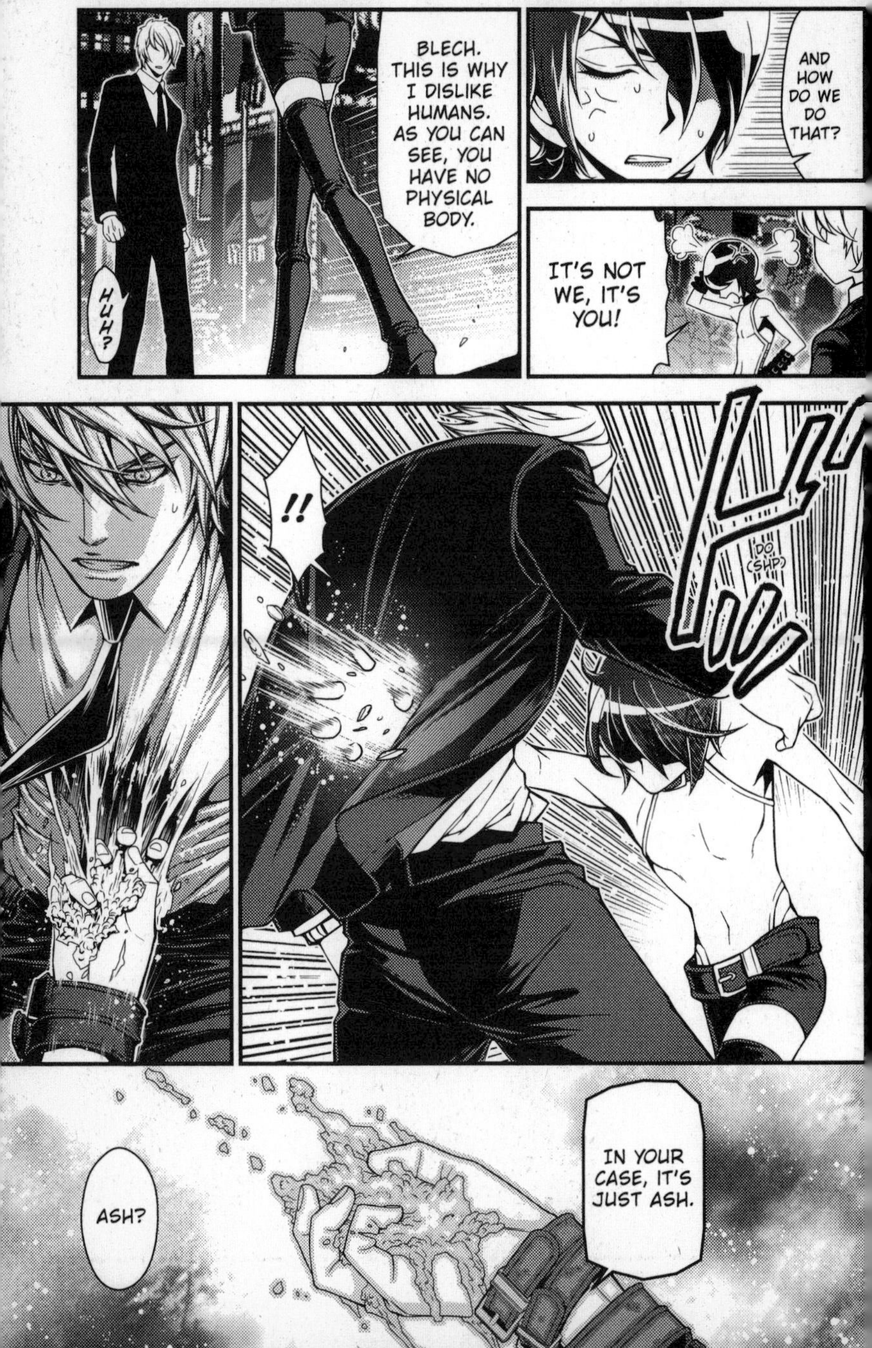
AND HOW DO WE DO THAT?
IT'S NOT WE, IT'S YOU!
BLECH. THIS IS WHY I DISLIKE HUMANS. AS YOU CAN SEE, YOU HAVE NO PHYSICAL BODY.
HUH?
!!
DO (SHP)
IN YOUR CASE, IT'S JUST ASH.
ASH?

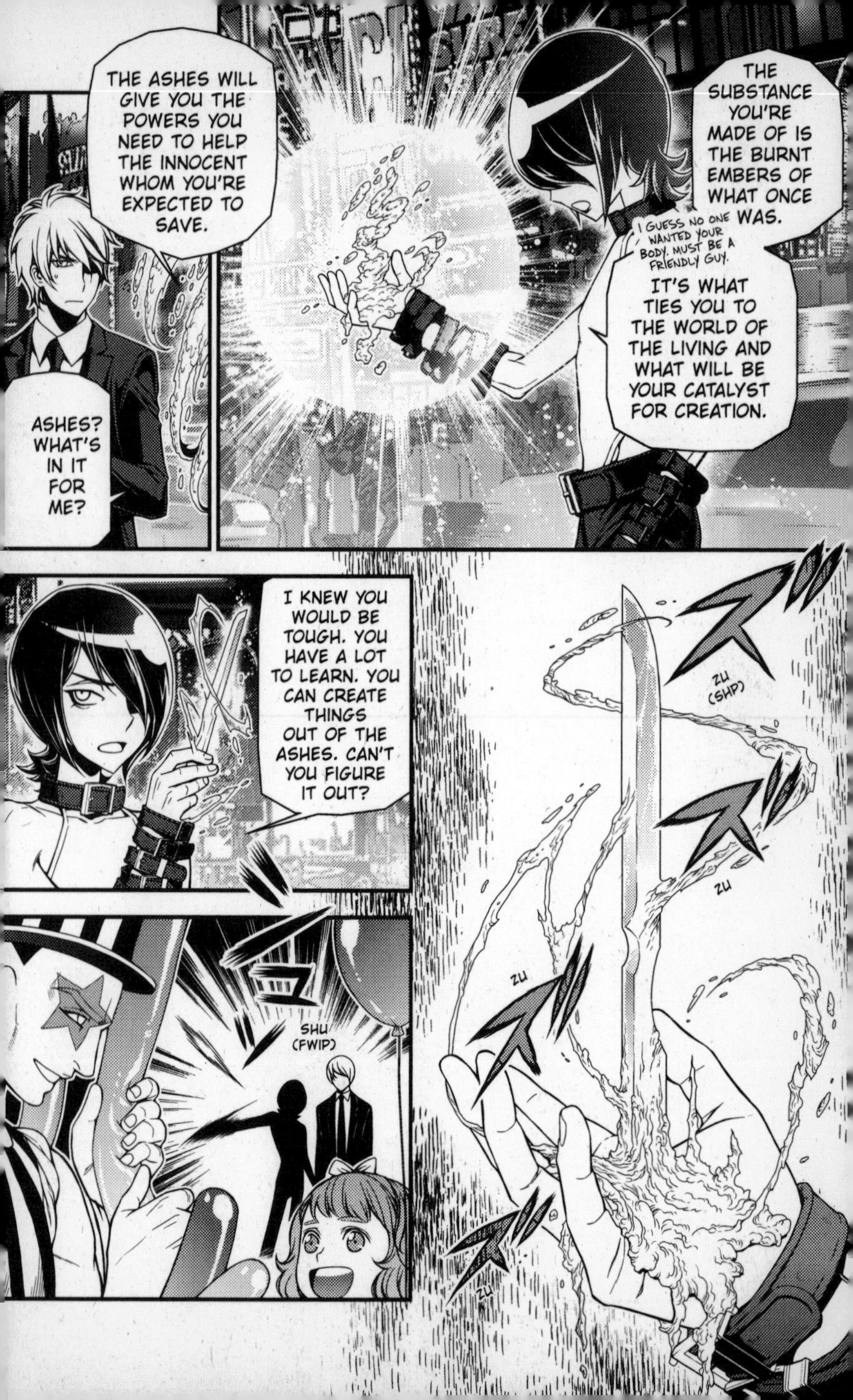
THE SUBSTANCE YOU'RE MADE OF IS THE BURNT EMBERS OF WHAT ONCE WAS.
I GUESS NO ONE WANTED YOUR BODY. MUST BE A FRIENDLY GUY.
IT'S WHAT TIES YOU TO THE WORLD OF THE LIVING AND WHAT WILL BE YOUR CATALYST FOR CREATION.
THE ASHES WILL GIVE YOU THE POWERS YOU NEED TO HELP THE INNOCENT WHOM YOU'RE EXPECTED TO SAVE.
ASHES? WHAT'S IN IT FOR ME?
ZU (SHP)
ZU
ZU
ZU
I KNEW YOU WOULD BE TOUGH. YOU HAVE A LOT TO LEARN. YOU CAN CREATE THINGS OUT OF THE ASHES. CAN'T YOU FIGURE IT OUT?
SHU (FWIP)

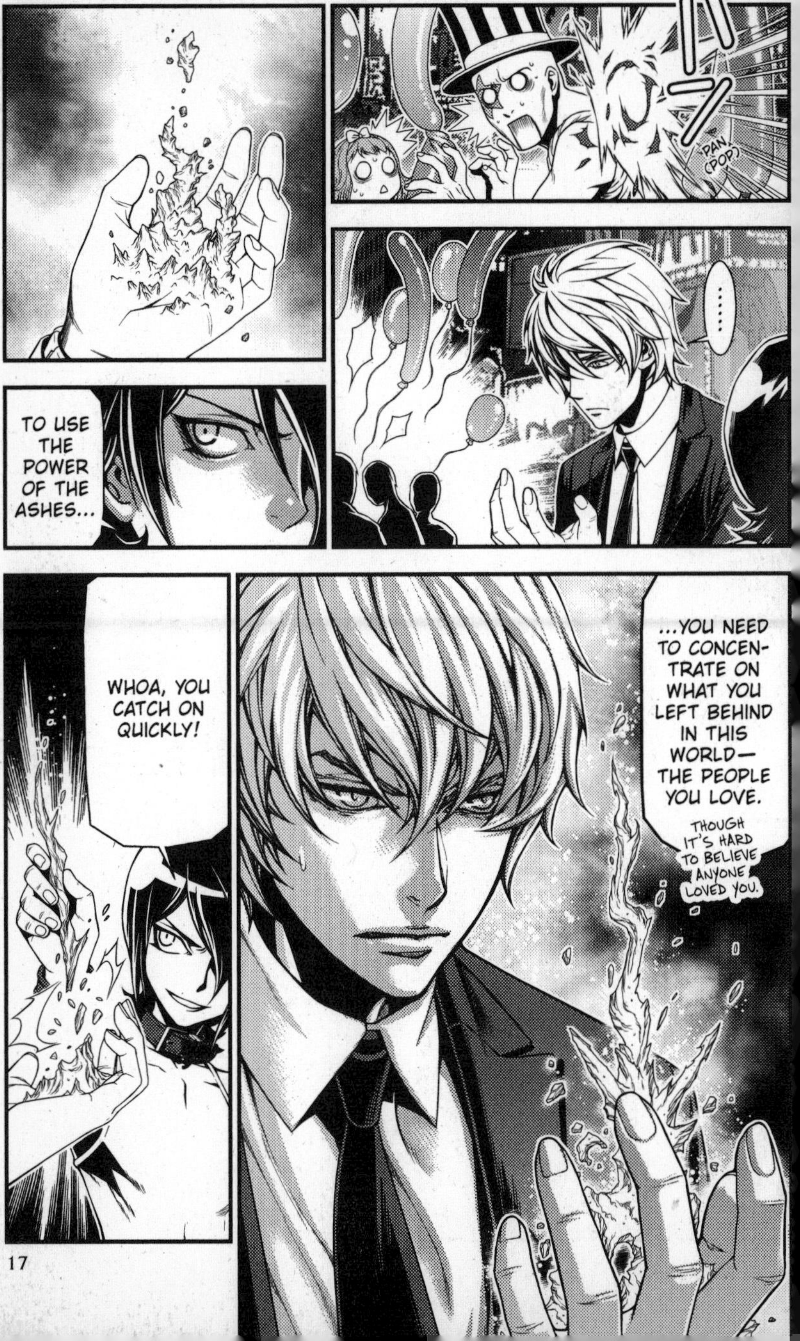

PAN (POP)
......
TO USE THE POWER OF THE ASHES...
...YOU NEED TO CONCEN-TRATE ON WHAT YOU LEFT BEHIND IN THIS WORLD—THE PEOPLE YOU LOVE.
THOUGH IT'S HARD TO BELIEVE ANYONE LOVED YOU.
WHOA, YOU CATCH ON QUICKLY!

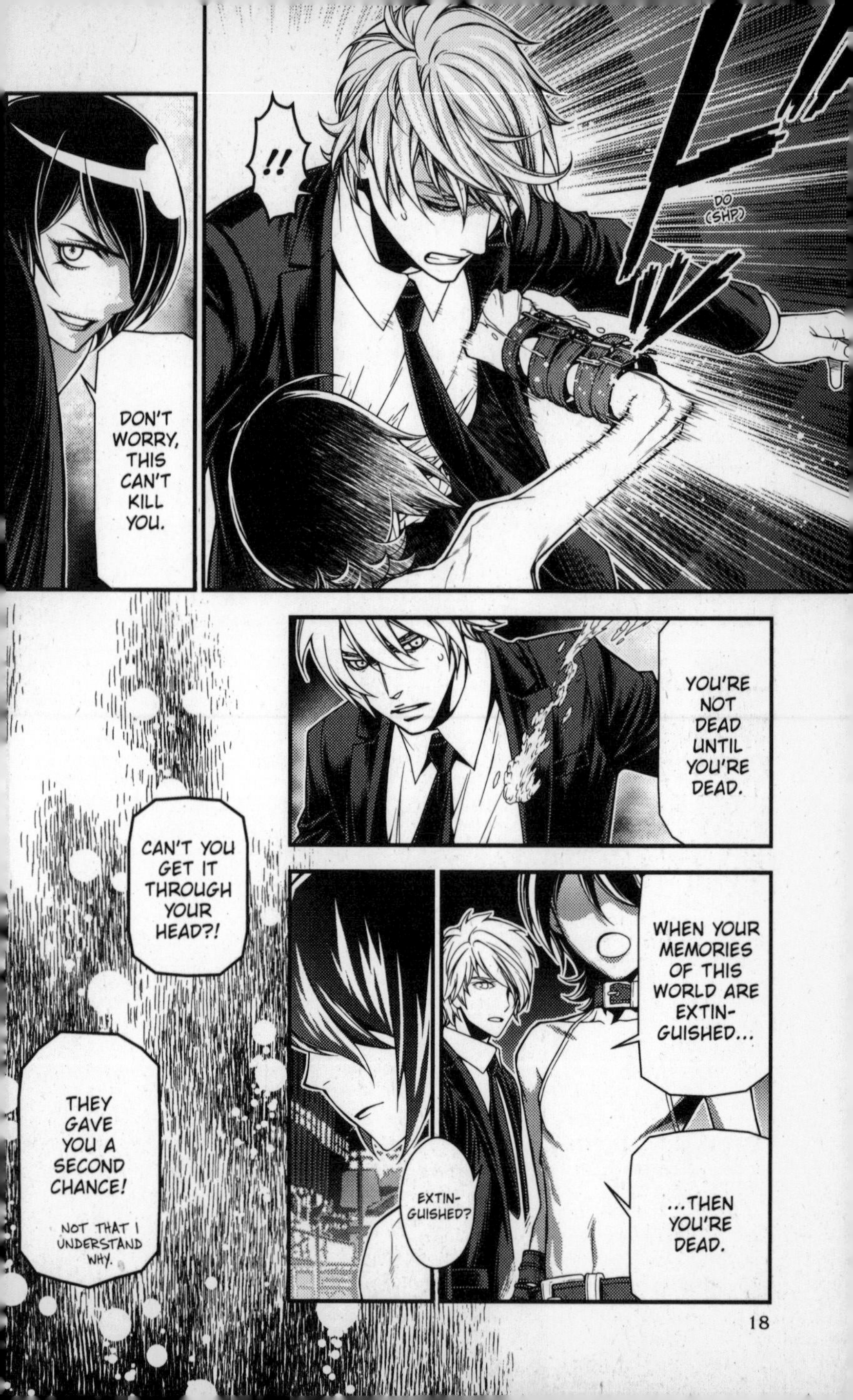
!!
DO (SHP)
DON'T WORRY, THIS CAN'T KILL YOU.
YOU'RE NOT DEAD UNTIL YOU'RE DEAD.
WHEN YOUR MEMORIES OF THIS WORLD ARE EXTIN-GUISHED...
...THEN YOU'RE DEAD.
EXTIN-GUISHED?
CAN'T YOU GET IT THROUGH YOUR HEAD?!
THEY GAVE YOU A SECOND CHANCE!
NOT THAT I UNDERSTAND WHY.

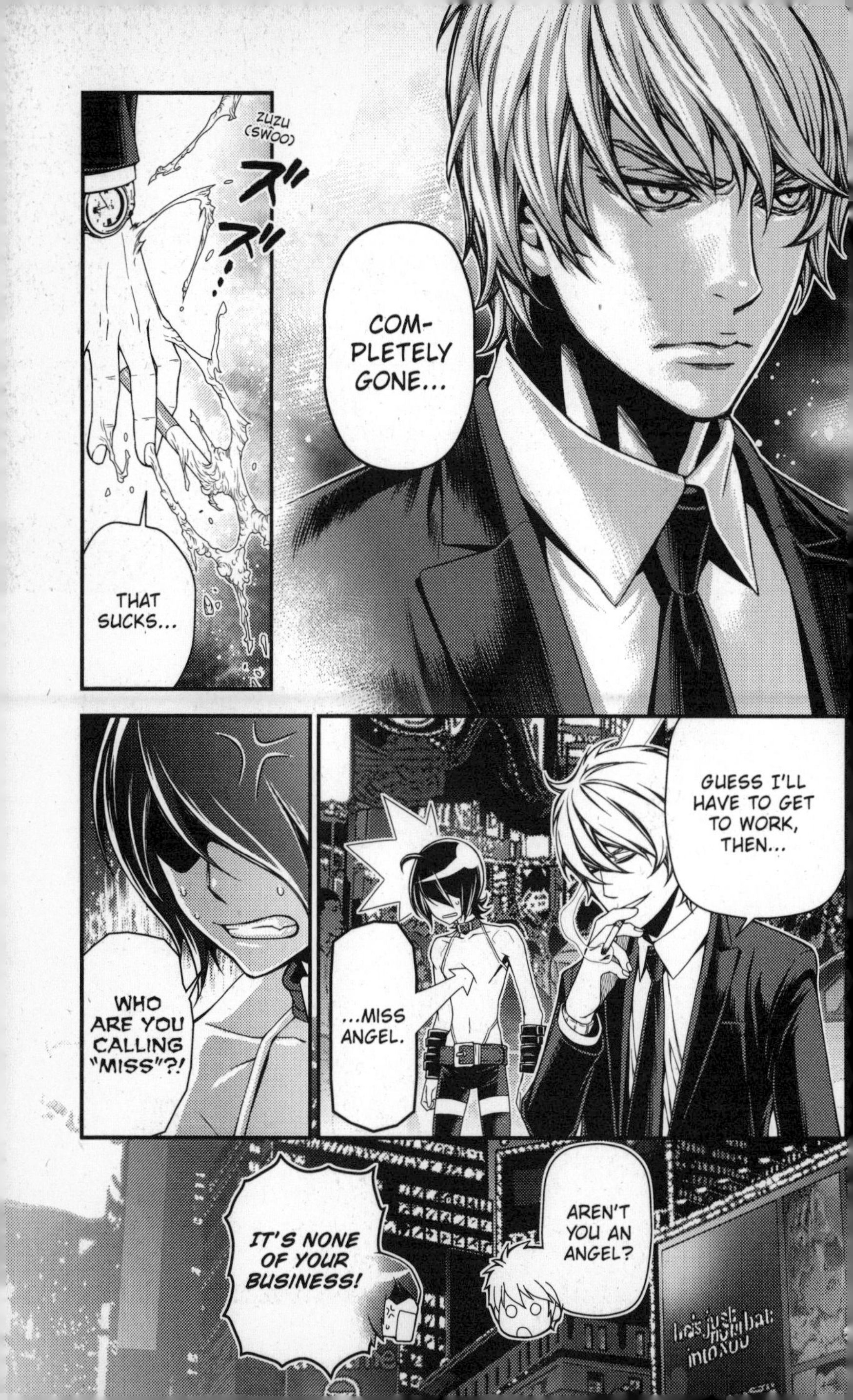
COM-PLETELY GONE...
ZUZU (SWOO)
THAT SUCKS...
GUESS I'LL HAVE TO GET TO WORK, THEN...
...MISS ANGEL.
WHO ARE YOU CALLING "MISS"?!
AREN'T YOU AN ANGEL?
IT'S NONE OF YOUR BUSINESS!

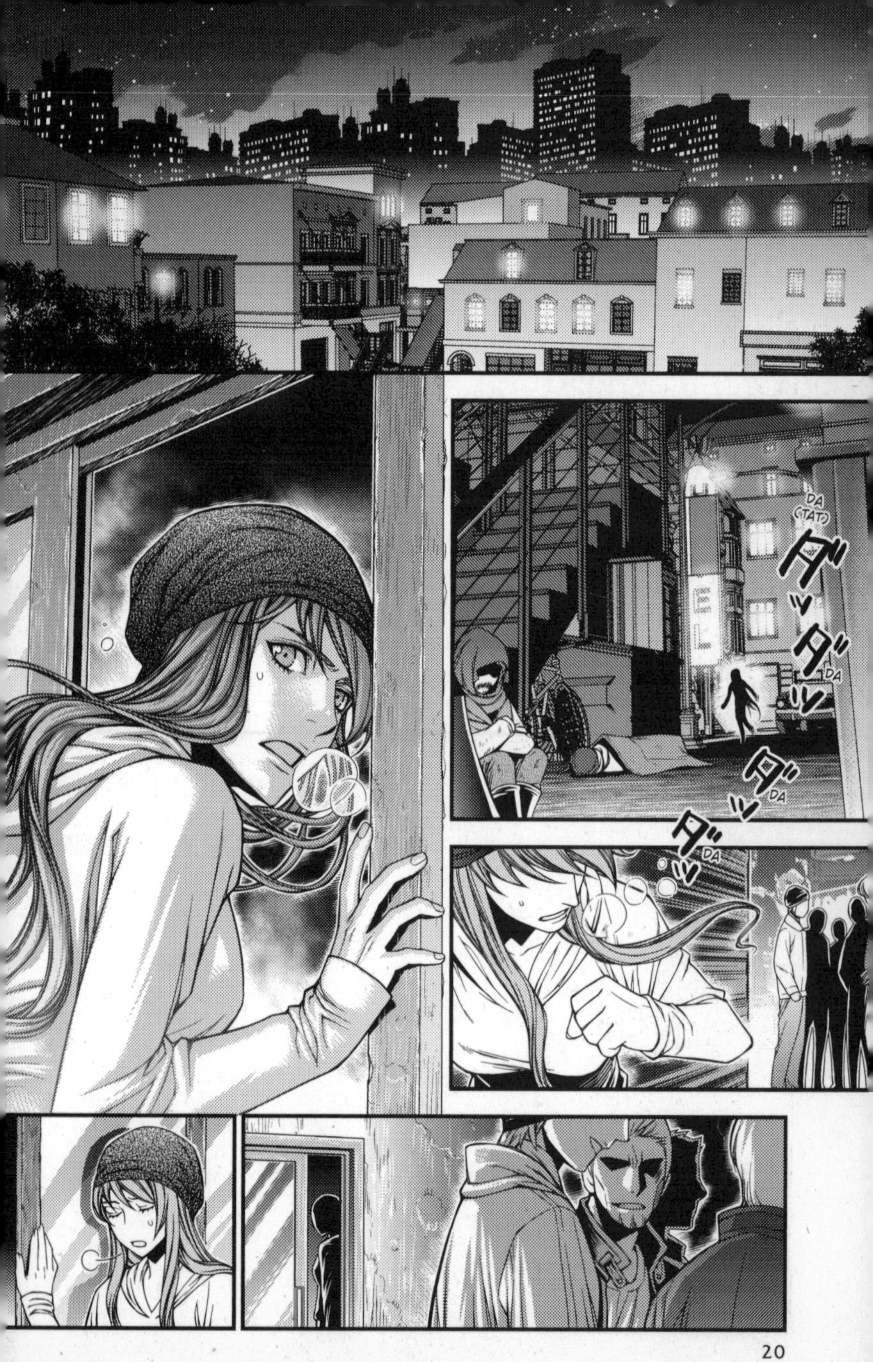
DA (TAT)
ダッ
DA
ダッ
DA
ダッ
DA
ダッ

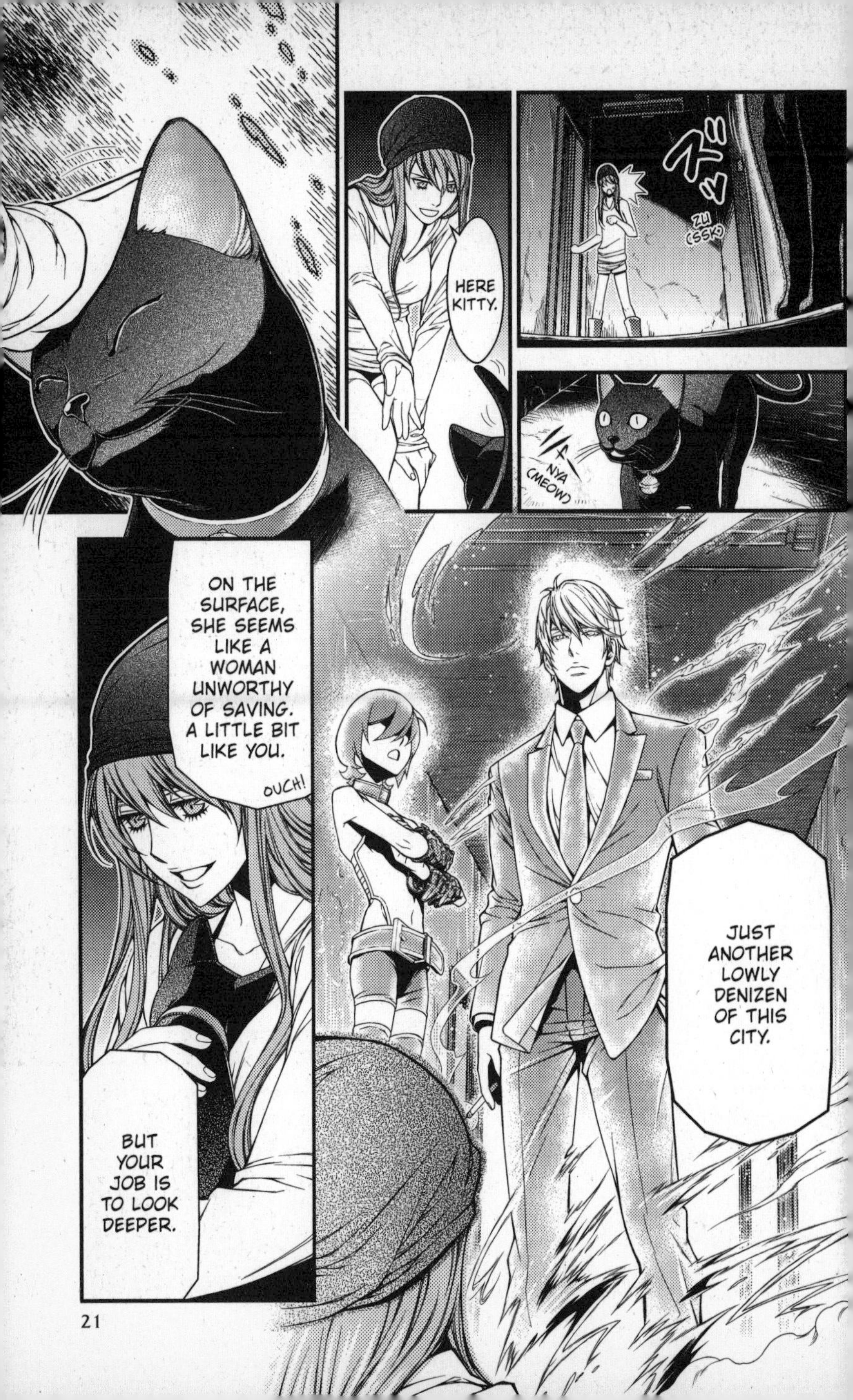
ZU (SSK)
NYA (MEOW)
HERE KITTY.
JUST ANOTHER LOWLY DENIZEN OF THIS CITY.
ON THE SURFACE, SHE SEEMS LIKE A WOMAN UNWORTHY OF SAVING. A LITTLE BIT LIKE YOU.
OUCH!
BUT YOUR JOB IS TO LOOK DEEPER.

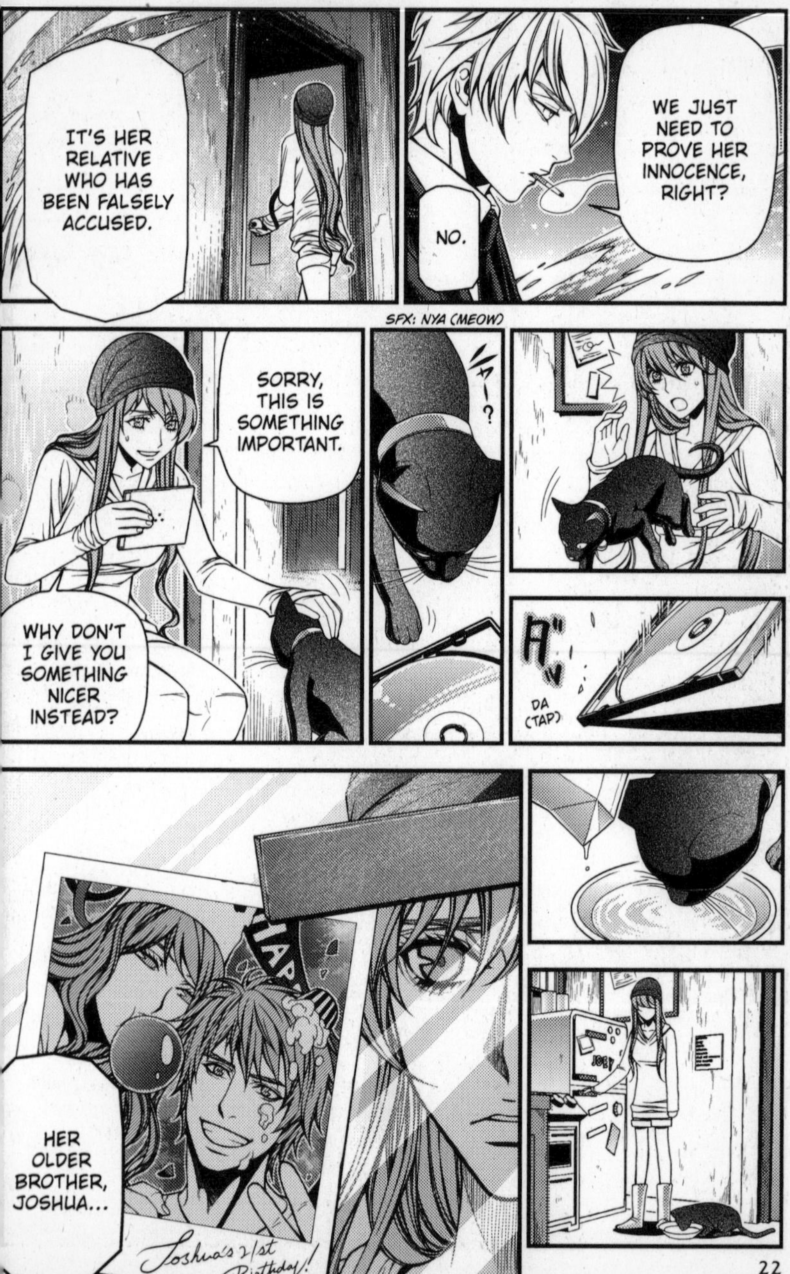
WE JUST NEED TO PROVE HER INNOCENCE, RIGHT?
NO.
IT'S HER RELATIVE WHO HAS BEEN FALSELY ACCUSED.
DA (TAP)
ニャー？
SFX: NYA (MEOW)
SORRY, THIS IS SOMETHING IMPORTANT.
WHY DON'T I GIVE YOU SOMETHING NICER INSTEAD?
HER OLDER BROTHER, JOSHUA...
Joshua's 21st Birthday!

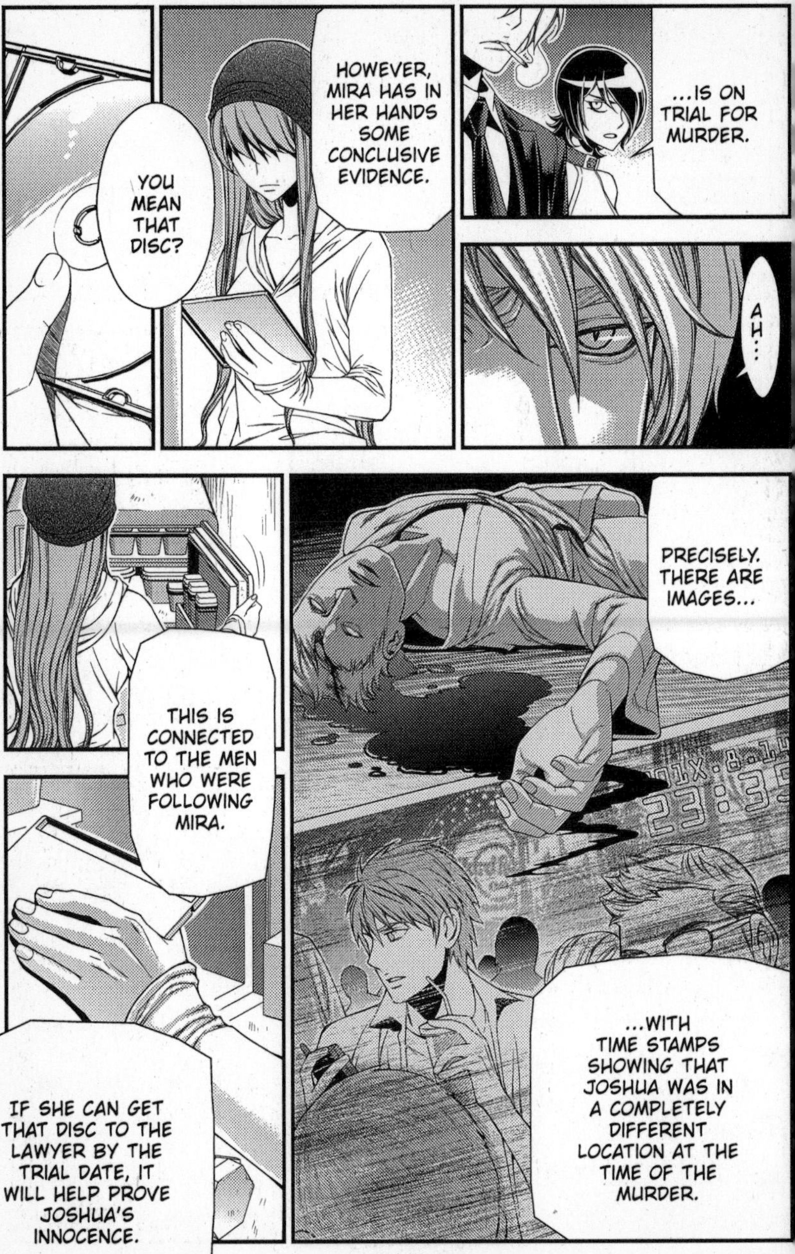
...IS ON TRIAL FOR MURDER.
AH...
HOWEVER, MIRA HAS IN HER HANDS SOME CONCLUSIVE EVIDENCE.
YOU MEAN THAT DISC?
PRECISELY. THERE ARE IMAGES...
...WITH TIME STAMPS SHOWING THAT JOSHUA WAS IN A COMPLETELY DIFFERENT LOCATION AT THE TIME OF THE MURDER.
THIS IS CONNECTED TO THE MEN WHO WERE FOLLOWING MIRA.
IF SHE CAN GET THAT DISC TO THE LAWYER BY THE TRIAL DATE, IT WILL HELP PROVE JOSHUA'S INNOCENCE.

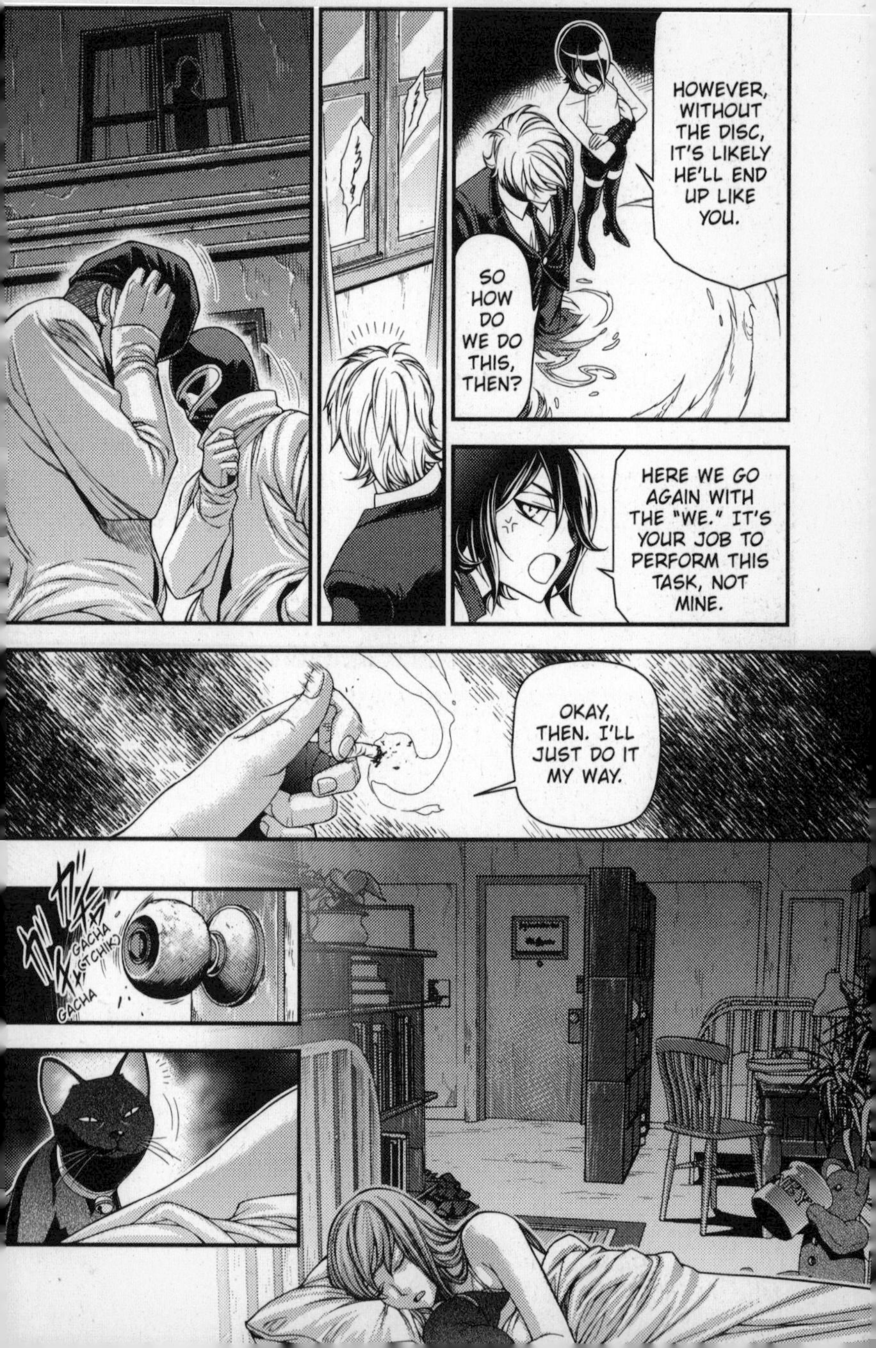
HOWEVER, WITHOUT THE DISC, IT'S LIKELY HE'LL END UP LIKE YOU.
SO HOW DO WE DO THIS, THEN?
HERE WE GO AGAIN WITH THE "WE." IT'S YOUR JOB TO PERFORM THIS TASK, NOT MINE.
OKAY, THEN. I'LL JUST DO IT MY WAY.
GACHA (STCHIK)
GACHA

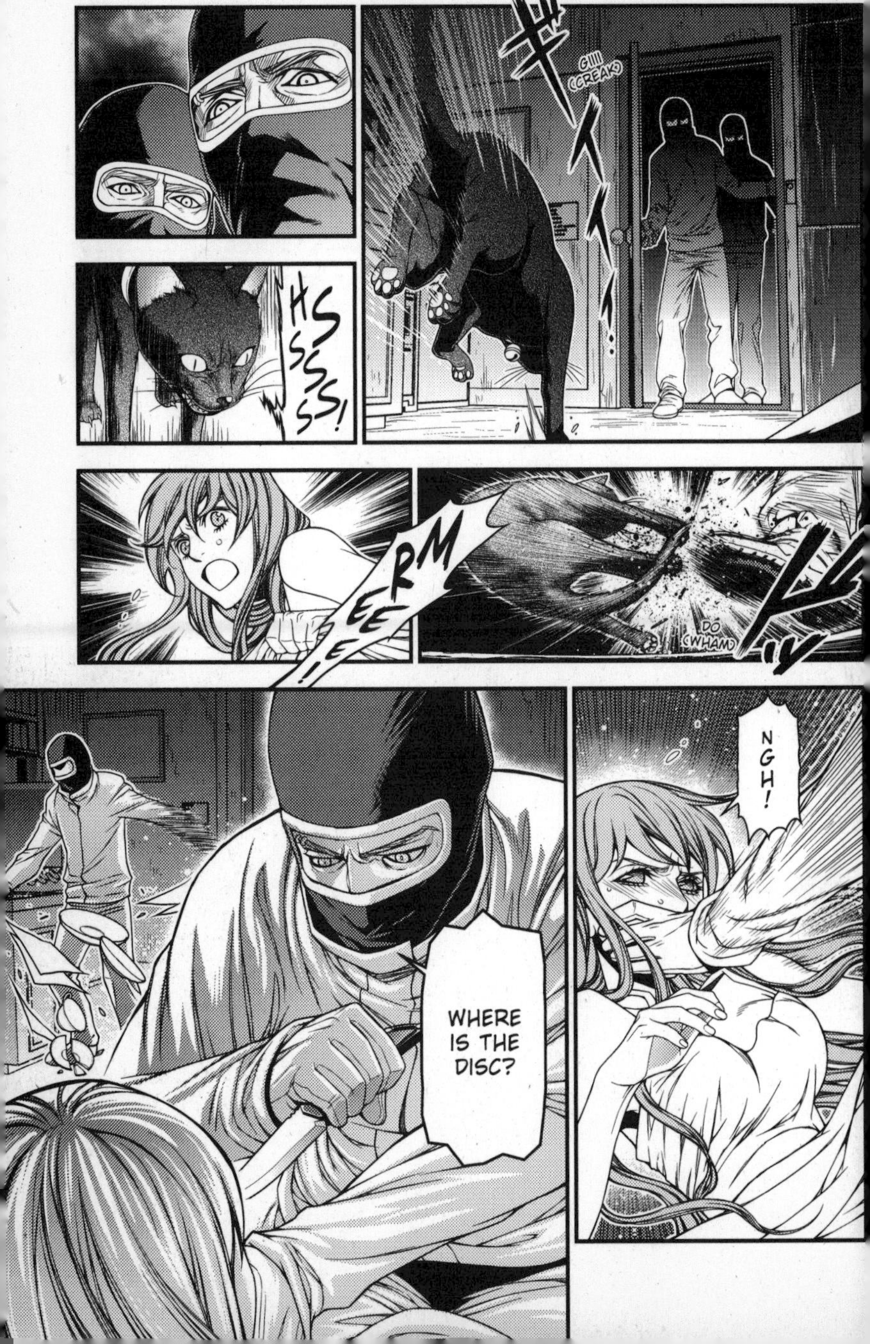
GIIII (CREAK)
HSSSSS!
DO (WHAM)
RMEEEE!
NGH!
WHERE IS THE DISC?

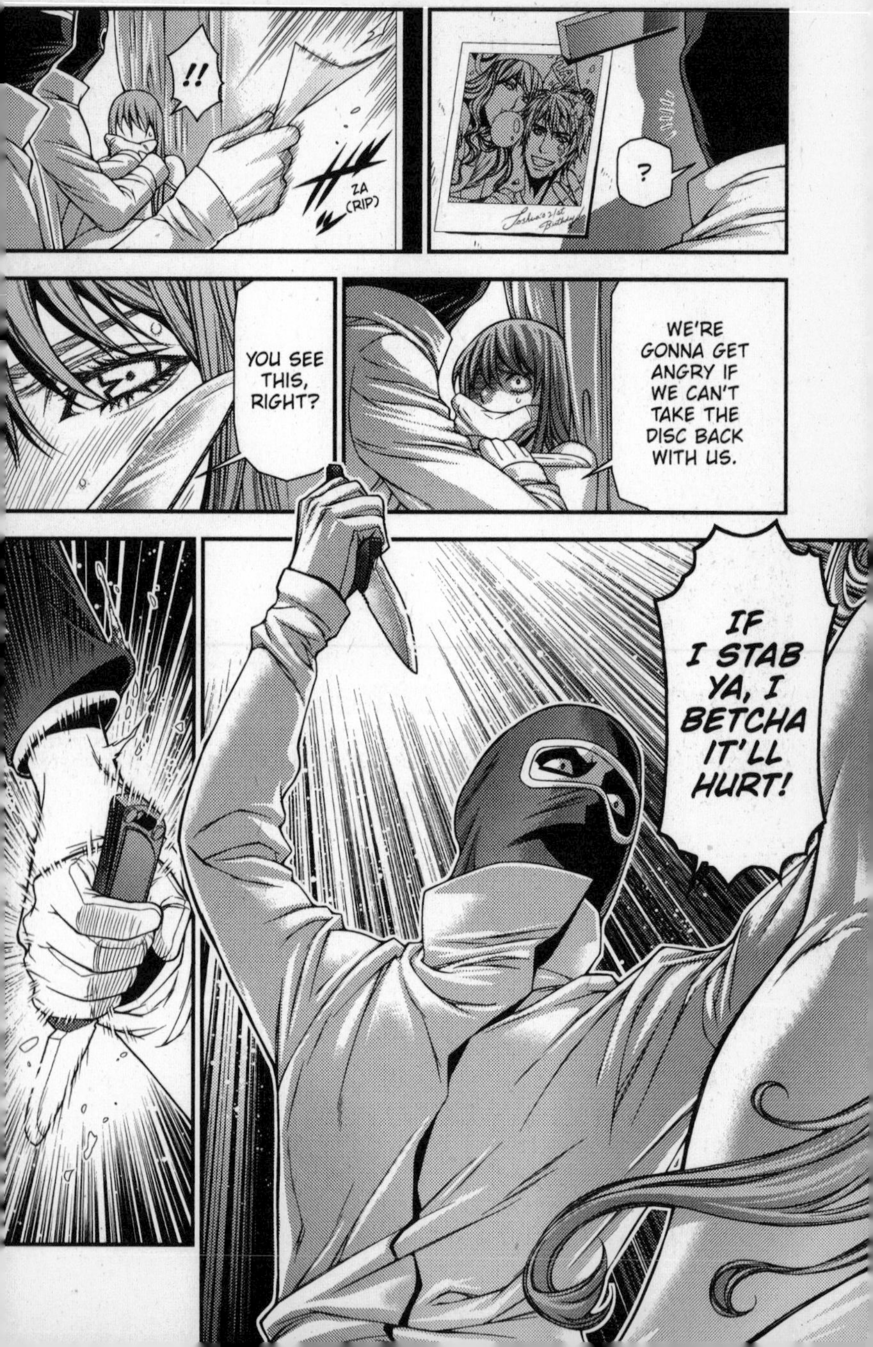
?
!!
ZA (RIP)
WE'RE GONNA GET ANGRY IF WE CAN'T TAKE THE DISC BACK WITH US.
YOU SEE THIS, RIGHT?
IF I STAB YA, I BETCHA IT'LL HURT!

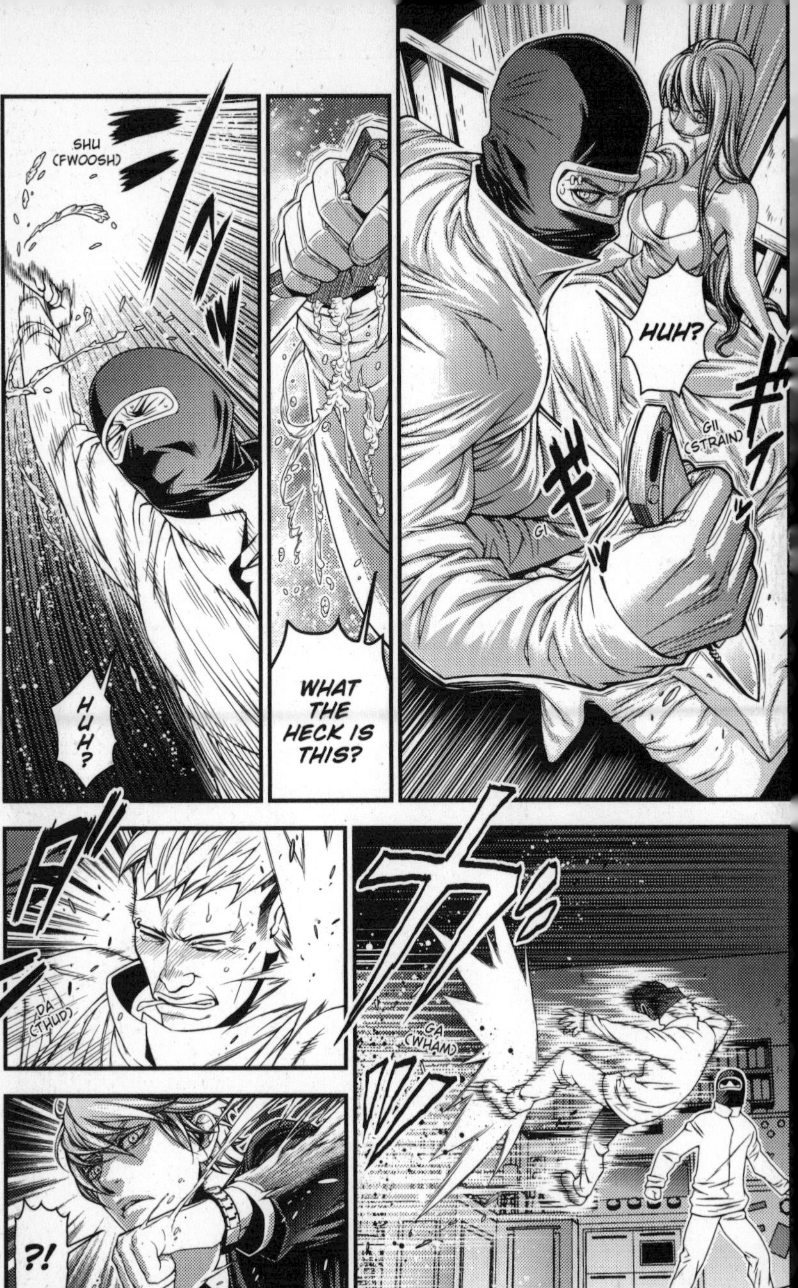
HUH?
GII (STRAIN)
GI
WHAT THE HECK IS THIS?
SHU (FWOOSH)
HUH?
GA (WHAM)
DA (THUD)
?!

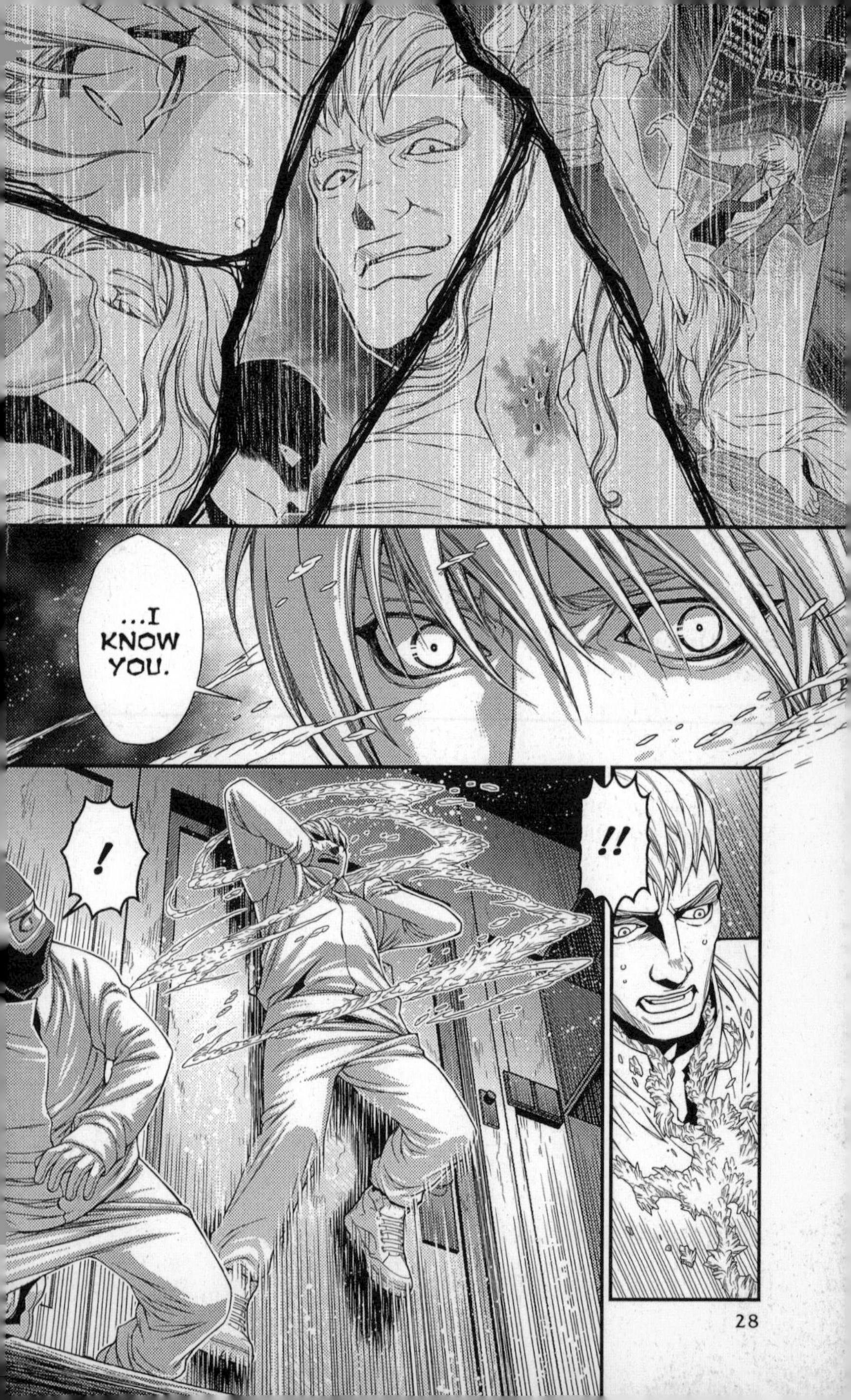
...I KNOW YOU.
!!
!

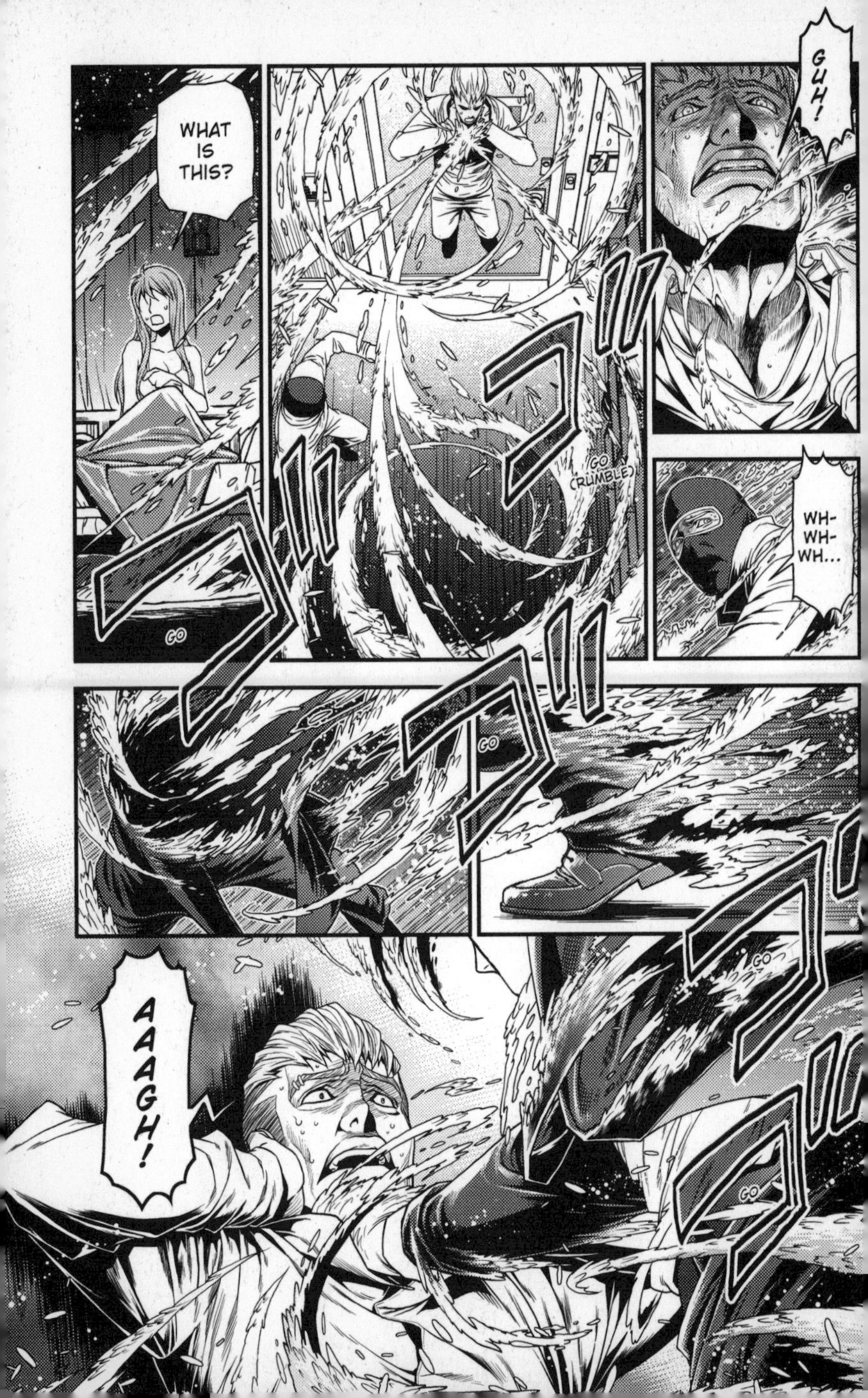
GUH!
WH- WH- WH...
GO (RUMBLE)
WHAT IS THIS?
GO
GO
GO
AAAGH!
GO

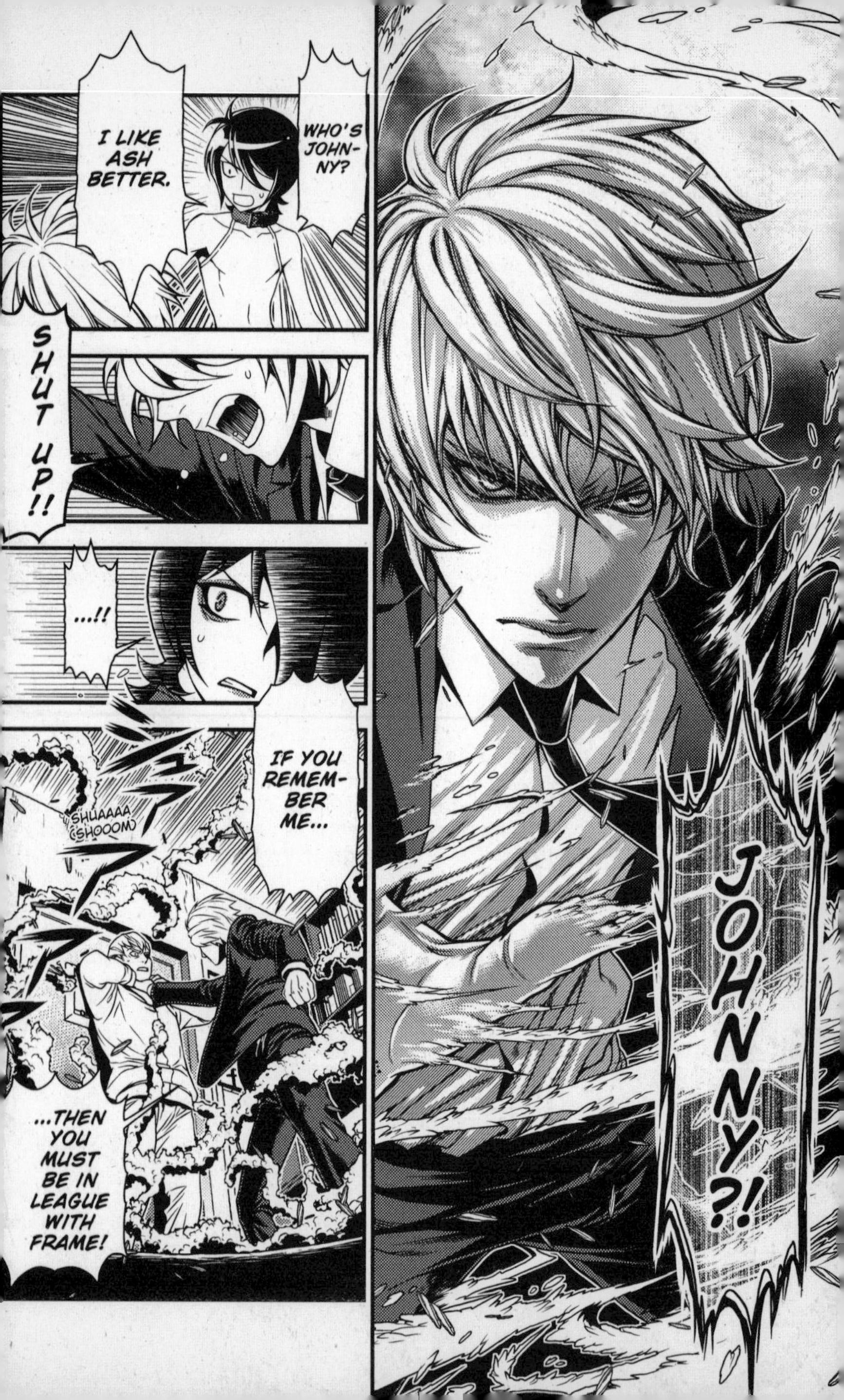
JOHNNY?!
WHO'S JOHNNY?
I LIKE ASH BETTER.
SHUT UP!!
...!!
IF YOU REMEMBER ME...
SHUAAAA (SHOOOM)
...THEN YOU MUST BE IN LEAGUE WITH FRAME!

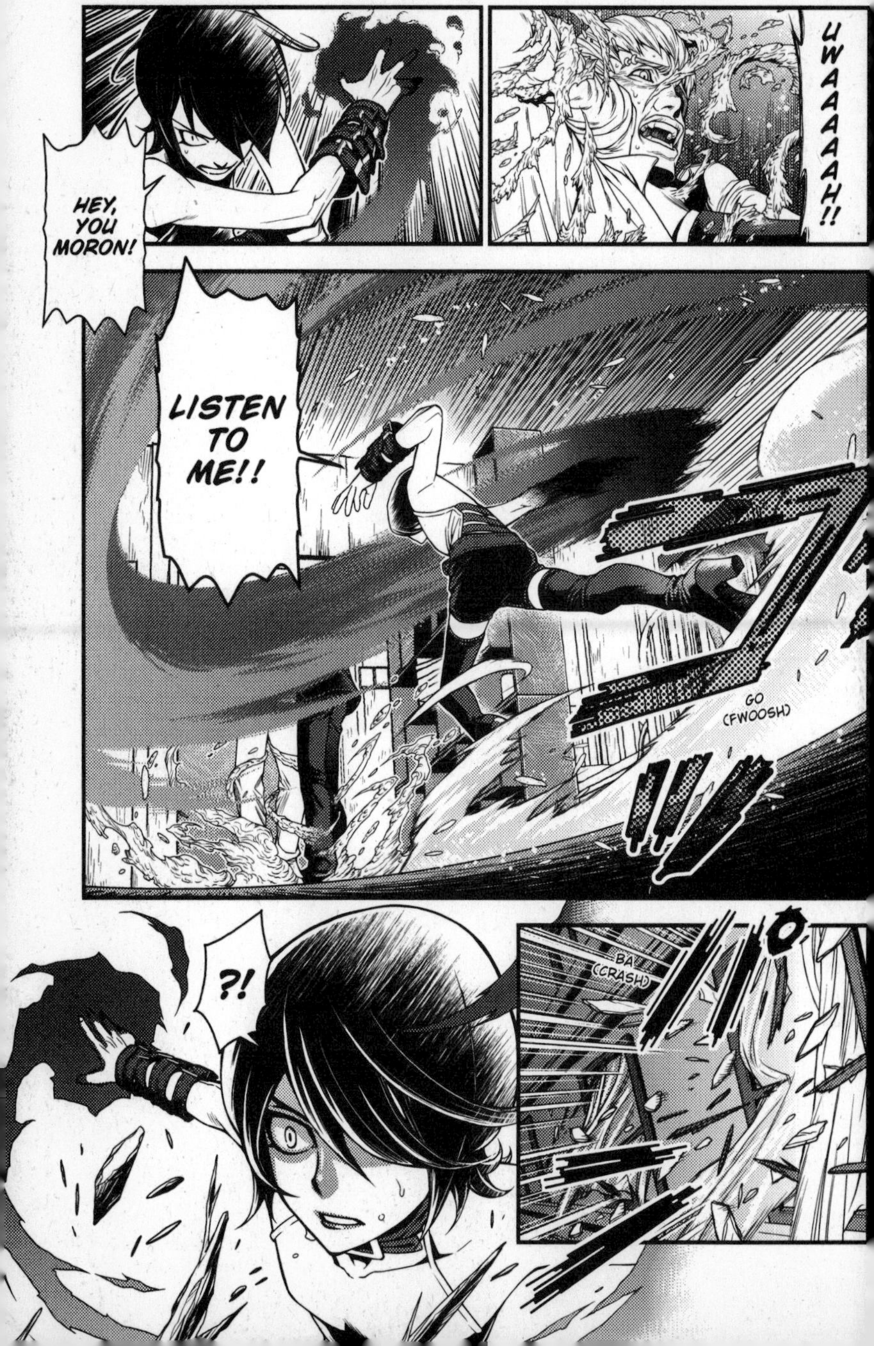
UWAAAAAAH!!
HEY, YOU MORON!
LISTEN TO ME!!
GO (FWOOSH)
BA (CRASH)
?!

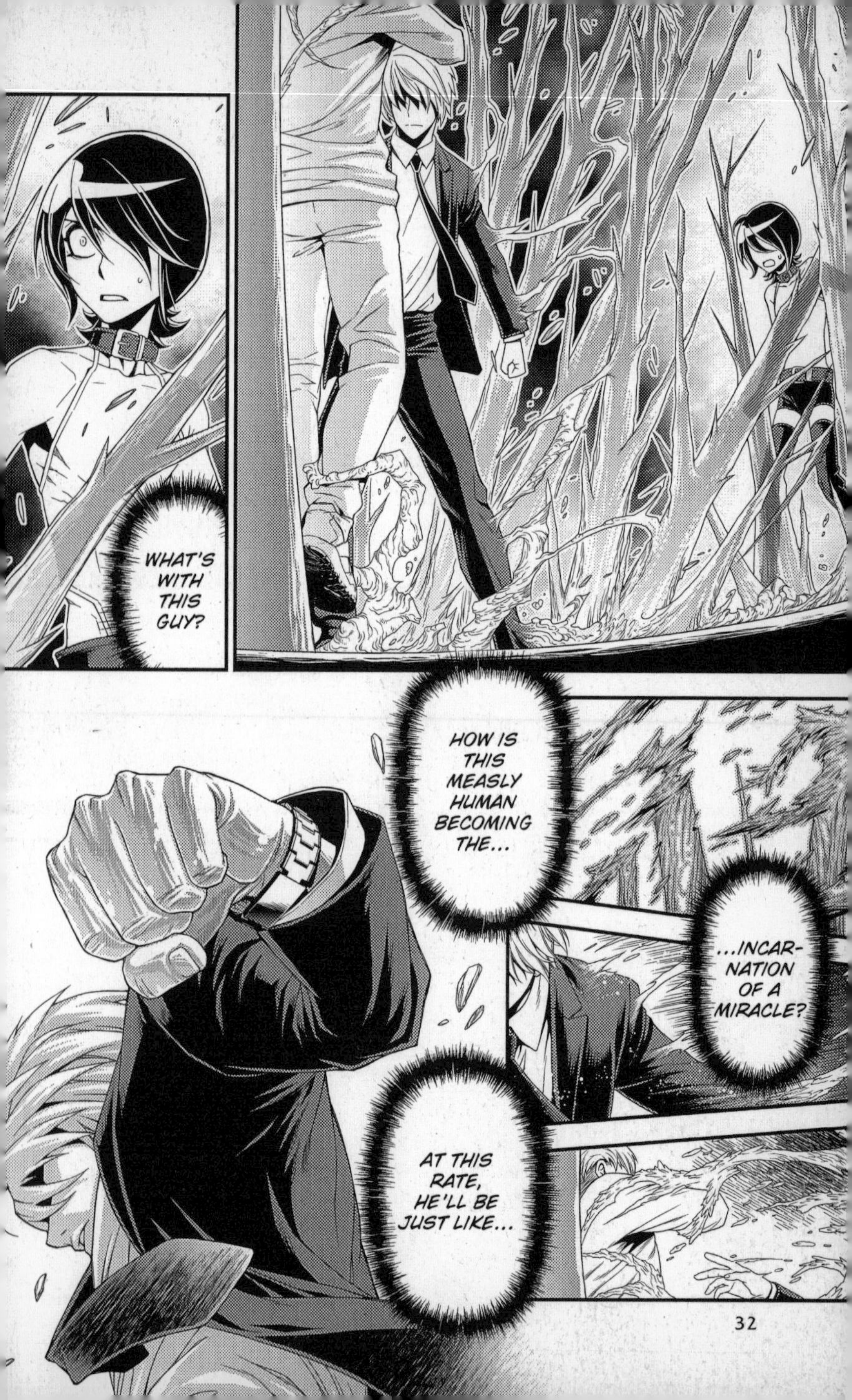
WHAT'S WITH THIS GUY?
HOW IS THIS MEASLY HUMAN BECOMING THE...
...INCARNATION OF A MIRACLE?
AT THIS RATE, HE'LL BE JUST LIKE...

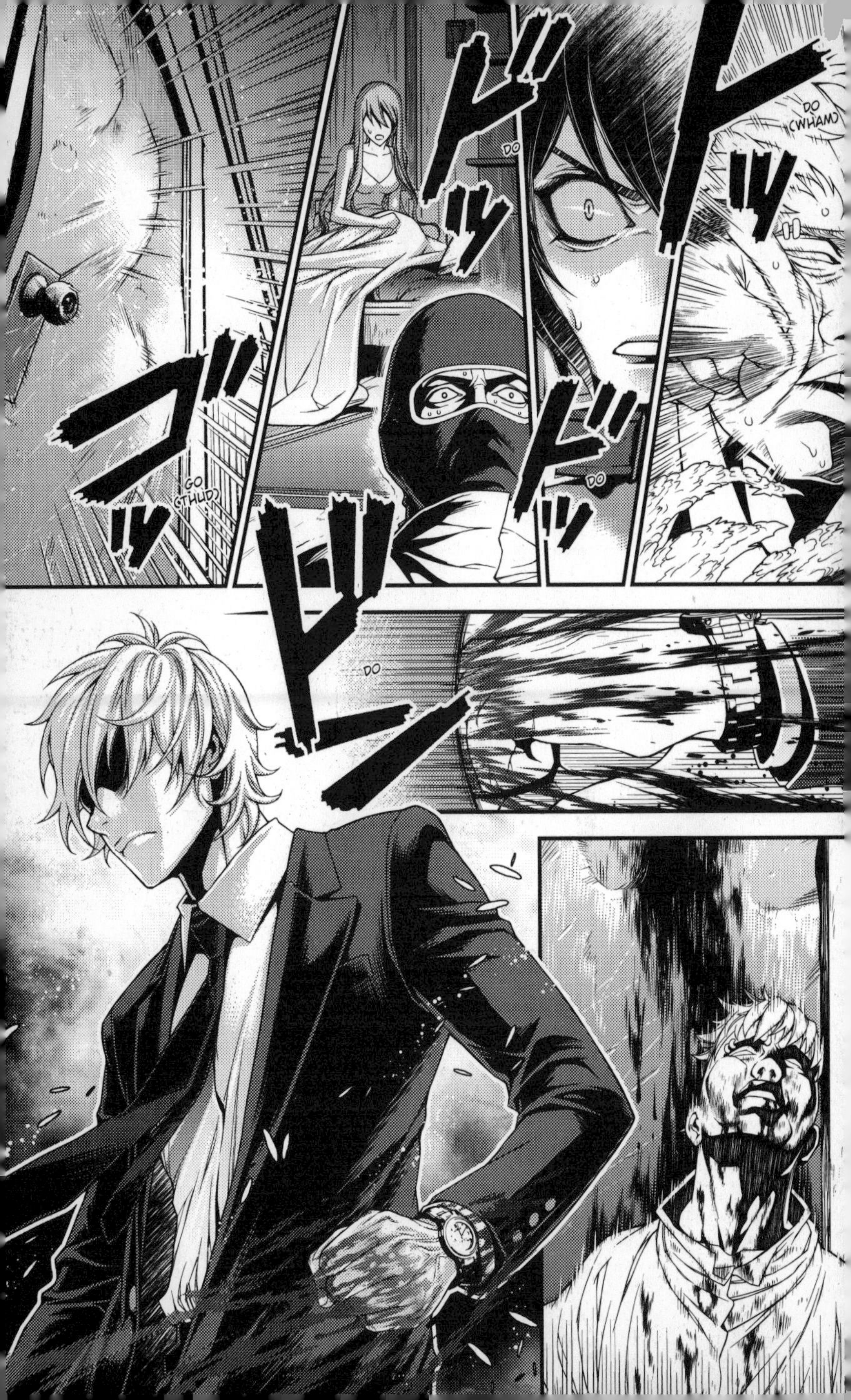
DO (WHAM)
DO
DO
GO (THUD)
DO

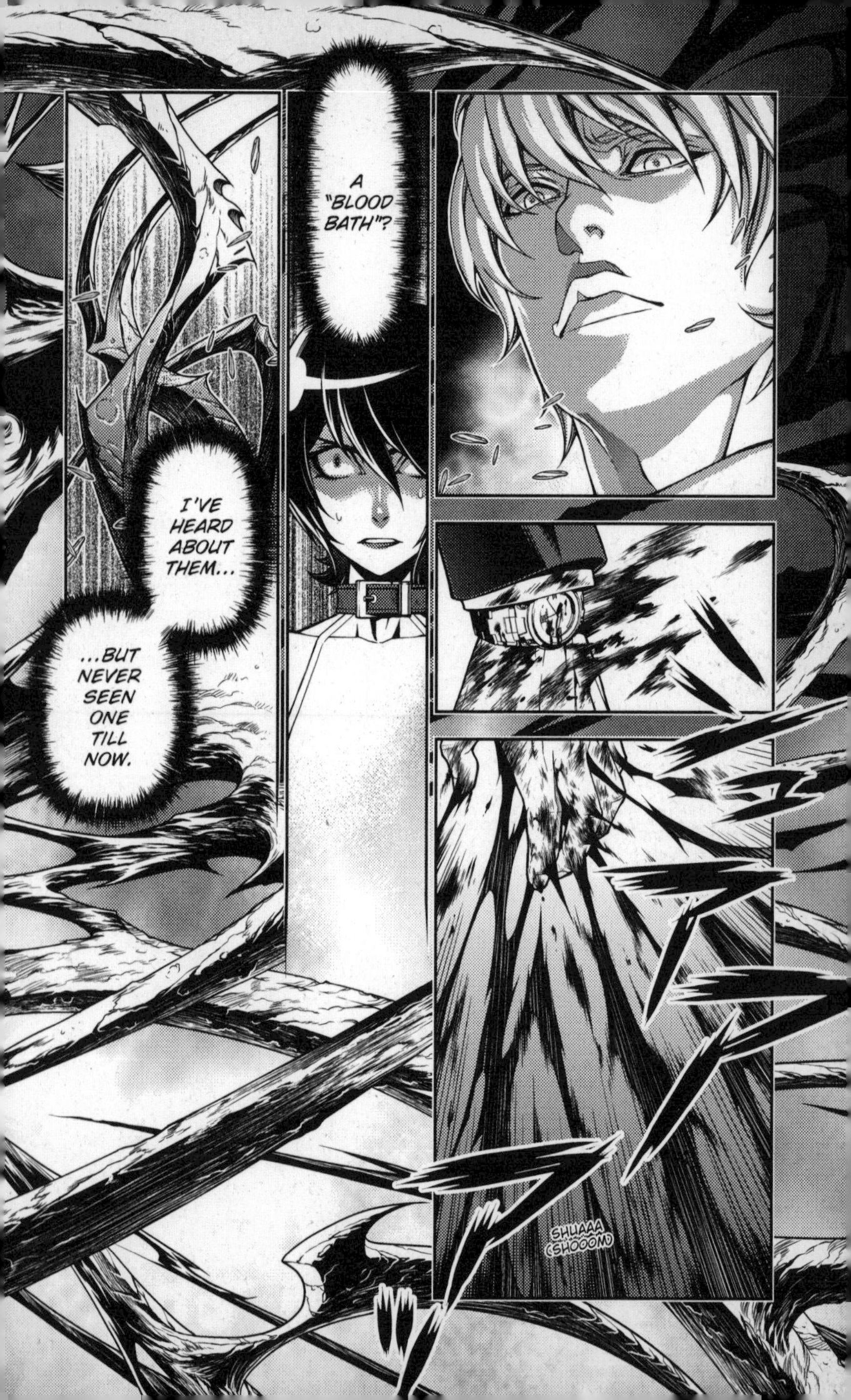
SHUAAA (SHOOOM)
A "BLOOD BATH"?
I'VE HEARD ABOUT THEM...
...BUT NEVER SEEN ONE TILL NOW.

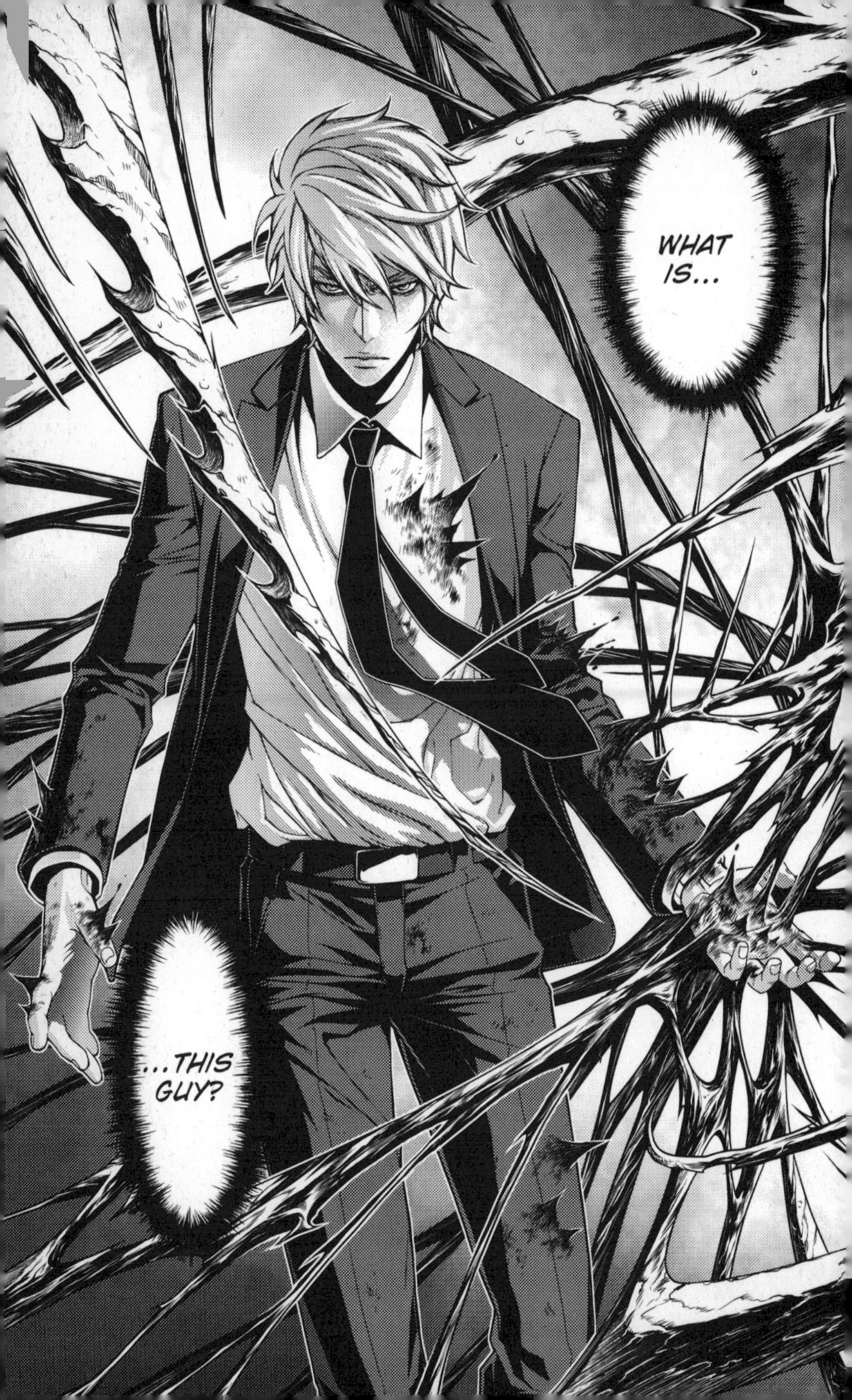
WHAT IS...
...THIS GUY?

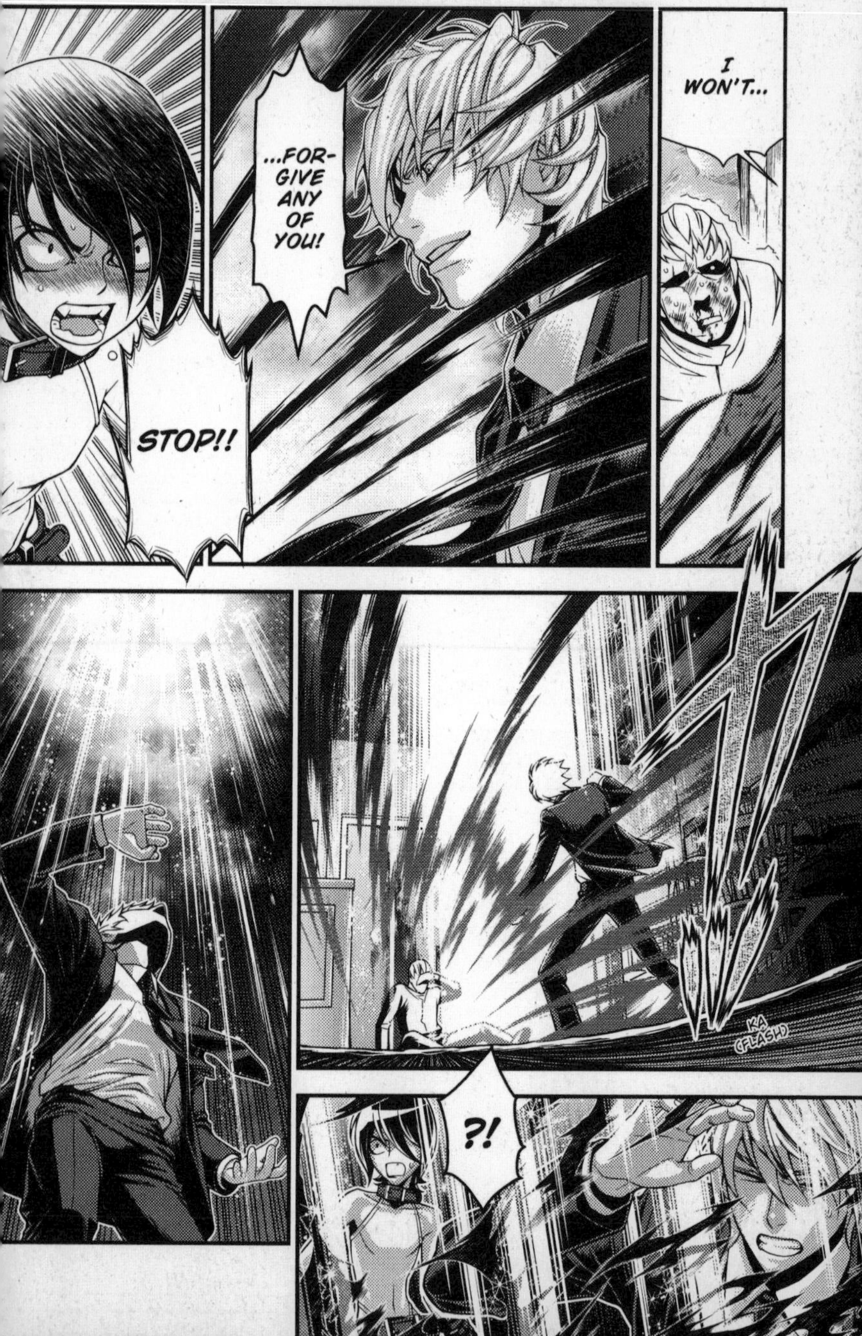
I WON'T...
...FOR-GIVE ANY OF YOU!
STOP!!
KA (FLASH)
?!

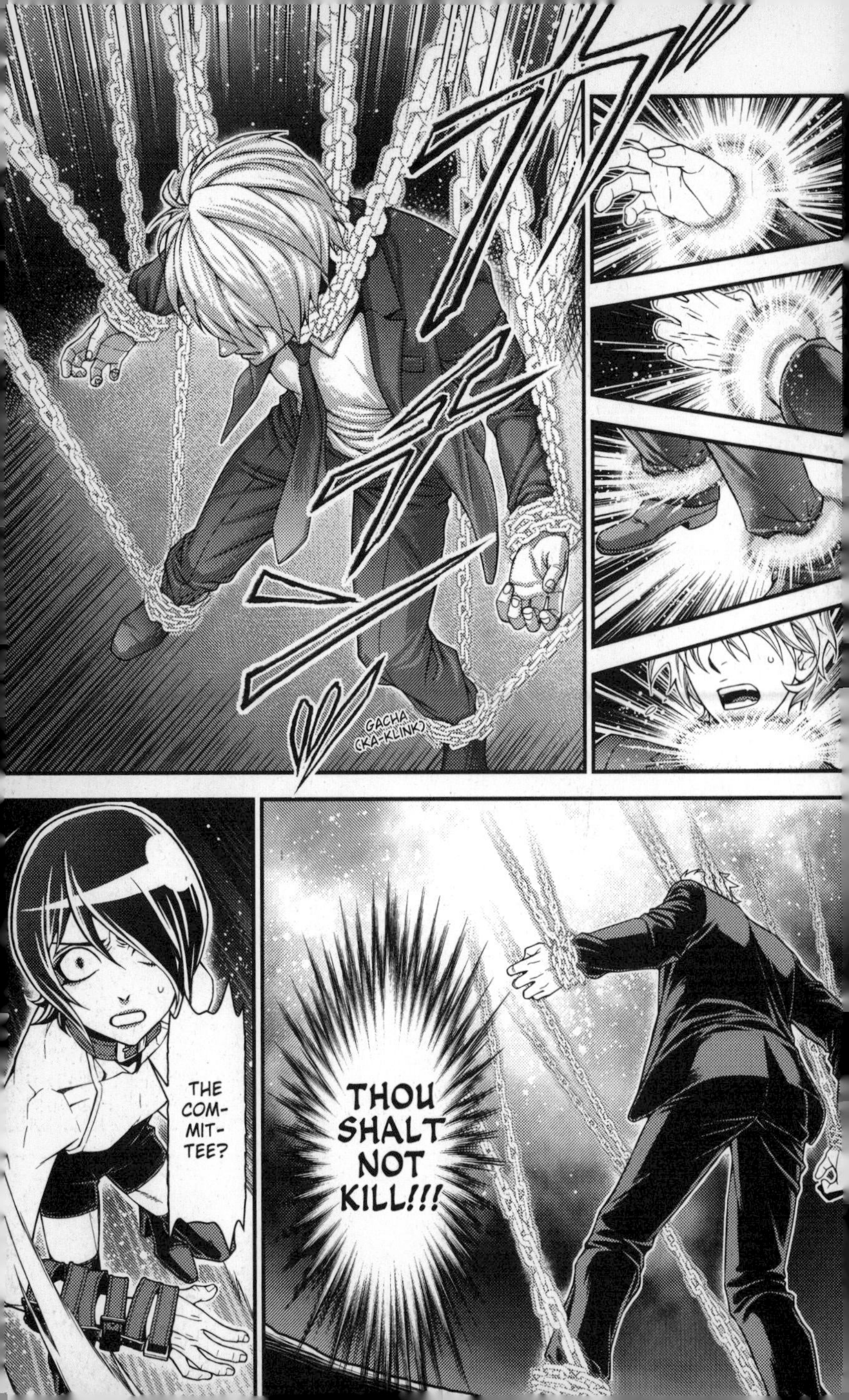
GACHA (KA-KLINK)
THOU SHALT NOT KILL!!!
THE COM-MIT-TEE?

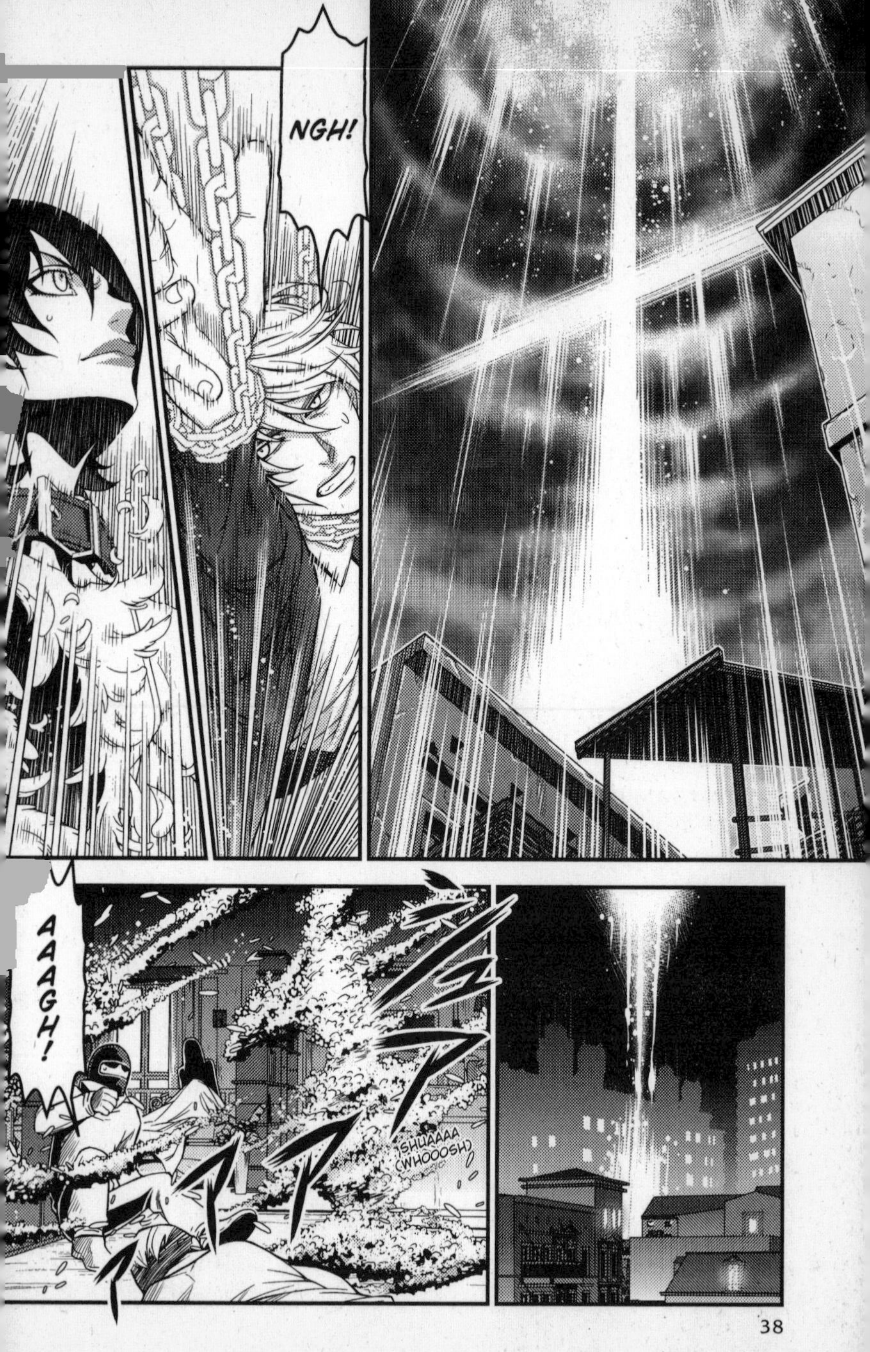
NGH!
AAAGH!
SHUAAAA (WHOOOSH)

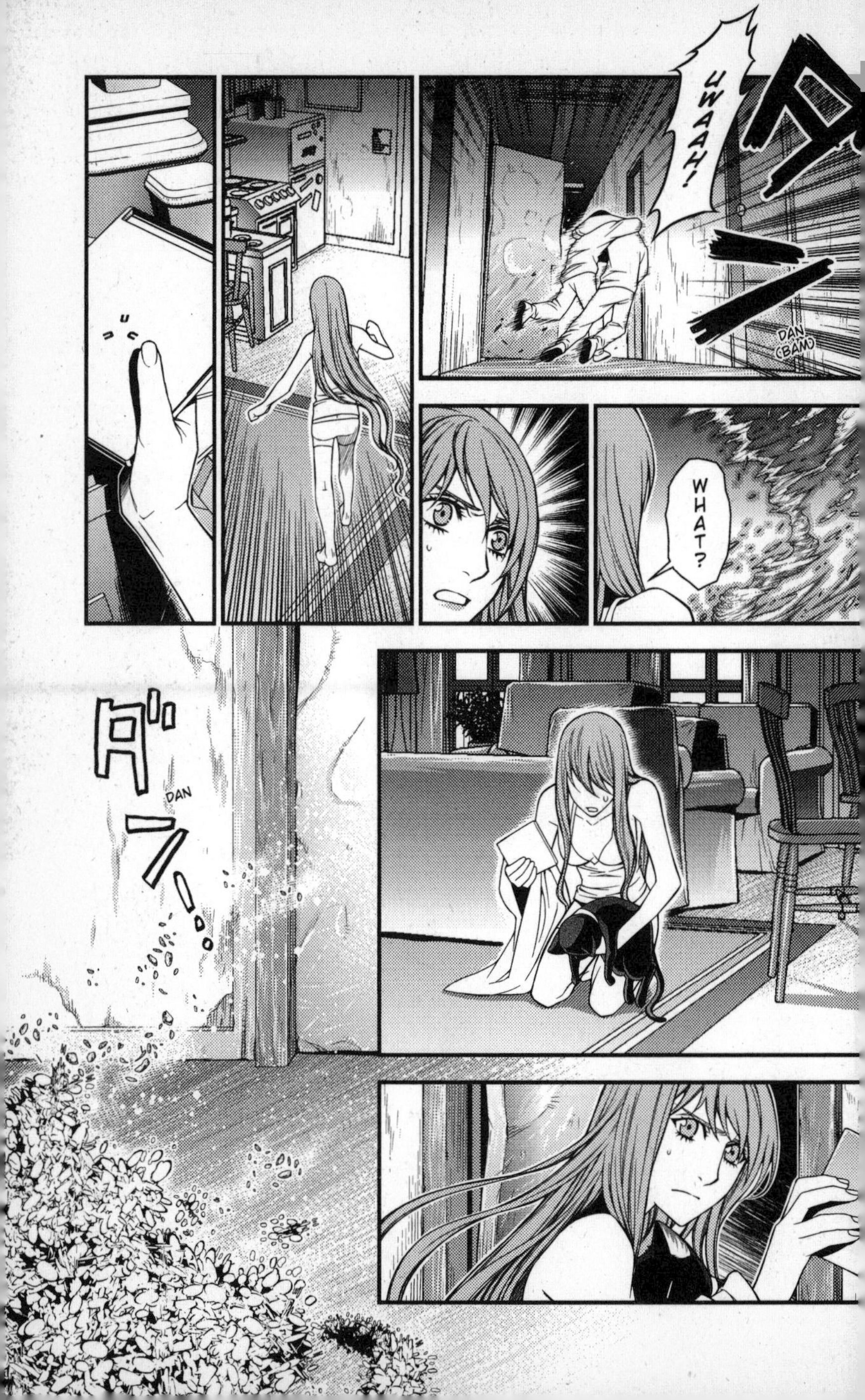
UWAAH!
DAN (BAM)
WHAT?
DAN

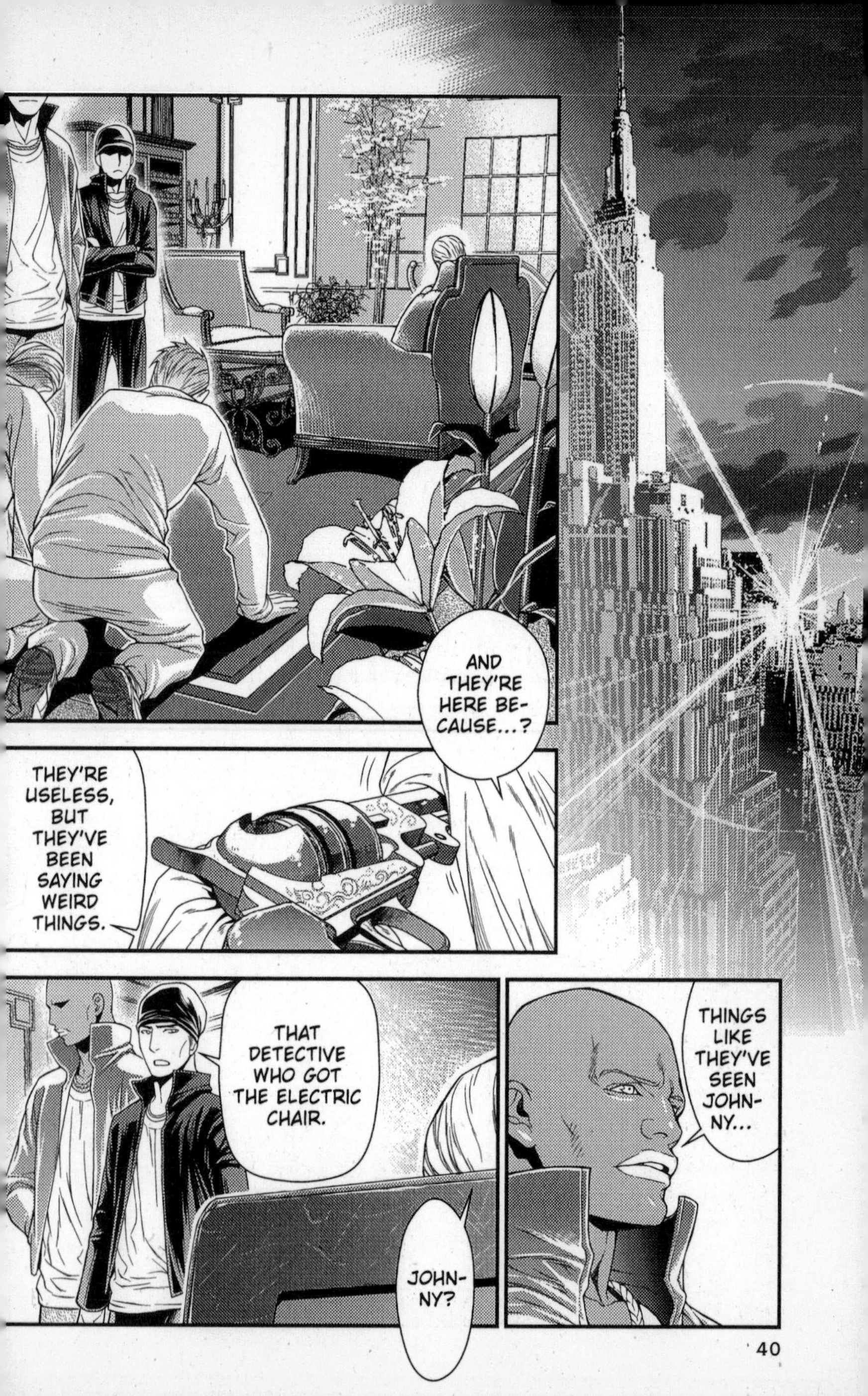
AND THEY'RE HERE BE-CAUSE...?
THEY'RE USELESS, BUT THEY'VE BEEN SAYING WEIRD THINGS.
THINGS LIKE THEY'VE SEEN JOHN-NY...
JOHN-NY?
THAT DETECTIVE WHO GOT THE ELECTRIC CHAIR.

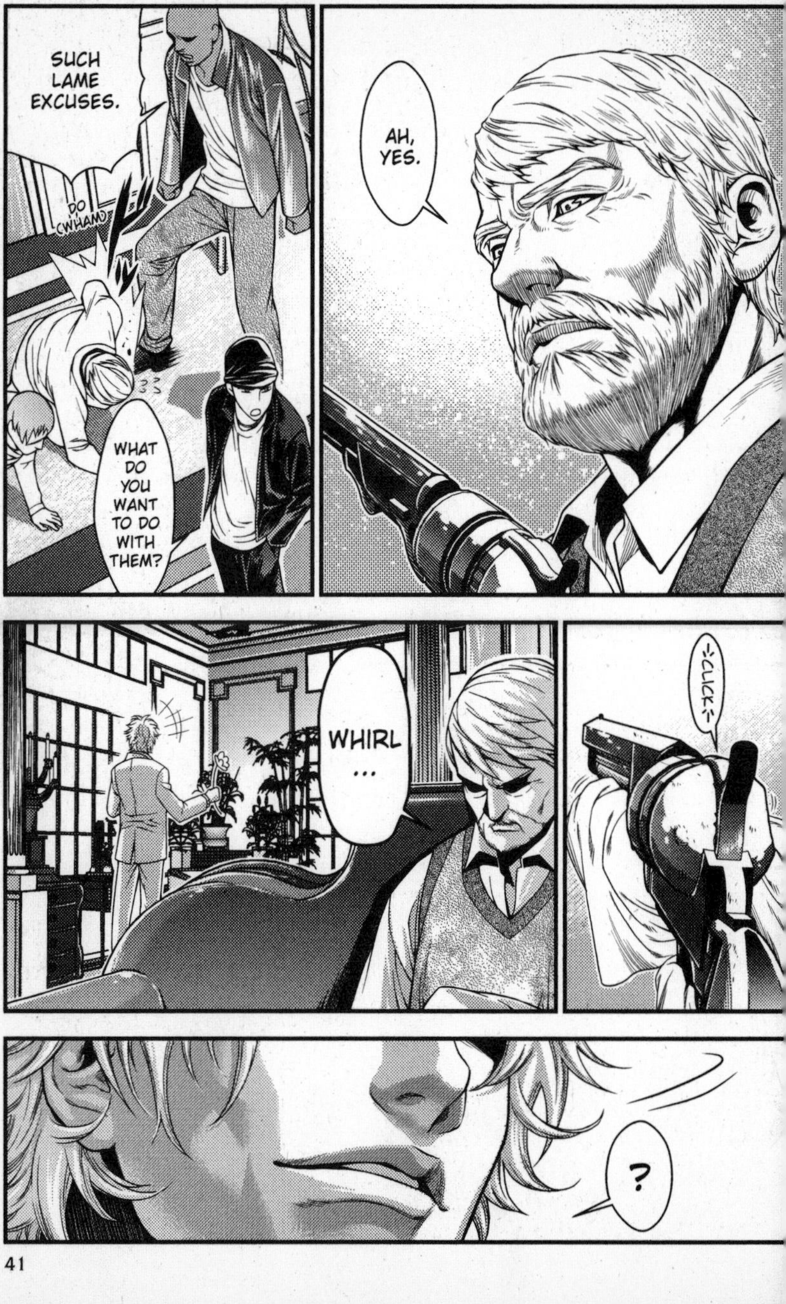
AH, YES.
SUCH LAME EXCUSES.
DO (WHAM)
WHAT DO YOU WANT TO DO WITH THEM?
-CLICK-
WHIRL ...
?

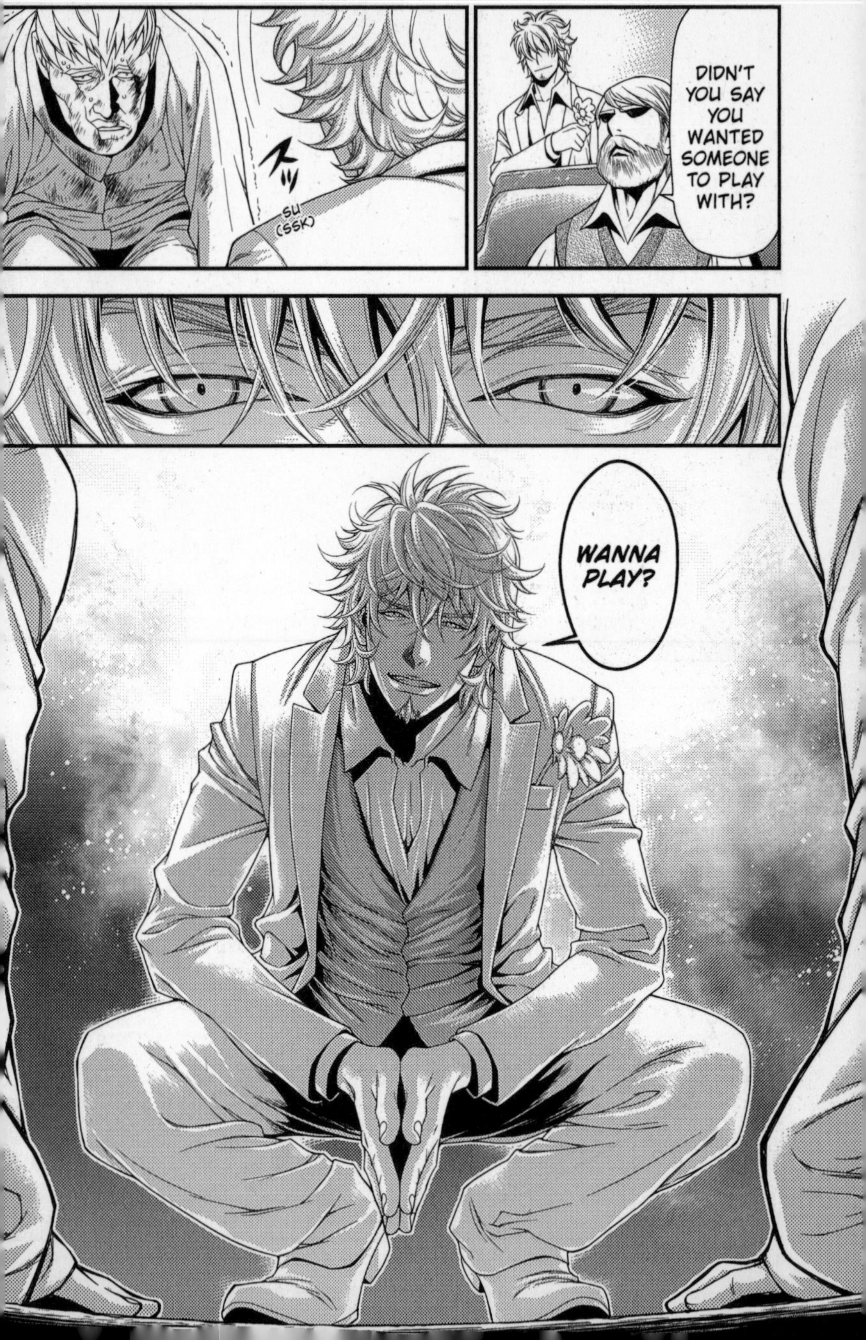
DIDN'T YOU SAY YOU WANTED SOMEONE TO PLAY WITH?
スッ
SU (SSK)
WANNA PLAY?

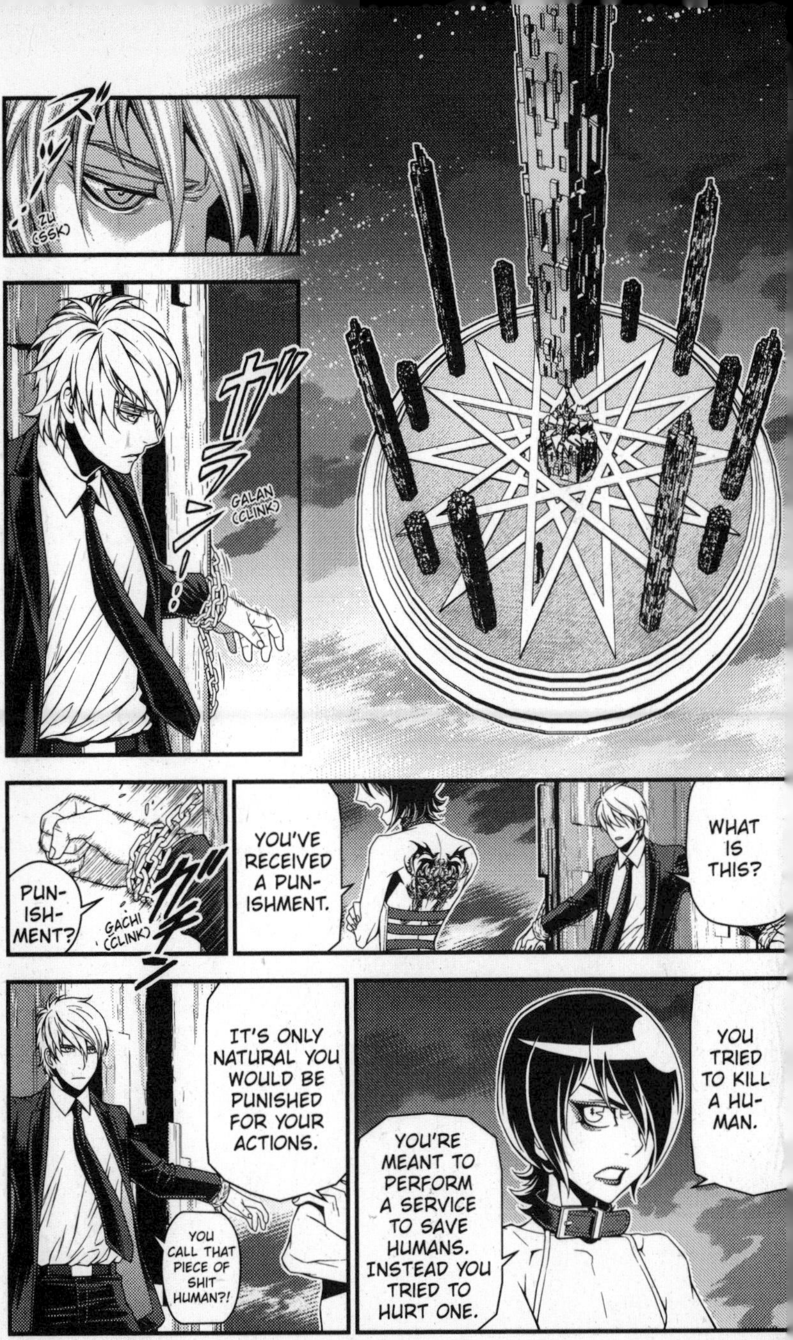

ZU (SSK)
GALAN (CLINK)
WHAT IS THIS?
YOU'VE RECEIVED A PUNISHMENT.
GACHI (CLINK)
PUNISHMENT?
YOU TRIED TO KILL A HUMAN.
YOU'RE MEANT TO PERFORM A SERVICE TO SAVE HUMANS. INSTEAD YOU TRIED TO HURT ONE.
IT'S ONLY NATURAL YOU WOULD BE PUNISHED FOR YOUR ACTIONS.
YOU CALL THAT PIECE OF SHIT HUMAN?!

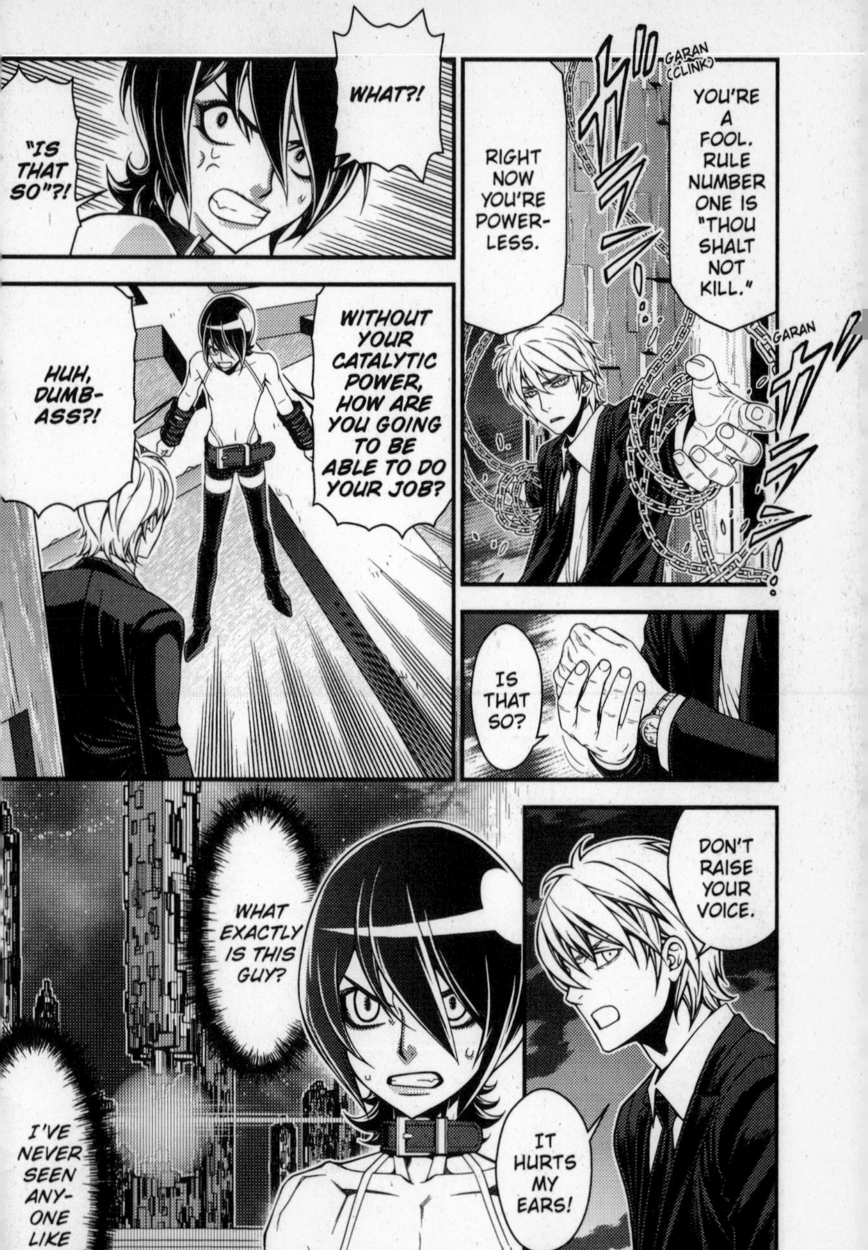
GARAN (CLINK)
YOU'RE A FOOL. RULE NUMBER ONE IS "THOU SHALT NOT KILL."
RIGHT NOW YOU'RE POWER-LESS.
GARAN
WITHOUT YOUR CATALYTIC POWER, HOW ARE YOU GOING TO BE ABLE TO DO YOUR JOB?
HUH, DUMB-ASS?!
IS THAT SO?
WHAT?!
"IS THAT SO"?!
DON'T RAISE YOUR VOICE.
IT HURTS MY EARS!
WHAT EXACTLY IS THIS GUY?
I'VE NEVER SEEN ANY-ONE LIKE HIM.

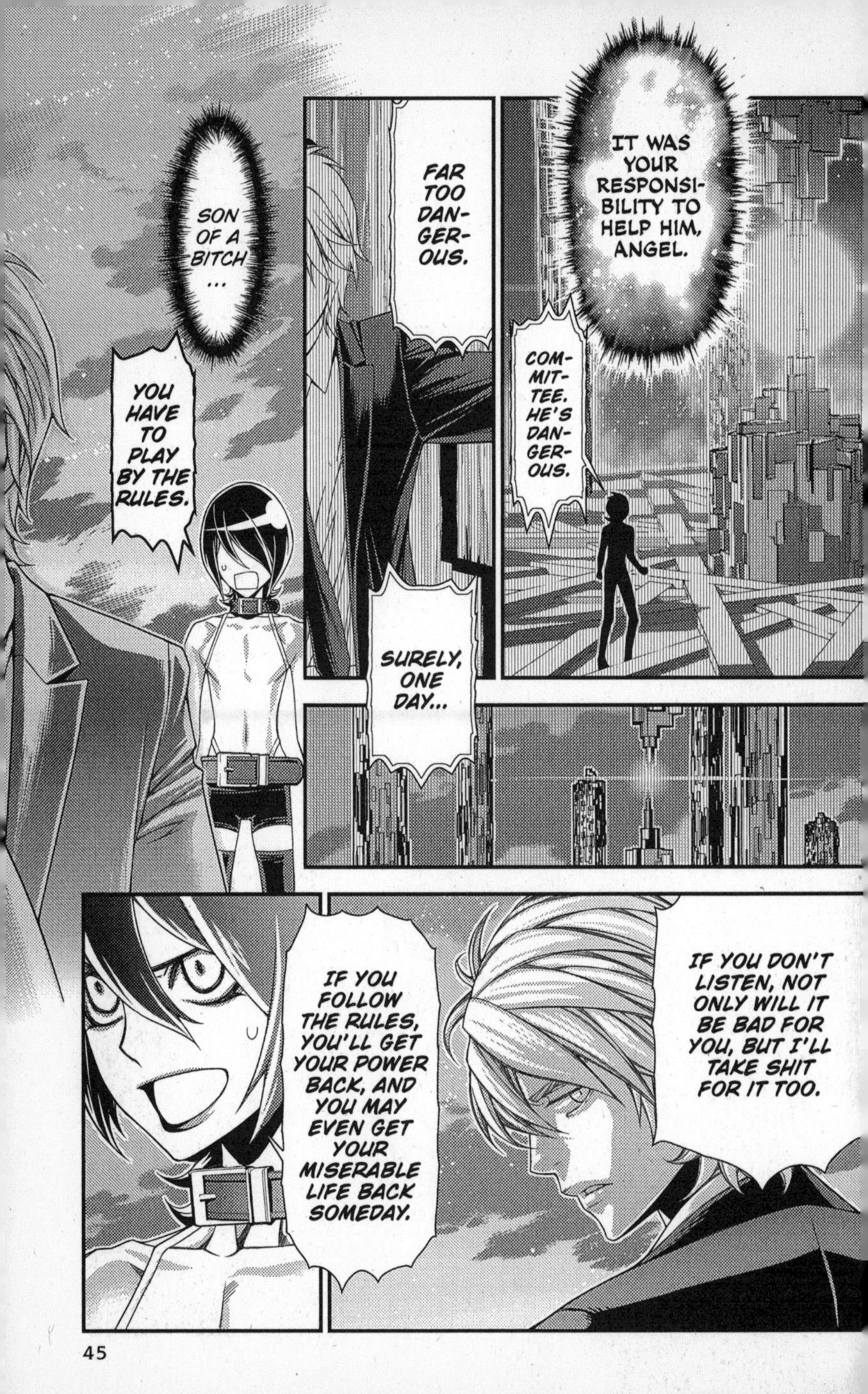
IT WAS YOUR RESPONSIBILITY TO HELP HIM, ANGEL.
COMMITTEE. HE'S DANGEROUS.
FAR TOO DANGEROUS.
SURELY, ONE DAY...
SON OF A BITCH...
YOU HAVE TO PLAY BY THE RULES.
IF YOU DON'T LISTEN, NOT ONLY WILL IT BE BAD FOR YOU, BUT I'LL TAKE SHIT FOR IT TOO.
IF YOU FOLLOW THE RULES, YOU'LL GET YOUR POWER BACK, AND YOU MAY EVEN GET YOUR MISERABLE LIFE BACK SOMEDAY.

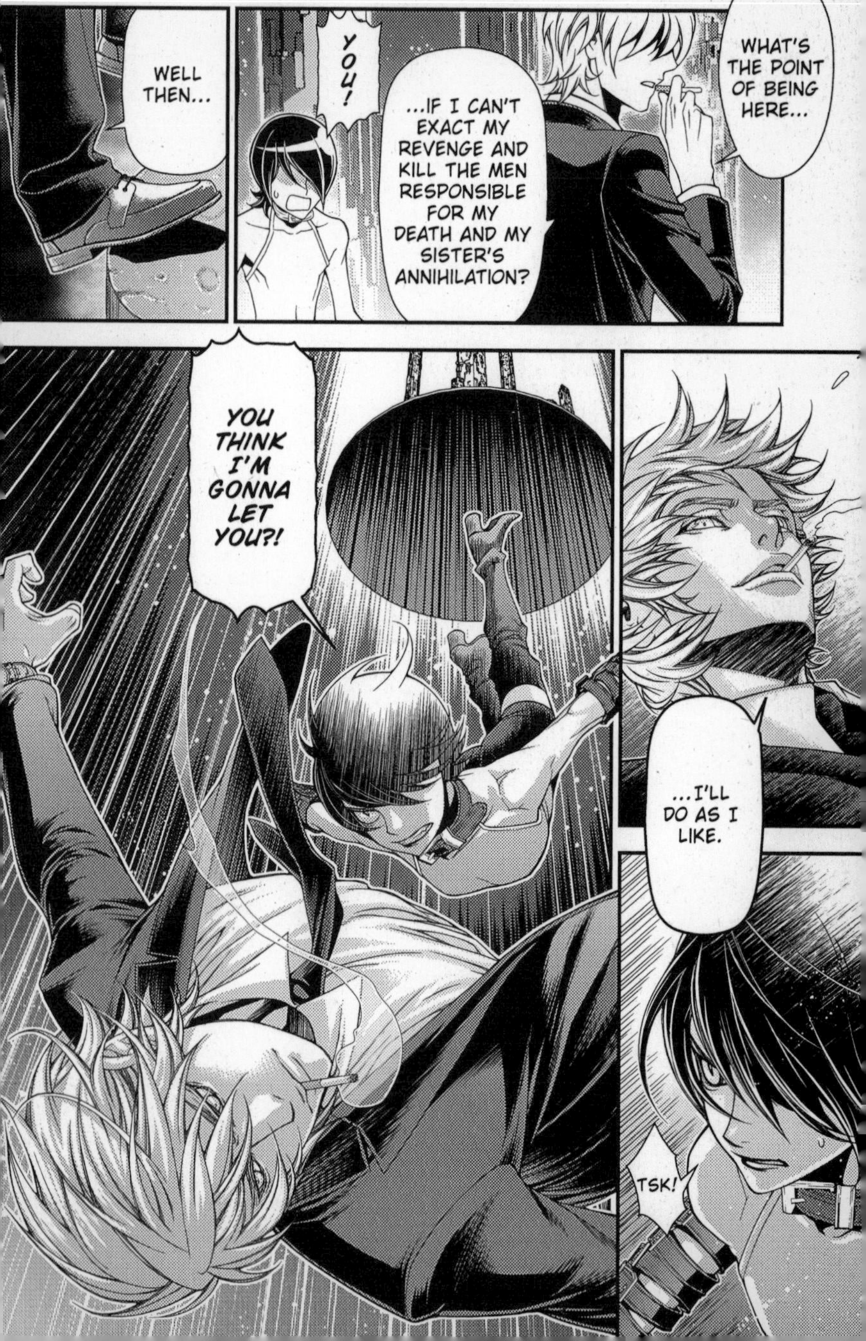
WHAT'S THE POINT OF BEING HERE...
...IF I CAN'T EXACT MY REVENGE AND KILL THE MEN RESPONSIBLE FOR MY DEATH AND MY SISTER'S ANNIHILATION?
YOU!
WELL THEN...
...I'LL DO AS I LIKE.
TSK!
YOU THINK I'M GONNA LET YOU?!

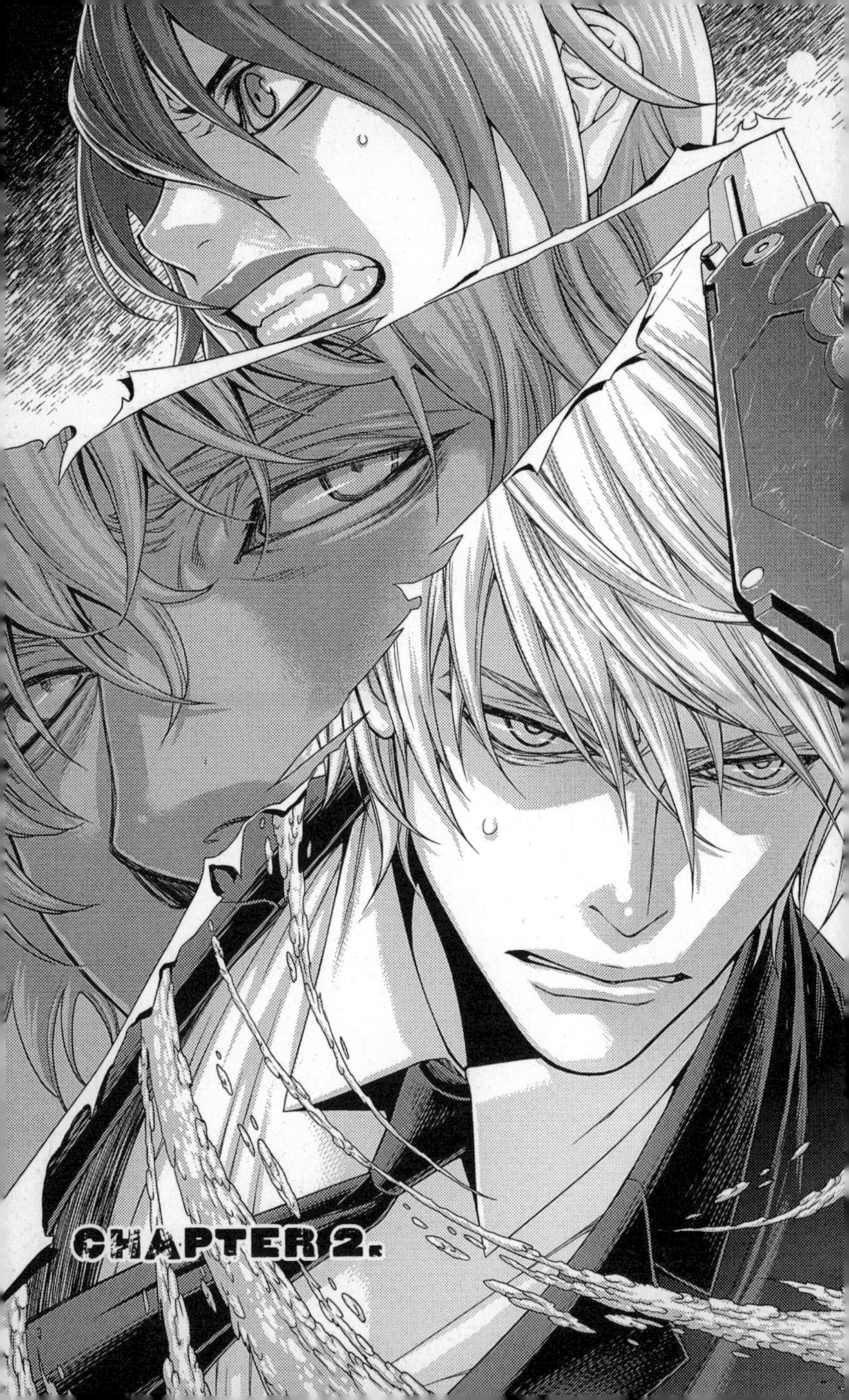
CHAPTER 2.

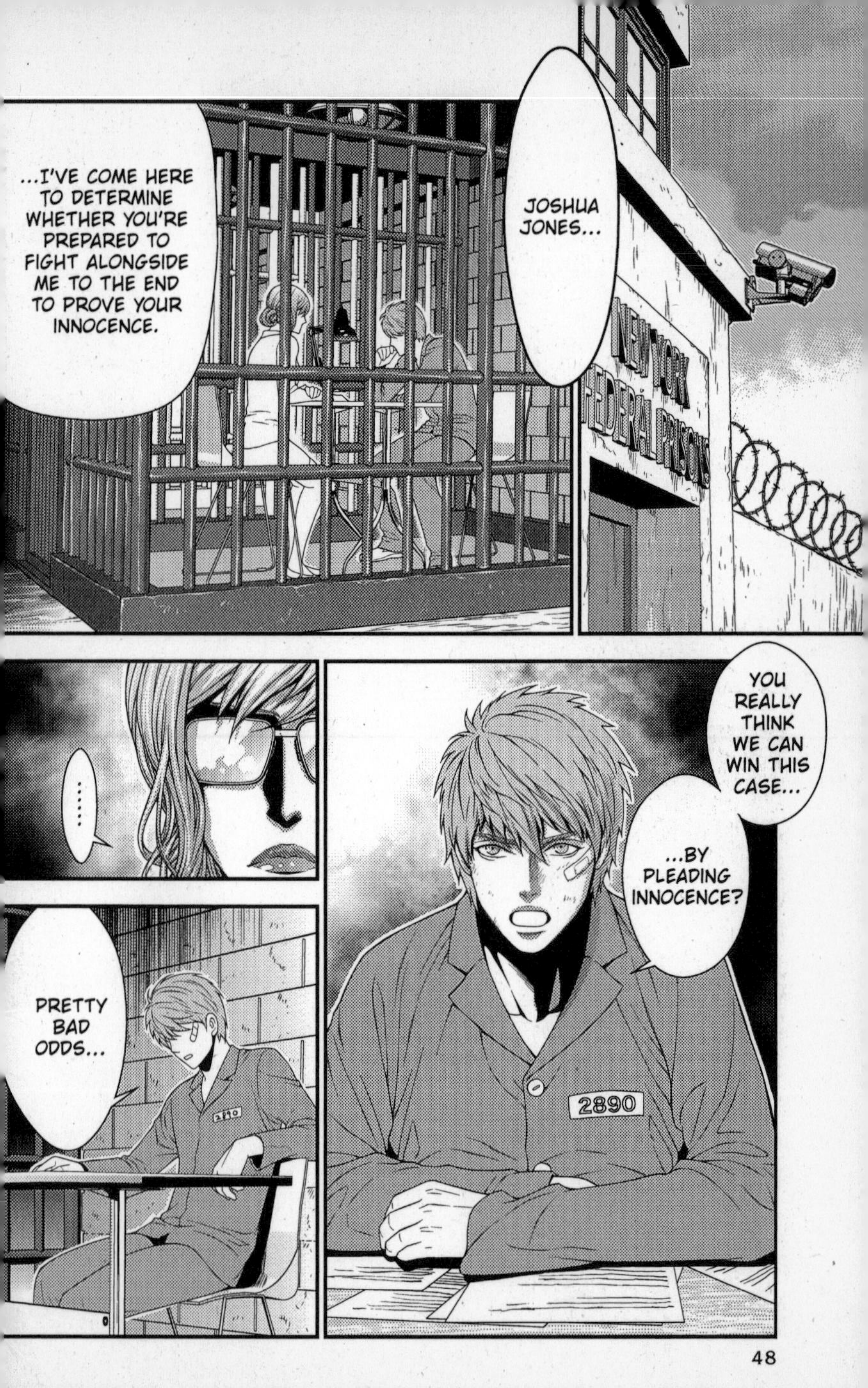
JOSHUA JONES...
NEW YORK FEDERAL PRISONS
...I'VE COME HERE TO DETERMINE WHETHER YOU'RE PREPARED TO FIGHT ALONGSIDE ME TO THE END TO PROVE YOUR INNOCENCE.
YOU REALLY THINK WE CAN WIN THIS CASE...
...BY PLEADING INNOCENCE?
2890
......
PRETTY BAD ODDS...

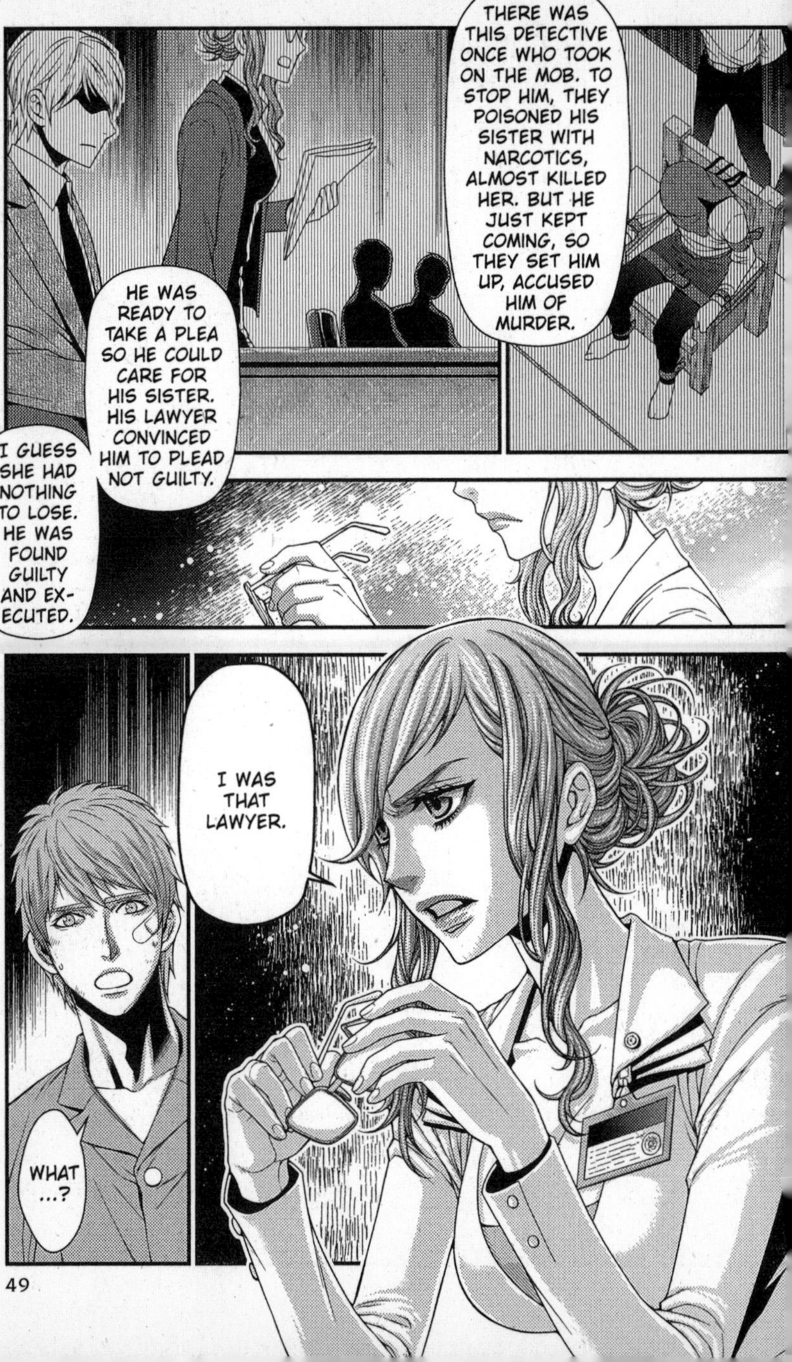
THERE WAS THIS DETECTIVE ONCE WHO TOOK ON THE MOB. TO STOP HIM, THEY POISONED HIS SISTER WITH NARCOTICS, ALMOST KILLED HER. BUT HE JUST KEPT COMING, SO THEY SET HIM UP, ACCUSED HIM OF MURDER.
HE WAS READY TO TAKE A PLEA SO HE COULD CARE FOR HIS SISTER. HIS LAWYER CONVINCED HIM TO PLEAD NOT GUILTY.
I GUESS SHE HAD NOTHING TO LOSE. HE WAS FOUND GUILTY AND EX-ECUTED.
I WAS THAT LAWYER.
WHAT ...?

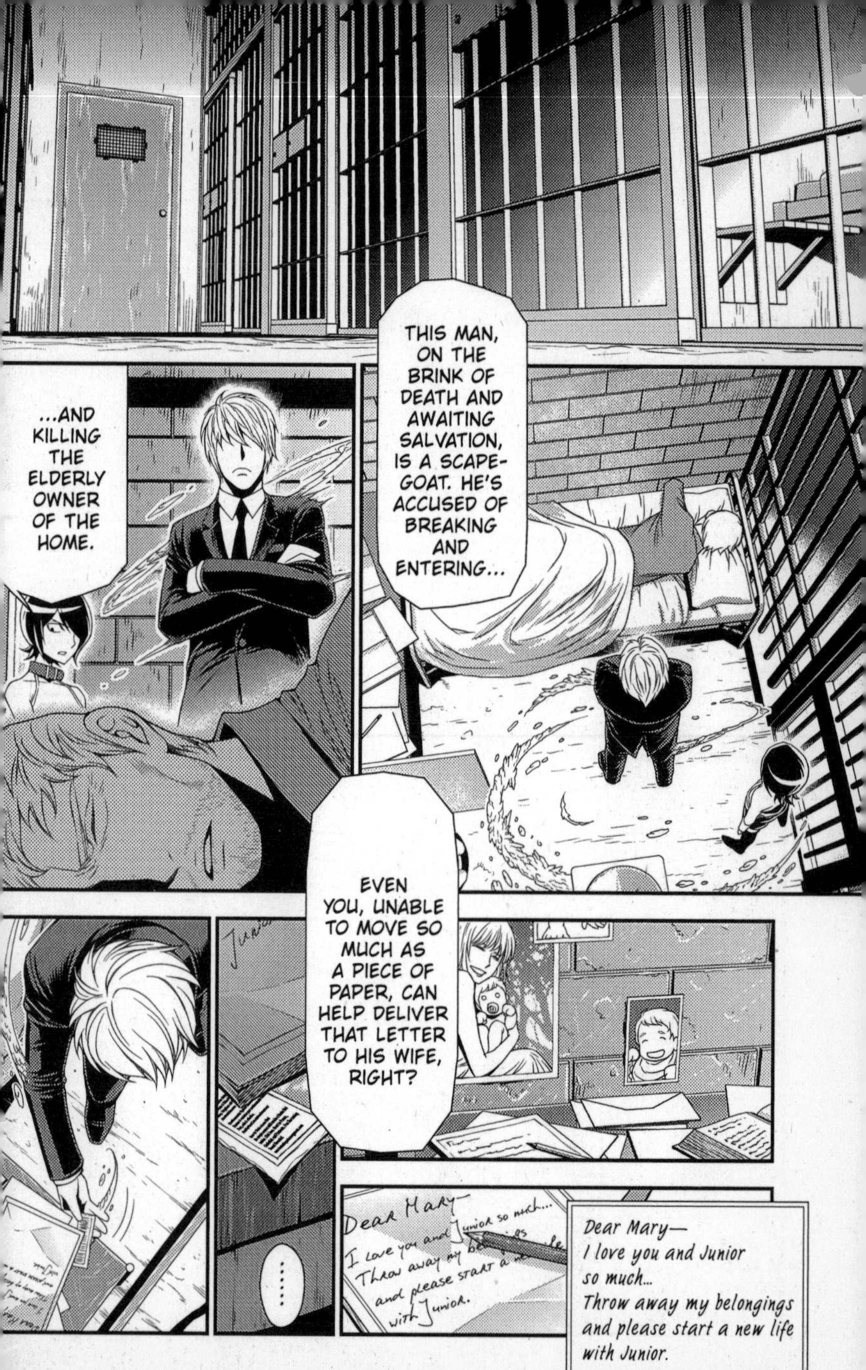
THIS MAN, ON THE BRINK OF DEATH AND AWAITING SALVATION, IS A SCAPE-GOAT. HE'S ACCUSED OF BREAKING AND ENTERING...
...AND KILLING THE ELDERLY OWNER OF THE HOME.
EVEN YOU, UNABLE TO MOVE SO MUCH AS A PIECE OF PAPER, CAN HELP DELIVER THAT LETTER TO HIS WIFE, RIGHT?
Dear Mary— I love you and Junior so much... Throw away my belongings and please start a new life with Junior.
......

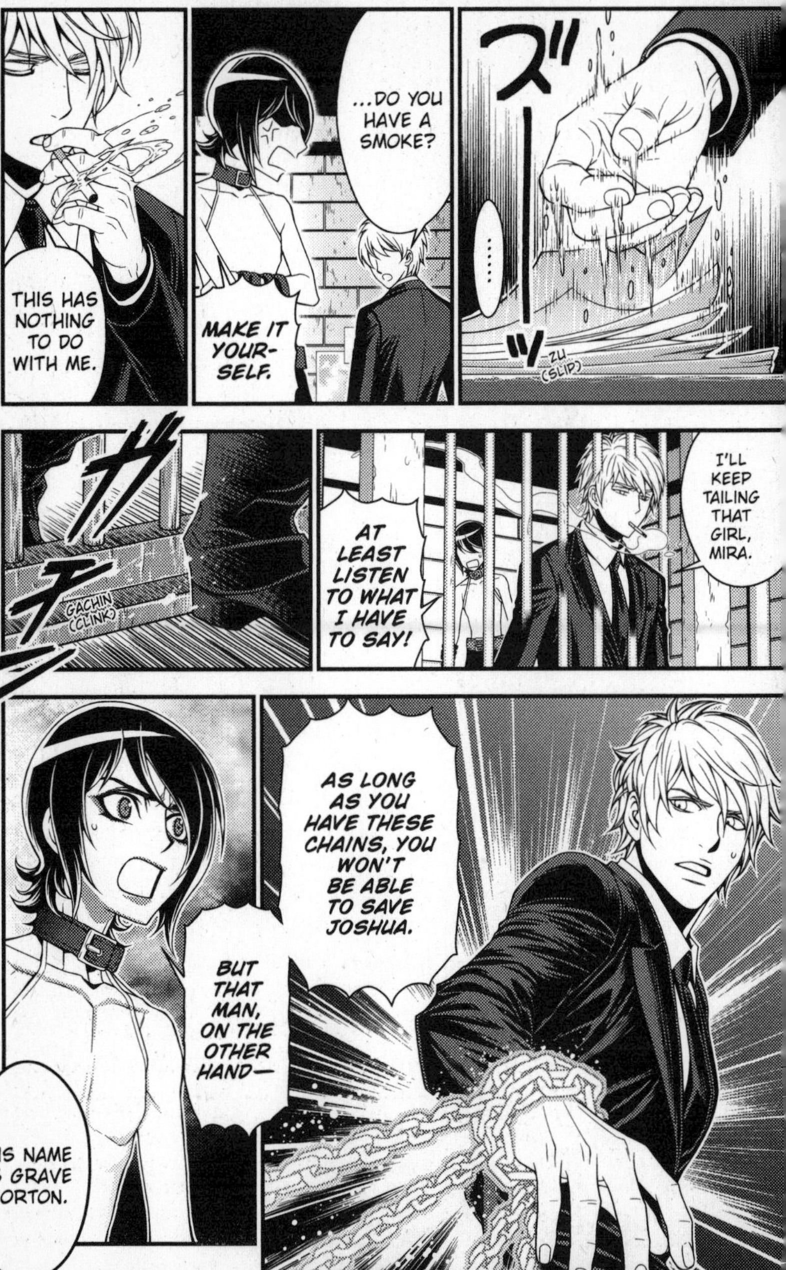
ズ
......
ZU (SLIP)
...DO YOU HAVE A SMOKE?
MAKE IT YOURSELF.
THIS HAS NOTHING TO DO WITH ME.
I'LL KEEP TAILING THAT GIRL, MIRA.
AT LEAST LISTEN TO WHAT I HAVE TO SAY!
GACHIN (CLINK)
AS LONG AS YOU HAVE THESE CHAINS, YOU WON'T BE ABLE TO SAVE JOSHUA.
BUT THAT MAN, ON THE OTHER HAND—
HIS NAME IS GRAVE NORTON.

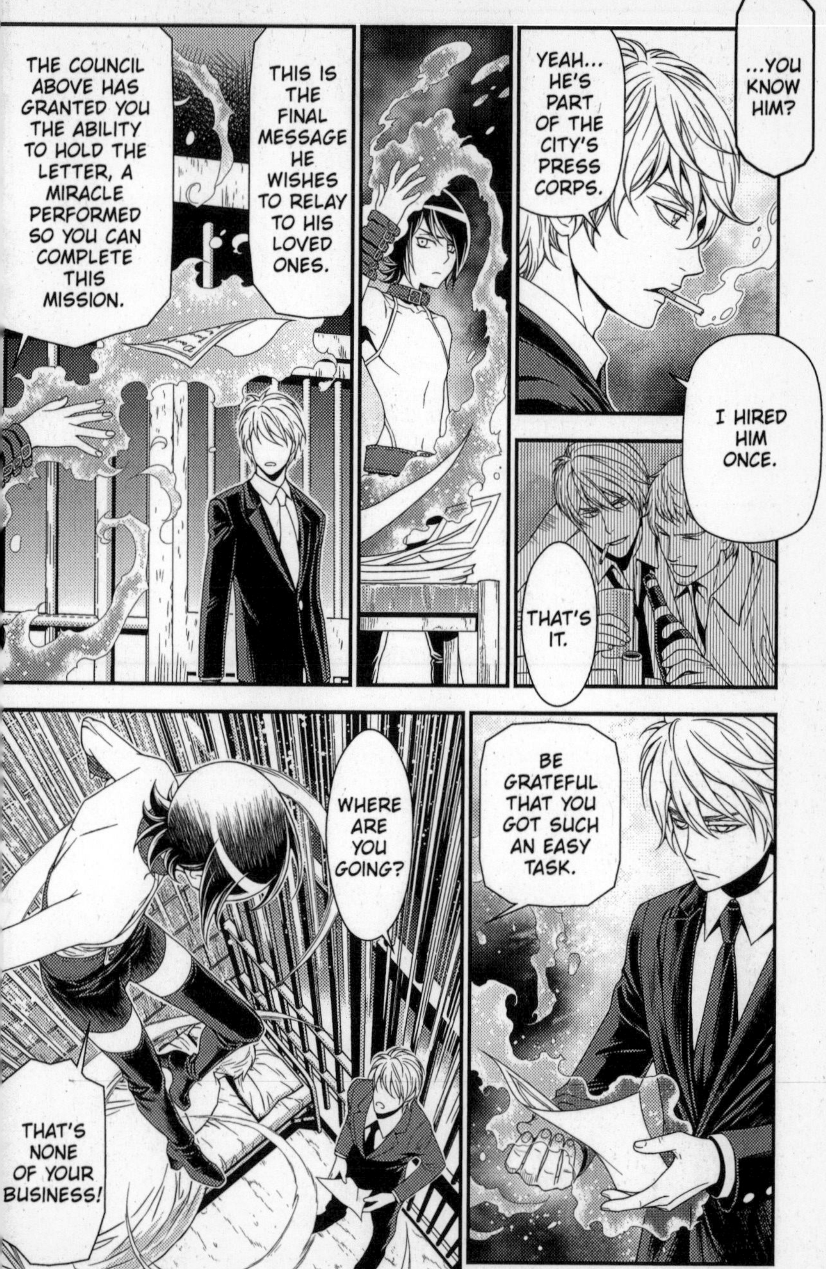
...YOU KNOW HIM?
YEAH... HE'S PART OF THE CITY'S PRESS CORPS.
I HIRED HIM ONCE.
THAT'S IT.
THIS IS THE FINAL MESSAGE HE WISHES TO RELAY TO HIS LOVED ONES.
THE COUNCIL ABOVE HAS GRANTED YOU THE ABILITY TO HOLD THE LETTER, A MIRACLE PERFORMED SO YOU CAN COMPLETE THIS MISSION.
BE GRATEFUL THAT YOU GOT SUCH AN EASY TASK.
WHERE ARE YOU GOING?
THAT'S NONE OF YOUR BUSINESS!

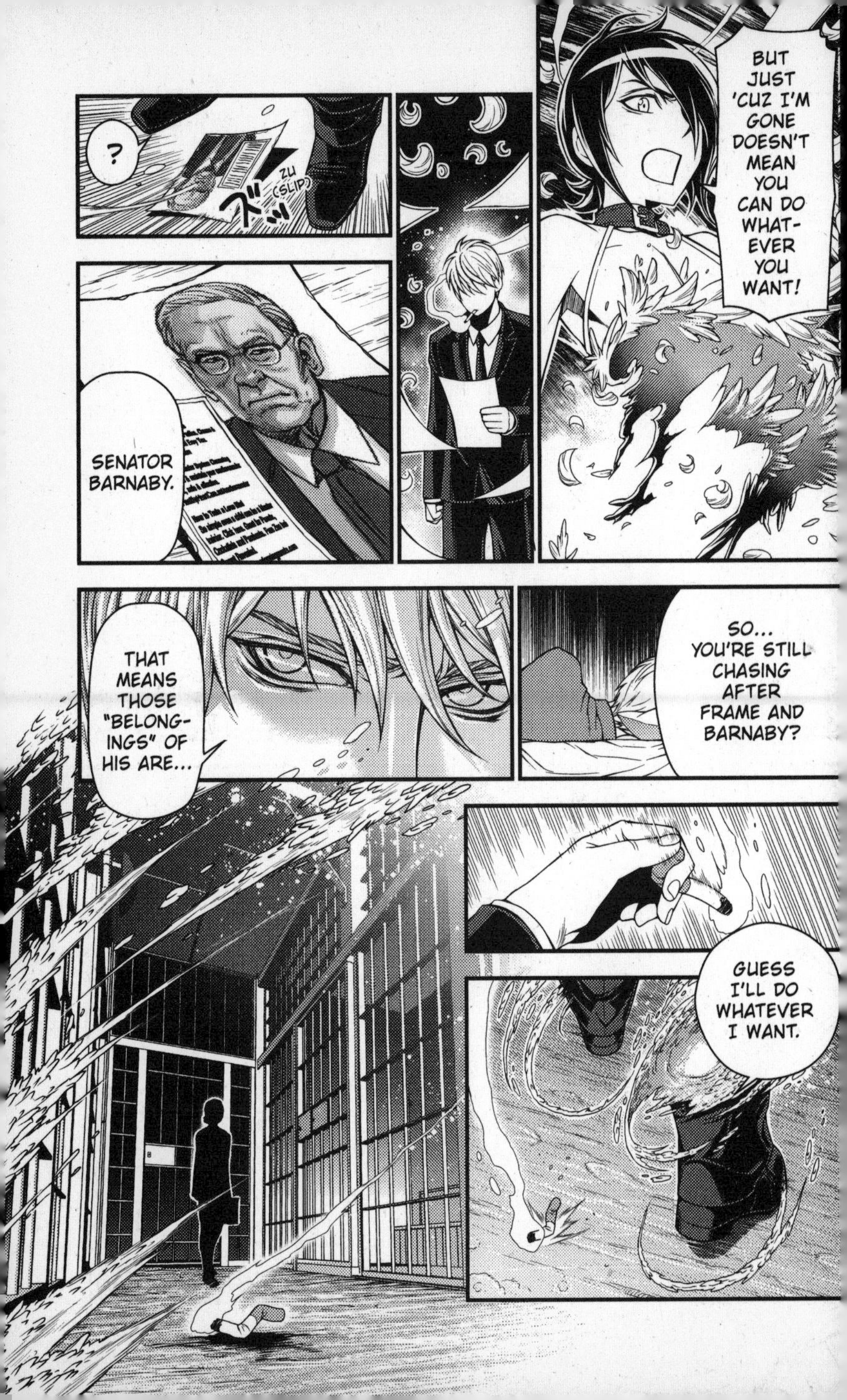
BUT JUST 'CUZ I'M GONE DOESN'T MEAN YOU CAN DO WHAT-EVER YOU WANT!
?
ZU (SLIP)
SENATOR BARNABY.
SO... YOU'RE STILL CHASING AFTER FRAME AND BARNABY?
THAT MEANS THOSE "BELONG-INGS" OF HIS ARE...
GUESS I'LL DO WHATEVER I WANT.

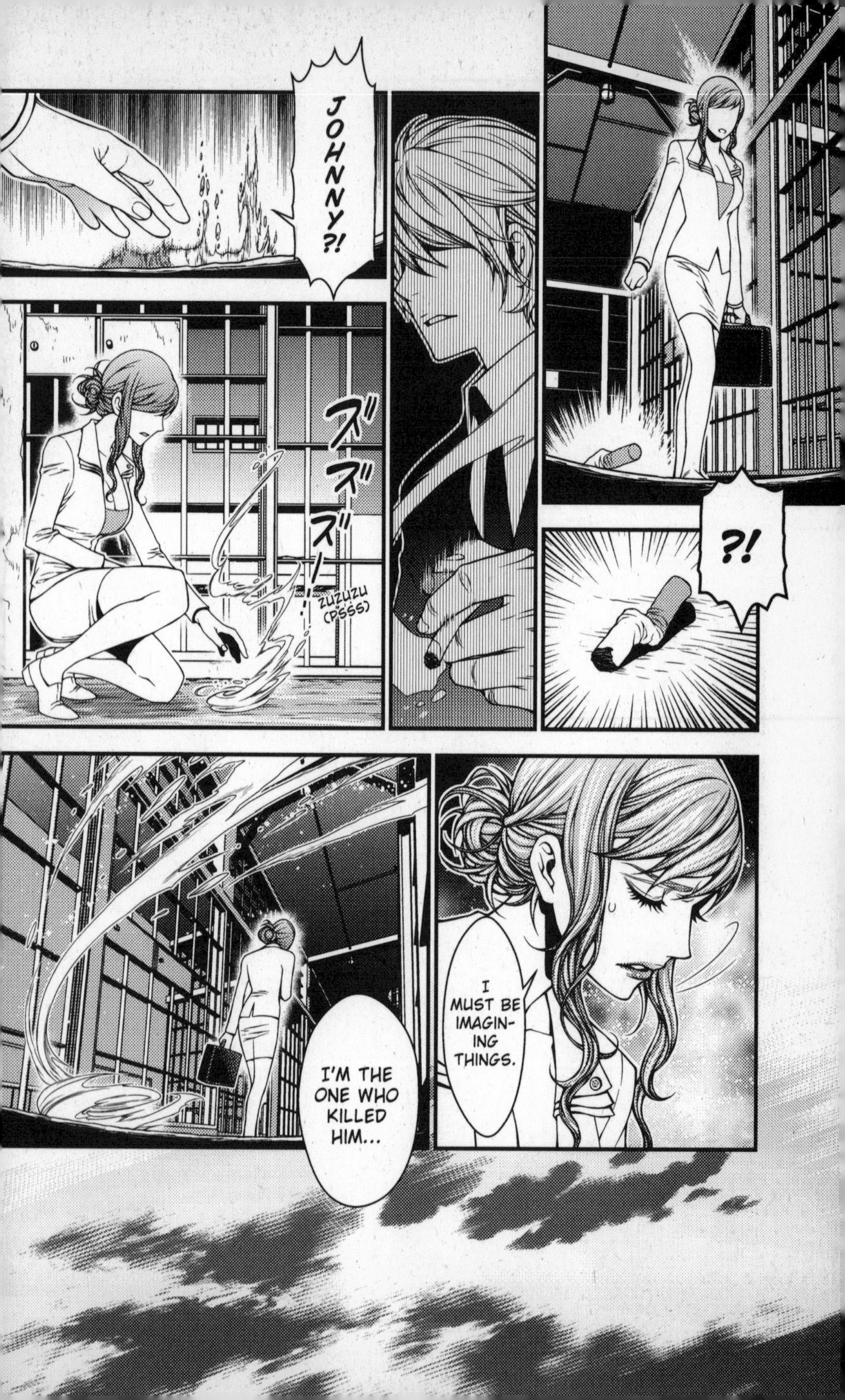
JOHNNY?!
?!
ズズズー
ZUZUZU (PSSS)
I MUST BE IMAGINING THINGS.
I'M THE ONE WHO KILLED HIM...

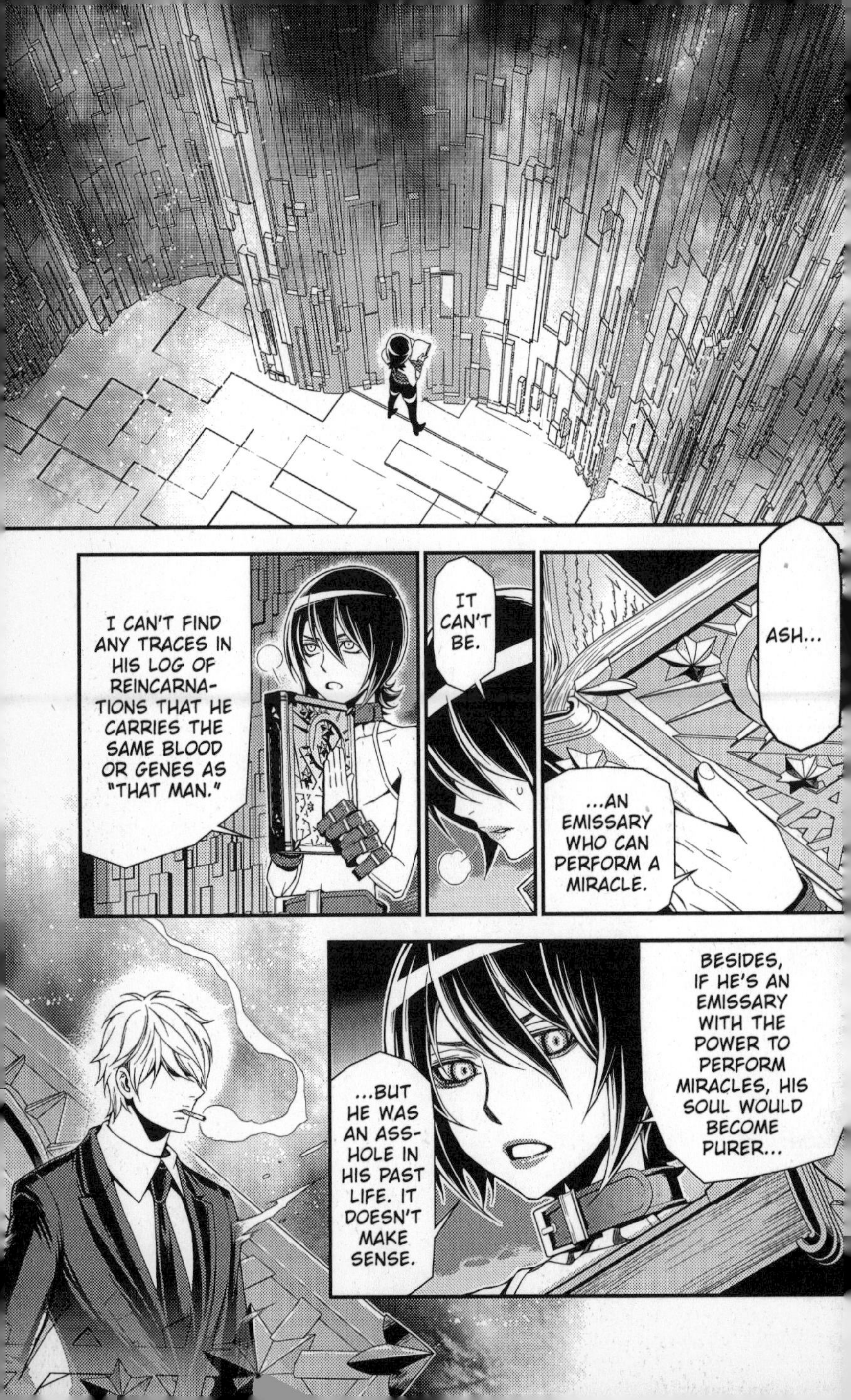
ASH...
...AN EMISSARY WHO CAN PERFORM A MIRACLE.
IT CAN'T BE.
I CAN'T FIND ANY TRACES IN HIS LOG OF REINCARNATIONS THAT HE CARRIES THE SAME BLOOD OR GENES AS "THAT MAN."
BESIDES, IF HE'S AN EMISSARY WITH THE POWER TO PERFORM MIRACLES, HIS SOUL WOULD BECOME PURER...
...BUT HE WAS AN ASSHOLE IN HIS PAST LIFE. IT DOESN'T MAKE SENSE.

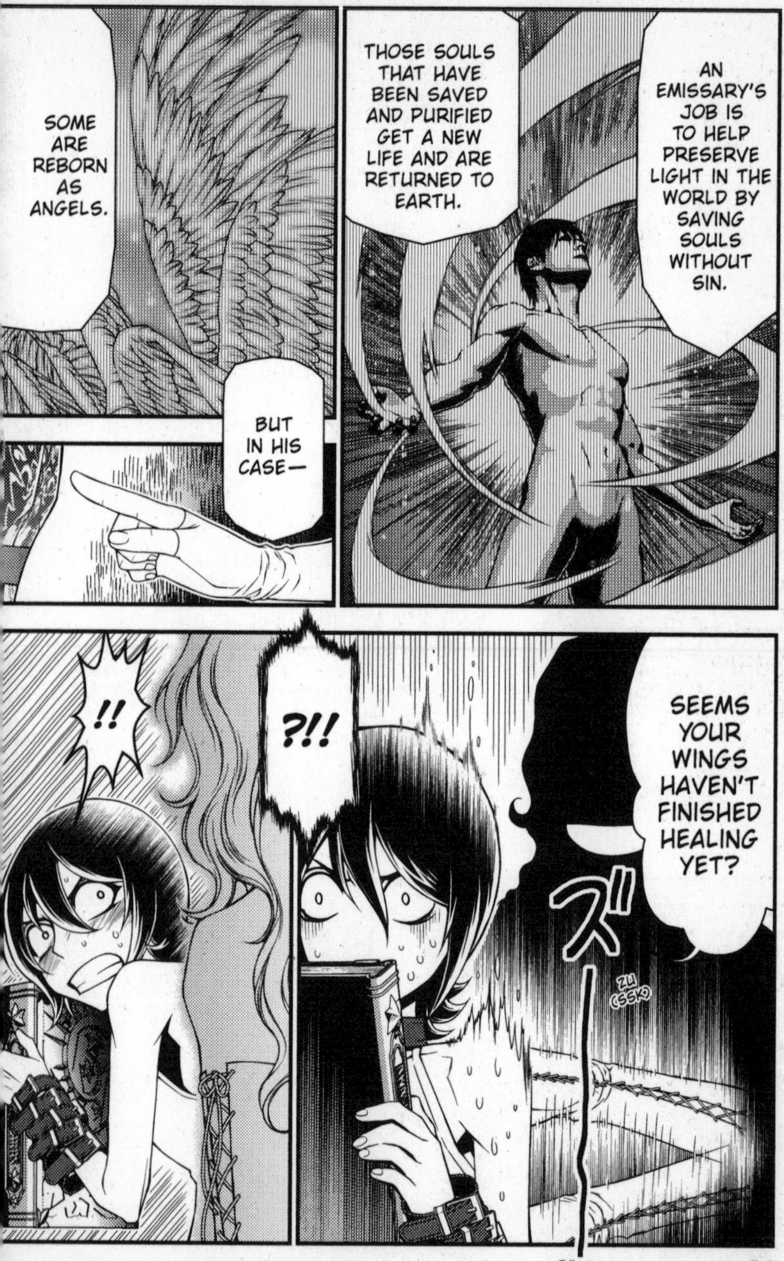
AN EMISSARY'S JOB IS TO HELP PRESERVE LIGHT IN THE WORLD BY SAVING SOULS WITHOUT SIN.
THOSE SOULS THAT HAVE BEEN SAVED AND PURIFIED GET A NEW LIFE AND ARE RETURNED TO EARTH.
SOME ARE REBORN AS ANGELS.
BUT IN HIS CASE—
SEEMS YOUR WINGS HAVEN'T FINISHED HEALING YET?
ズ
ZU (SSK)
?!!
!!

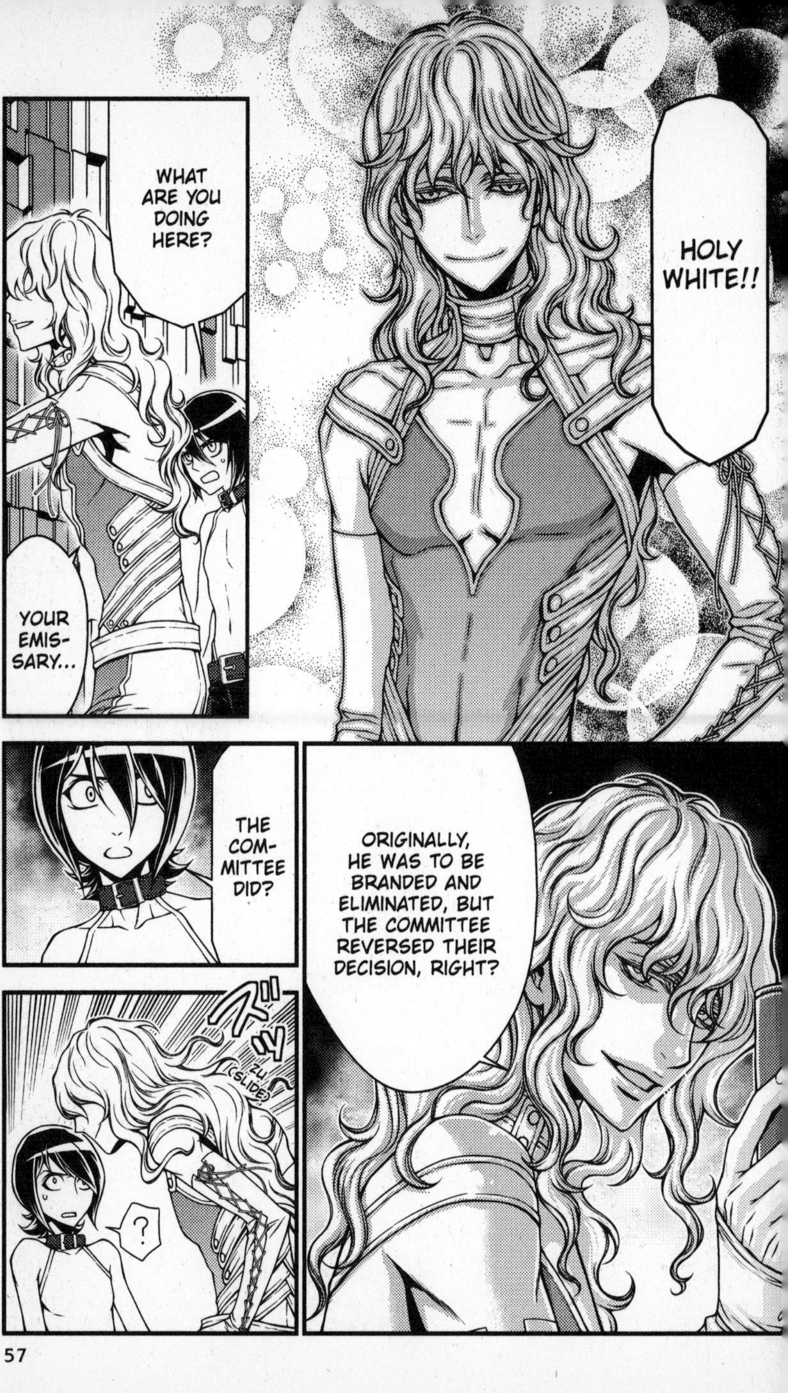
HOLY WHITE!!
WHAT ARE YOU DOING HERE?
YOUR EMIS-SARY...
ORIGINALLY, HE WAS TO BE BRANDED AND ELIMINATED, BUT THE COMMITTEE REVERSED THEIR DECISION, RIGHT?
THE COM-MITTEE DID?
ZU (SLIDE)
?

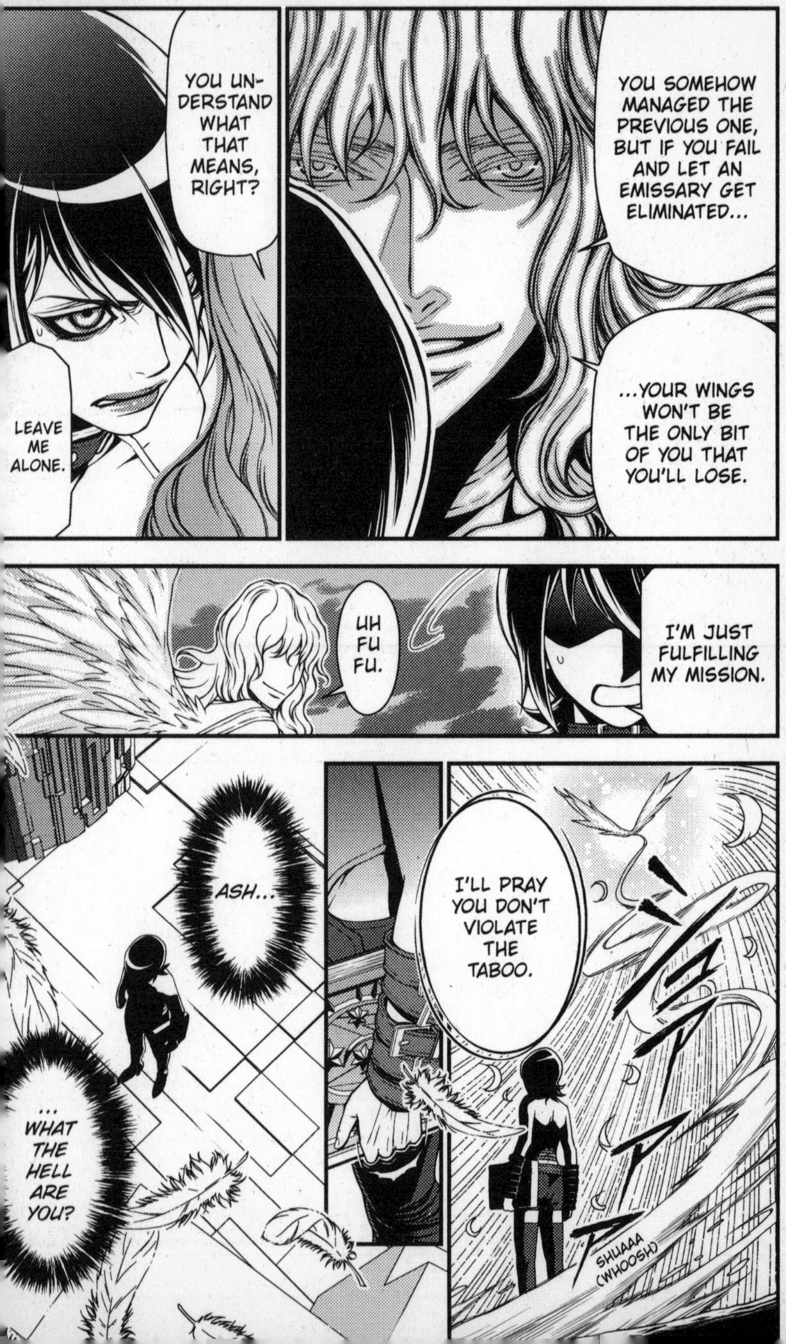
YOU SOMEHOW MANAGED THE PREVIOUS ONE, BUT IF YOU FAIL AND LET AN EMISSARY GET ELIMINATED...
...YOUR WINGS WON'T BE THE ONLY BIT OF YOU THAT YOU'LL LOSE.
YOU UN-DERSTAND WHAT THAT MEANS, RIGHT?
LEAVE ME ALONE.
I'M JUST FULFILLING MY MISSION.
UH FU FU.
I'LL PRAY YOU DON'T VIOLATE THE TABOO.
SHUAAA (WHOOSH)
ASH...
...WHAT THE HELL ARE YOU?

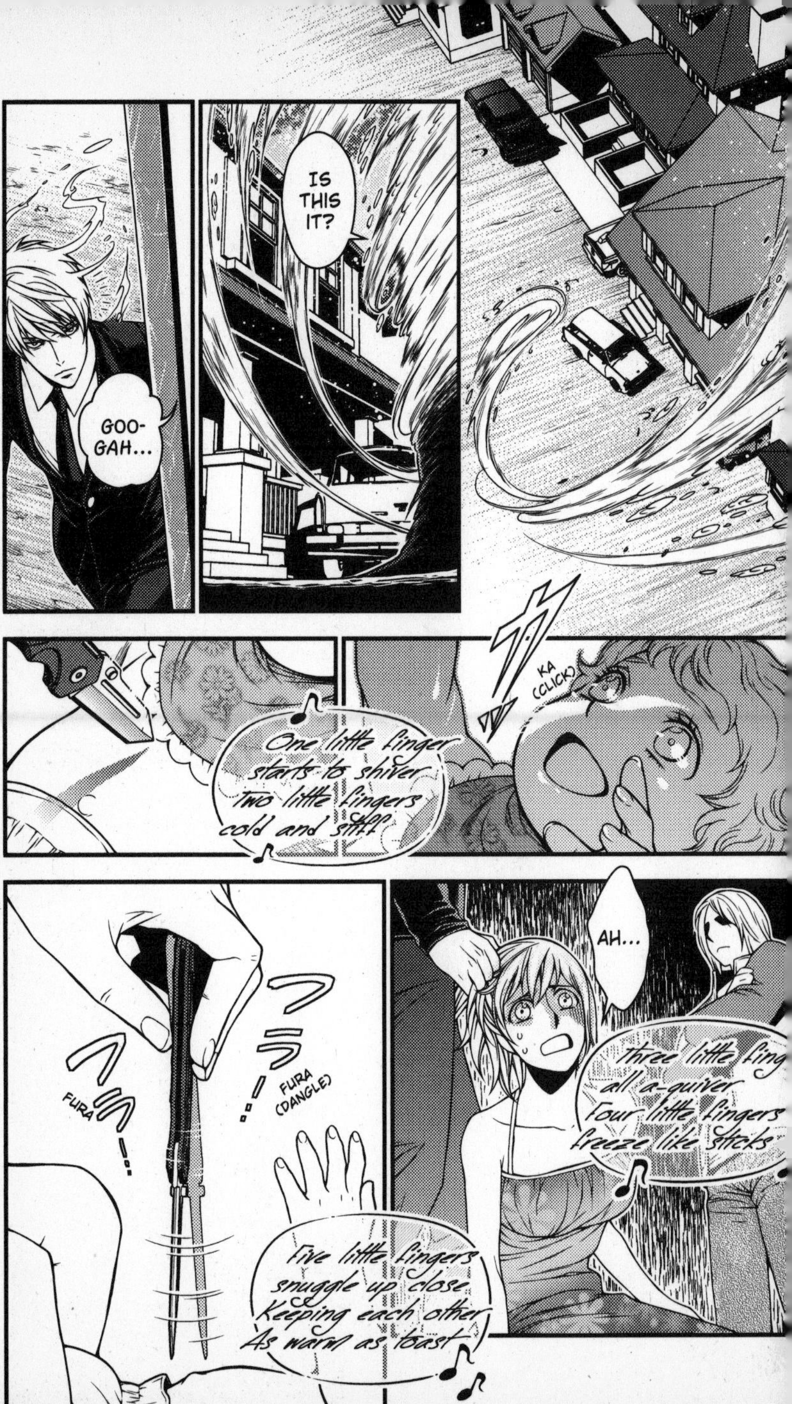
IS THIS IT?
GOO-GAH...
KA (CLICK)
One little finger starts to shiver Two little fingers cold and stiff
AH...
three little fing all a-quiver Four little fingers freeze like sticks
FURA (DANGLE)
FURA
Five little fingers snuggle up close Keeping each other As warm as toast

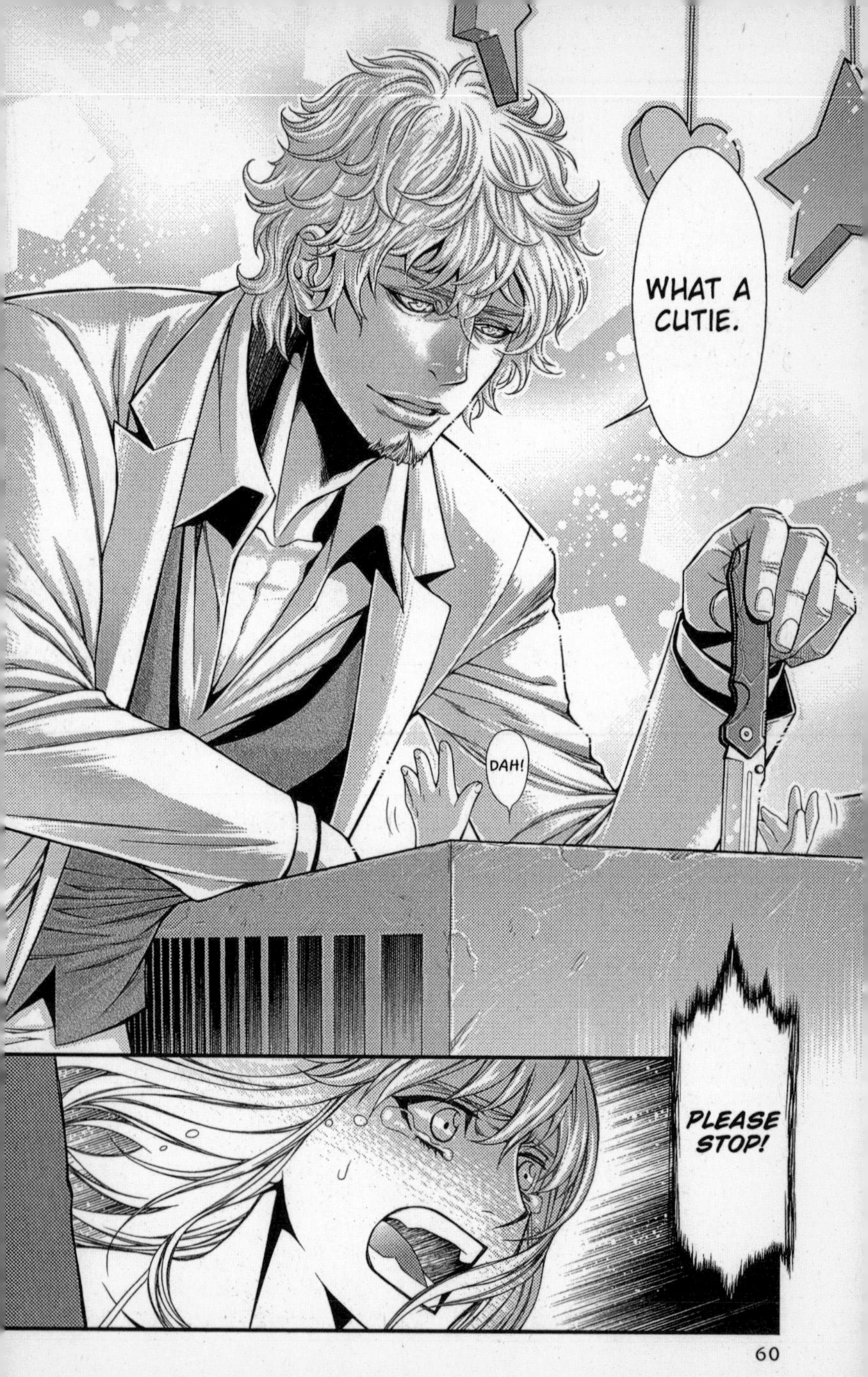
WHAT A CUTIE.
DAH!
PLEASE STOP!

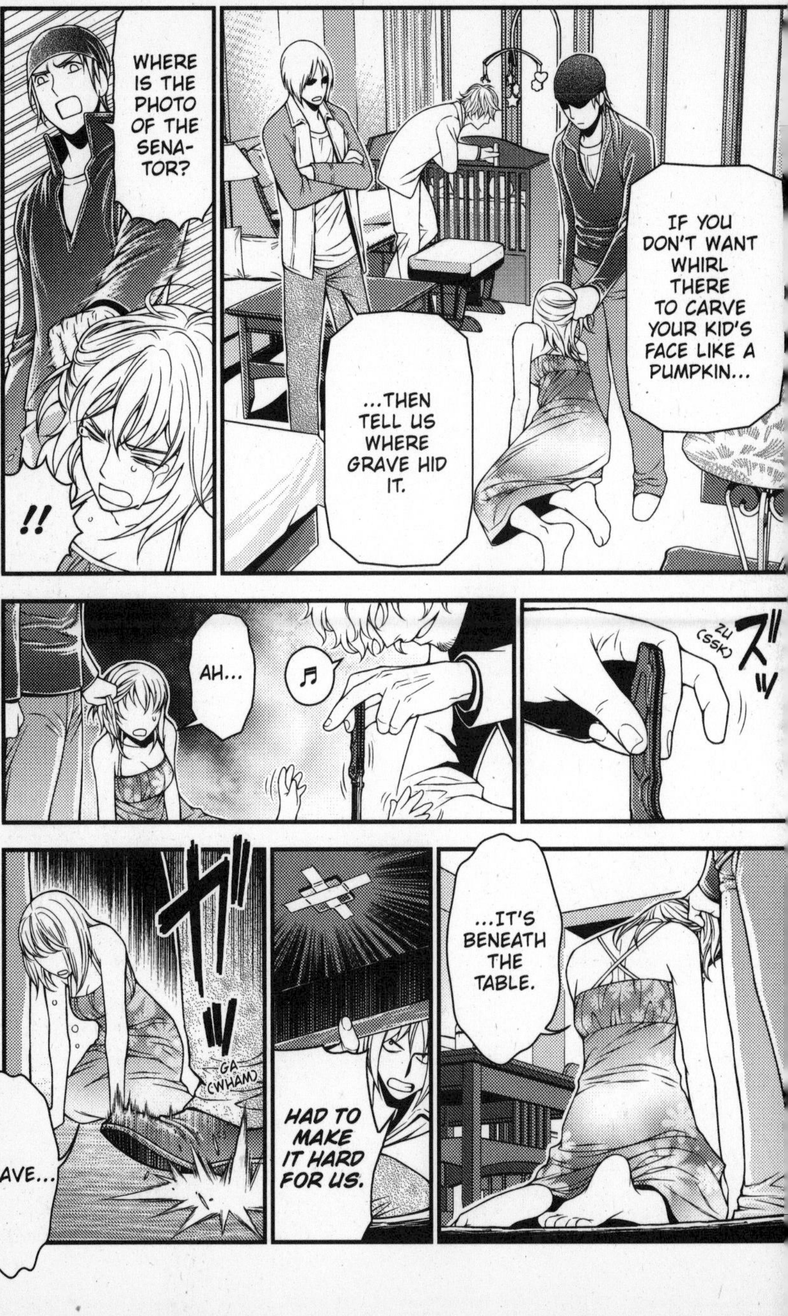
IF YOU DON'T WANT WHIRL THERE TO CARVE YOUR KID'S FACE LIKE A PUMPKIN...
...THEN TELL US WHERE GRAVE HID IT.
WHERE IS THE PHOTO OF THE SENA-TOR?
!!
ZU (SSK)
♪
AH...
...IT'S BENEATH THE TABLE.
HAD TO MAKE IT HARD FOR US.
GA (WHAM)
GRAVE...

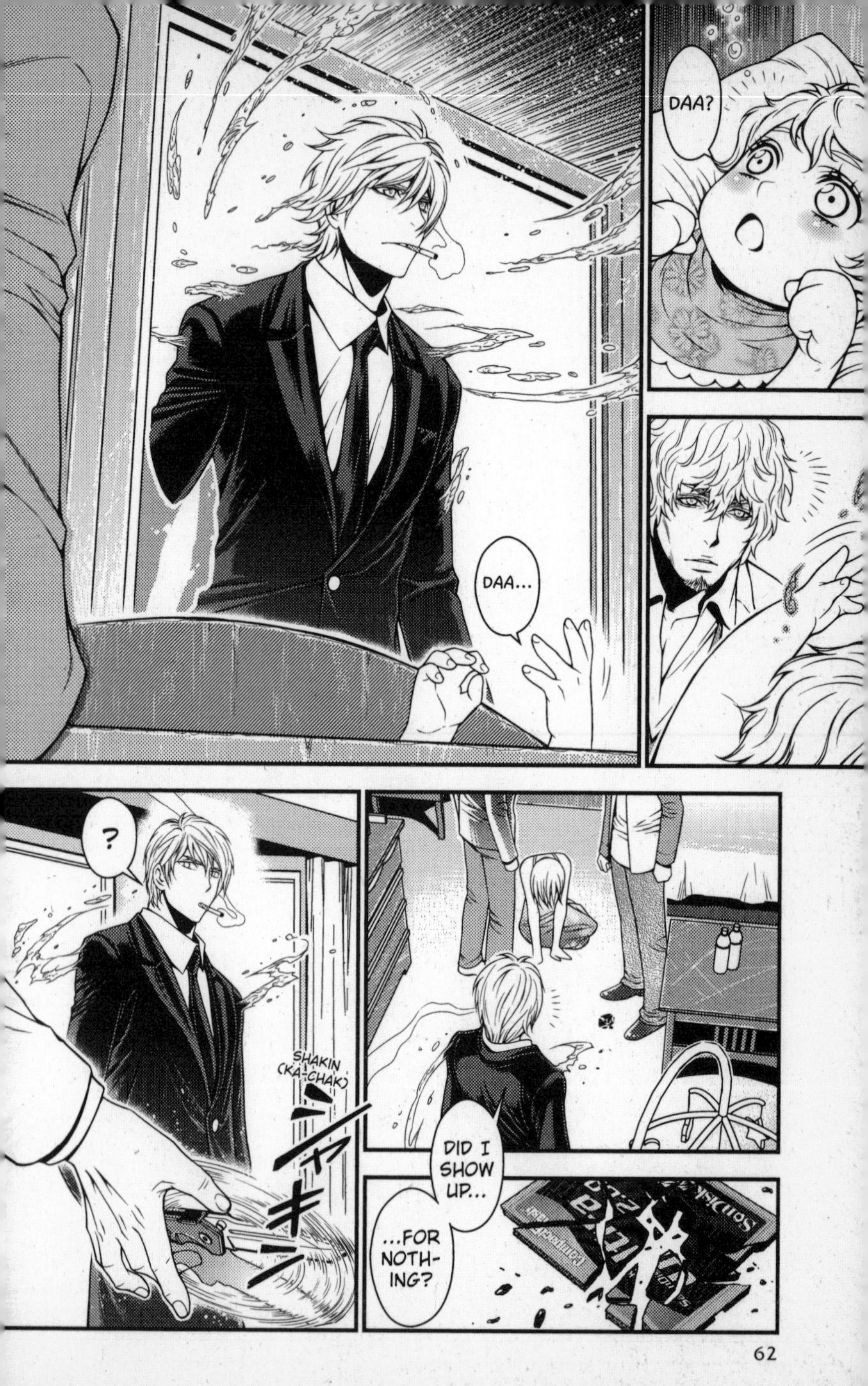
DAA?
DAA...
DID I SHOW UP...
...FOR NOTHING?
?
SHAKIN (KA-CHAK)

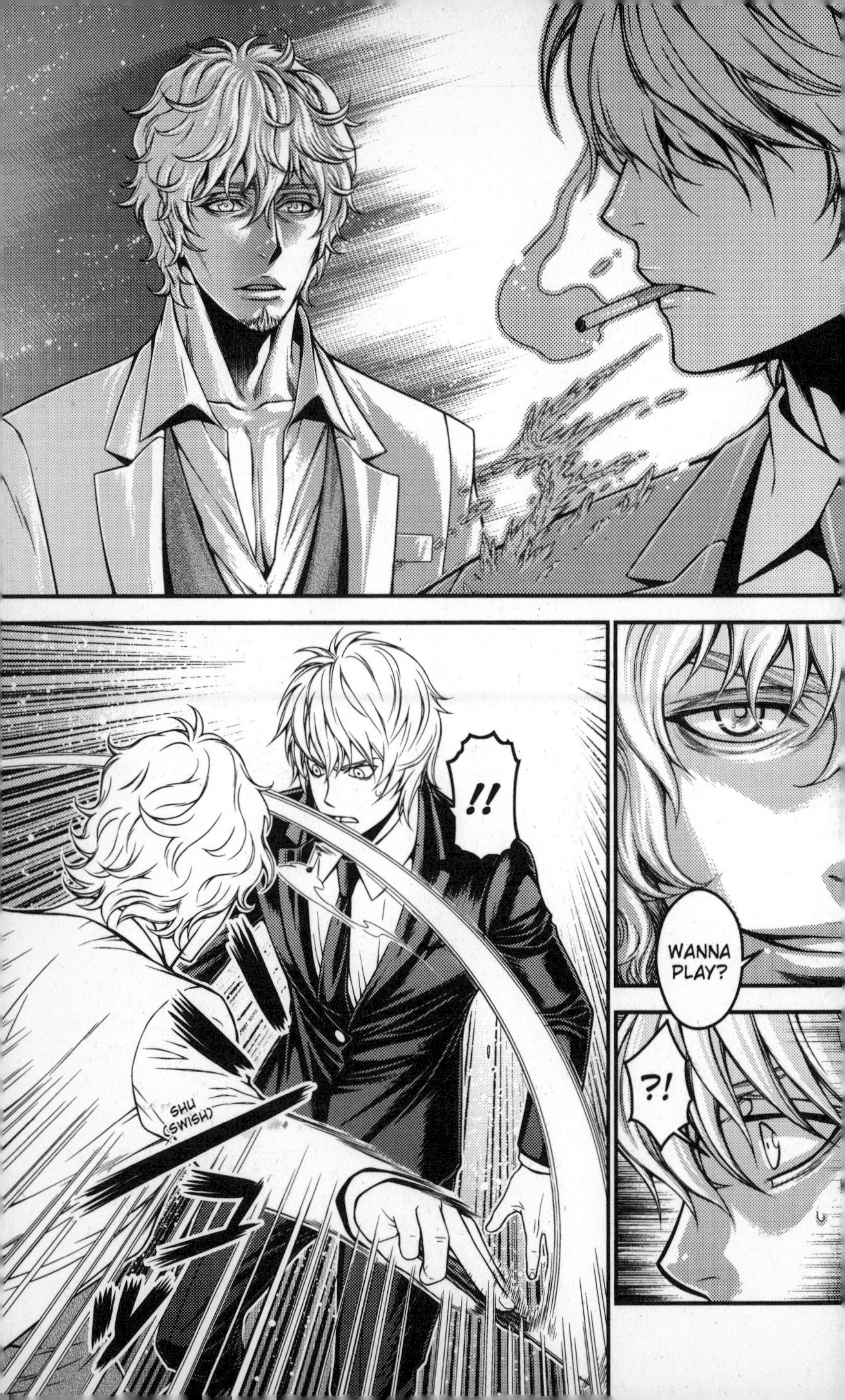
WANNA PLAY?
?!
!!
SHU (SWISH)

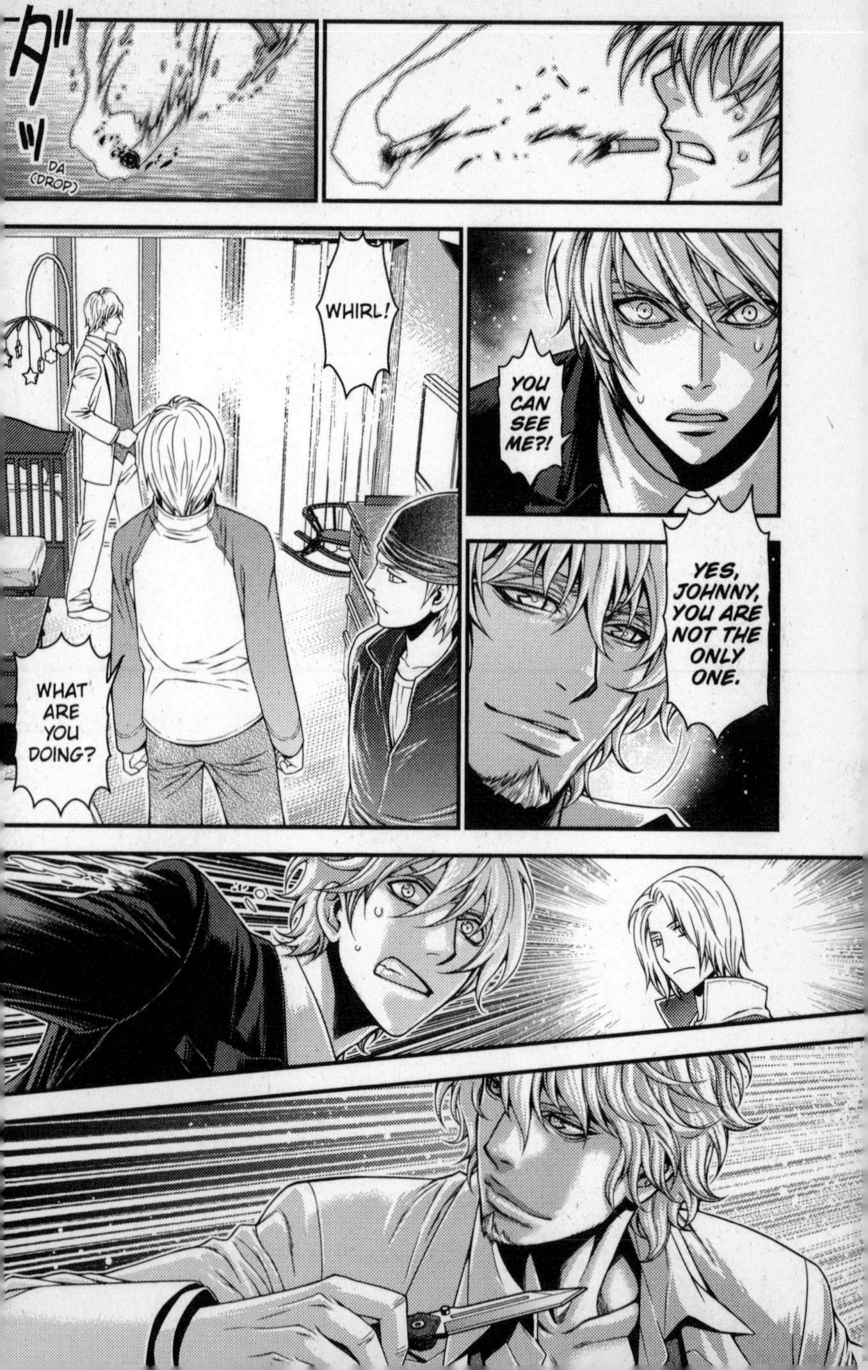
ダッ
DA (DROP)
YOU CAN SEE ME?!
YES, JOHNNY, YOU ARE NOT THE ONLY ONE.
WHIRL!
WHAT ARE YOU DOING?

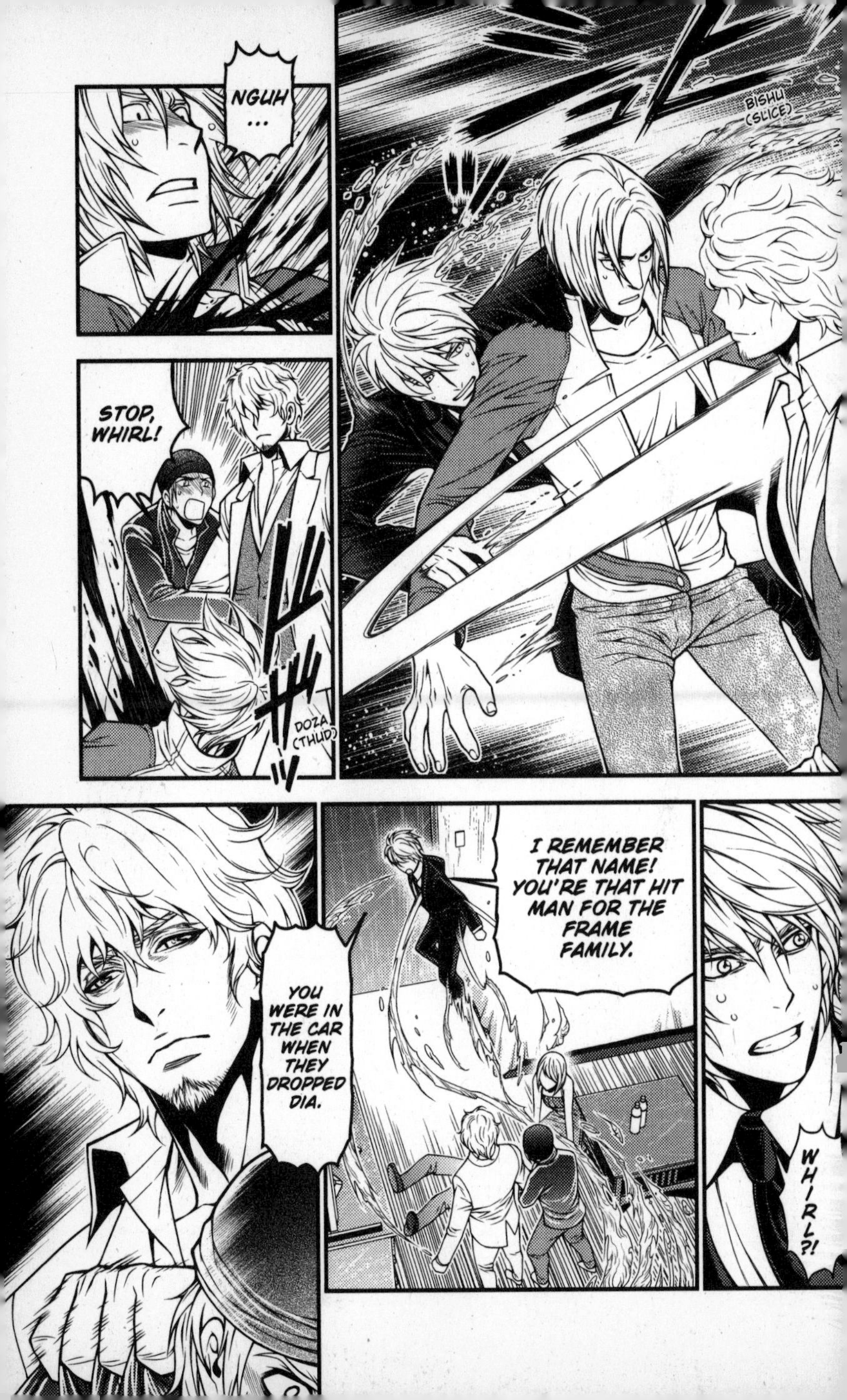
BISHU (SLICE)
NGUH ...
STOP, WHIRL!
DOZA (THUD)
WHIRL?!
I REMEMBER THAT NAME! YOU'RE THAT HIT MAN FOR THE FRAME FAMILY.
YOU WERE IN THE CAR WHEN THEY DROPPED DIA.

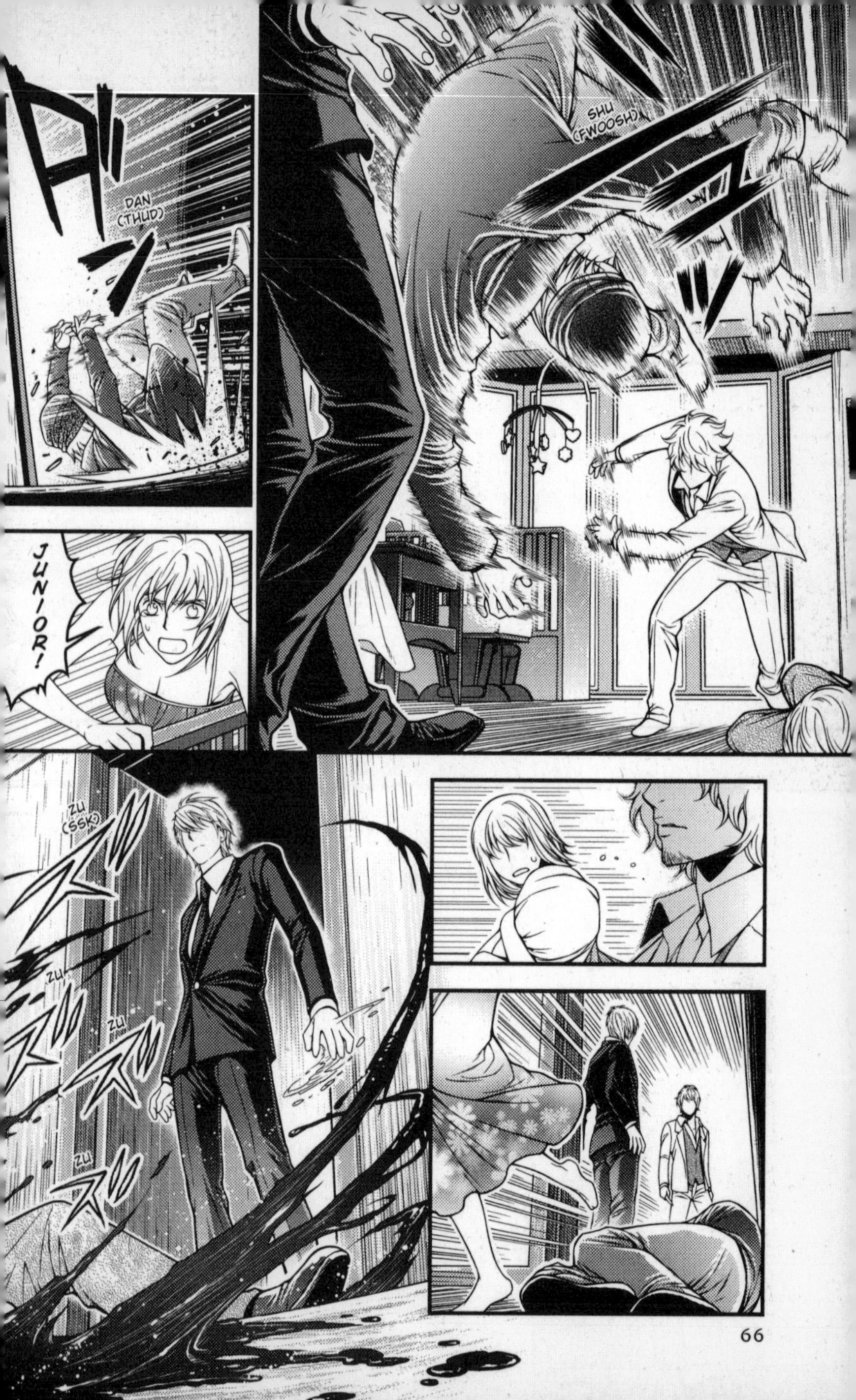
SHU
(FWOOSH)
DAN
(THUD)
JUNIOR!
ZU
(SSK)
ZU
ZU
ZU

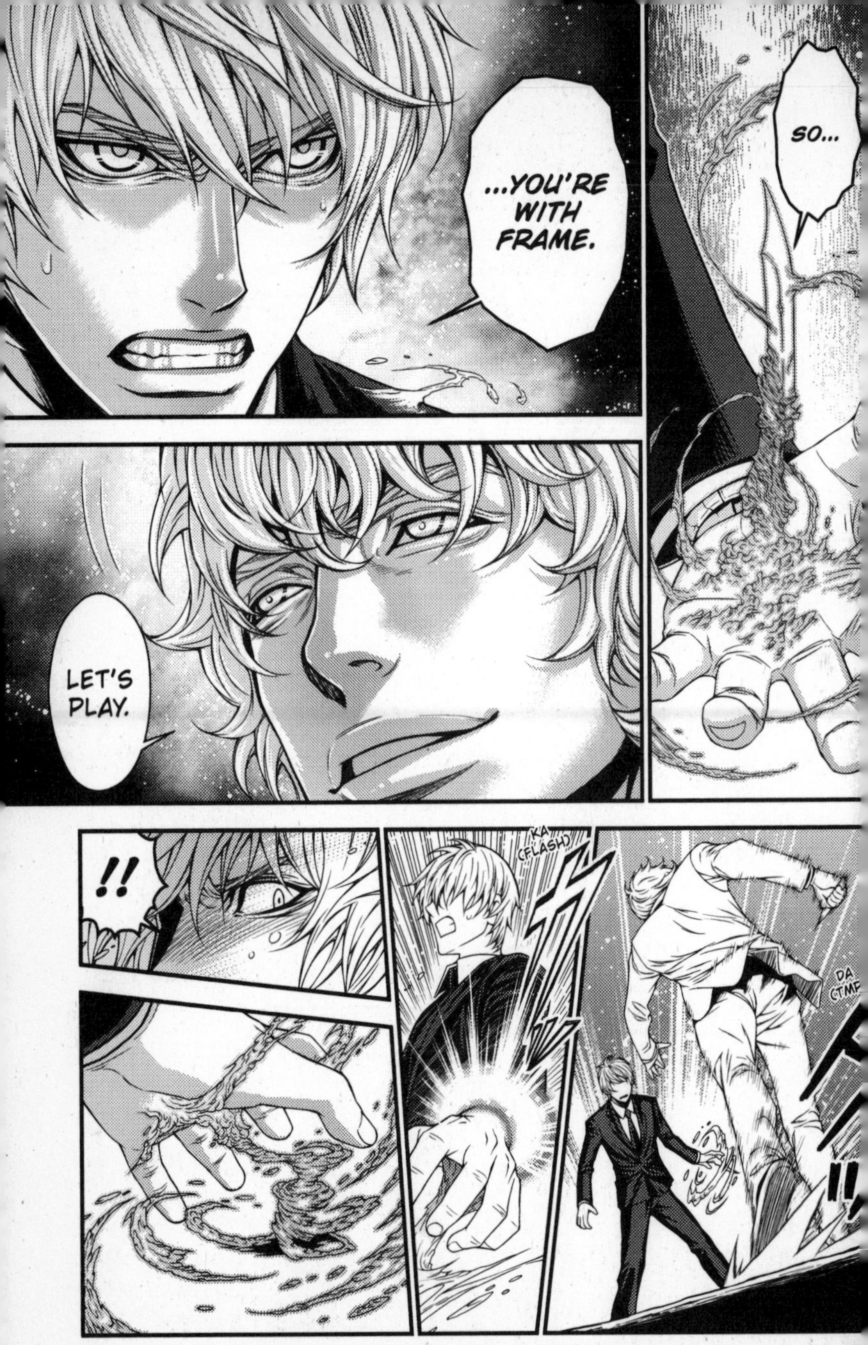
SO...
...YOU'RE WITH FRAME.
LET'S PLAY.
DA (TMP
!!
KA (FLASH)
!!

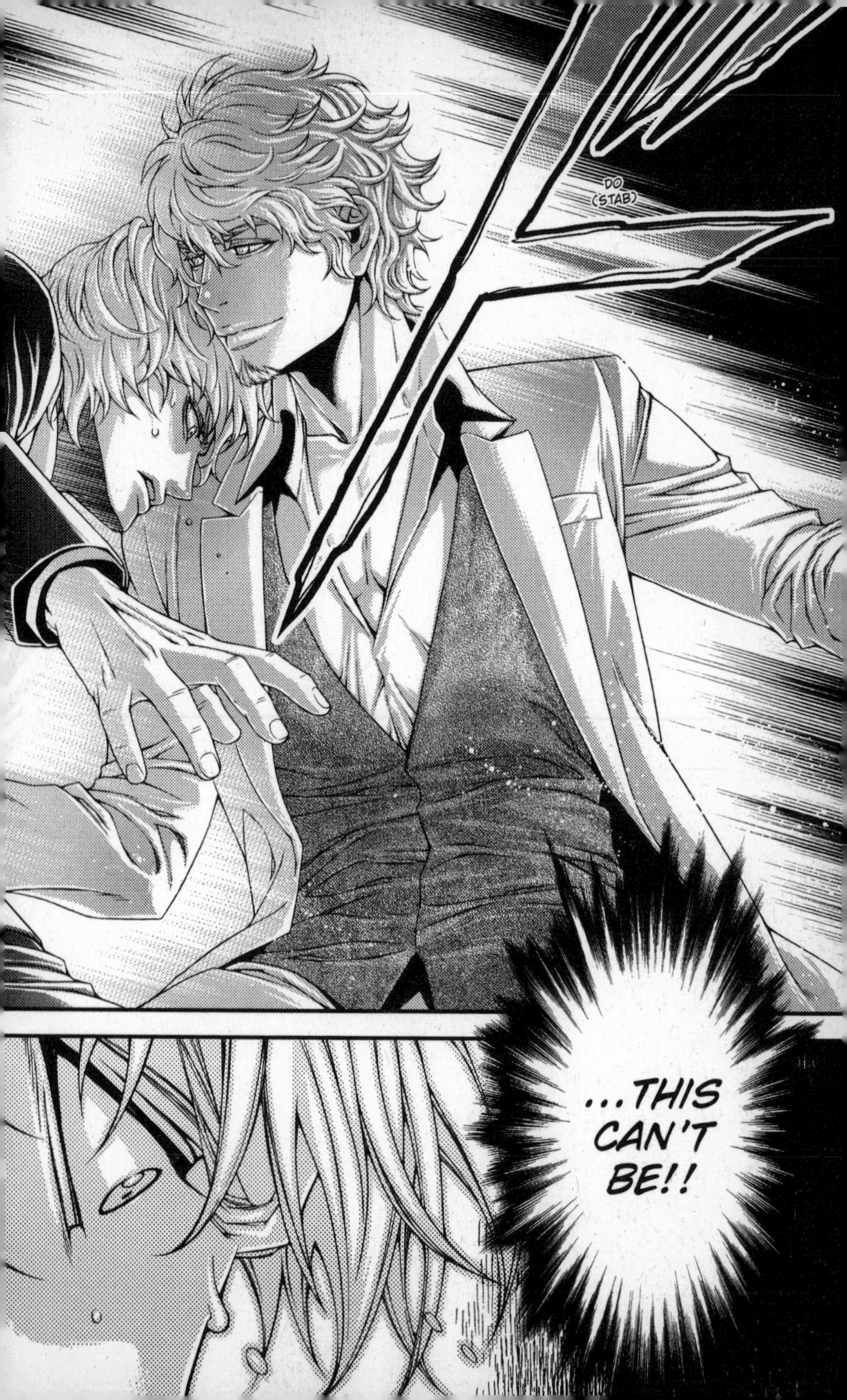
DO
(STAB)
...THIS CAN'T BE!!

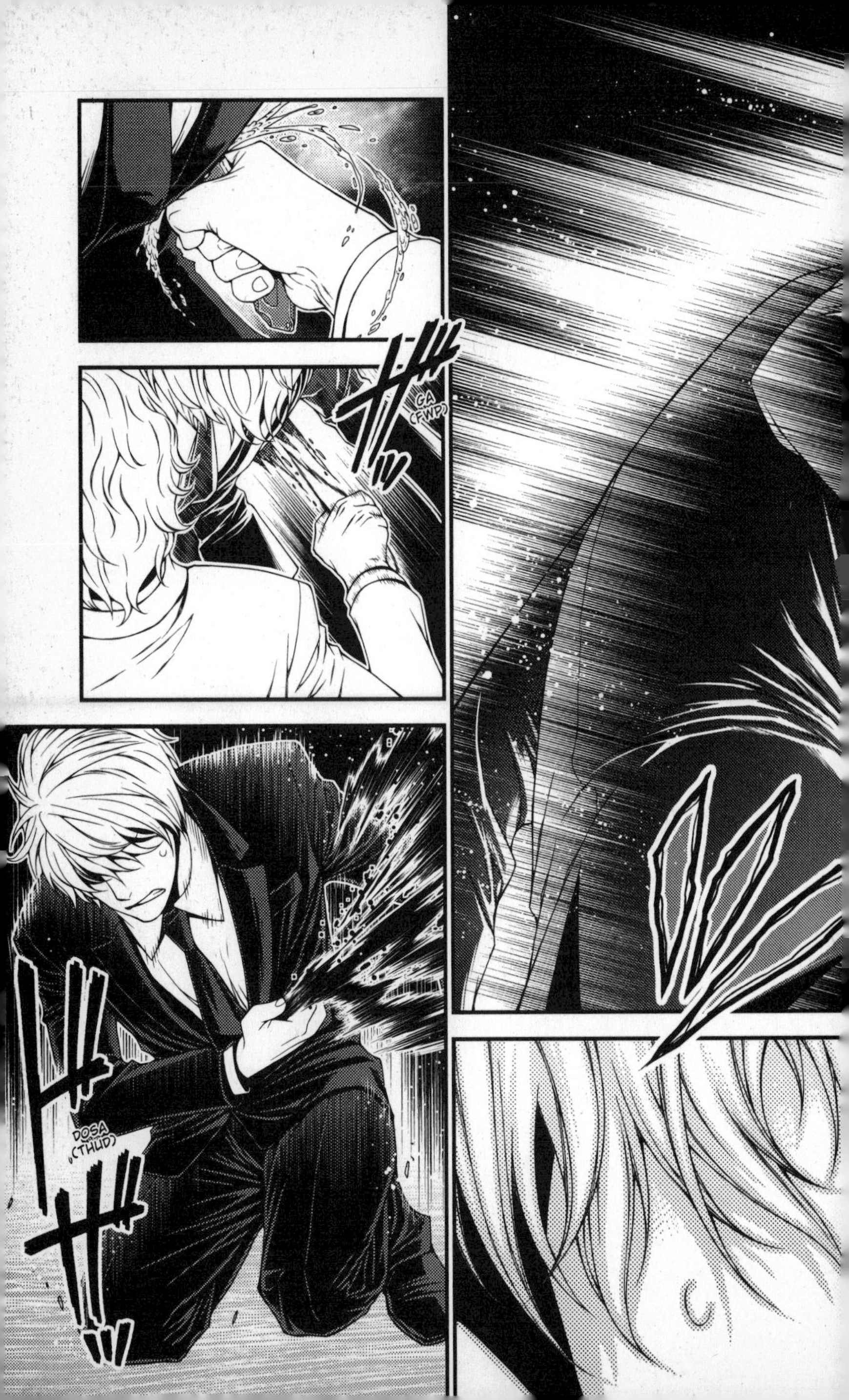
GA
(FWP)
DOSA
(THUD)

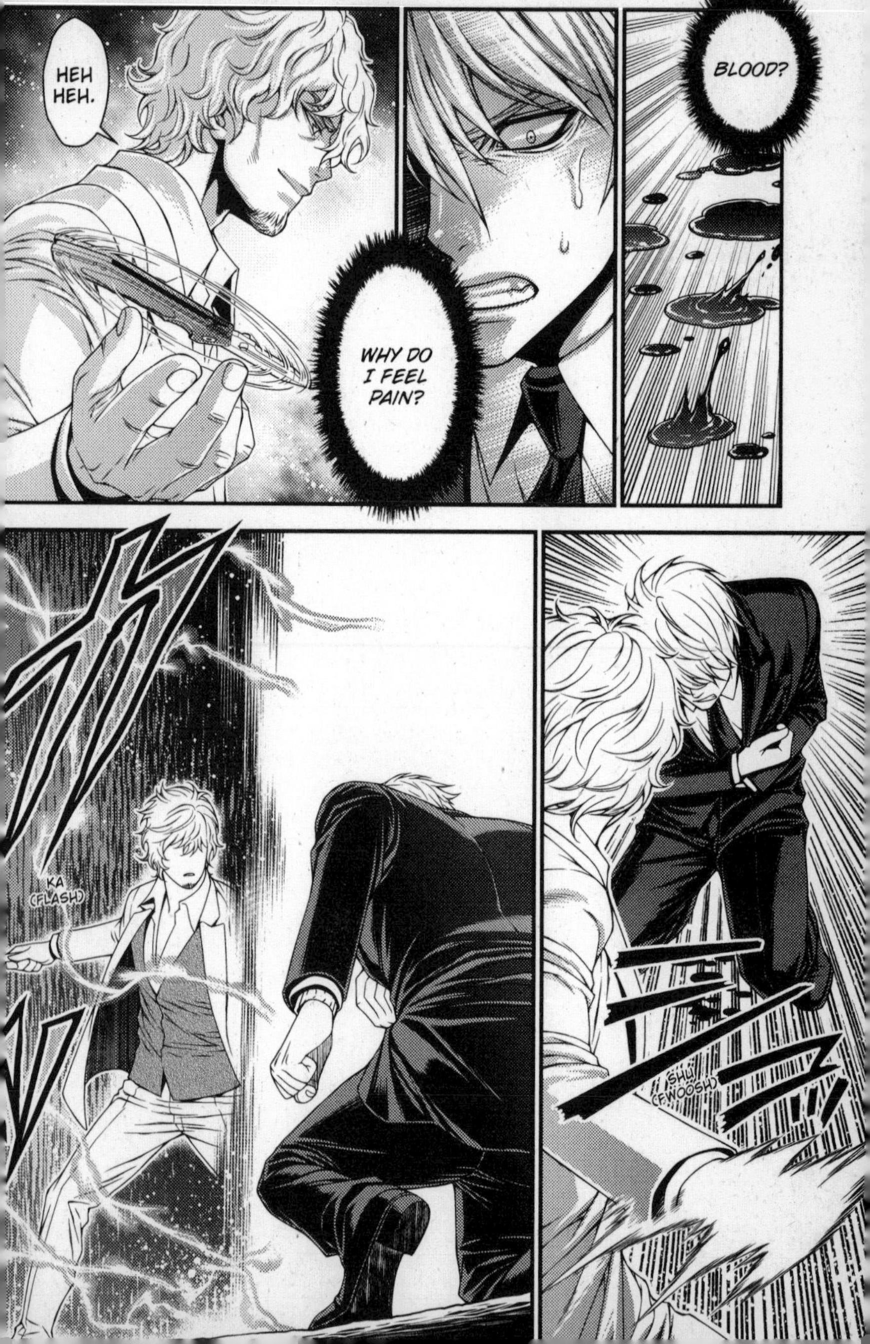
BLOOD?
WHY DO I FEEL PAIN?
HEH HEH.
SHU (FWOOSH)
KA (FLASH)

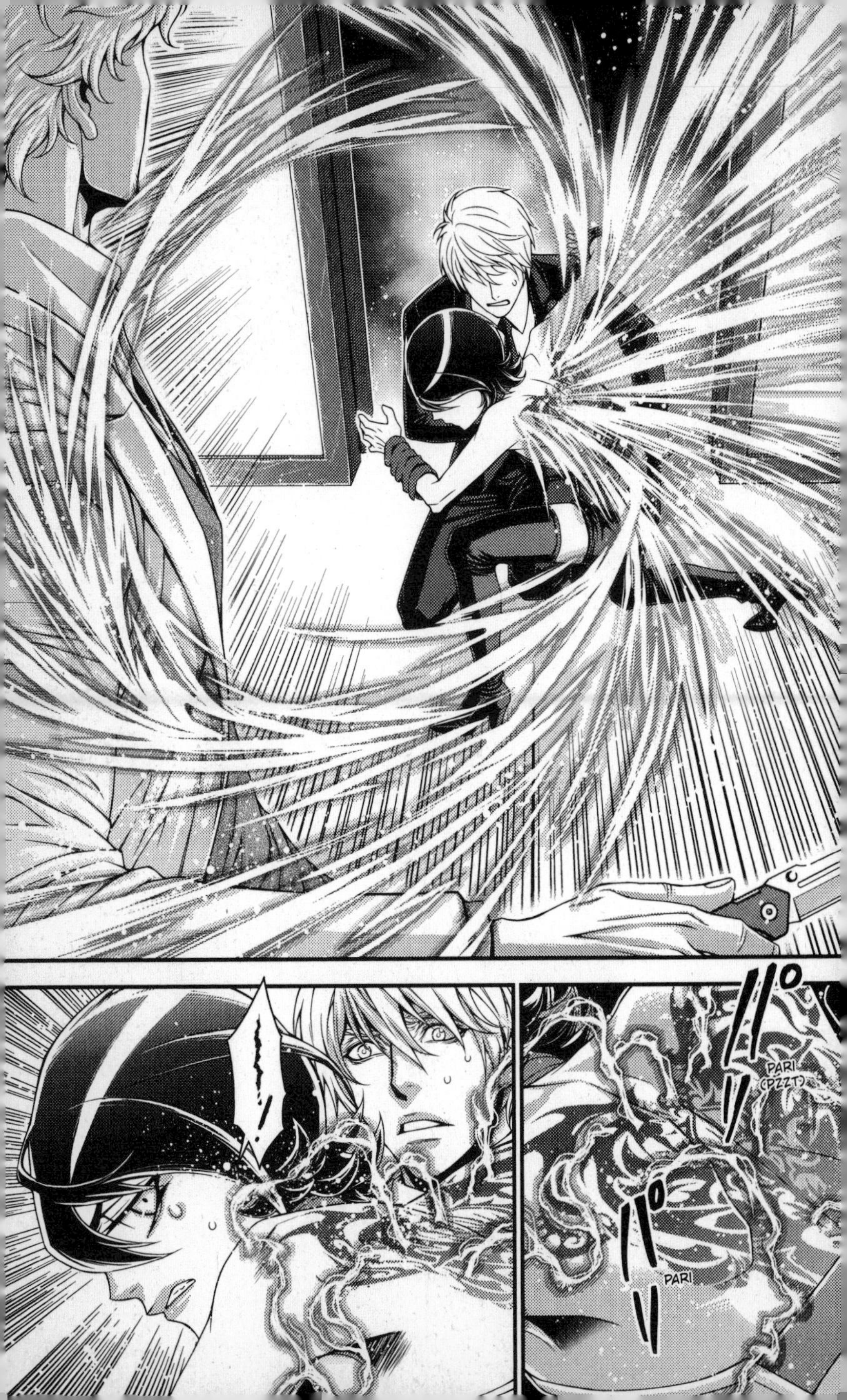
PARI (PZZT)
PARI
...!

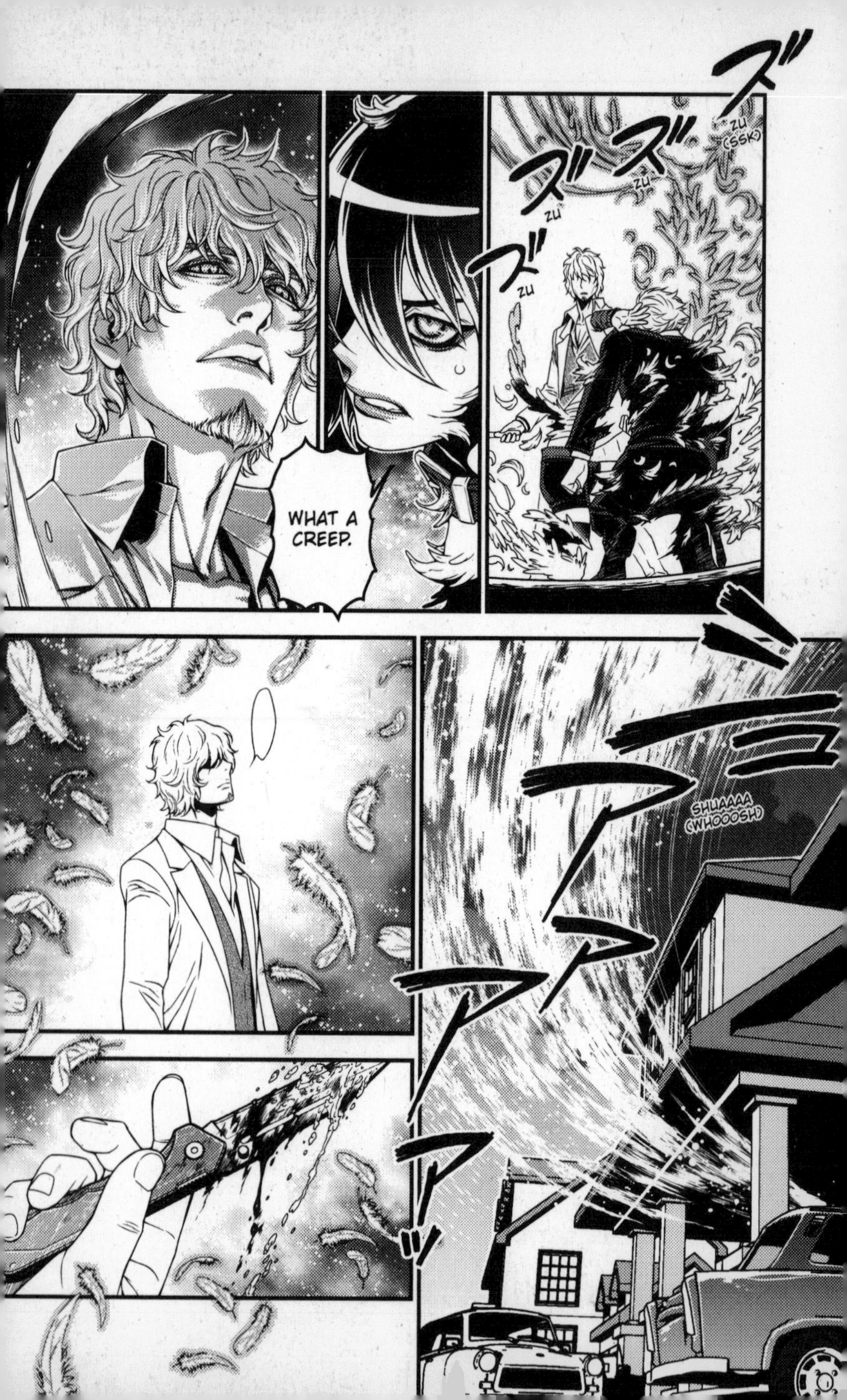
ZU (SSK)
ZU
ZU
ZU
WHAT A CREEP.
SHUAAAA (WHOOOSH)

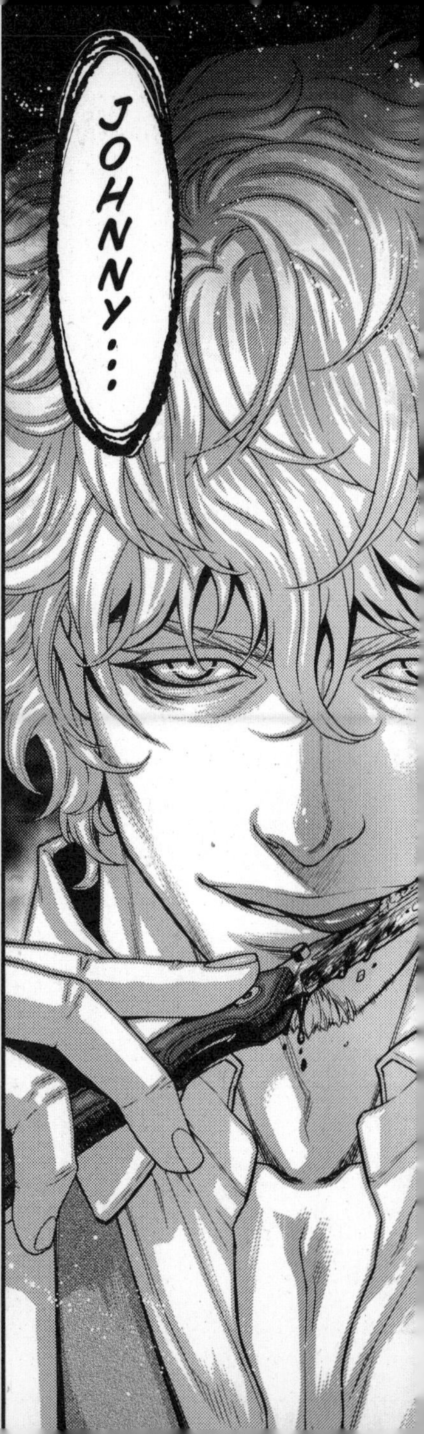
JOHNNY...
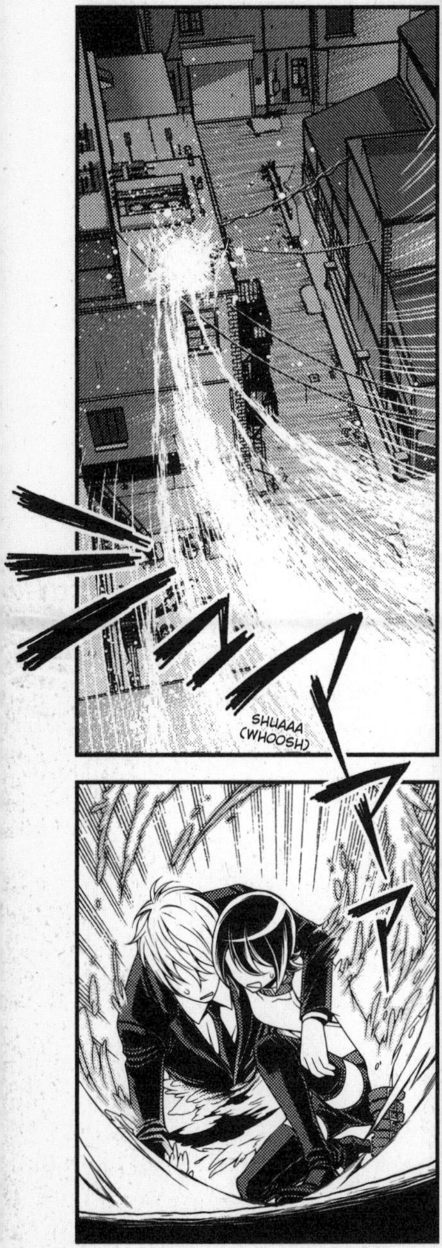
SHUAAA
(WHOOSH)

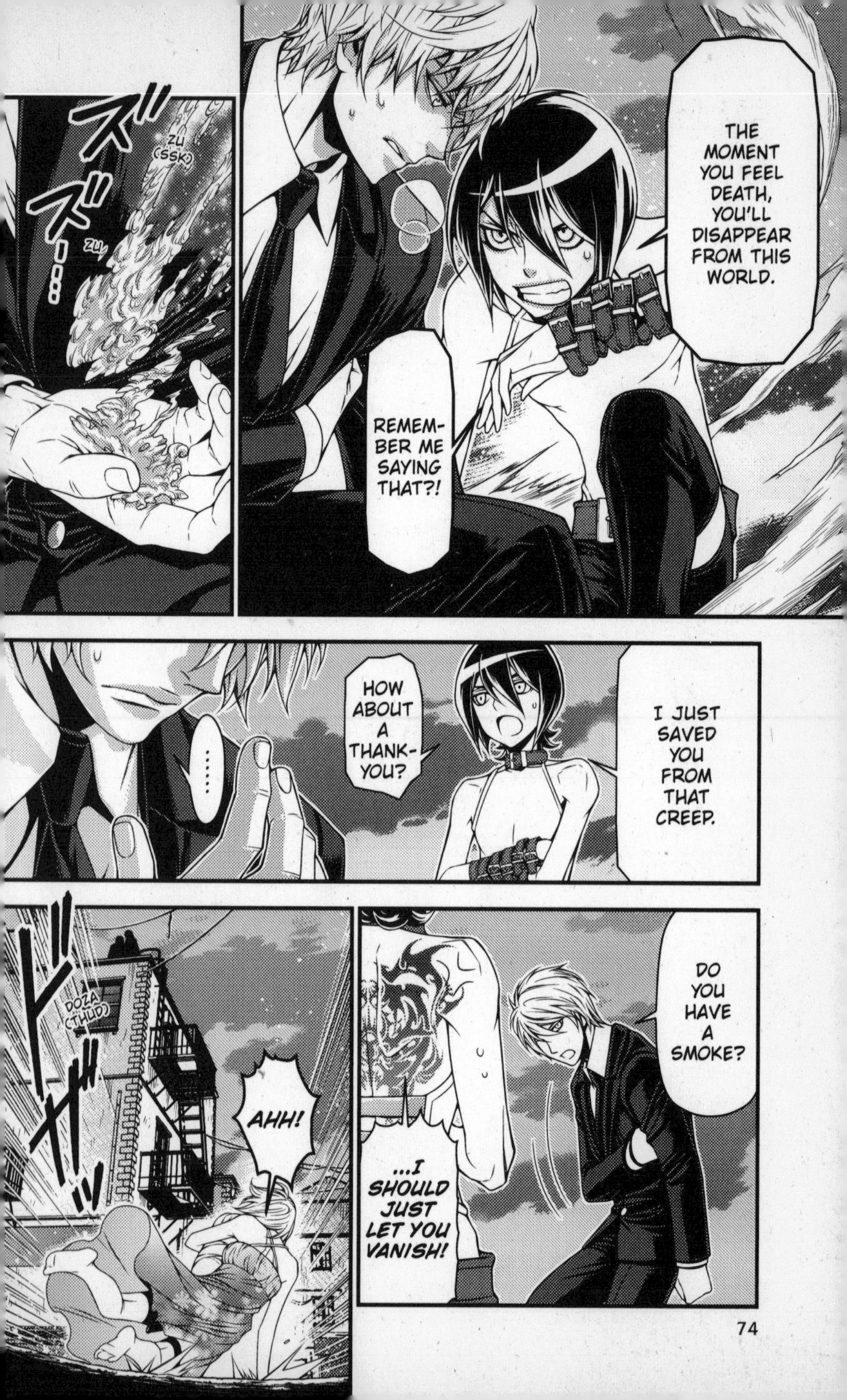

THE MOMENT YOU FEEL DEATH, YOU'LL DISAPPEAR FROM THIS WORLD.
REMEMBER ME SAYING THAT?!
ズ ZU (SSK)
ズ ZU
I JUST SAVED YOU FROM THAT CREEP.
HOW ABOUT A THANK-YOU?
......
DO YOU HAVE A SMOKE?
...I SHOULD JUST LET YOU VANISH!
AHH!
ドザ DOZA (THUD)

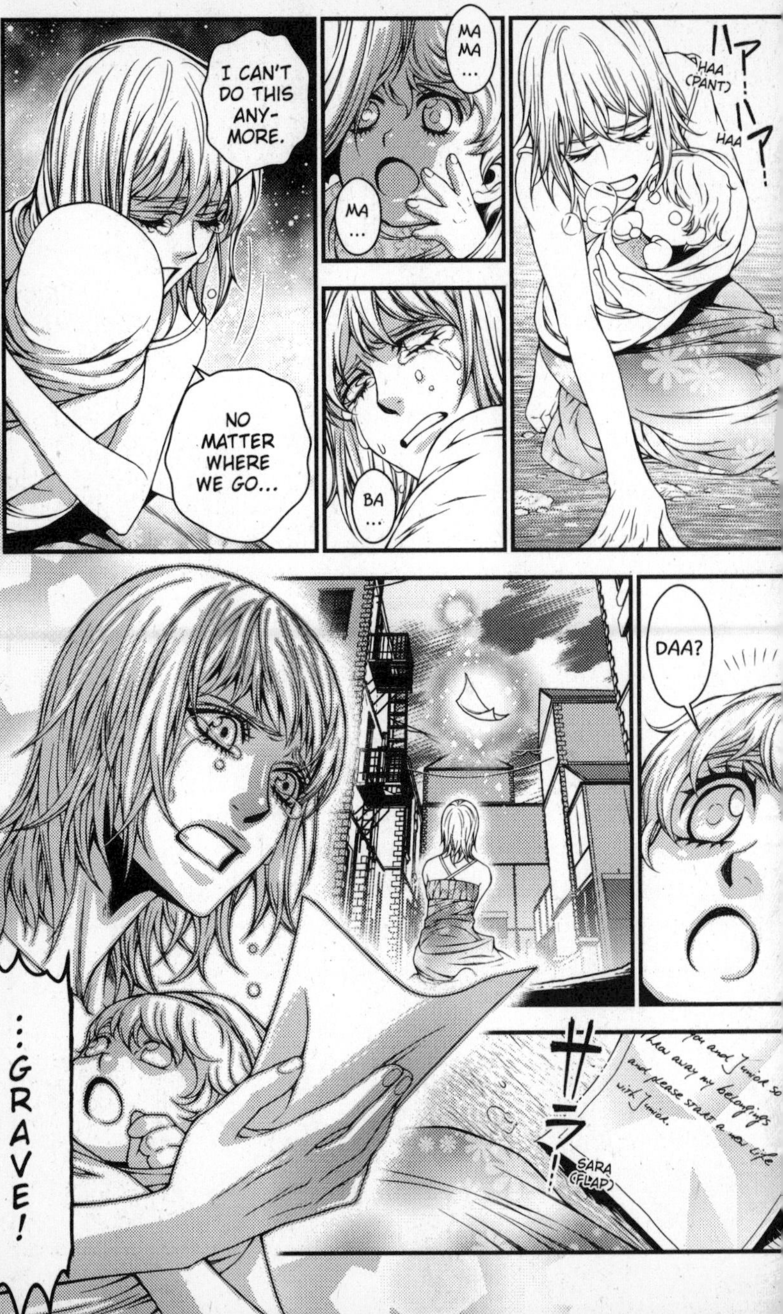
ハァ…ハァ…
HAA (PANT)
HAA
MA MA ...
MA ...
BA ...
I CAN'T DO THIS ANYMORE.
NO MATTER WHERE WE GO...
DAA?
you and Junior so
throw away my belongings
and please start a new life
with Junior.
サラ
SARA (FLAP)
...GRAVE!

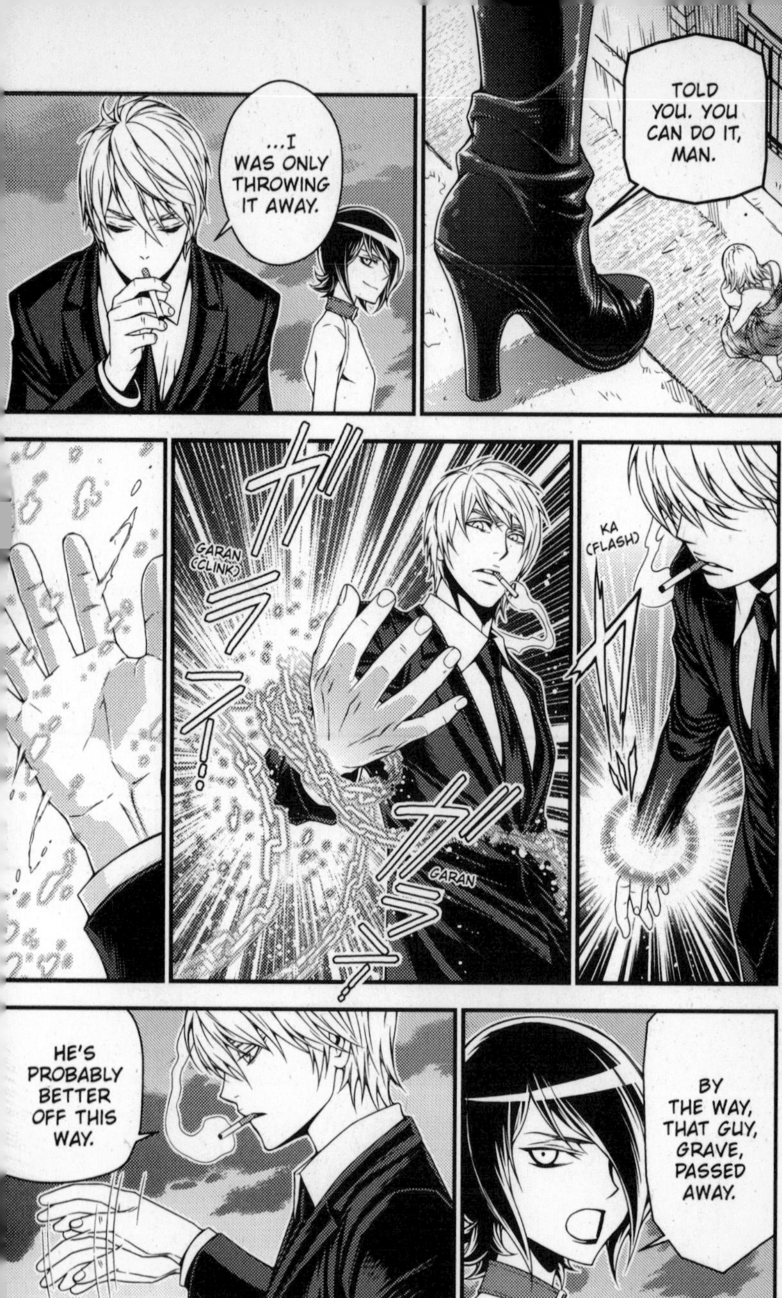
TOLD YOU. YOU CAN DO IT, MAN.
...I WAS ONLY THROWING IT AWAY.
KA (FLASH)
GARAN (CLINK)
GARAN
BY THE WAY, THAT GUY, GRAVE, PASSED AWAY.
HE'S PROBABLY BETTER OFF THIS WAY.

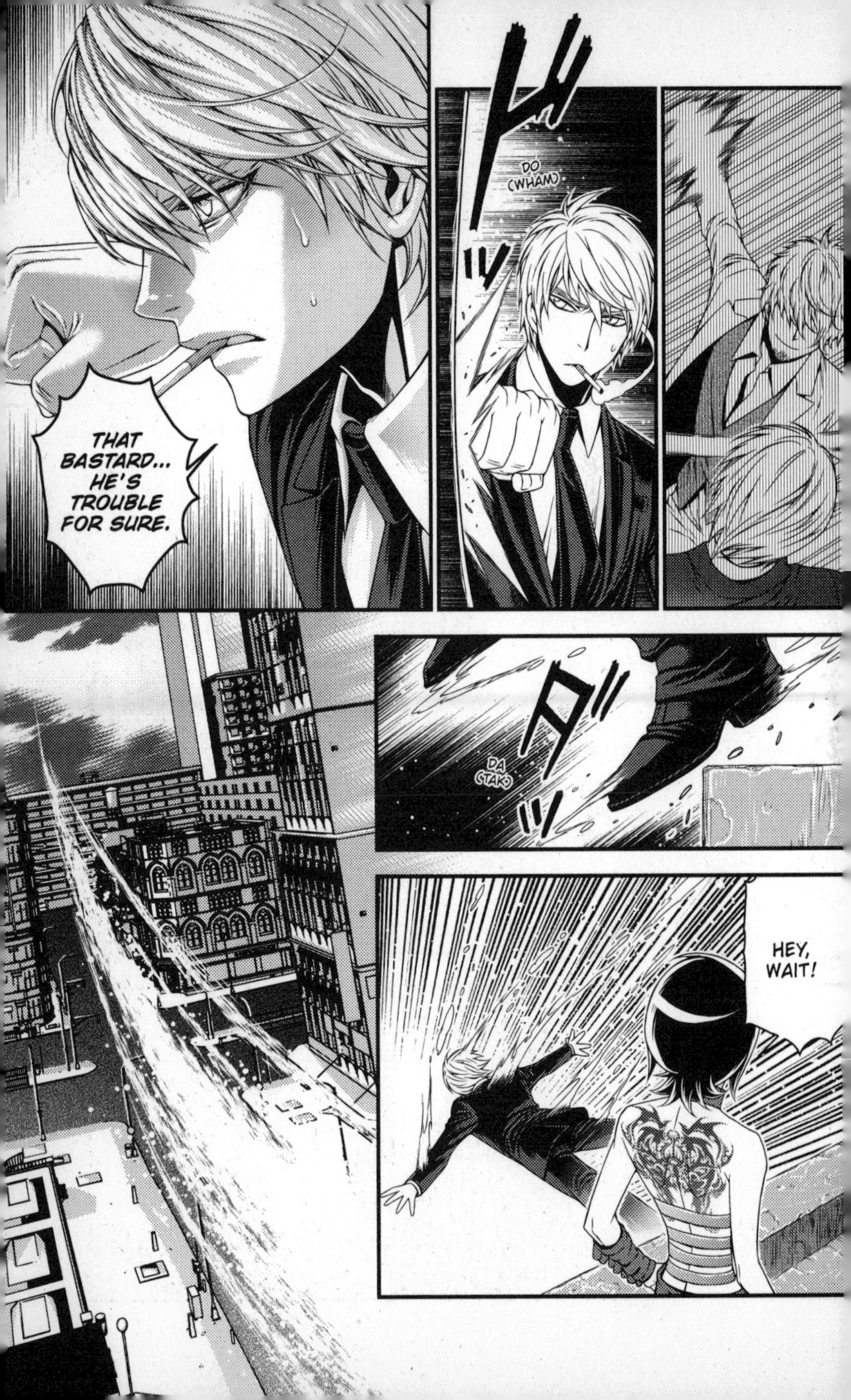
DO
(WHAM)
THAT BASTARD... HE'S TROUBLE FOR SURE.
DA
(TAK)
HEY, WAIT!

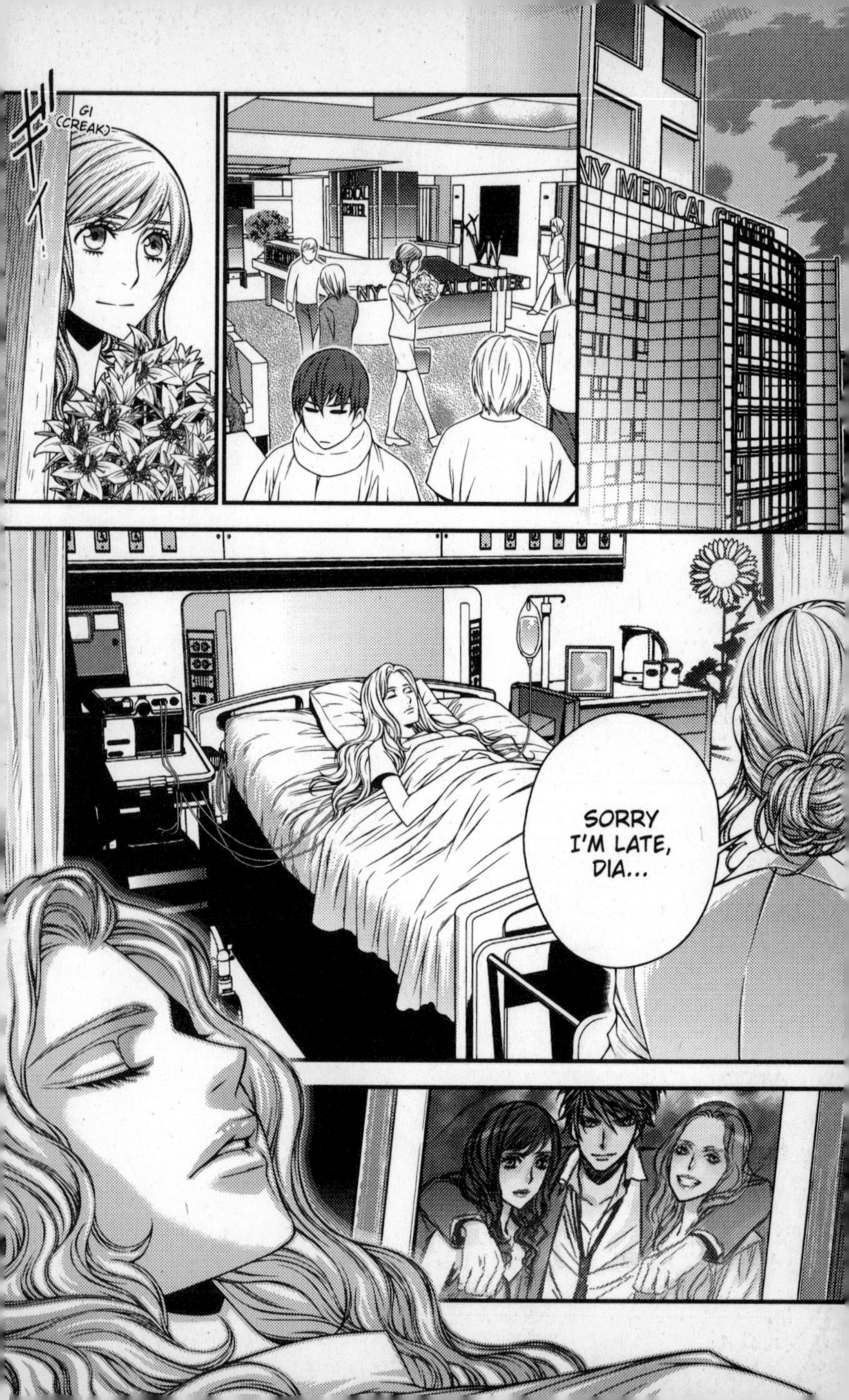
NY MEDICAL
NY
AL CENTER
ギイ！
GI
(CREAK)
SORRY I'M LATE, DIA...

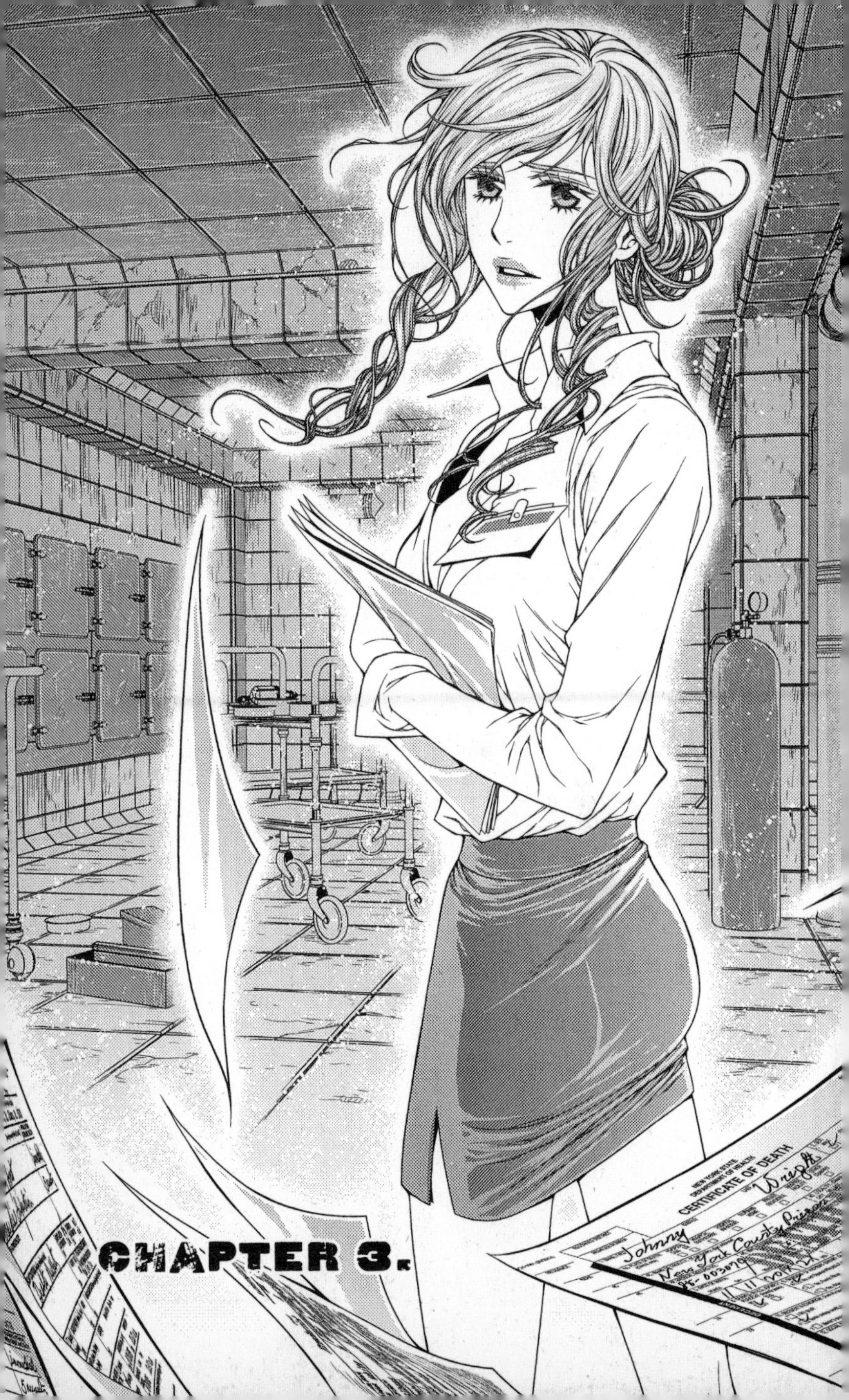
CHAPTER 3.
NEW YORK STATE
DEPARTMENT OF HEALTH
CERTIFICATE OF DEATH
Johnny
Wright
New York County Prison

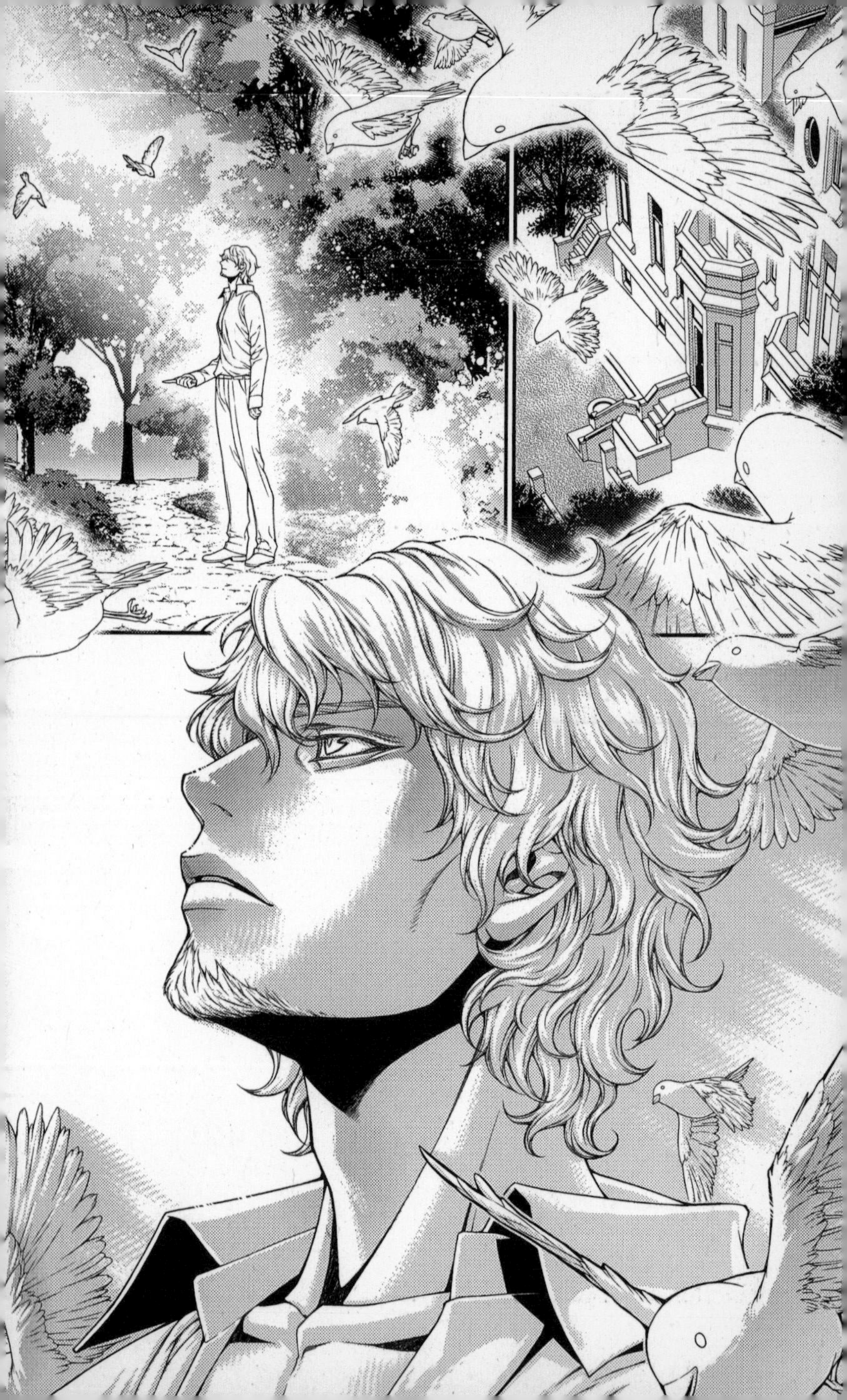

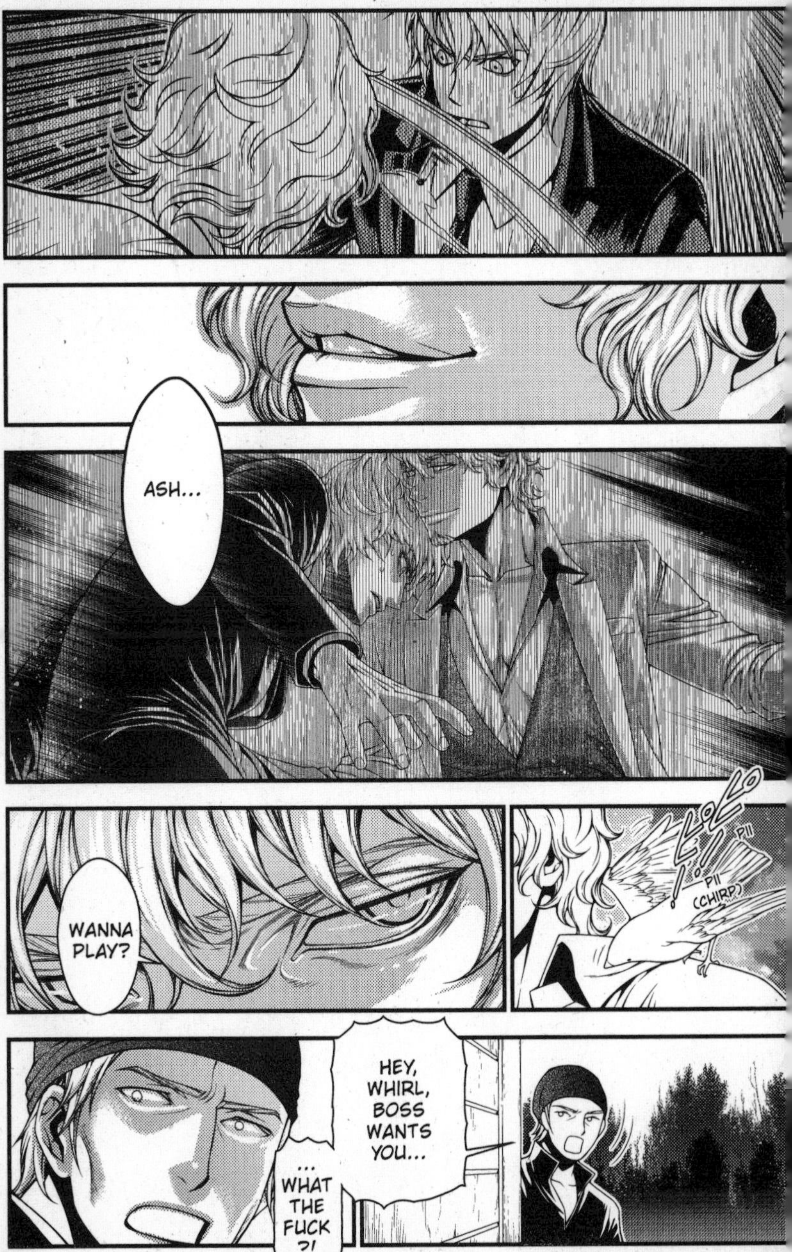
ASH...
PII PII (CHIRP)
WANNA PLAY?
HEY, WHIRL, BOSS WANTS YOU...
...WHAT THE FUCK?!

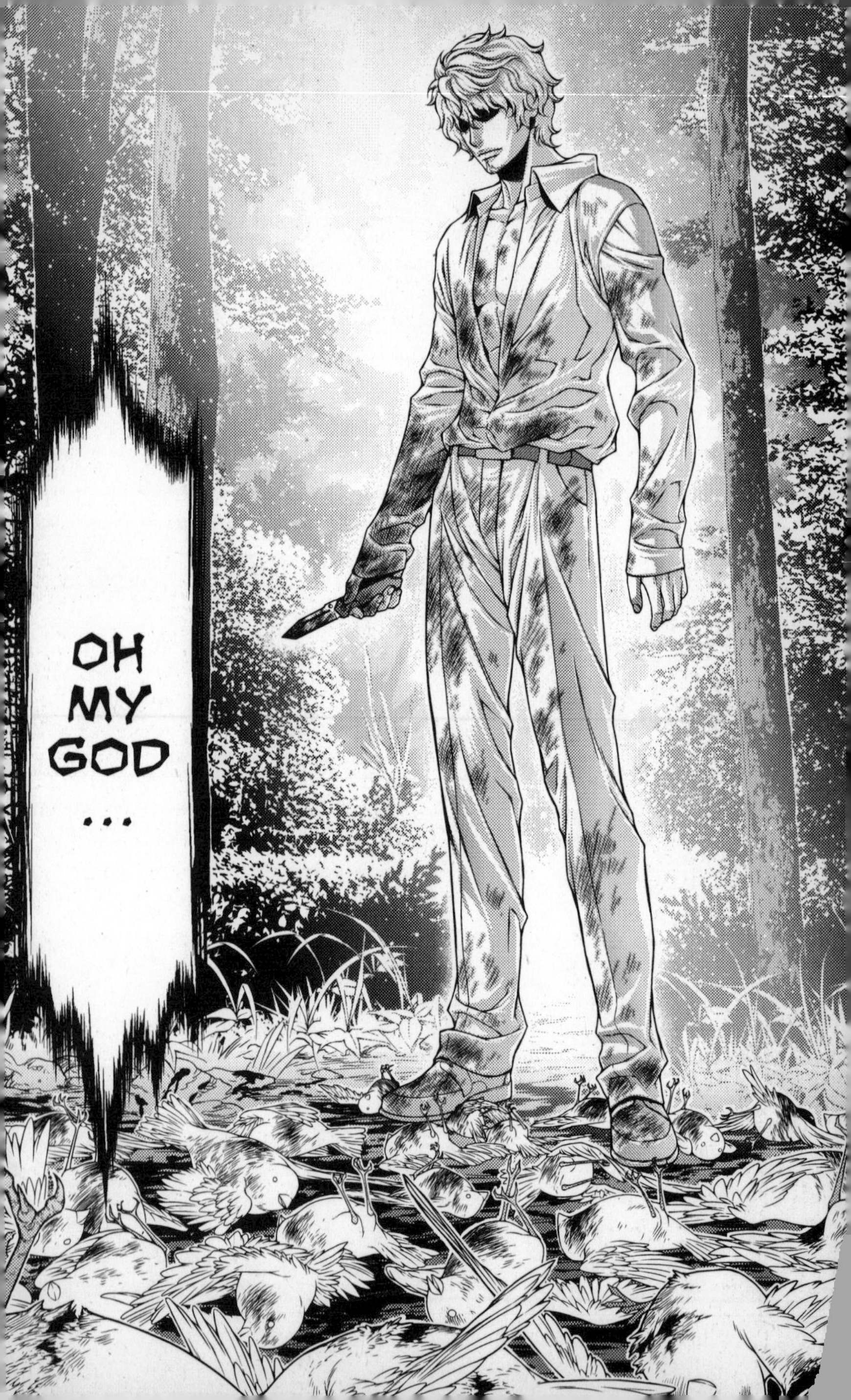
OH MY GOD ...

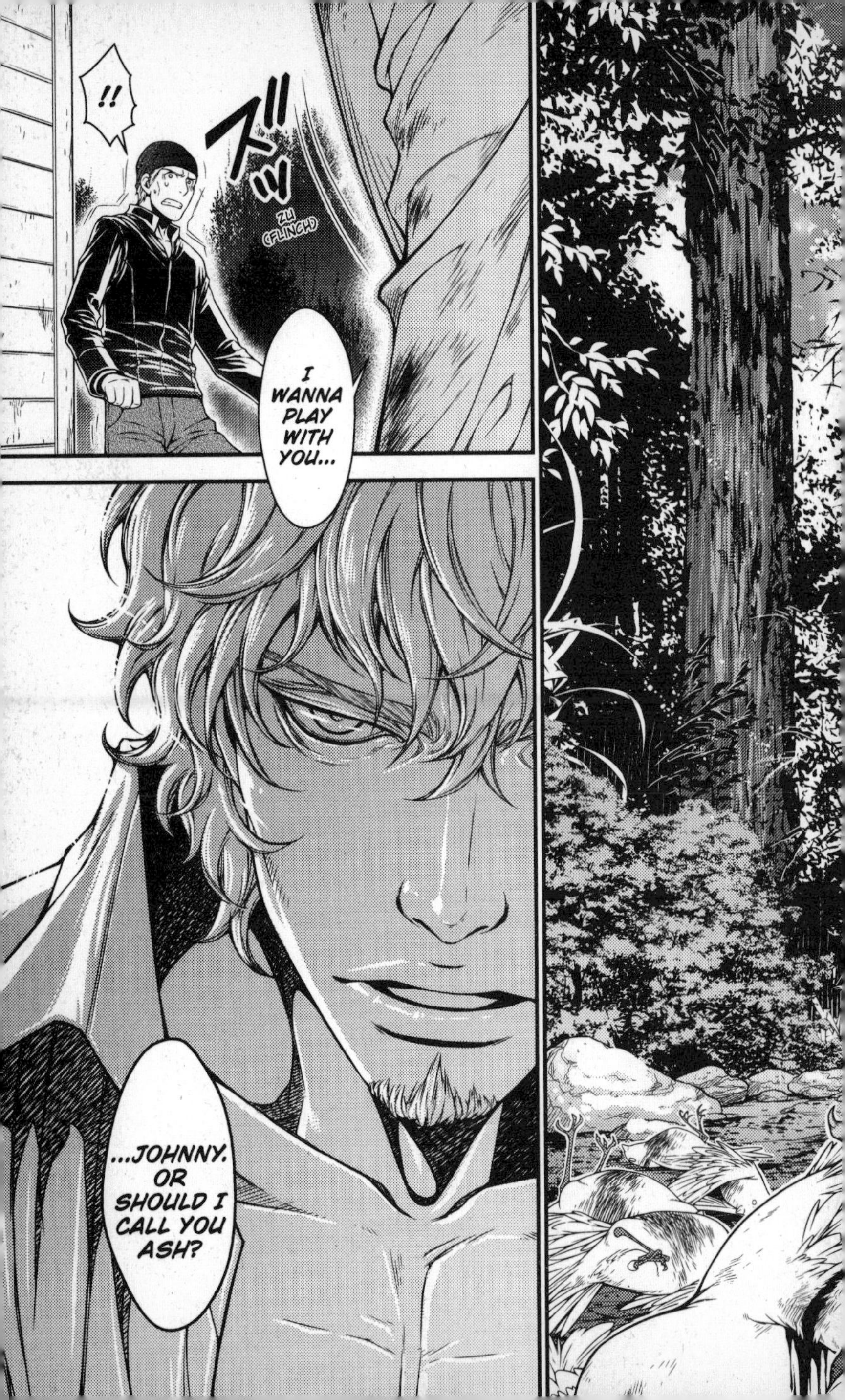
ズッ
ZU (FLINCH)
!!
I WANNA PLAY WITH YOU...
...JOHNNY. OR SHOULD I CALL YOU ASH?

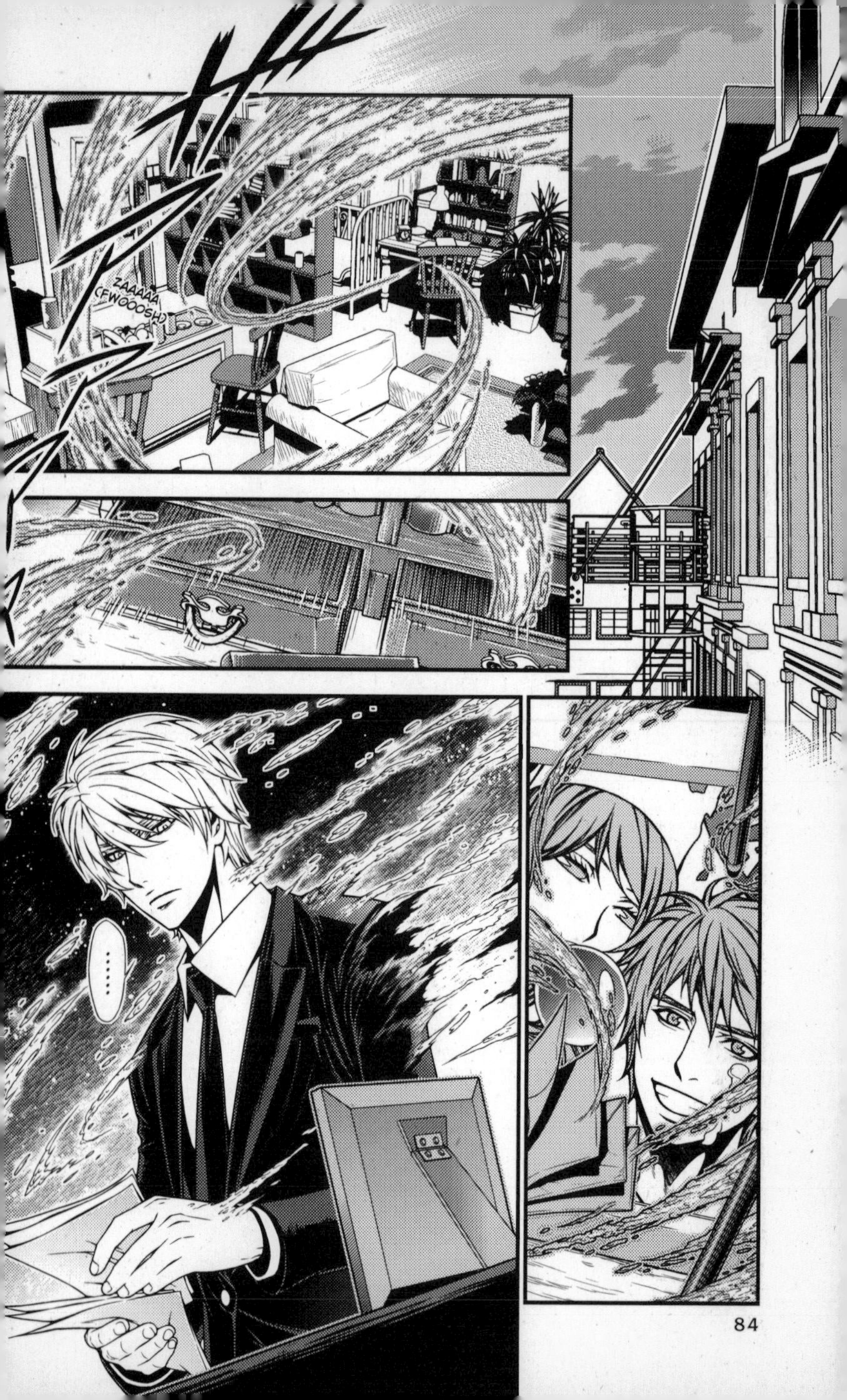
ZAAAAA (FWOOOSH)
......

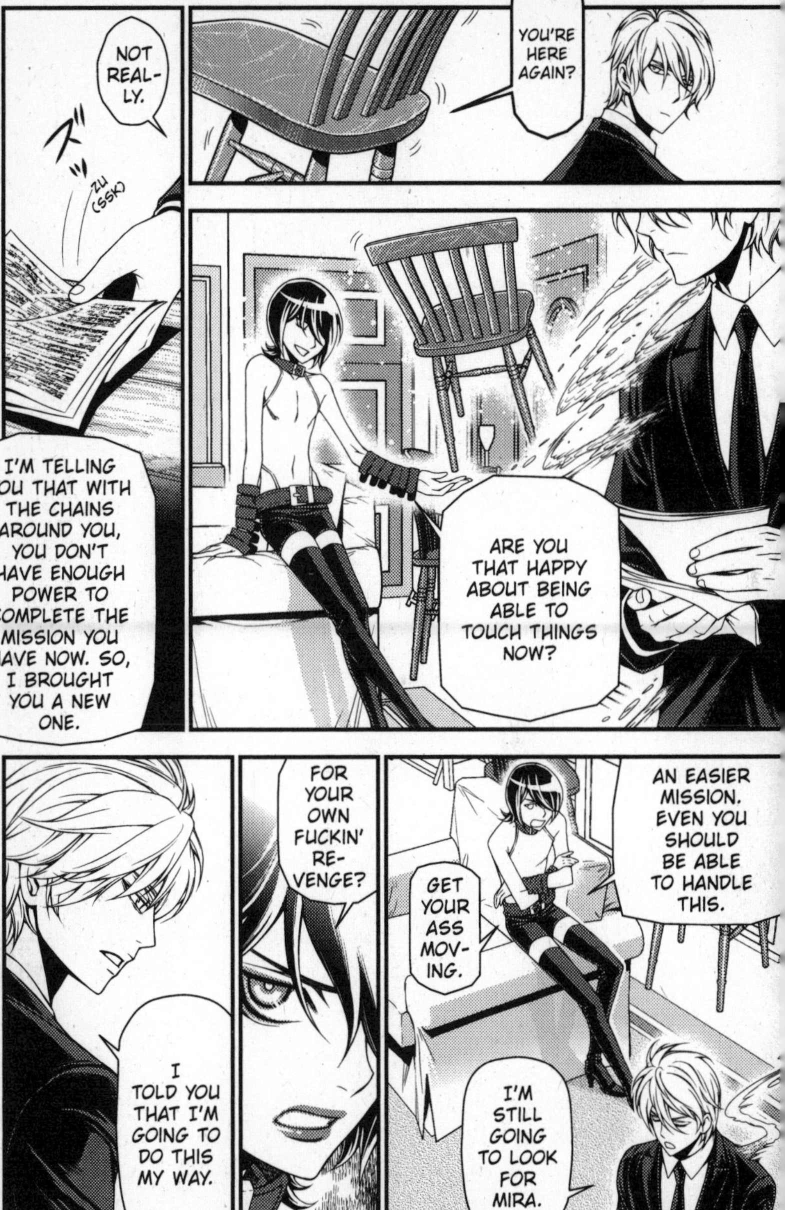
YOU'RE HERE AGAIN?
ARE YOU THAT HAPPY ABOUT BEING ABLE TO TOUCH THINGS NOW?
NOT REALLY.
ZU (SSK)
I'M TELLING YOU THAT WITH THE CHAINS AROUND YOU, YOU DON'T HAVE ENOUGH POWER TO COMPLETE THE MISSION YOU HAVE NOW. SO, I BROUGHT YOU A NEW ONE.
AN EASIER MISSION. EVEN YOU SHOULD BE ABLE TO HANDLE THIS.
GET YOUR ASS MOVING.
I'M STILL GOING TO LOOK FOR MIRA.
FOR YOUR OWN FUCKIN' REVENGE?
I TOLD YOU THAT I'M GOING TO DO THIS MY WAY.

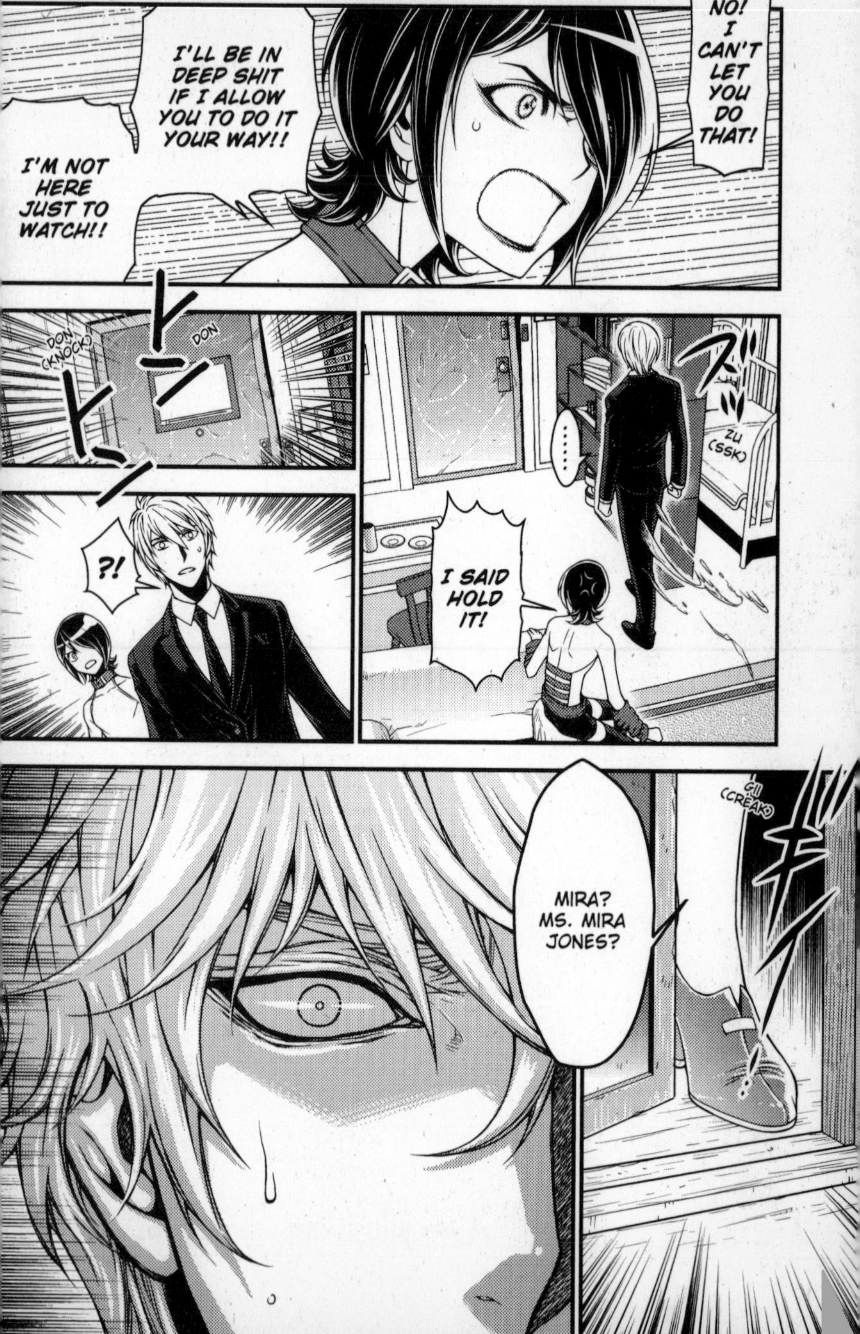
NO! I CAN'T LET YOU DO THAT!
I'LL BE IN DEEP SHIT IF I ALLOW YOU TO DO IT YOUR WAY!!
I'M NOT HERE JUST TO WATCH!!
ZU (SSK)
......
I SAID HOLD IT!
DON (KNOCK)
DON
?!
GII (CREAK)
MIRA? MS. MIRA JONES?

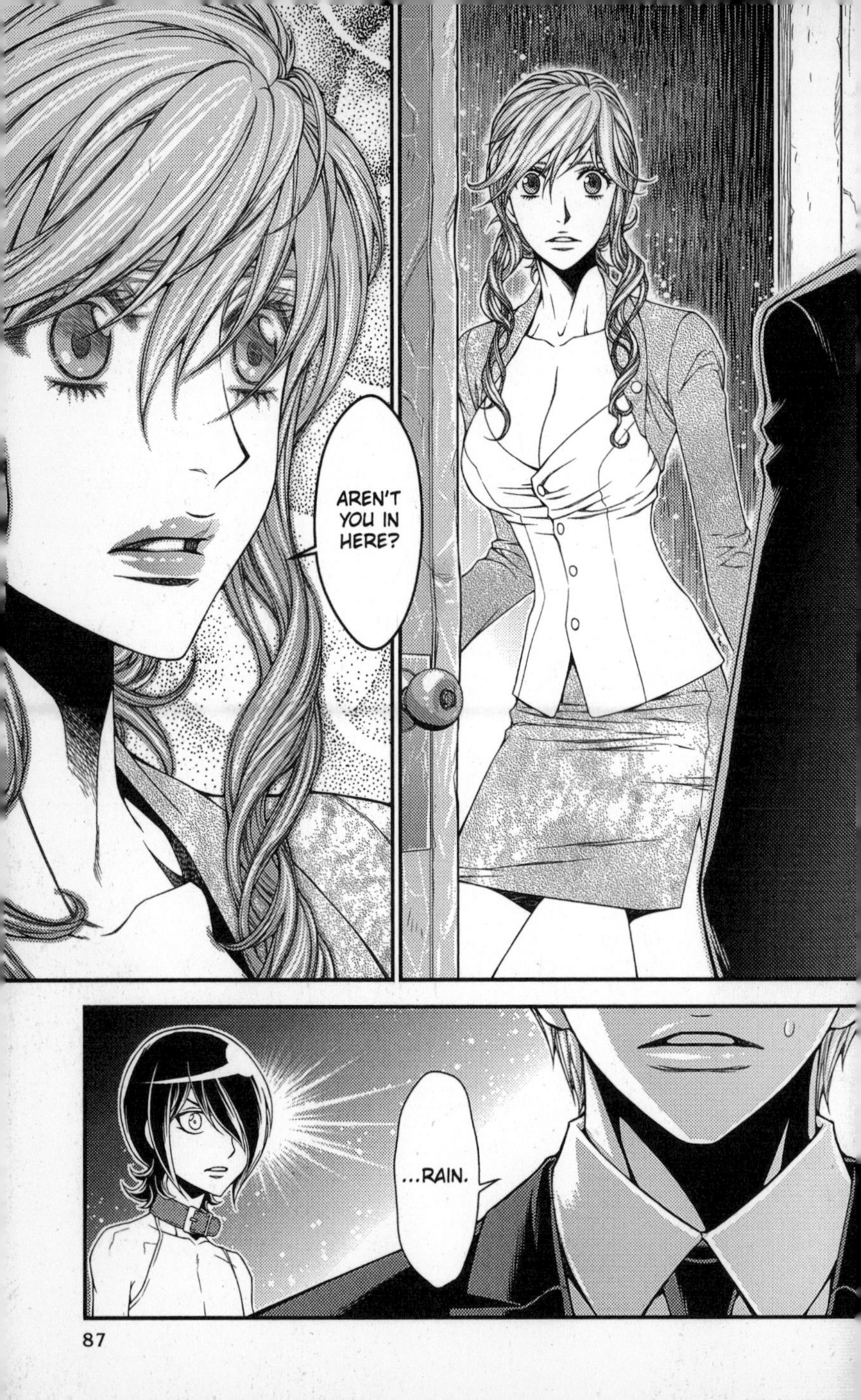
AREN'T YOU IN HERE?
...RAIN.

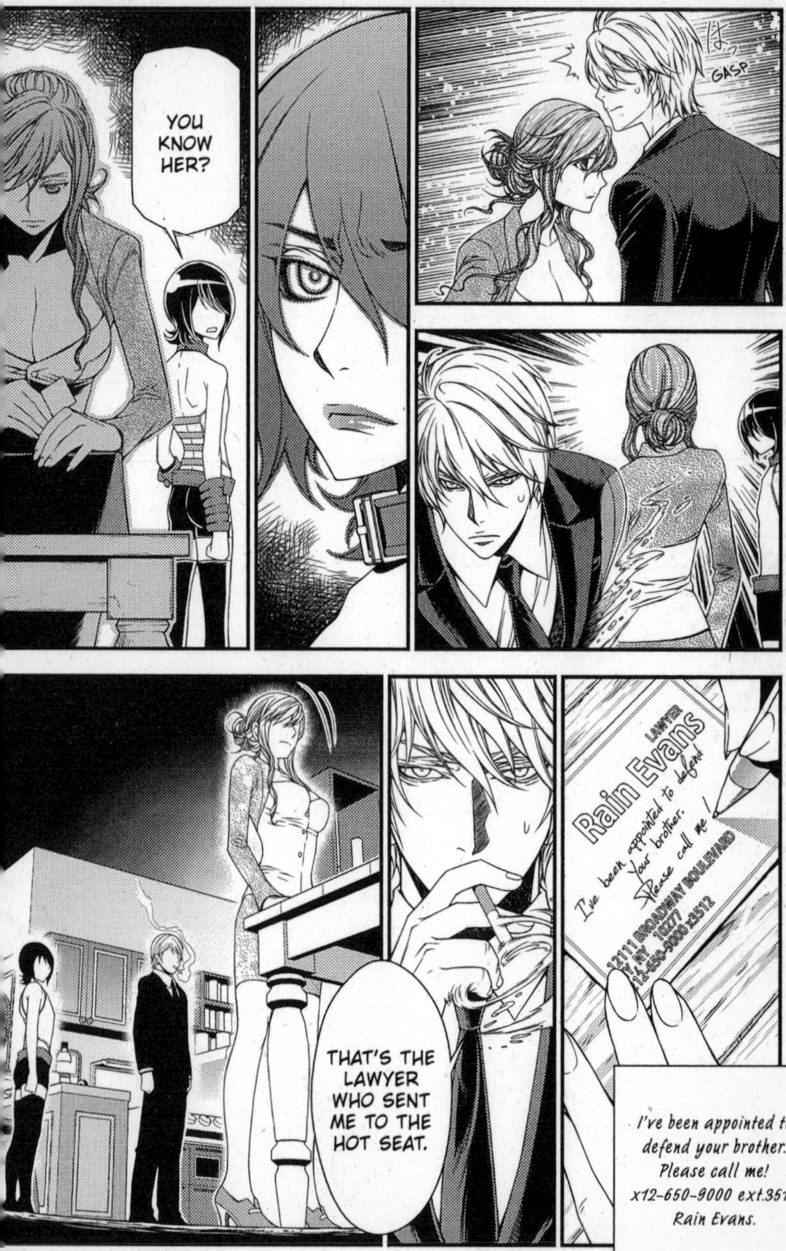
は
GASP
LAWYER
Rain Evans
I've been appointed to defend your brother. Please call me!
12111 BROADWAY BOULEVARD
THAT'S THE LAWYER WHO SENT ME TO THE HOT SEAT.
YOU KNOW HER?

I've been appointed to defend your brother. Please call me! x12-650-9000 ext.3512 Rain Evans.

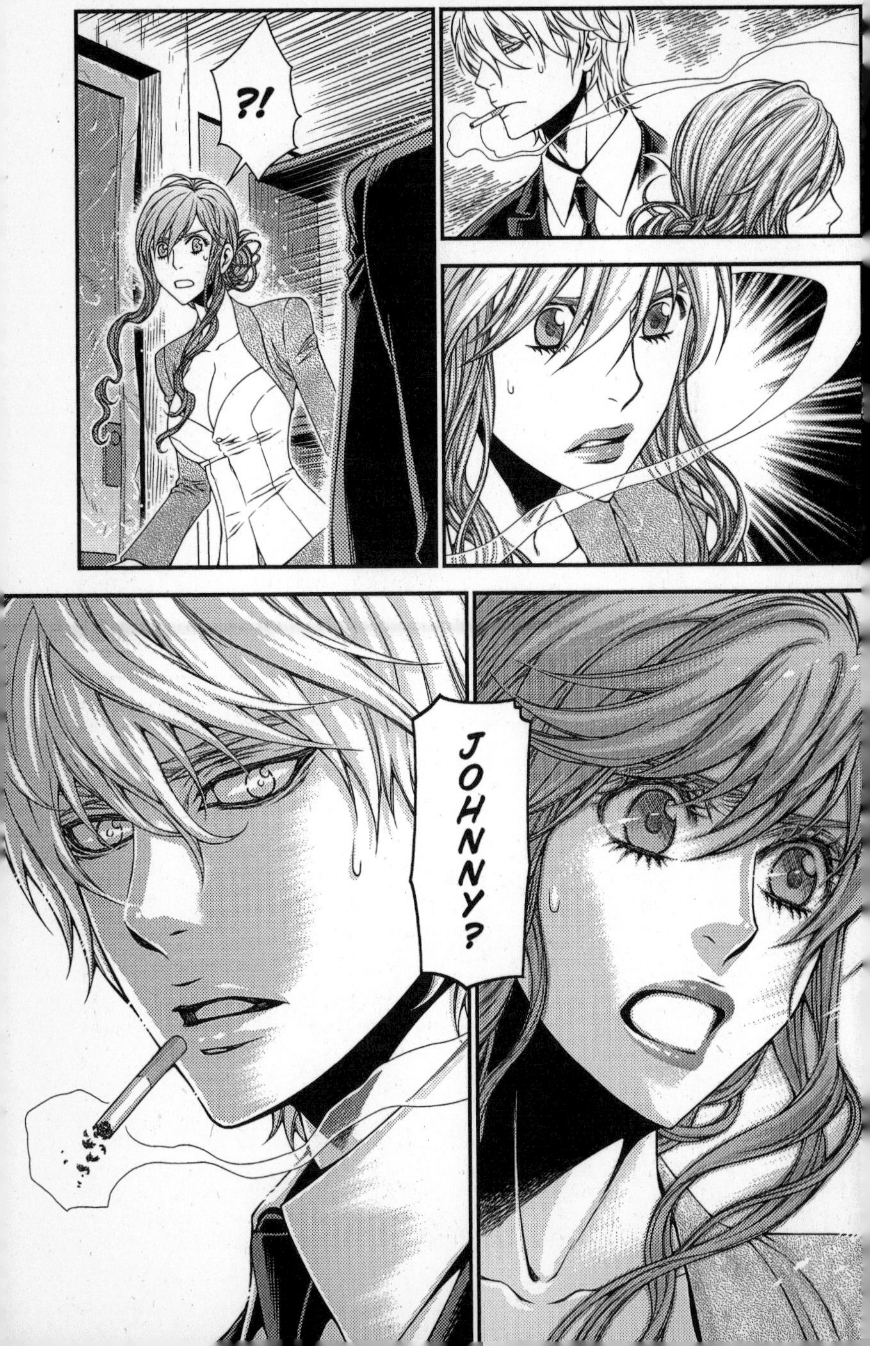
?!
JOHNNY?

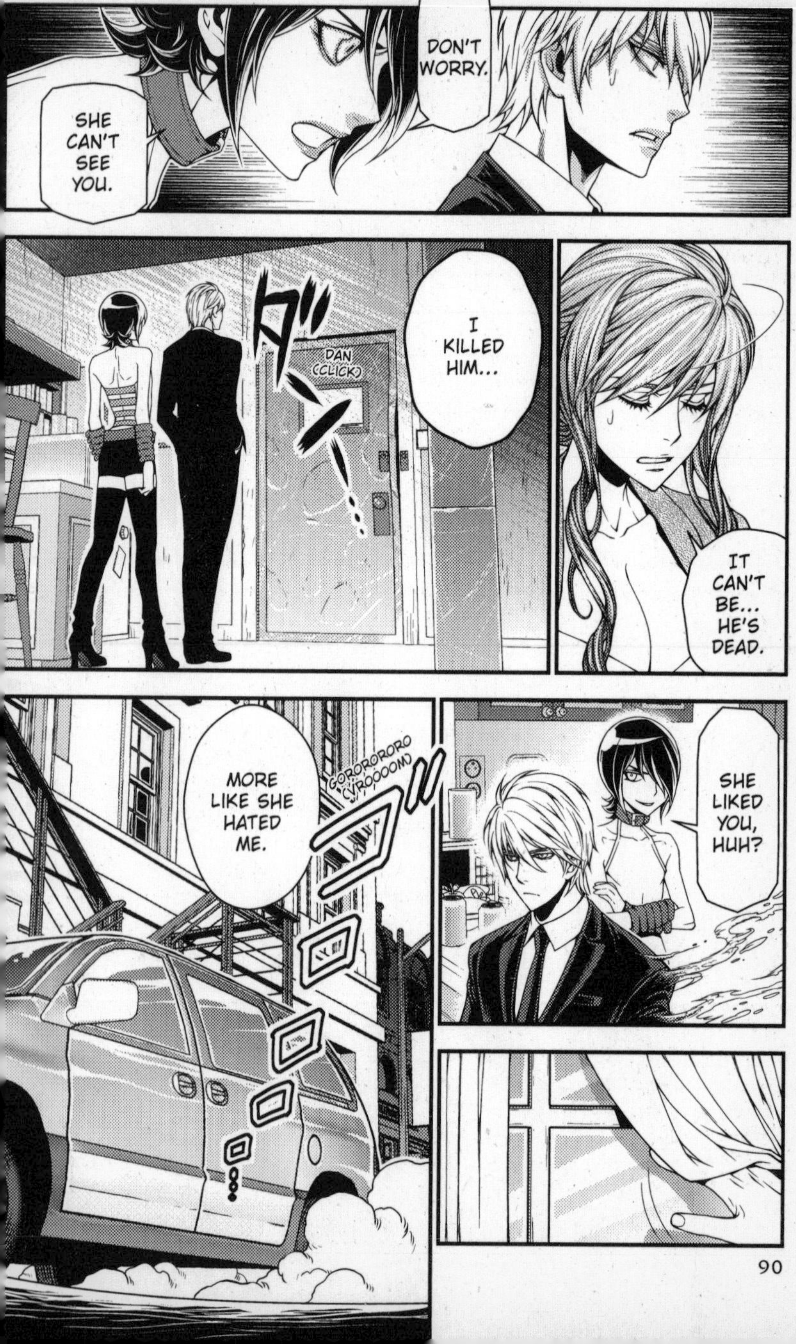
DON'T WORRY.
SHE CAN'T SEE YOU.
IT CAN'T BE... HE'S DEAD.
I KILLED HIM...
DAN (CLICK)
SHE LIKED YOU, HUH?
MORE LIKE SHE HATED ME.
GORORORORO (VROOOOM)

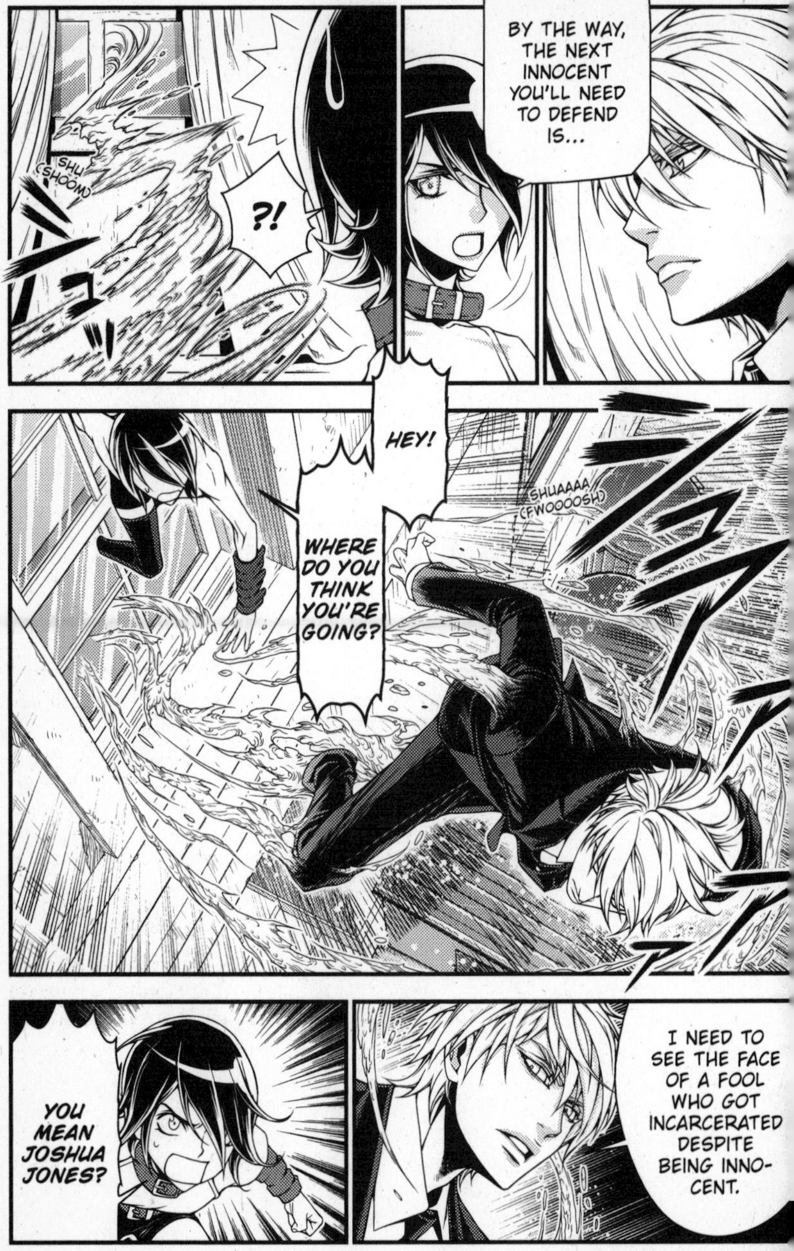
BY THE WAY, THE NEXT INNOCENT YOU'LL NEED TO DEFEND IS...
SHU (SHOOM)
?!
HEY!
WHERE DO YOU THINK YOU'RE GOING?
SHUAAAA (FWOOOOSH)
I NEED TO SEE THE FACE OF A FOOL WHO GOT INCARCERATED DESPITE BEING INNO-CENT.
YOU MEAN JOSHUA JONES?

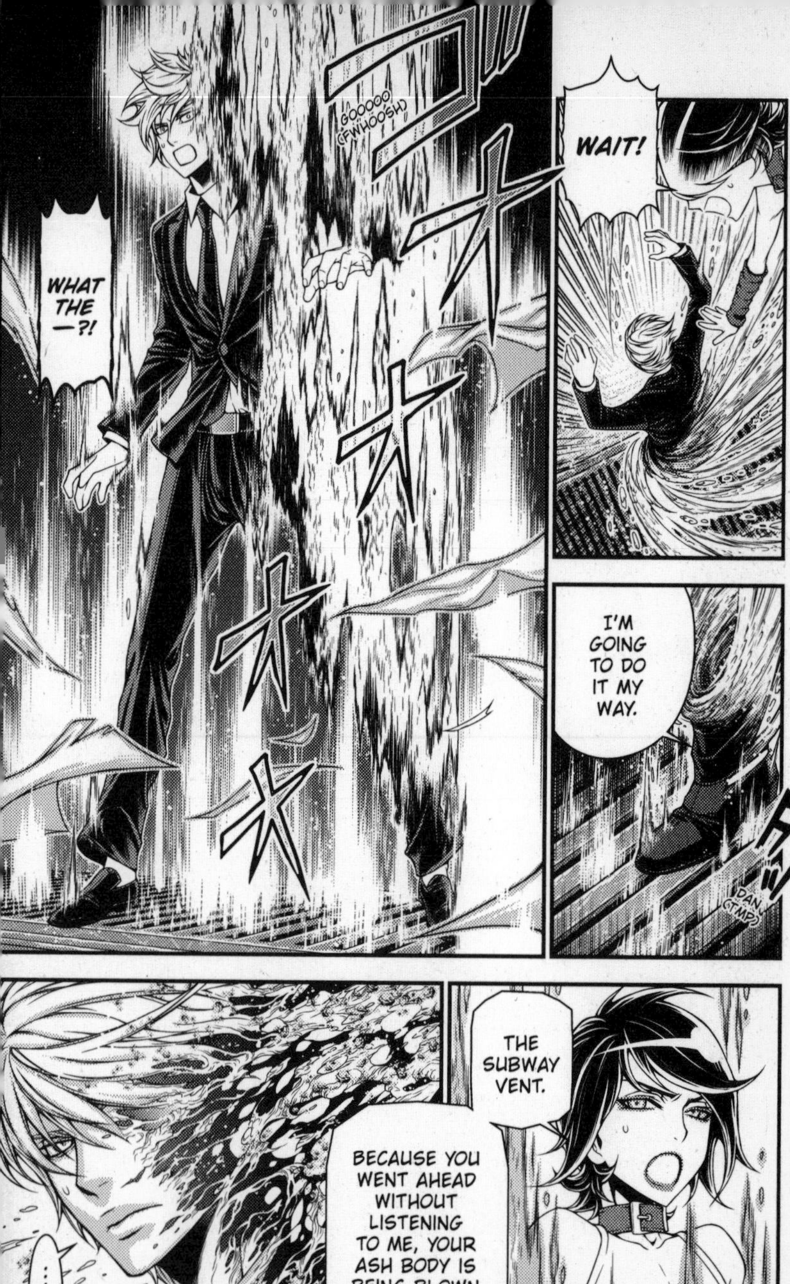
WAIT!
I'M GOING TO DO IT MY WAY.
DAN (TMP)
GOOOOO (FWHOOSH)
WHAT THE—?!
THE SUBWAY VENT.
BECAUSE YOU WENT AHEAD WITHOUT LISTENING TO ME, YOUR ASH BODY IS BEING BLOWN AWAY.
......

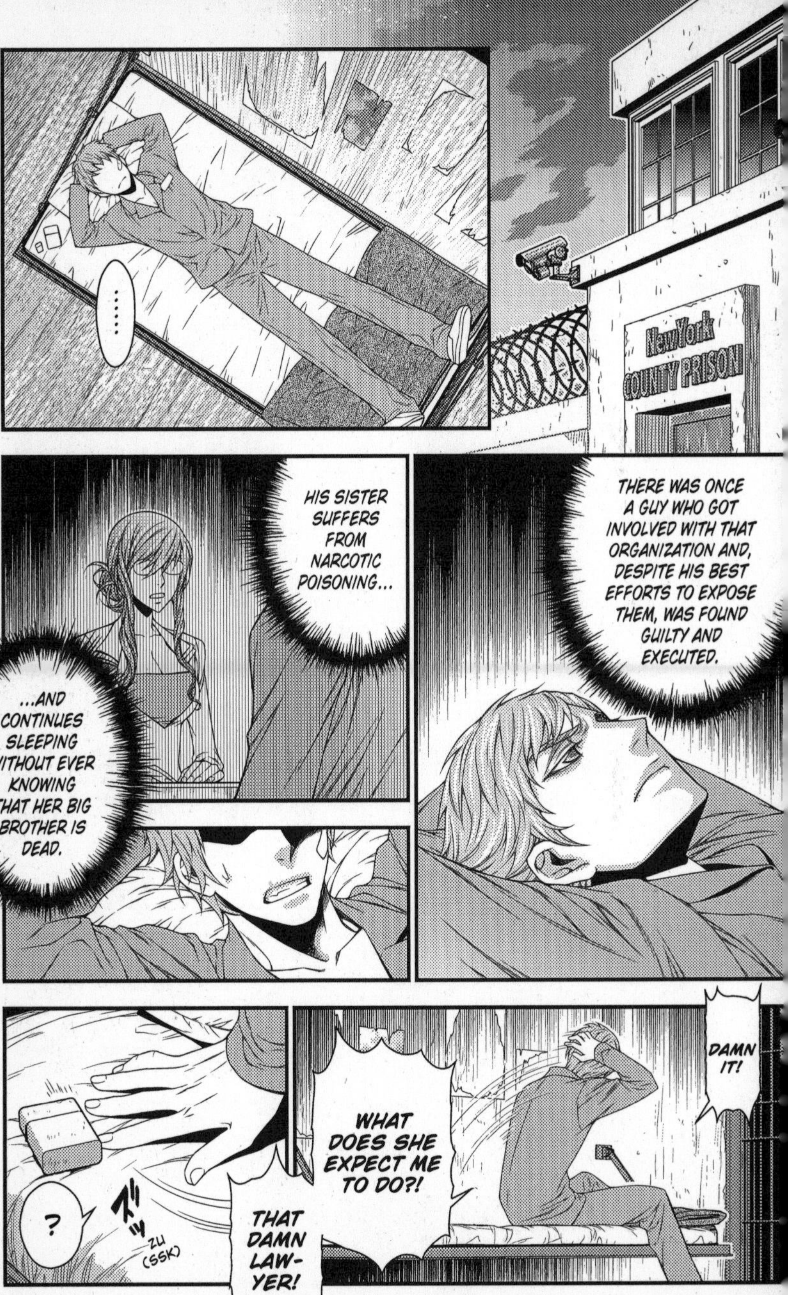
……
THERE WAS ONCE A GUY WHO GOT INVOLVED WITH THAT ORGANIZATION AND, DESPITE HIS BEST EFFORTS TO EXPOSE THEM, WAS FOUND GUILTY AND EXECUTED.
HIS SISTER SUFFERS FROM NARCOTIC POISONING…
…AND CONTINUES SLEEPING WITHOUT EVER KNOWING THAT HER BIG BROTHER IS DEAD.
DAMN IT!
WHAT DOES SHE EXPECT ME TO DO?!
THAT DAMN LAW-YER!
?
ズッ
ZU (SSK)

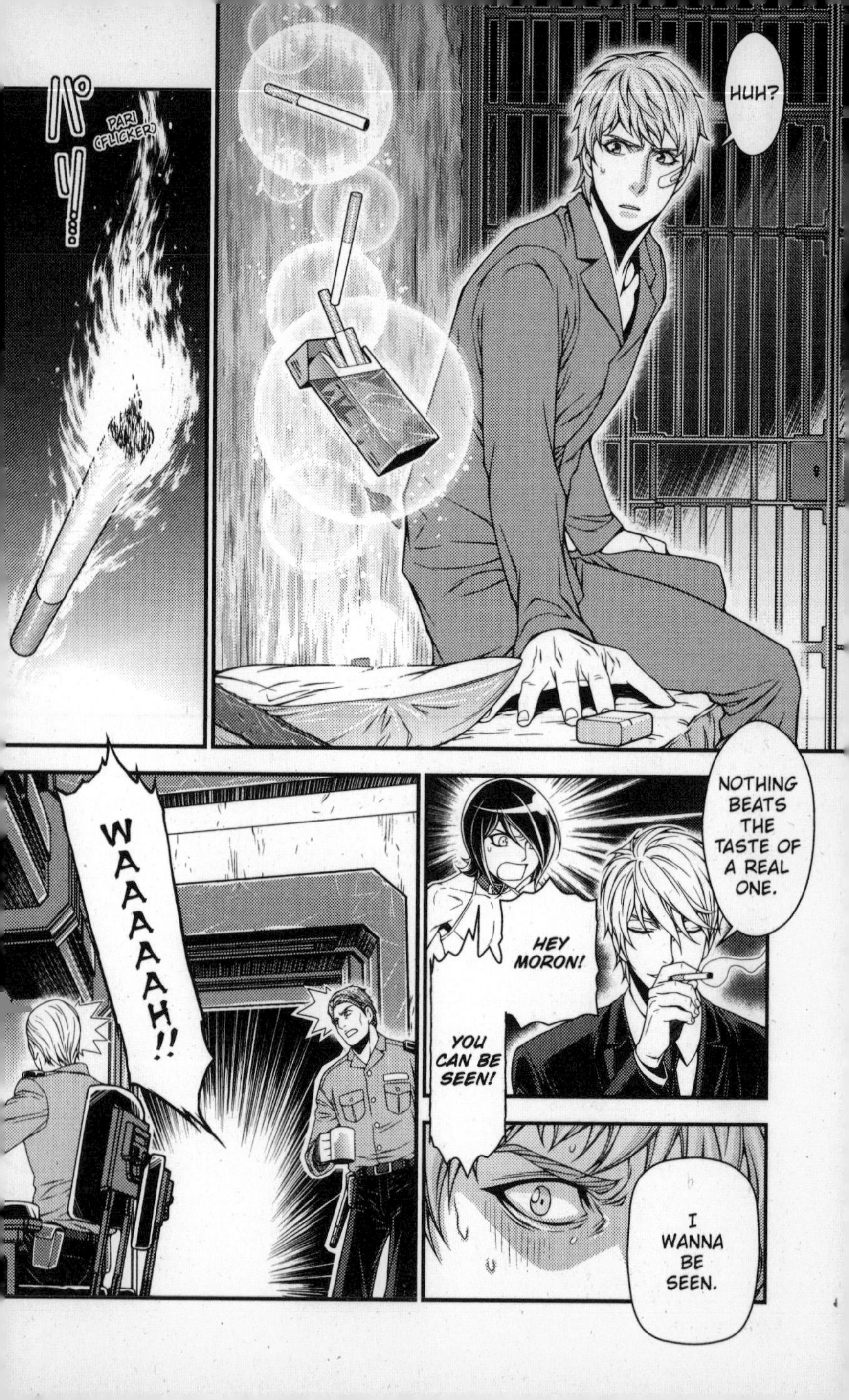

HUH?
PARI (FLICKER)
NOTHING BEATS THE TASTE OF A REAL ONE.
HEY MORON!
YOU CAN BE SEEN!
I WANNA BE SEEN.
WAAAAAAH!!

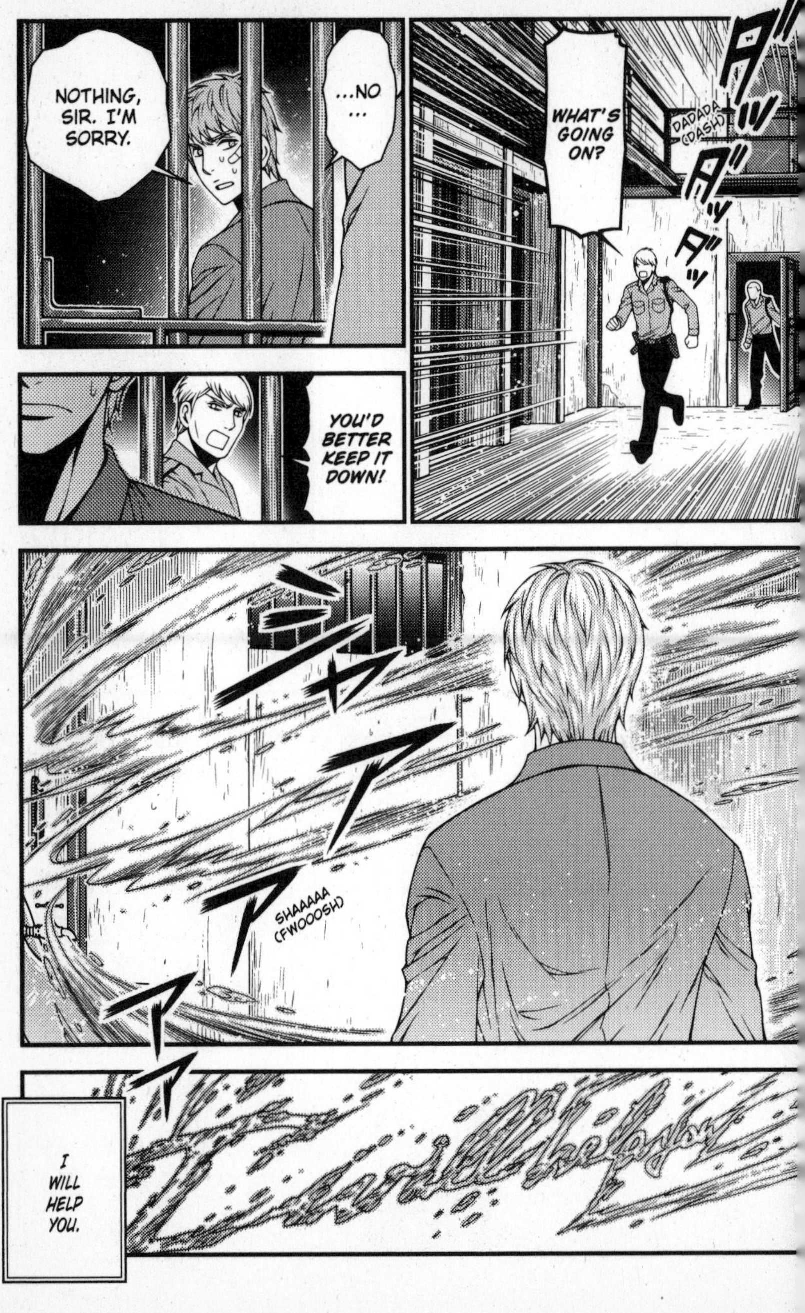
WHAT'S GOING ON?
DADADA (DASH)
...NO ...
NOTHING, SIR. I'M SORRY.
YOU'D BETTER KEEP IT DOWN!
SHAAAAA (FWOOOSH)
I WILL HELP YOU.

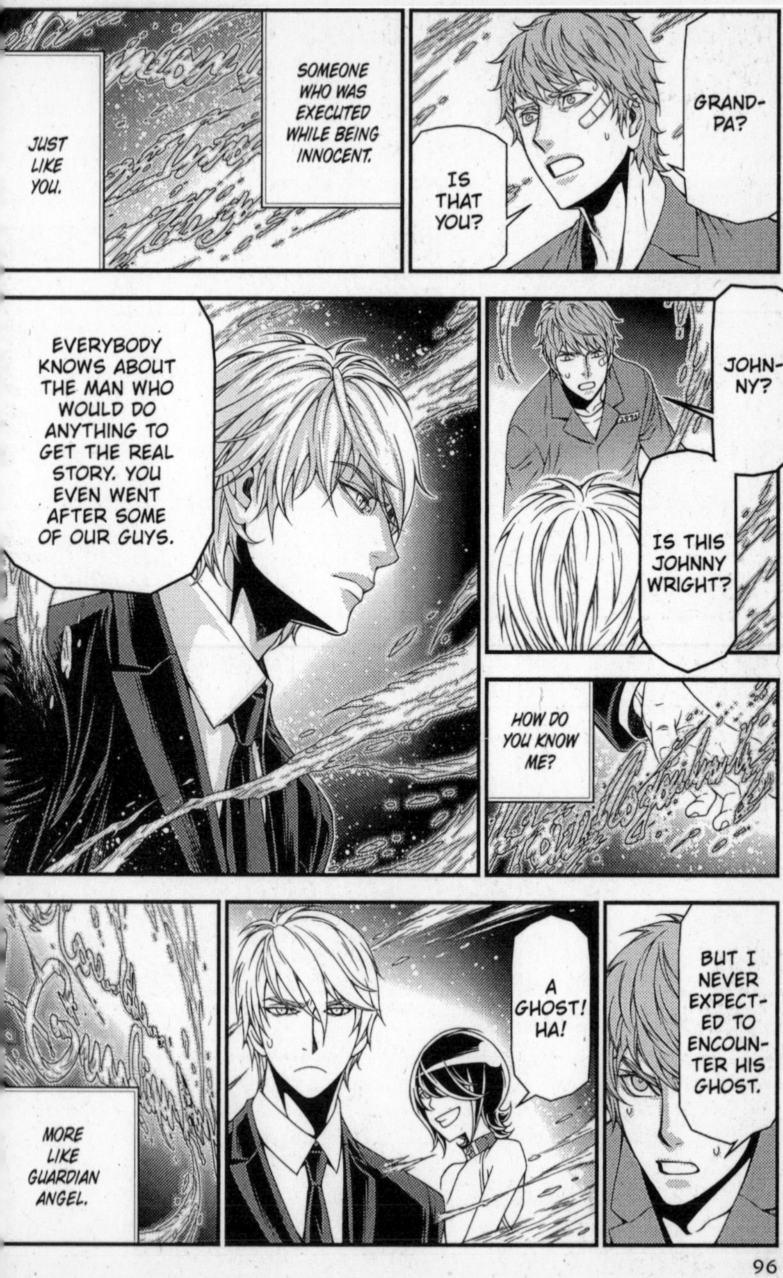
GRAND-PA?
IS THAT YOU?
SOMEONE WHO WAS EXECUTED WHILE BEING INNOCENT.
JUST LIKE YOU.
JOHN-NY?
IS THIS JOHNNY WRIGHT?
HOW DO YOU KNOW ME?
EVERYBODY KNOWS ABOUT THE MAN WHO WOULD DO ANYTHING TO GET THE REAL STORY. YOU EVEN WENT AFTER SOME OF OUR GUYS.
BUT I NEVER EXPECT-ED TO ENCOUN-TER HIS GHOST.
A GHOST! HA!
MORE LIKE GUARDIAN ANGEL.

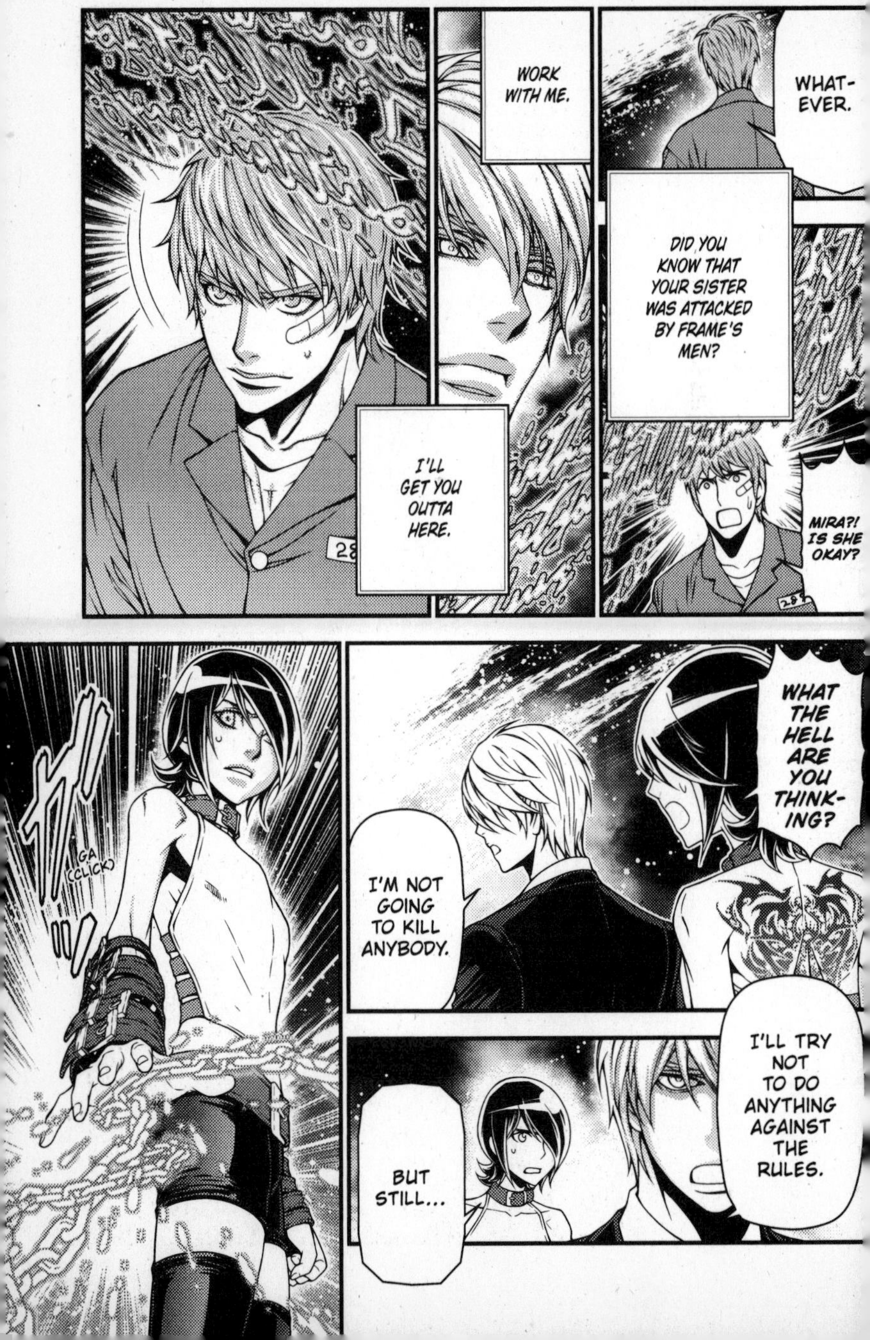
WHAT-EVER.
DID YOU KNOW THAT YOUR SISTER WAS ATTACKED BY FRAME'S MEN?
MIRA?! IS SHE OKAY?
WORK WITH ME.
I'LL GET YOU OUTTA HERE.
WHAT THE HELL ARE YOU THINKING?
I'M NOT GOING TO KILL ANYBODY.
I'LL TRY NOT TO DO ANYTHING AGAINST THE RULES.
BUT STILL...
GA (CLICK)

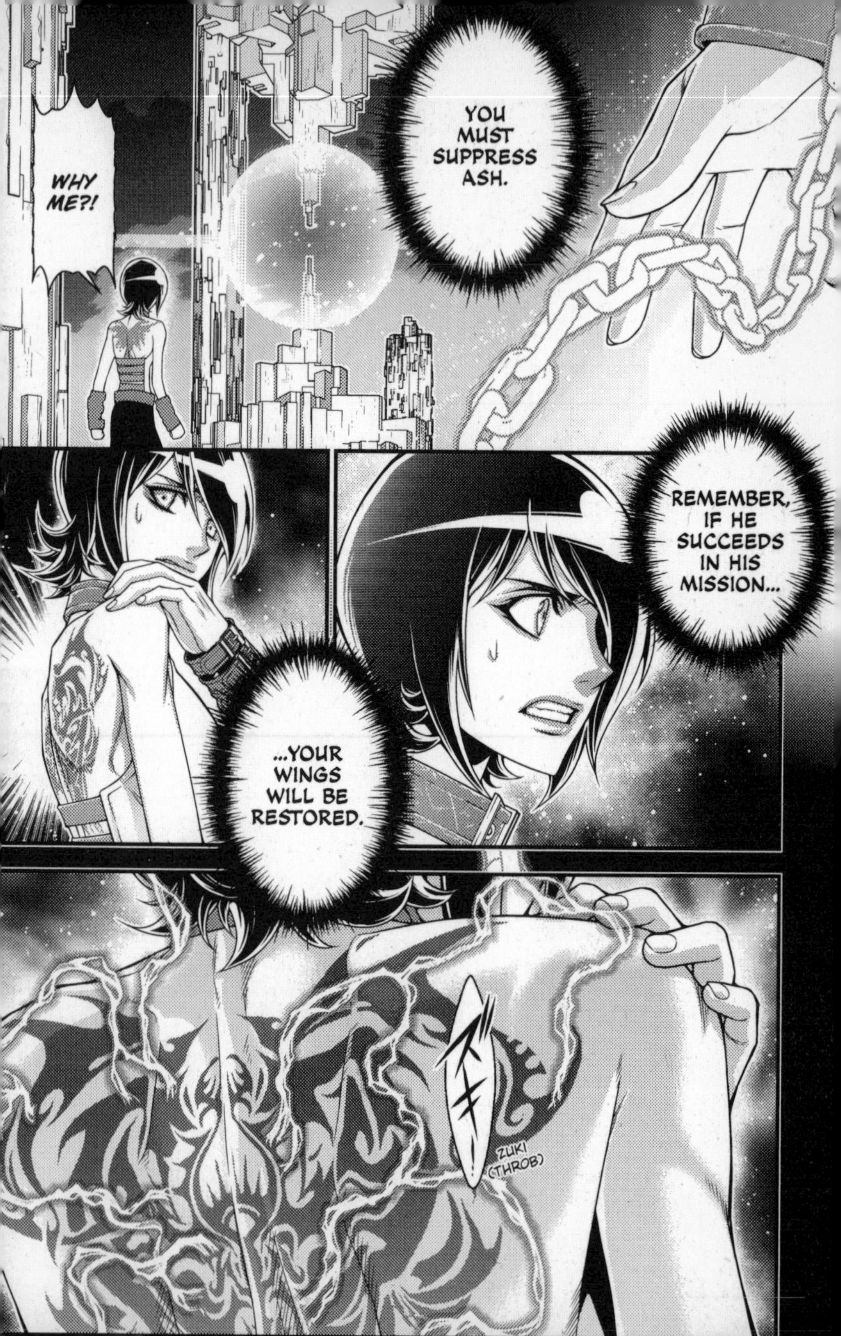
YOU MUST SUPPRESS ASH.
WHY ME?!
REMEMBER, IF HE SUCCEEDS IN HIS MISSION...
...YOUR WINGS WILL BE RESTORED.
ZUKI (THROB)

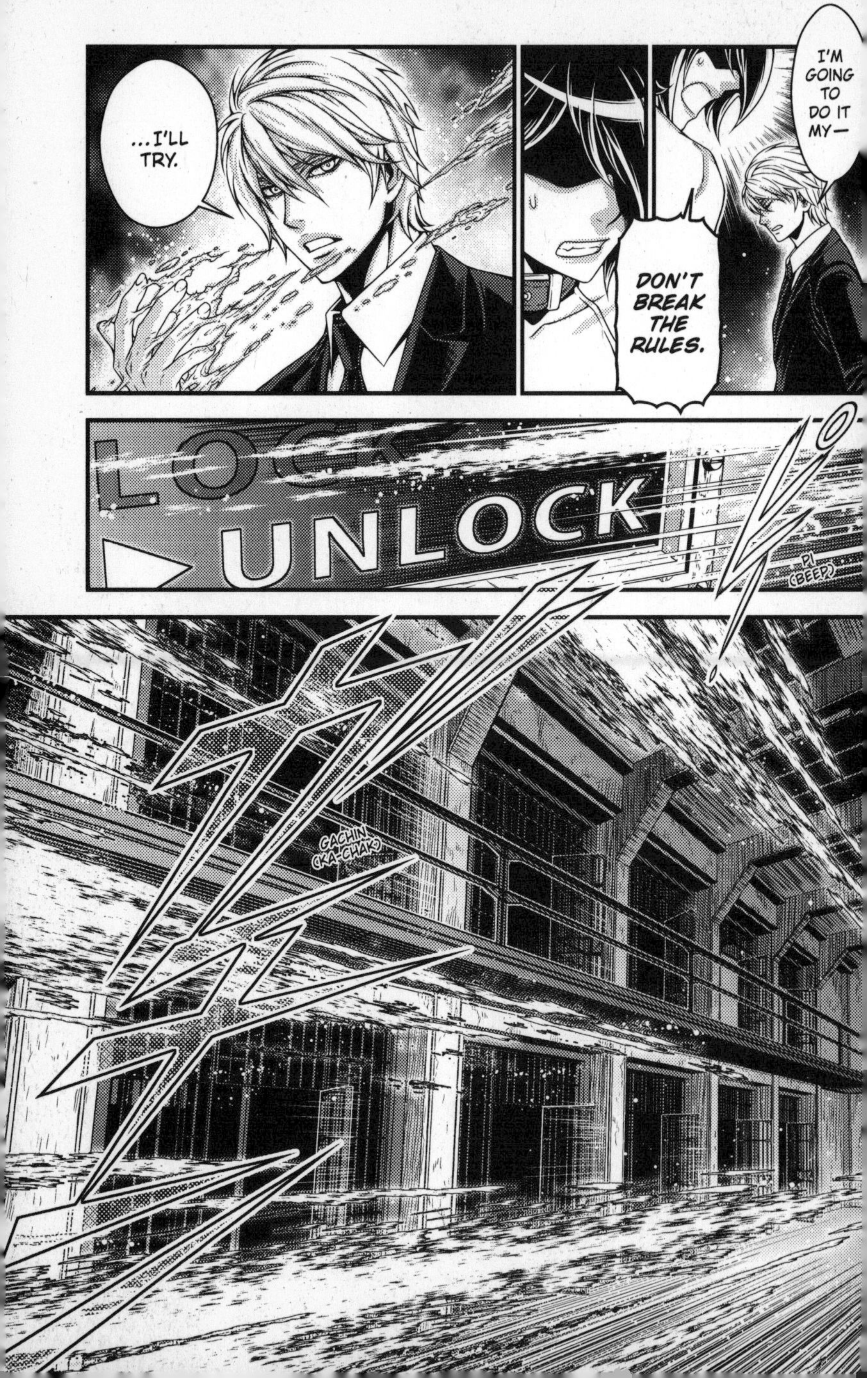
I'M GOING TO DO IT MY—
DON'T BREAK THE RULES.
...I'LL TRY.
UNLOCK
PI (BEEP)
GACHIN (KA-CHAK)

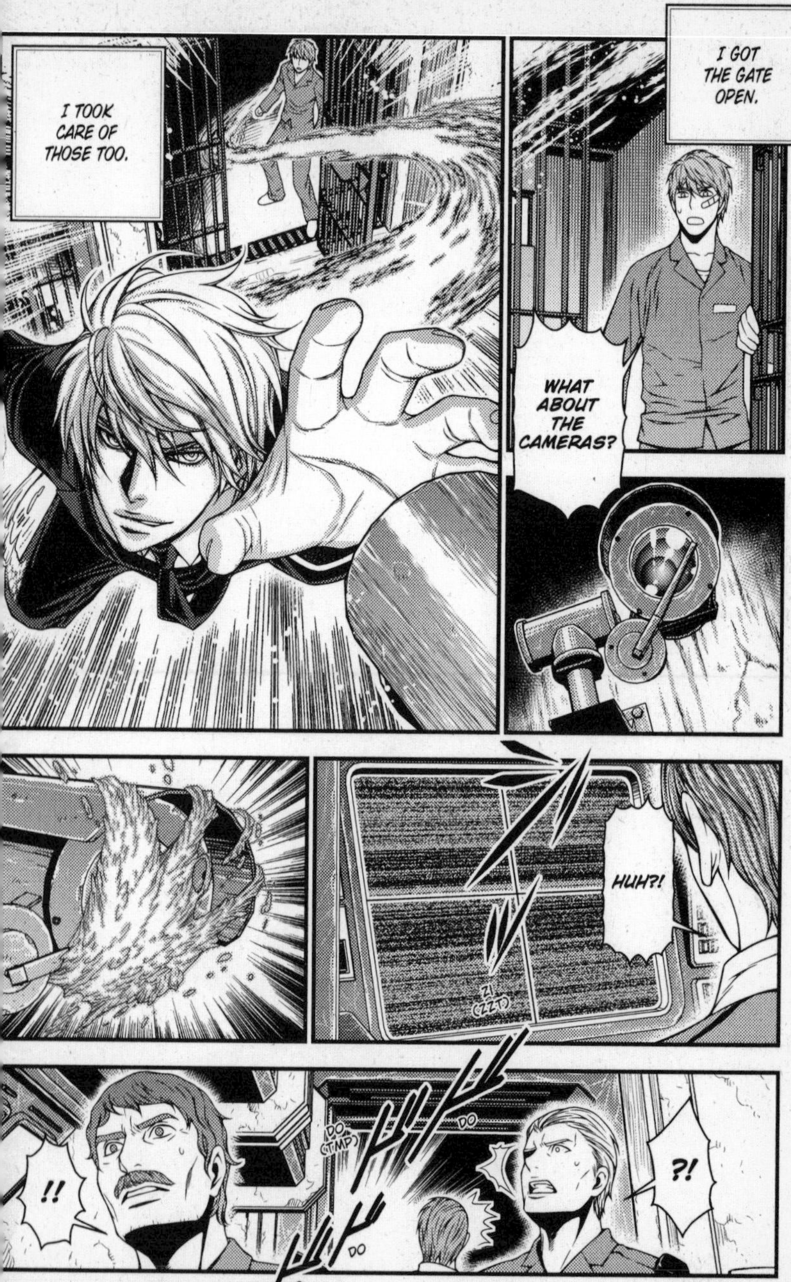
I GOT THE GATE OPEN.
WHAT ABOUT THE CAMERAS?
I TOOK CARE OF THOSE TOO.
HUH?!
ZI (ZZT)
?!
DO
DO (TMP)
!!
DO
DO

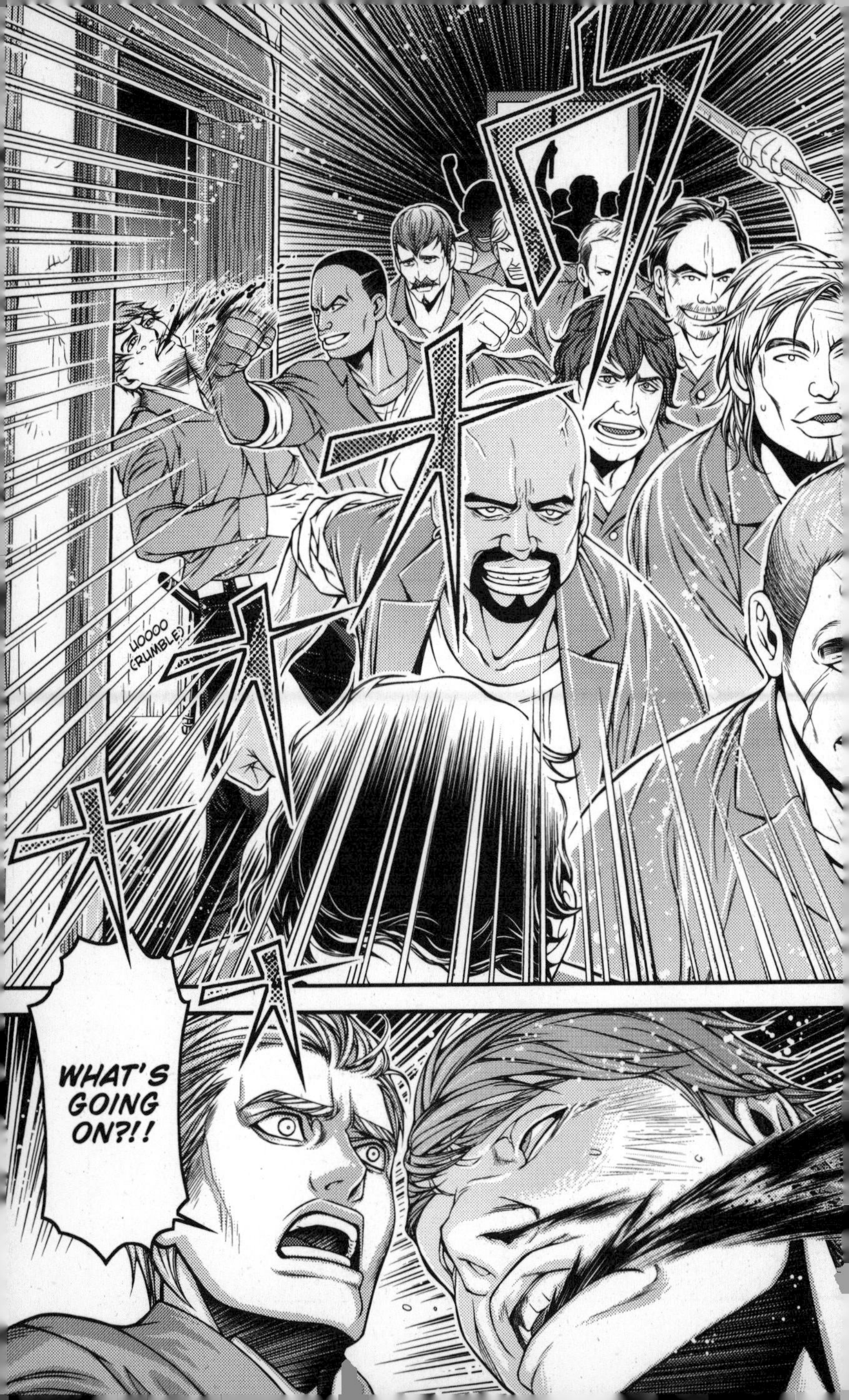
UOOOO (RUMBLE)
WHAT'S GOING ON?!!

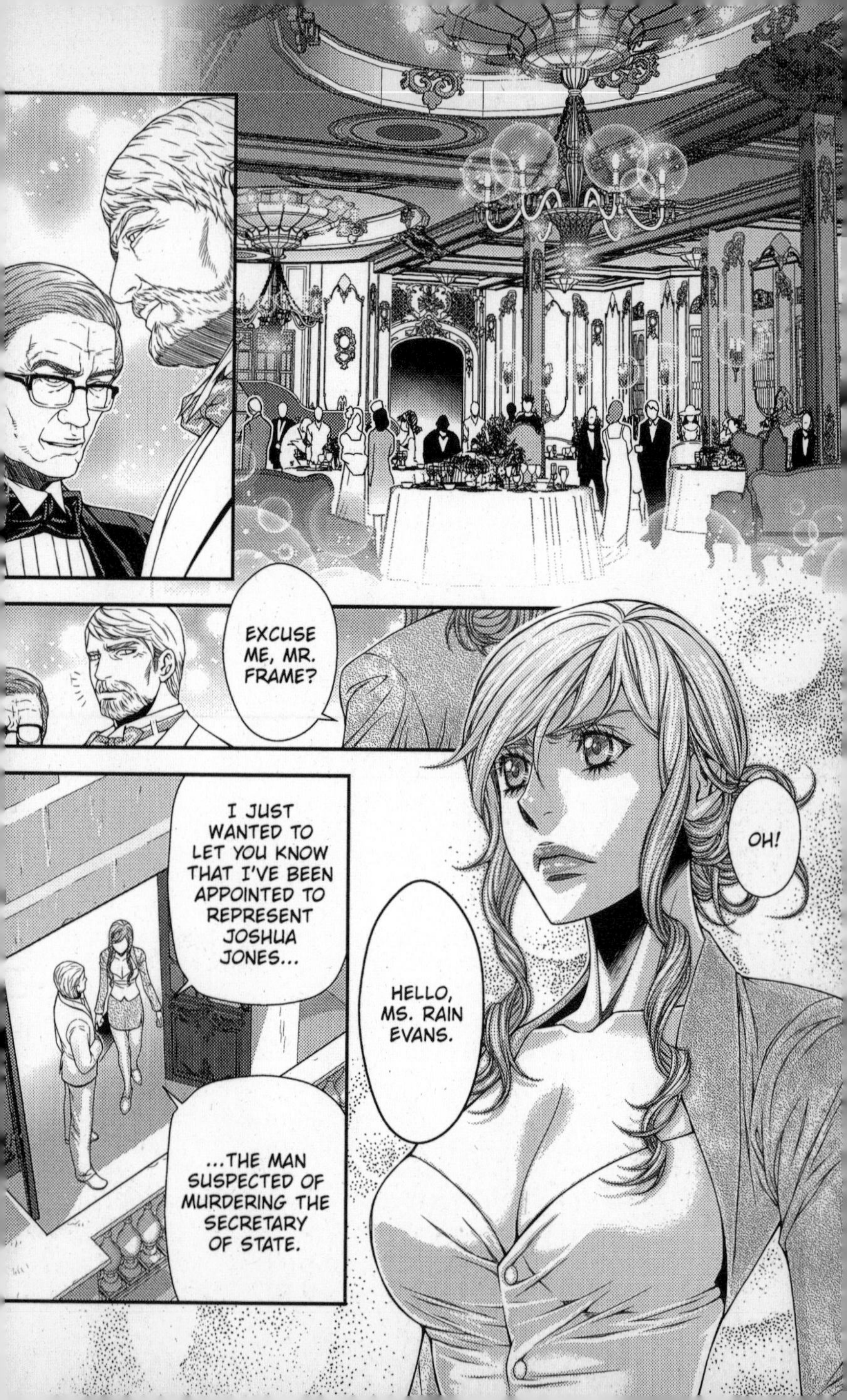
EXCUSE ME, MR. FRAME?
OH!
HELLO, MS. RAIN EVANS.
I JUST WANTED TO LET YOU KNOW THAT I'VE BEEN APPOINTED TO REPRESENT JOSHUA JONES...
...THE MAN SUSPECTED OF MURDERING THE SECRETARY OF STATE.

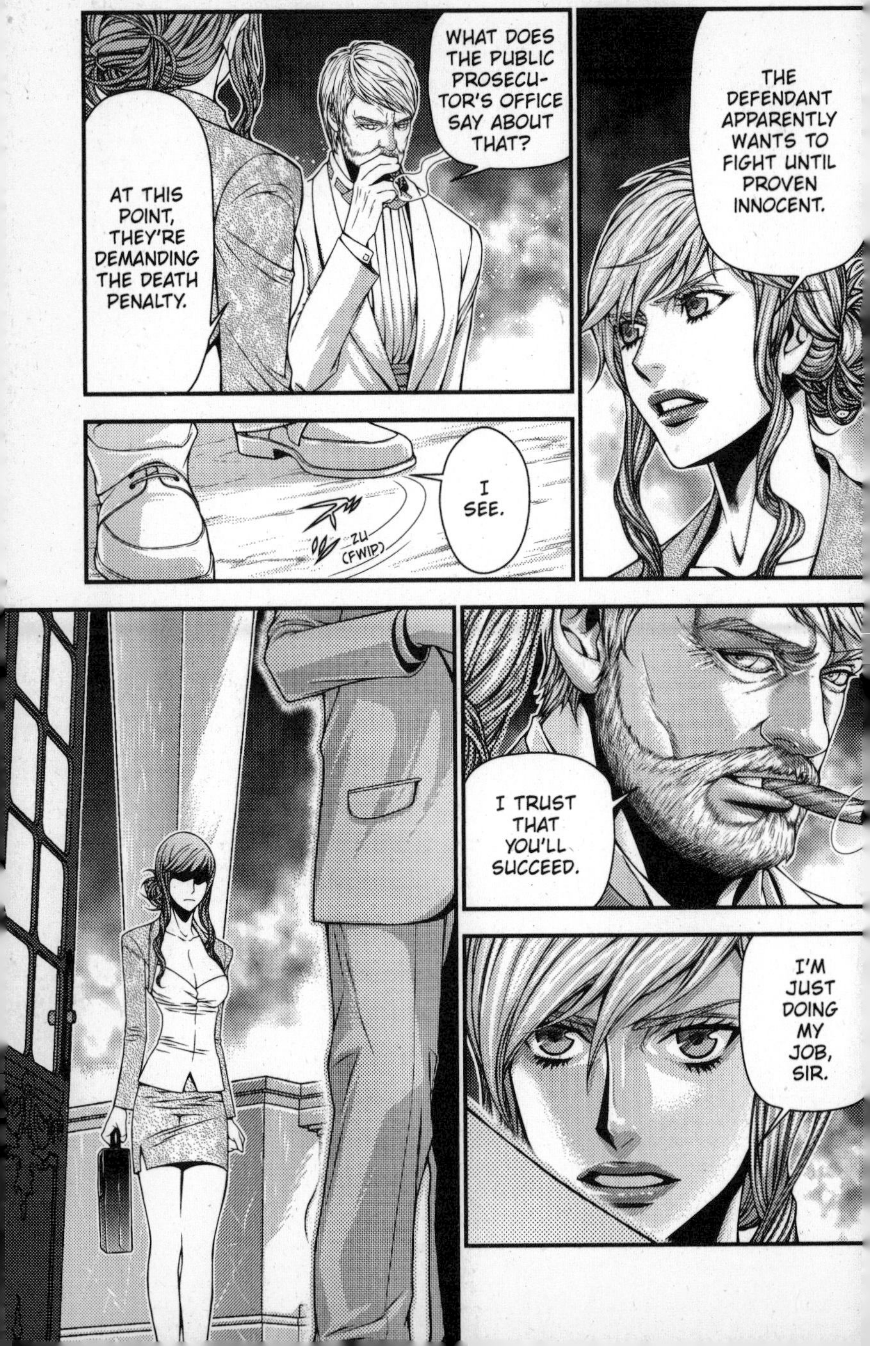
THE DEFENDANT APPARENTLY WANTS TO FIGHT UNTIL PROVEN INNOCENT.
WHAT DOES THE PUBLIC PROSECU-TOR'S OFFICE SAY ABOUT THAT?
AT THIS POINT, THEY'RE DEMANDING THE DEATH PENALTY.
I SEE.
ZU (FWIP)
I TRUST THAT YOU'LL SUCCEED.
I'M JUST DOING MY JOB, SIR.

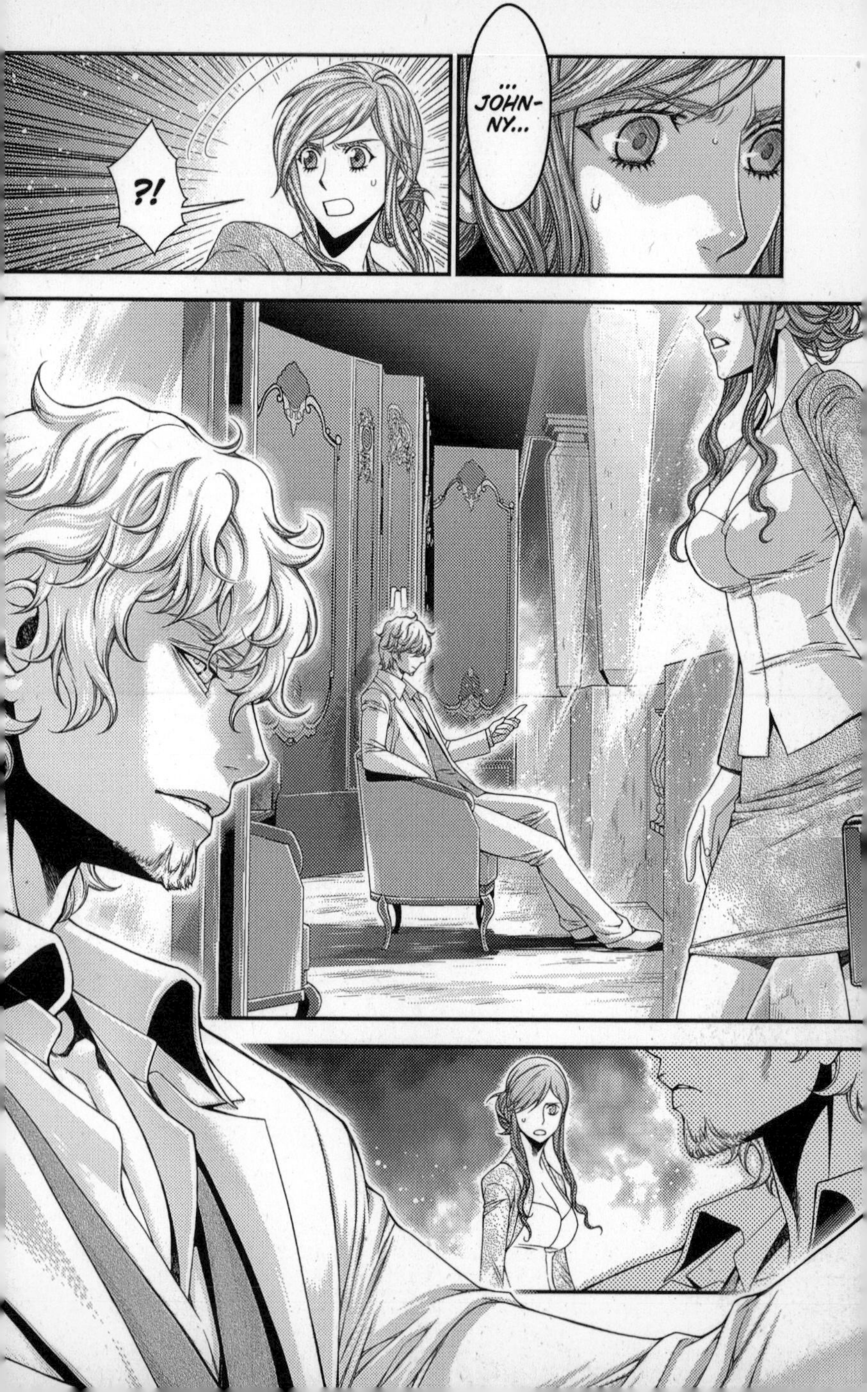
... JOHN-NY...
?!

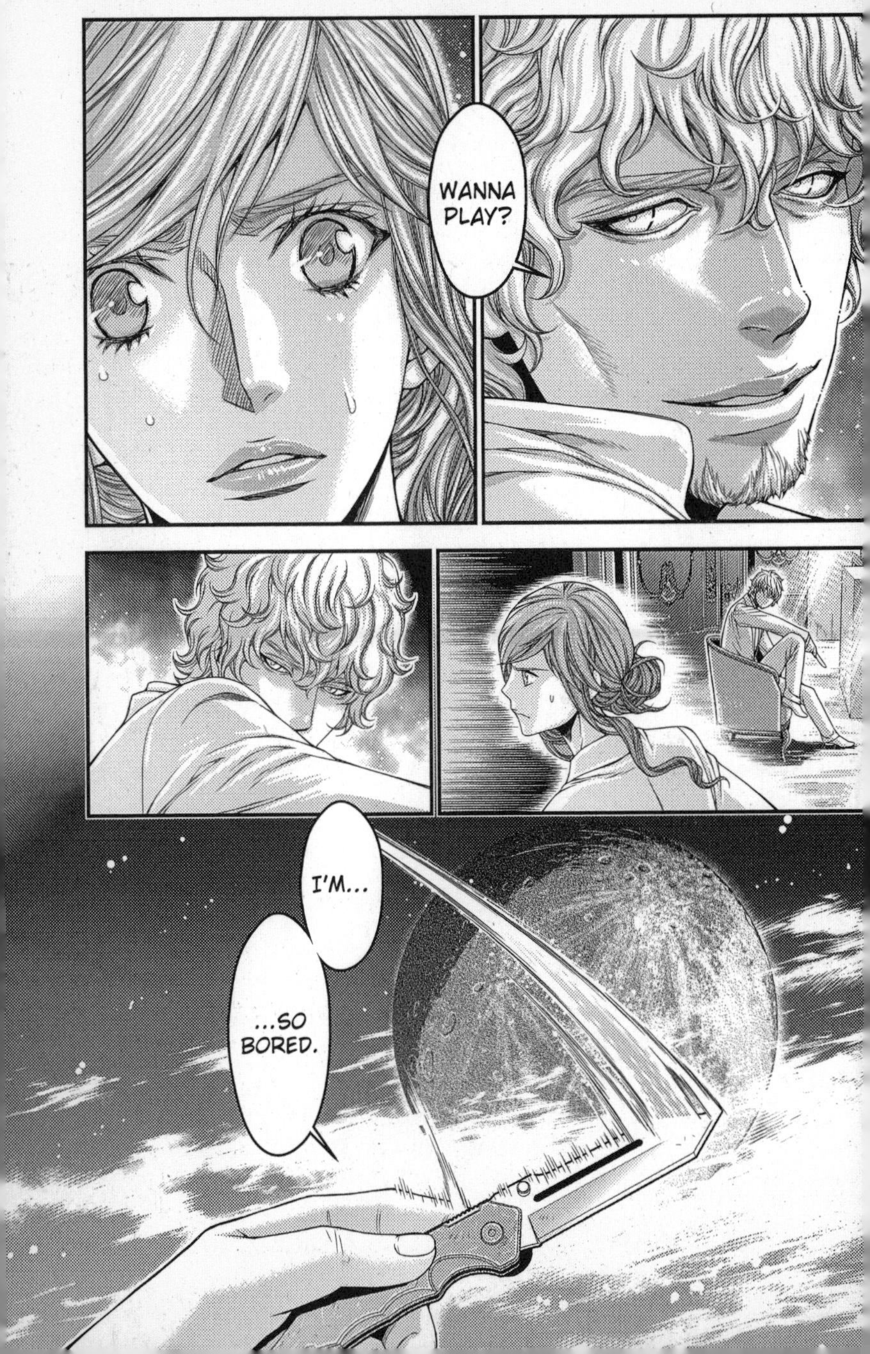
WANNA PLAY?
I'M...
...SO BORED.

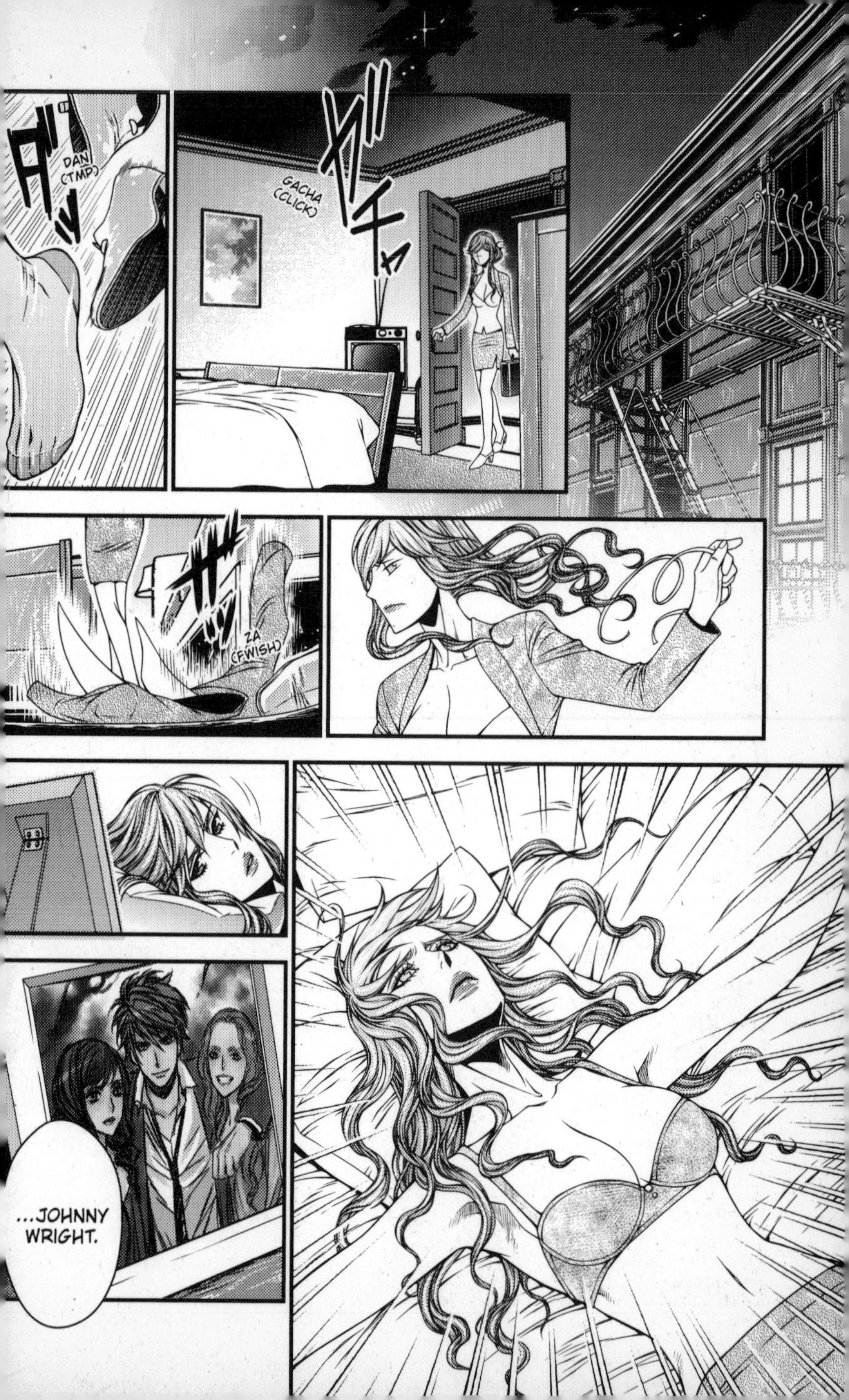
GACHA (CLICK)
DAN (TMP)
ZA (F-WISH)
...JOHNNY WRIGHT.

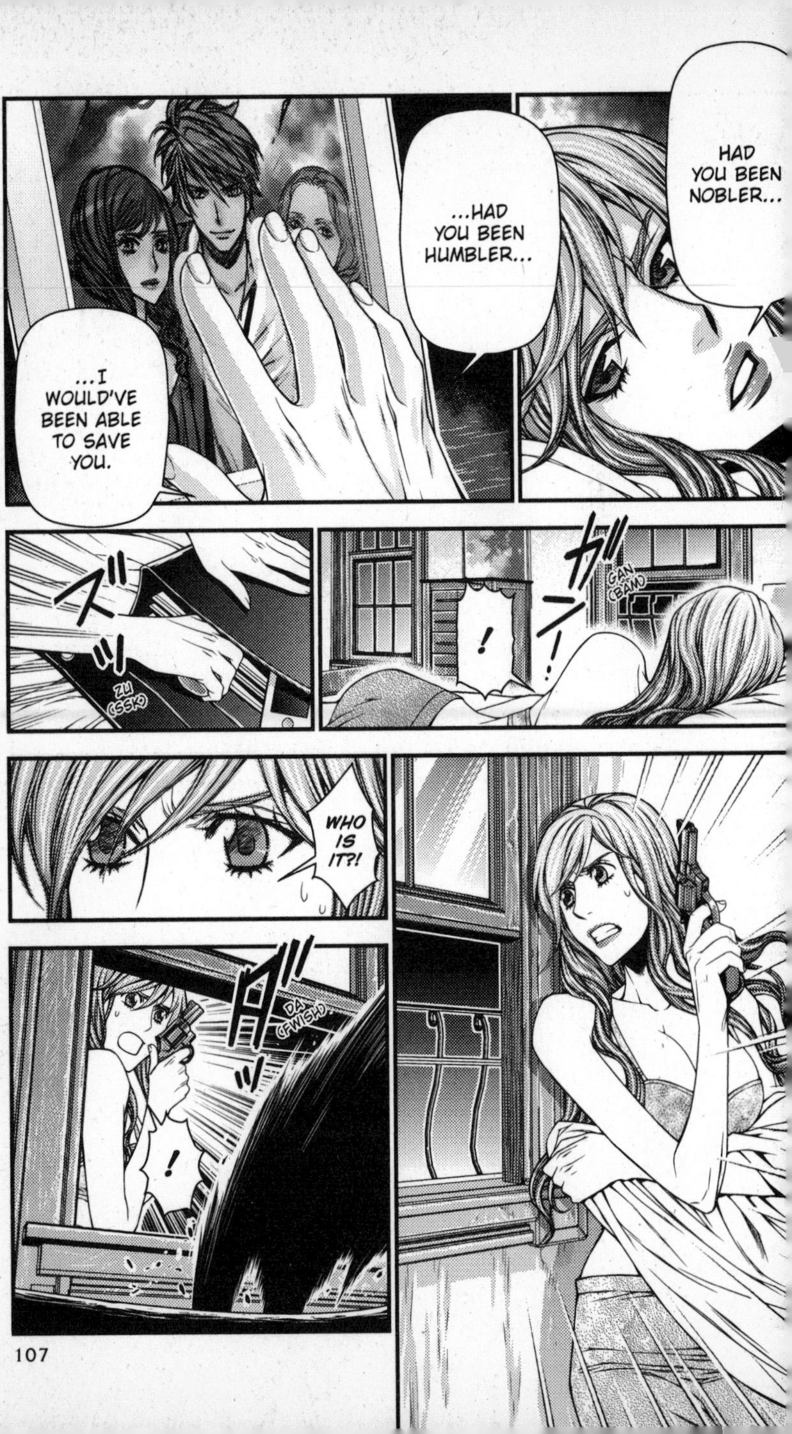
HAD YOU BEEN NOBLER...
...HAD YOU BEEN HUMBLER...
...I WOULD'VE BEEN ABLE TO SAVE YOU.
GAN (BAM)
!
ZU (SSK)
WHO IS IT?!
DA (FWISH)
!

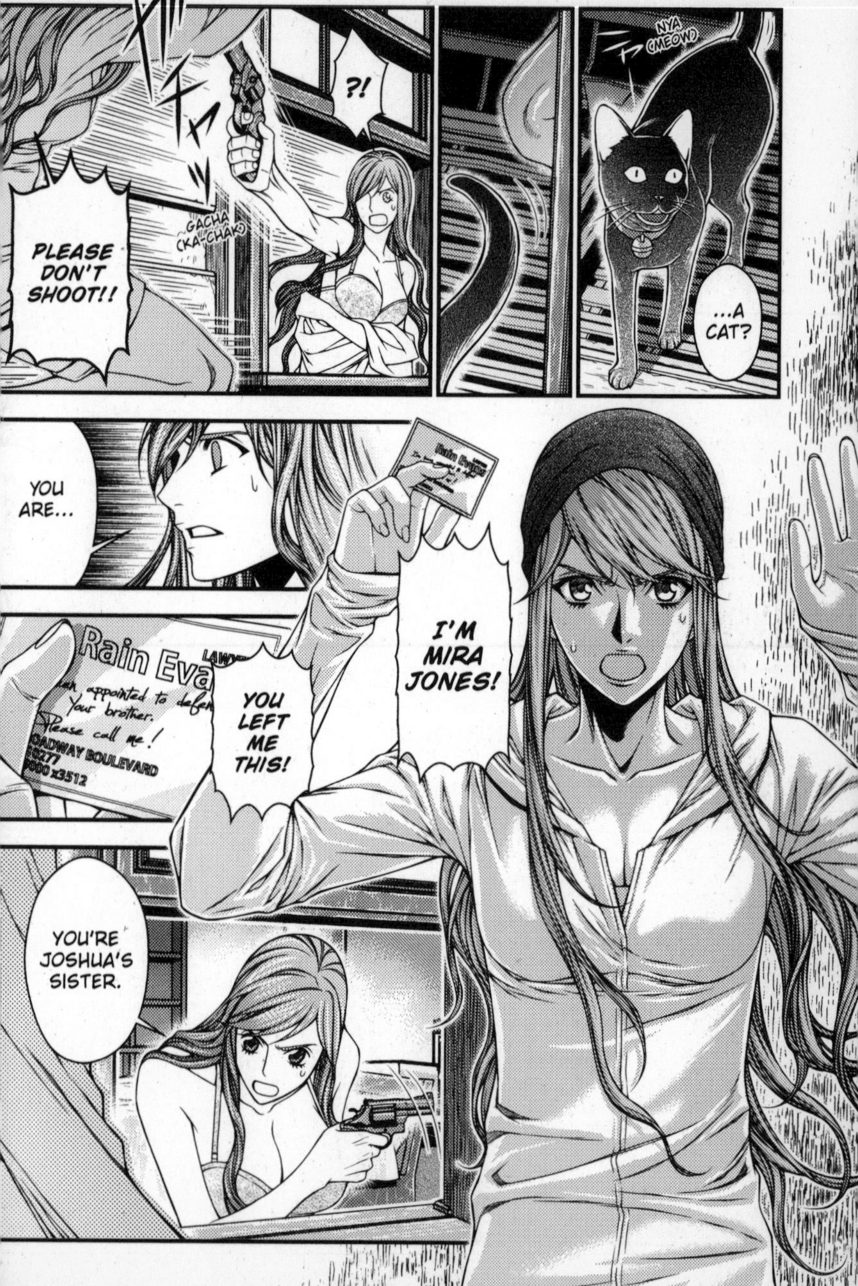
NYA (MEOW)
...A CAT?
?!
GACHA (KA-CHAK)
PLEASE DON'T SHOOT!!
I'M MIRA JONES!
YOU LEFT ME THIS!
YOU ARE...
Rain Eva
Your brother.
Please call me!
YOU'RE JOSHUA'S SISTER.

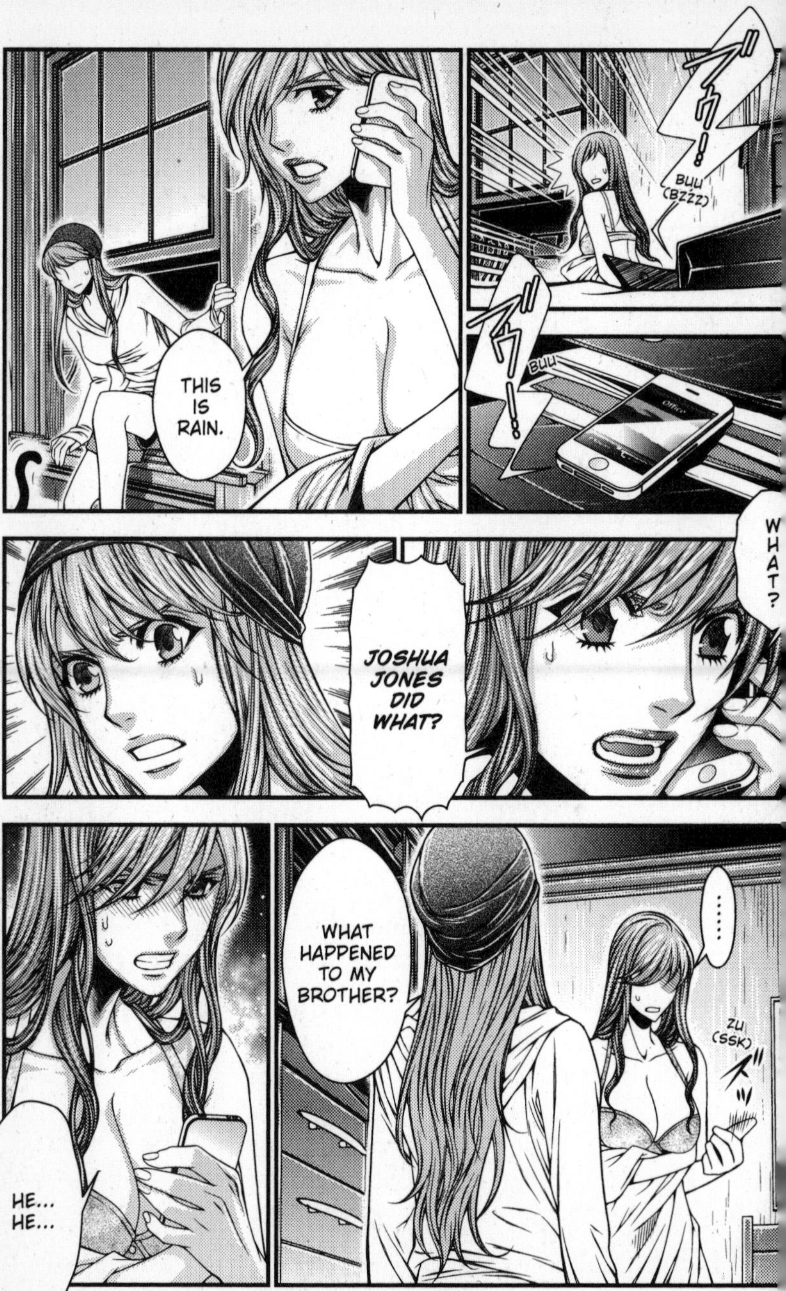
BUU (BZZZ)
BUU
THIS IS RAIN.
WHAT?
JOSHUA JONES DID WHAT?
......
ZU (SSK)
WHAT HAPPENED TO MY BROTHER?
HE... HE...

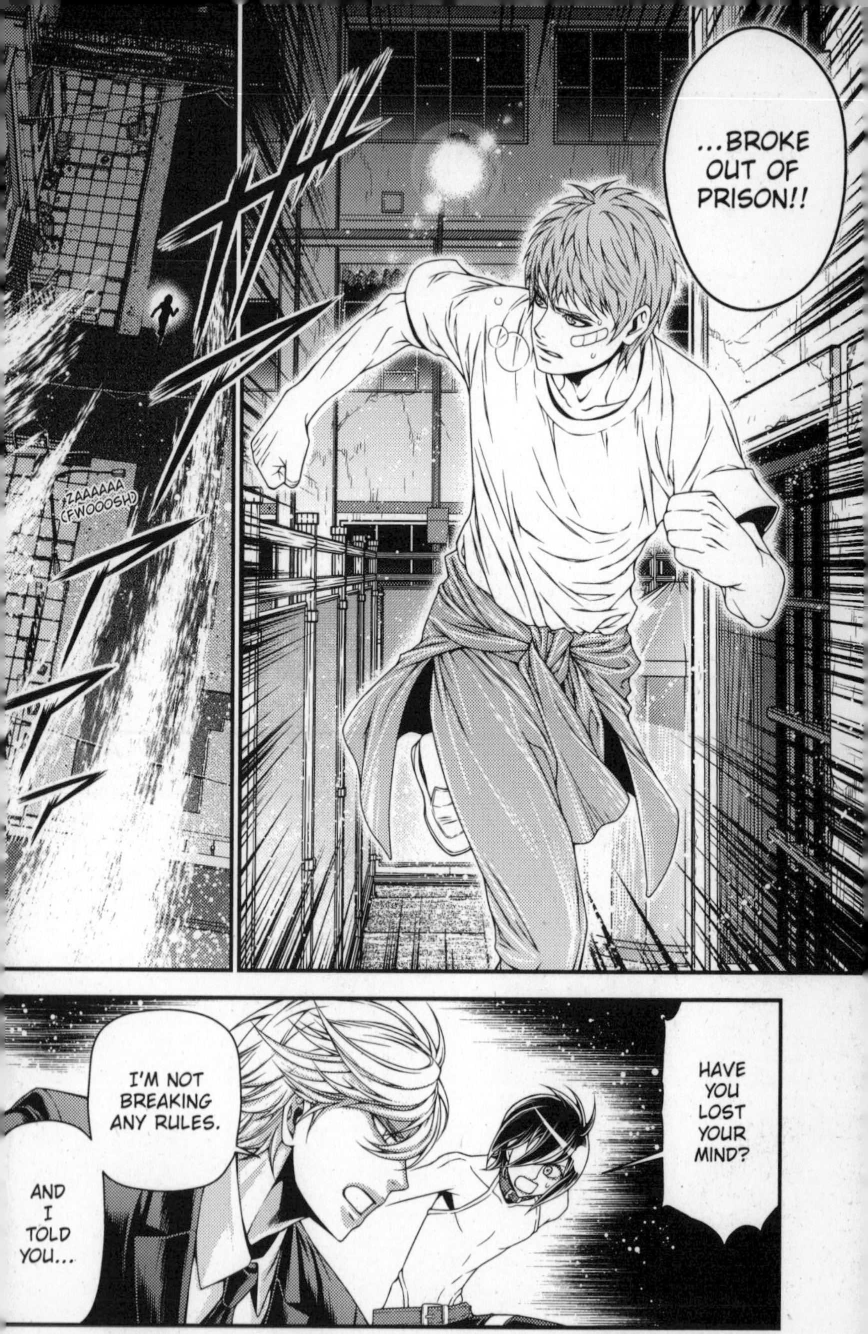
...BROKE OUT OF PRISON!!
ZAAAAAA (FWOOOSH)
HAVE YOU LOST YOUR MIND?
I'M NOT BREAKING ANY RULES.
AND I TOLD YOU...

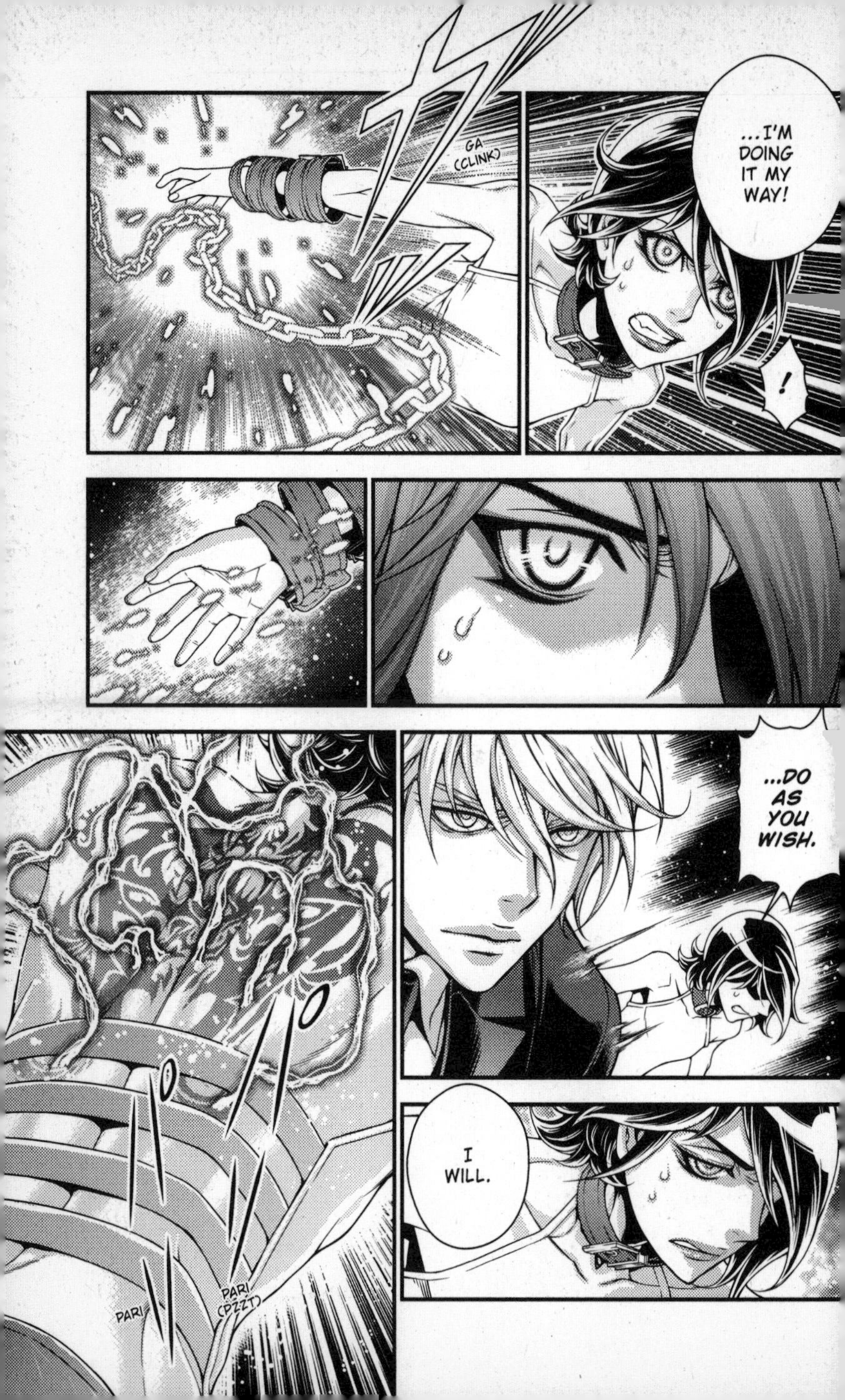
...I'M DOING IT MY WAY!
!
GA (CLINK)
...DO AS YOU WISH.
I WILL.
PARI (PZZT)
PARI

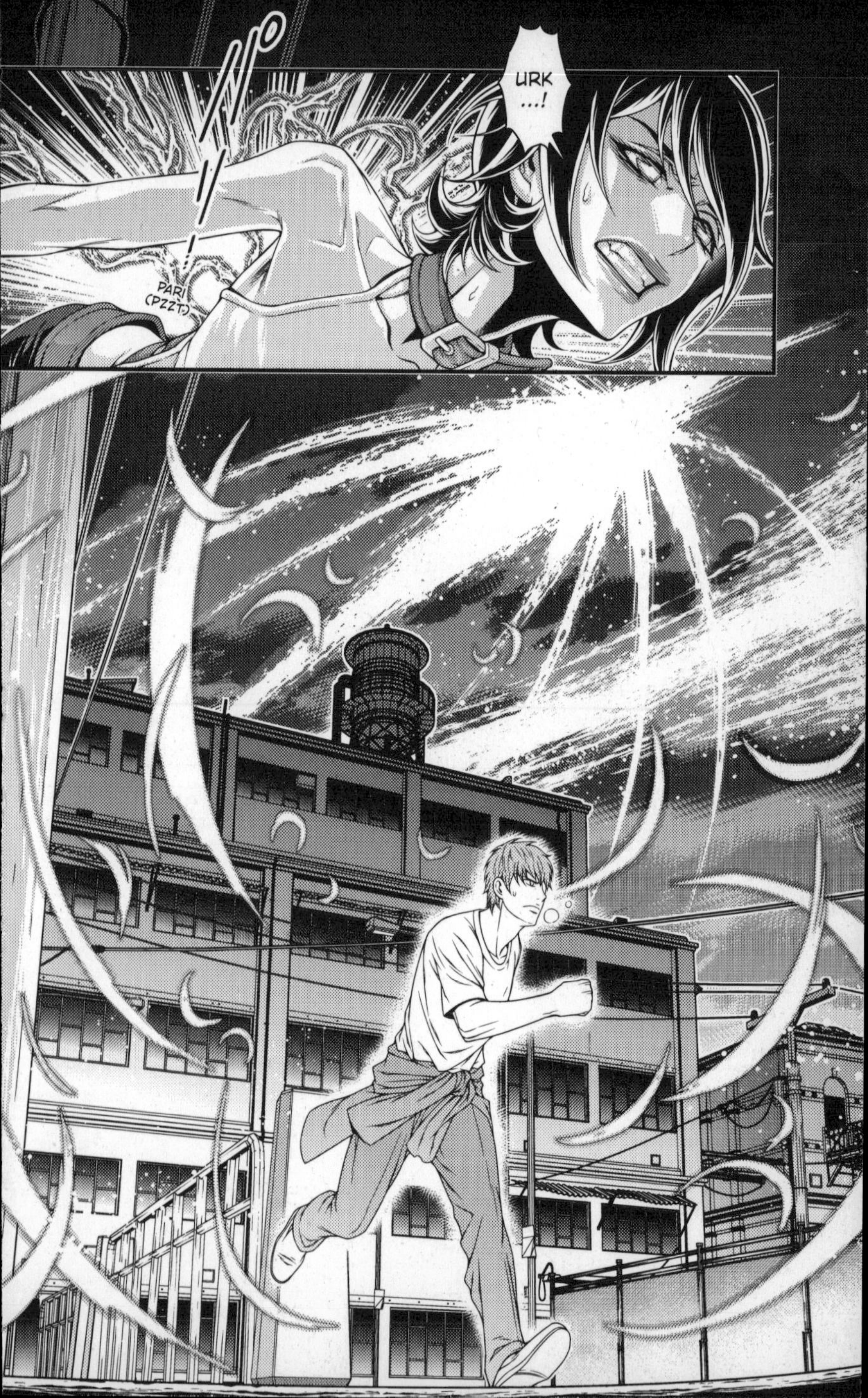
URK ...!
PARI (PZZT)

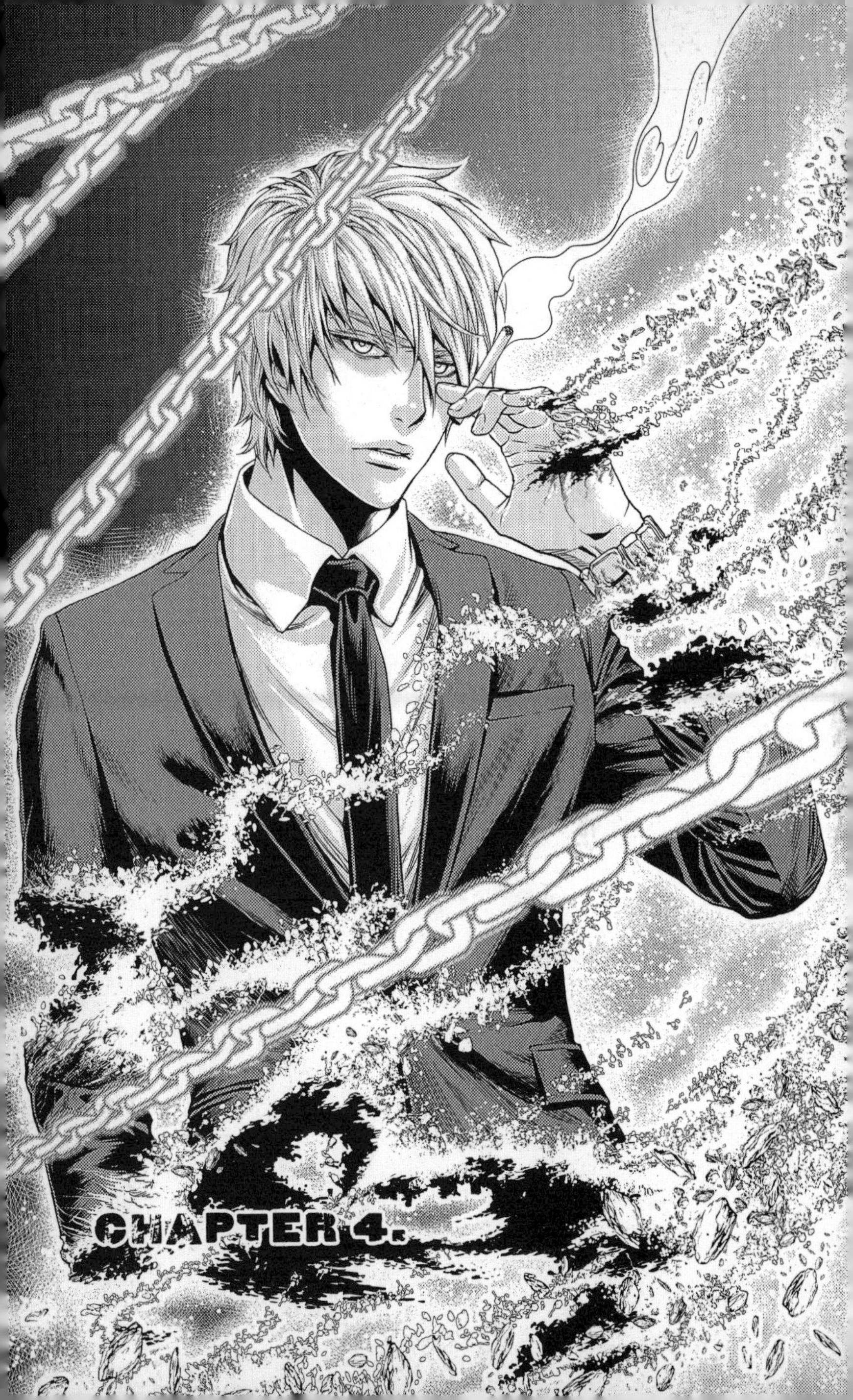
CHAPTER 4.

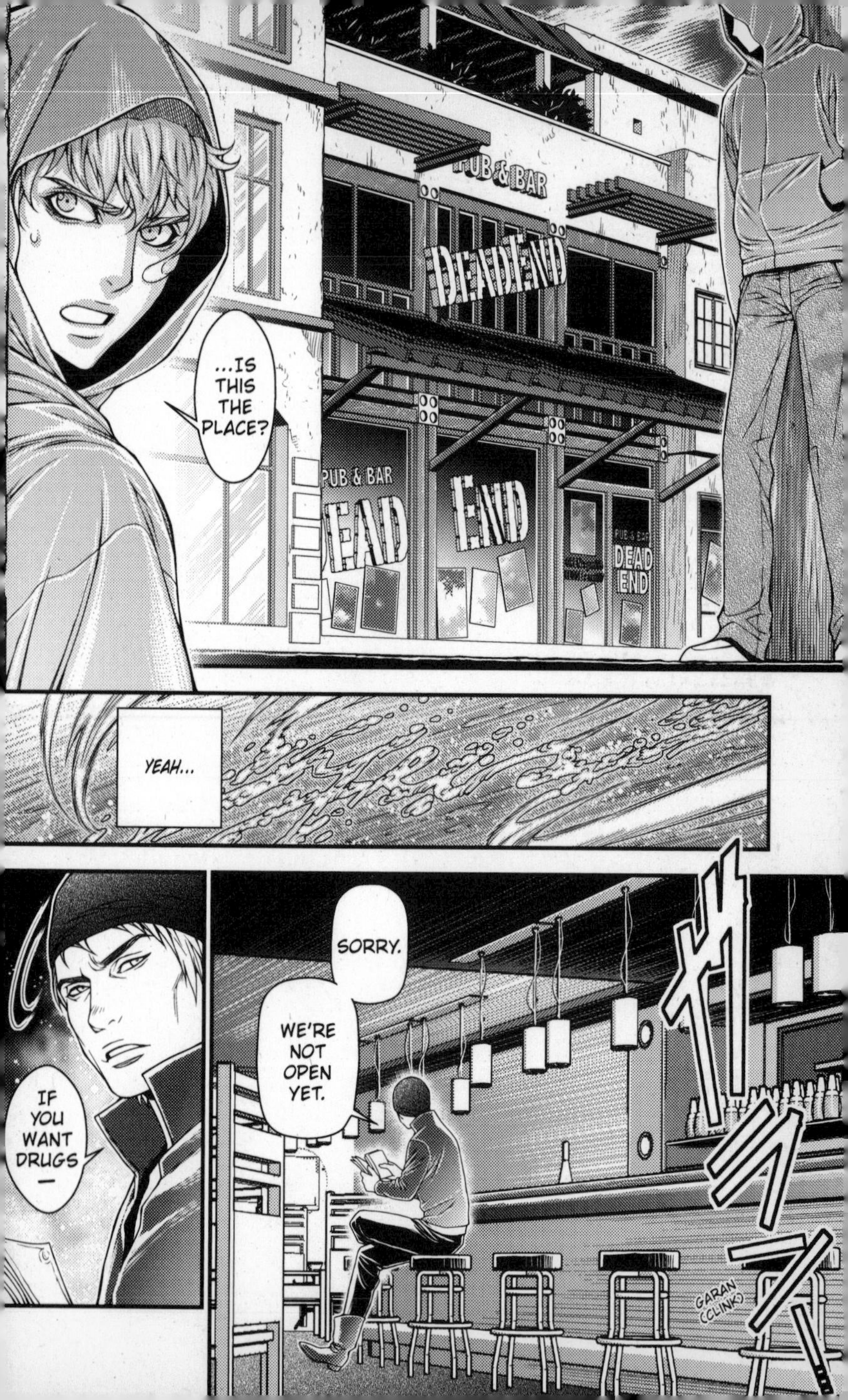
PUB & BAR
DEADEND
PUB & BAR
DEAD END
PUB & BAR
DEAD END
...IS THIS THE PLACE?
YEAH...
SORRY.
WE'RE NOT OPEN YET.
GARAN (CLINK)
IF YOU WANT DRUGS—

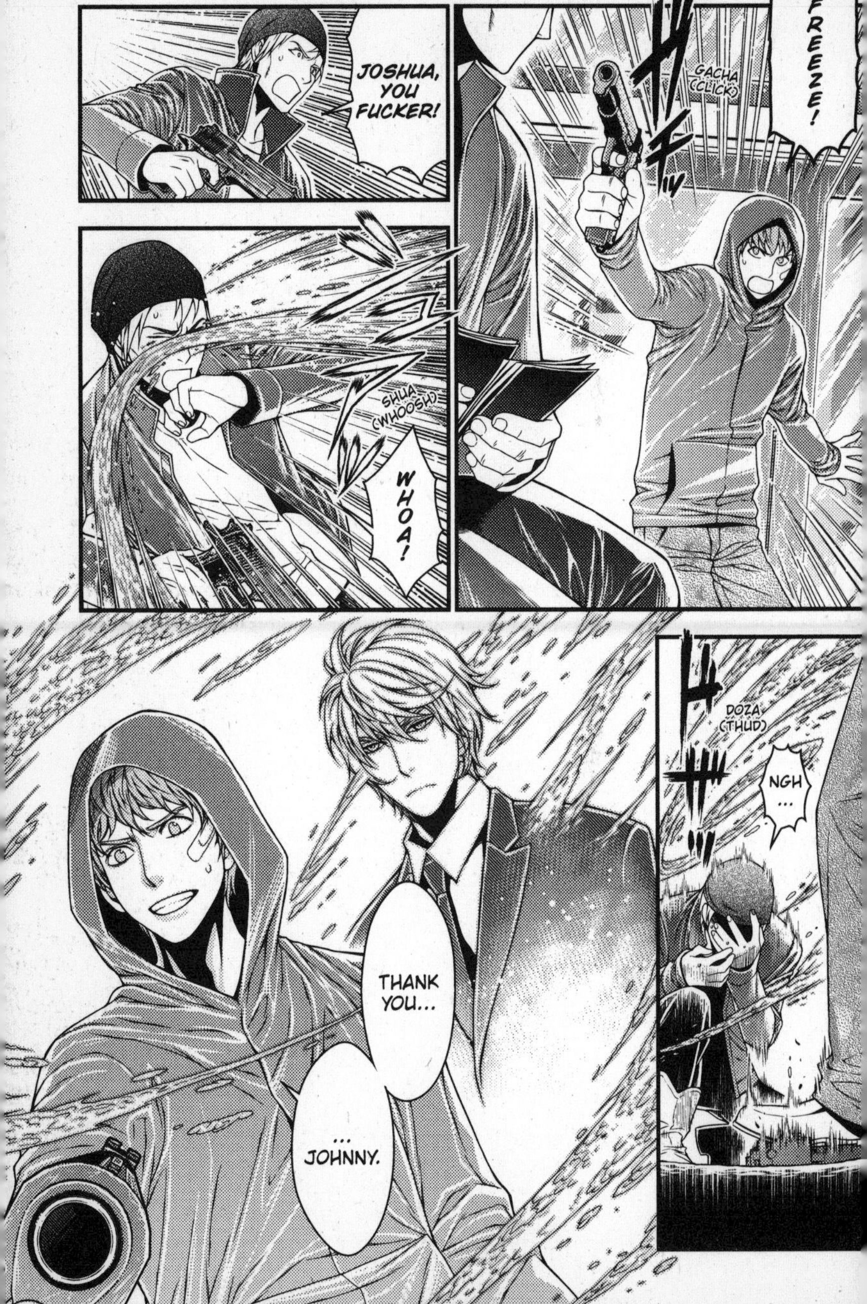
FREEZE!
GACHA (CLICK)
JOSHUA, YOU FUCKER!
SHUA (WHOOSH)
WHOA!
DOZA (THUD)
NGH ...
THANK YOU...
... JOHNNY.

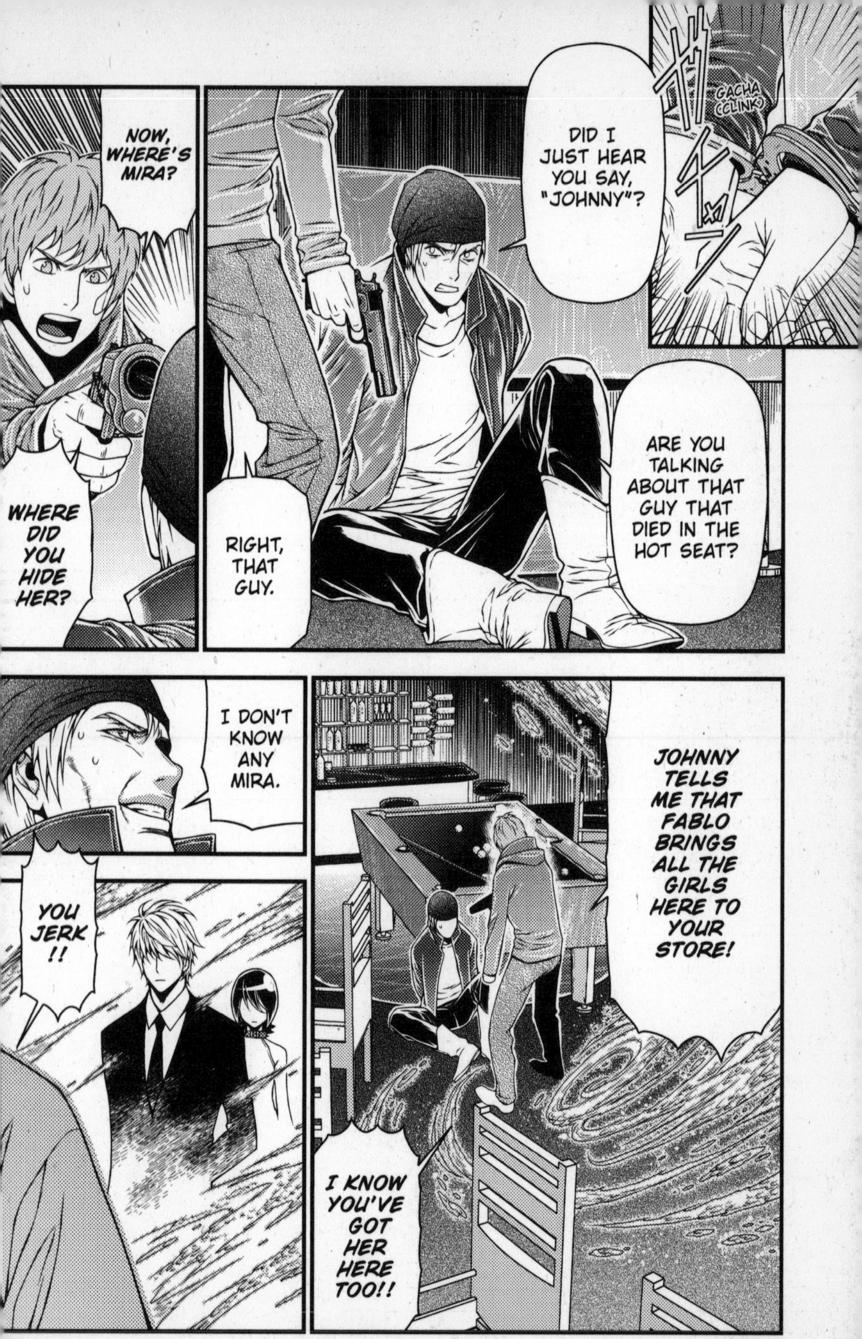
GACHA (CLINK)
DID I JUST HEAR YOU SAY, "JOHNNY"?
ARE YOU TALKING ABOUT THAT GUY THAT DIED IN THE HOT SEAT?
RIGHT, THAT GUY.
NOW, WHERE'S MIRA?
WHERE DID YOU HIDE HER?
JOHNNY TELLS ME THAT FABLO BRINGS ALL THE GIRLS HERE TO YOUR STORE!
I KNOW YOU'VE GOT HER HERE TOO!!
I DON'T KNOW ANY MIRA.
YOU JERK!!

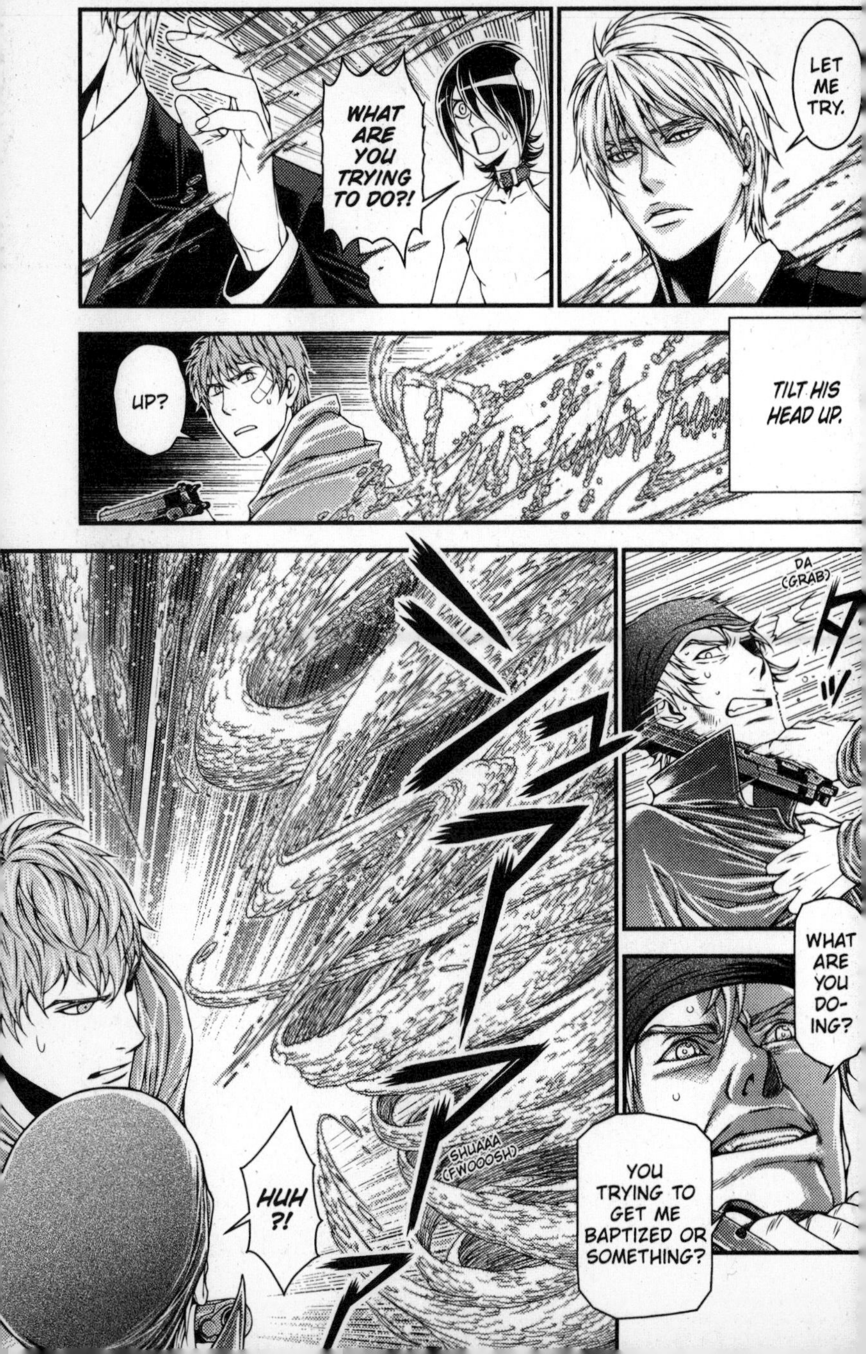
LET ME TRY.
WHAT ARE YOU TRYING TO DO?!
TILT HIS HEAD UP.
UP?
DA (GRAB)
WHAT ARE YOU DO-ING?
YOU TRYING TO GET ME BAPTIZED OR SOMETHING?
SHUAAA (FWOOOSH)
HUH?!

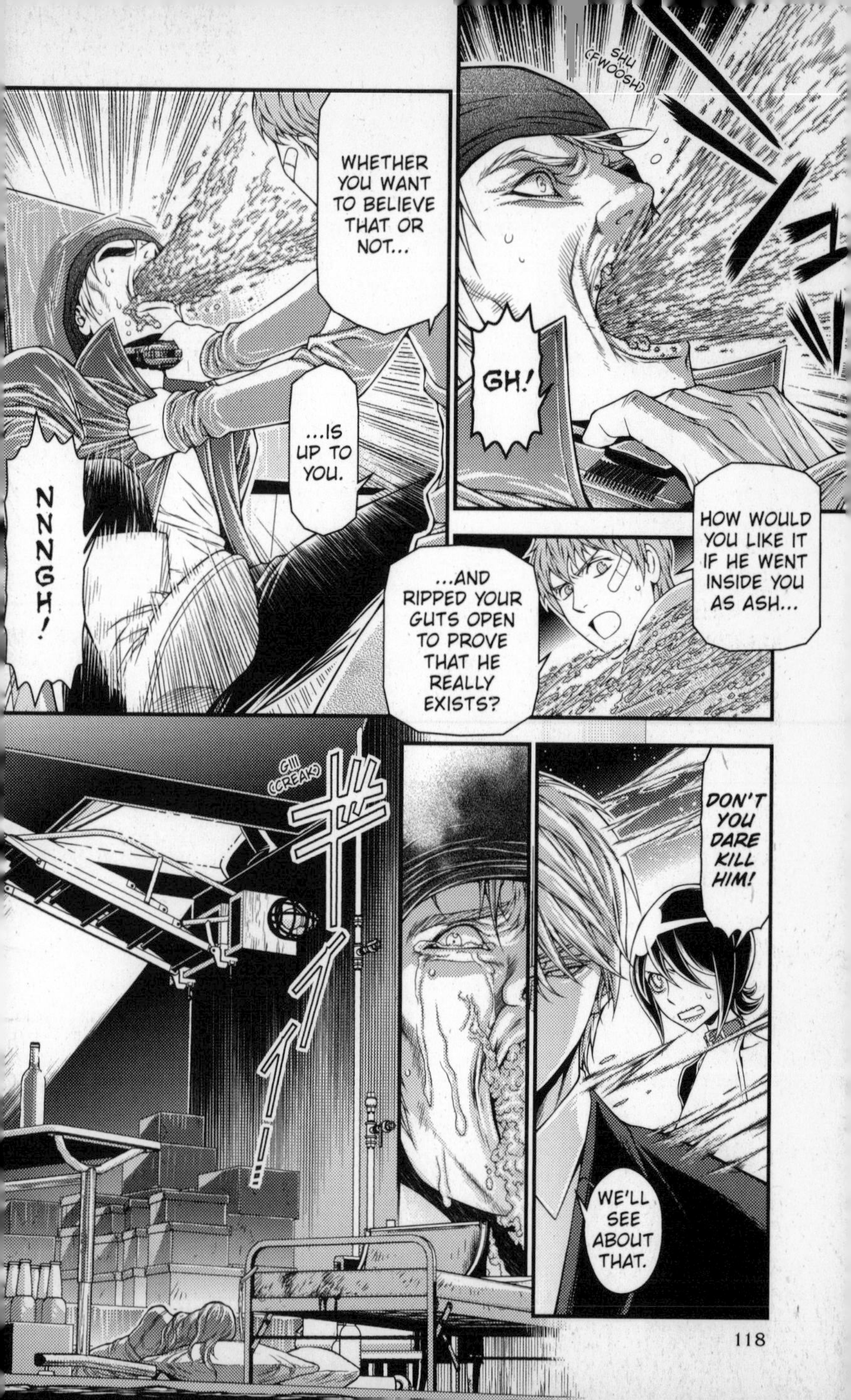
SHU (FWOOSH)
GH!
HOW WOULD YOU LIKE IT IF HE WENT INSIDE YOU AS ASH...
...AND RIPPED YOUR GUTS OPEN TO PROVE THAT HE REALLY EXISTS?
WHETHER YOU WANT TO BELIEVE THAT OR NOT...
...IS UP TO YOU.
NNNGH!
DON'T YOU DARE KILL HIM!
WE'LL SEE ABOUT THAT.
GIII (CREAK)

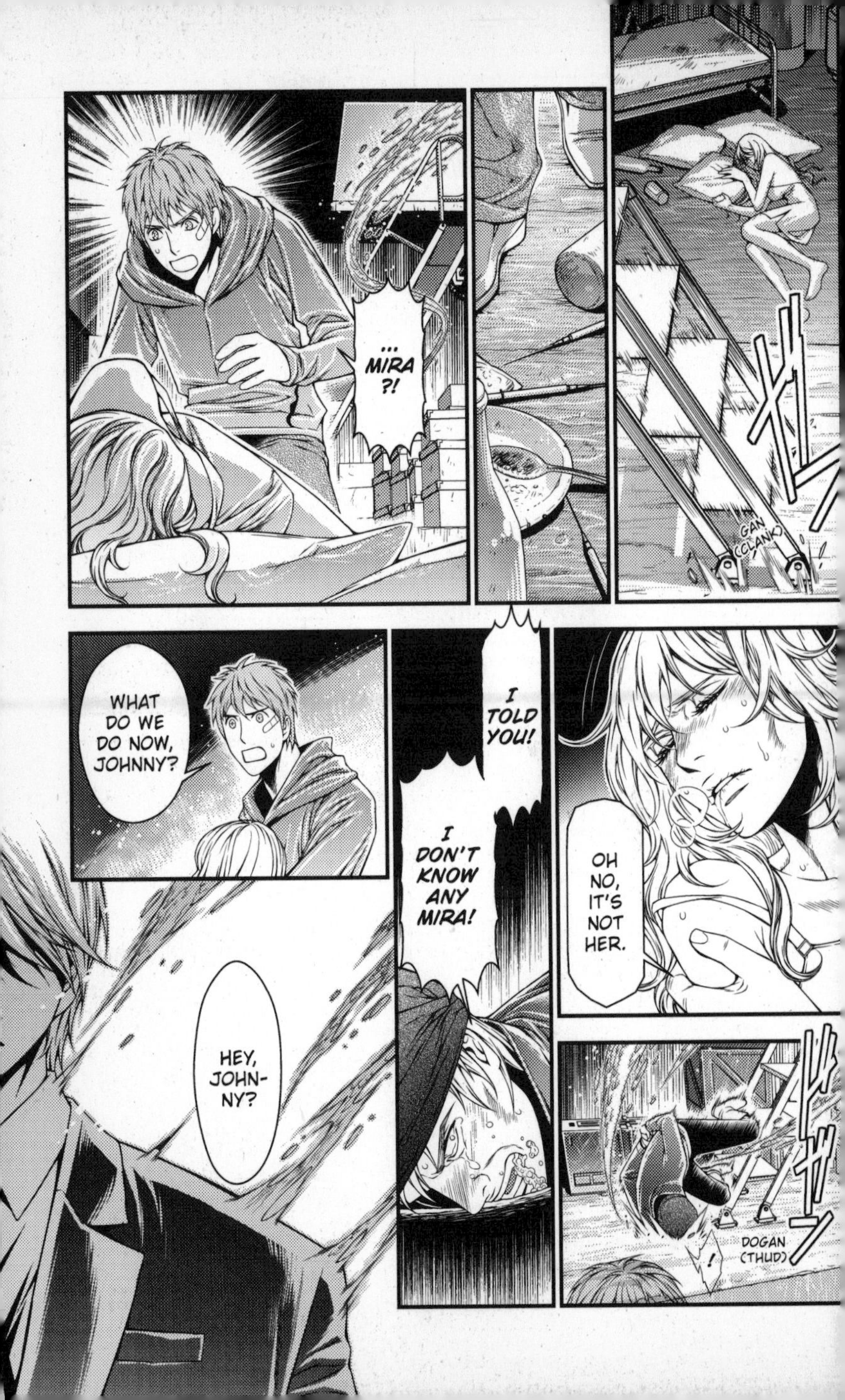
GAN (CLANK)
...MIRA?!
OH NO, IT'S NOT HER.
DOGAN (THUD)
!
I TOLD YOU!
I DON'T KNOW ANY MIRA!
WHAT DO WE DO NOW, JOHNNY?
HEY, JOHN-NY?

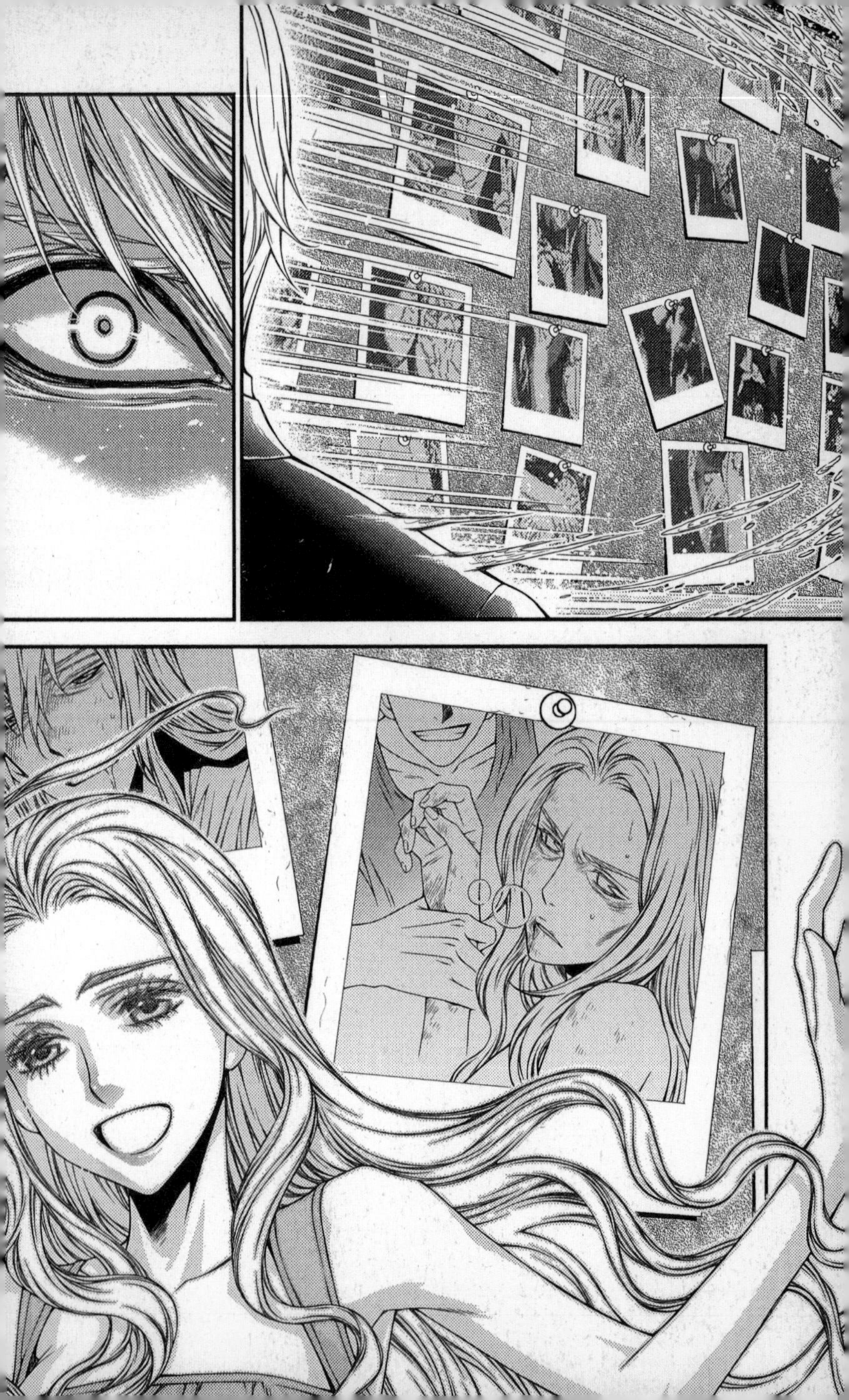

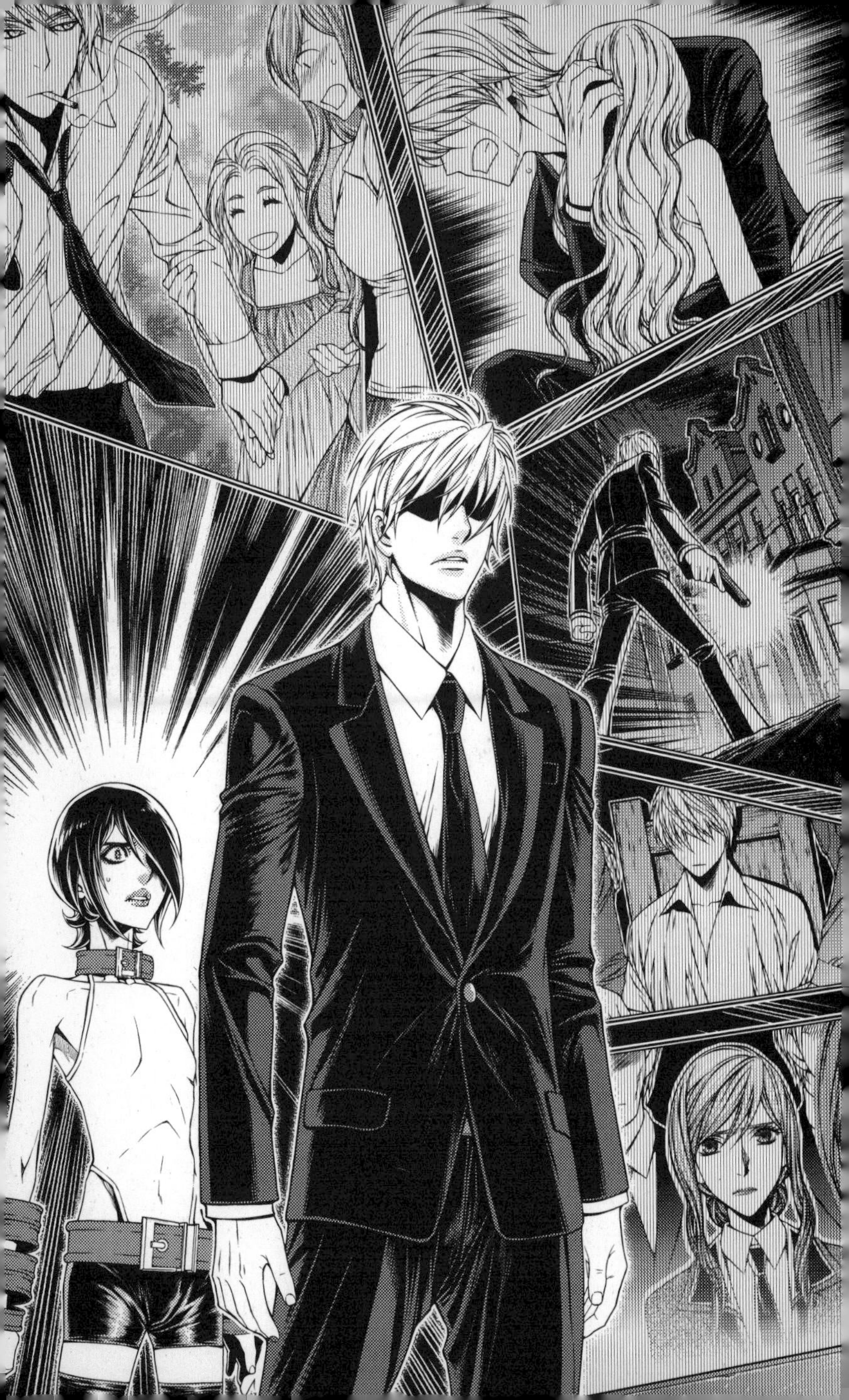

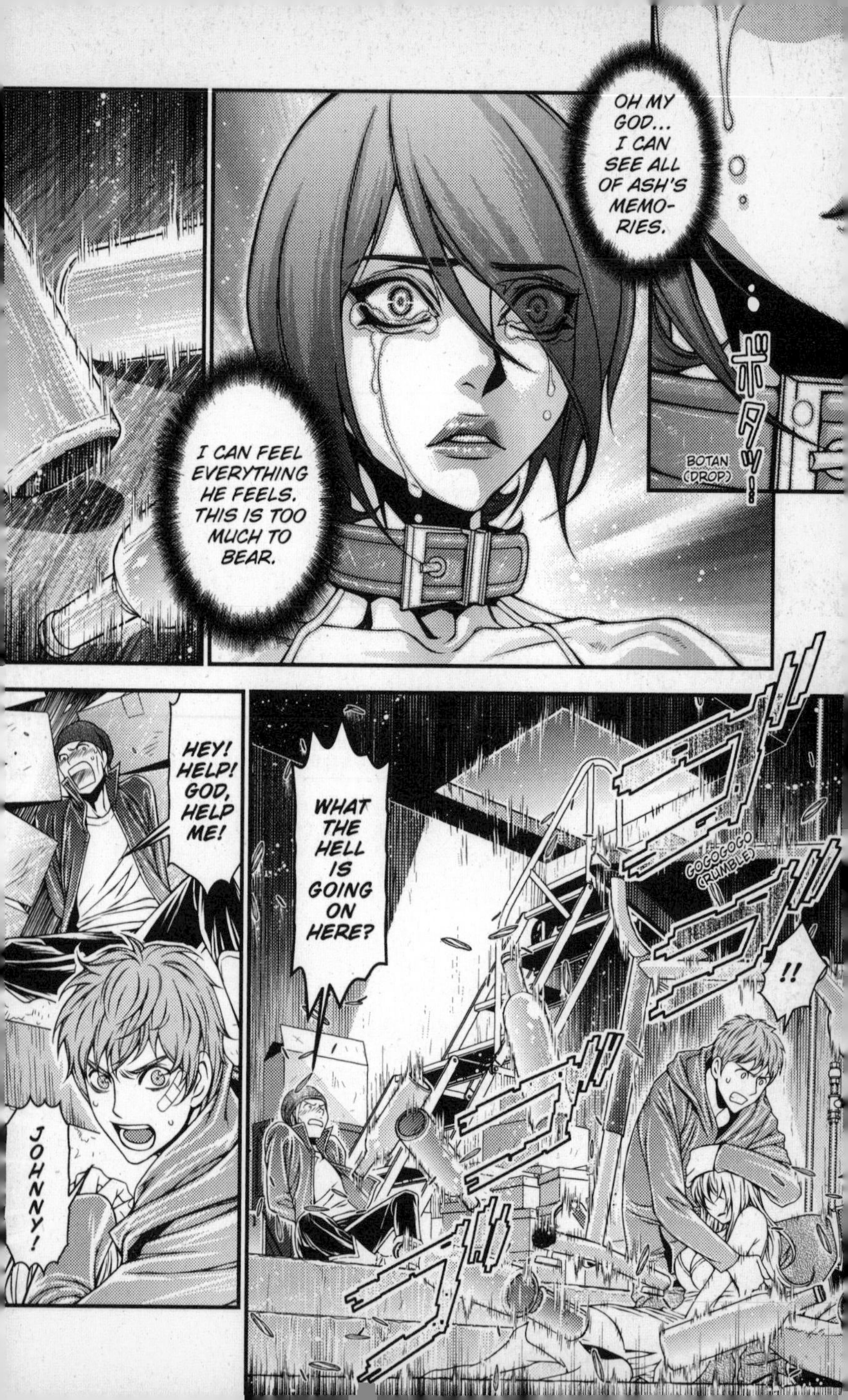
OH MY GOD... I CAN SEE ALL OF ASH'S MEMO-RIES.
BOTAN (DROP)
I CAN FEEL EVERYTHING HE FEELS. THIS IS TOO MUCH TO BEAR.
WHAT THE HELL IS GOING ON HERE?
GOGOGOGO (RUMBLE)
!!
HEY! HELP! GOD, HELP ME!
JOHNNY!

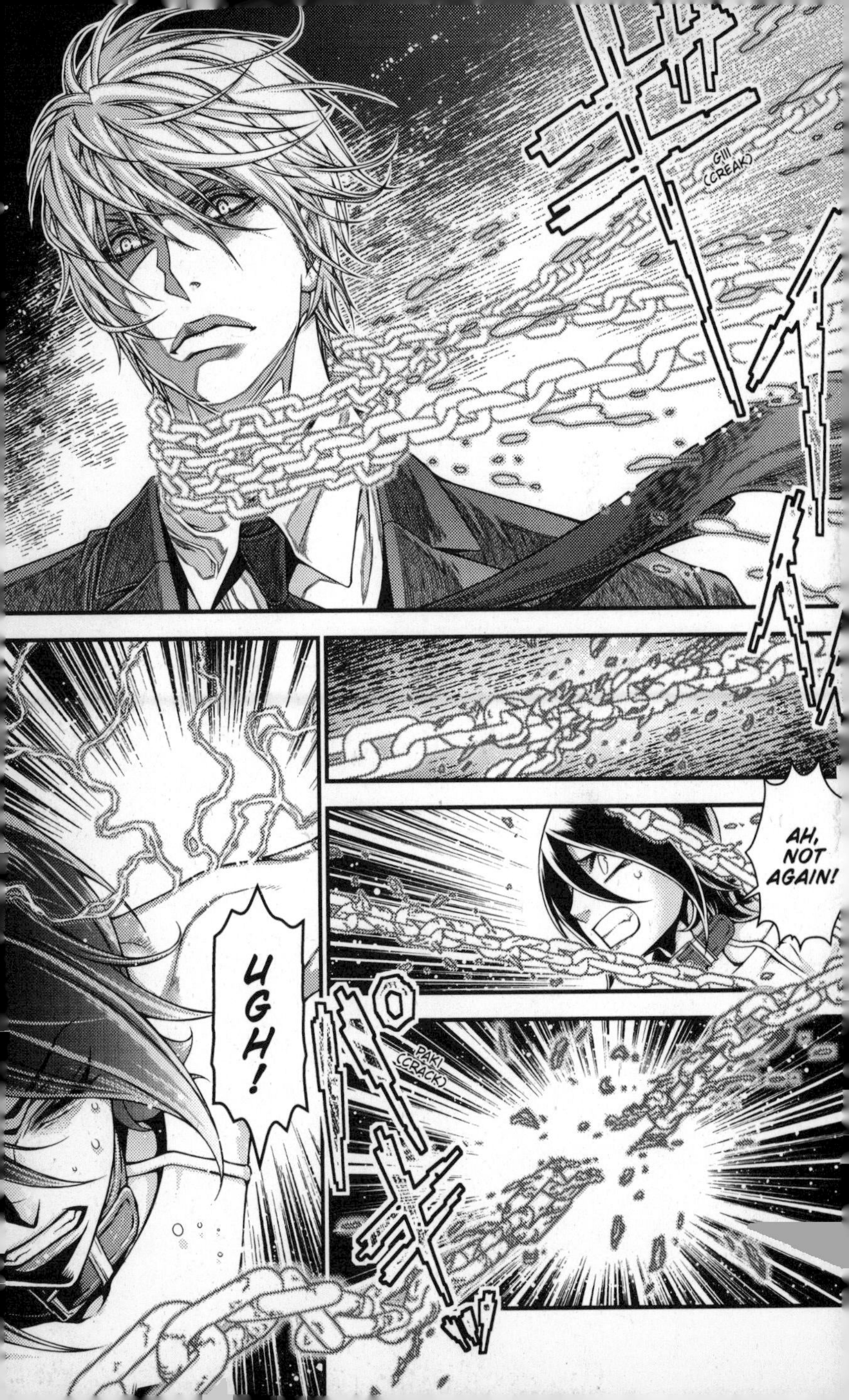
GIII
(CREAK)
AH, NOT AGAIN!
PAKI
(CRACK)
UGH!

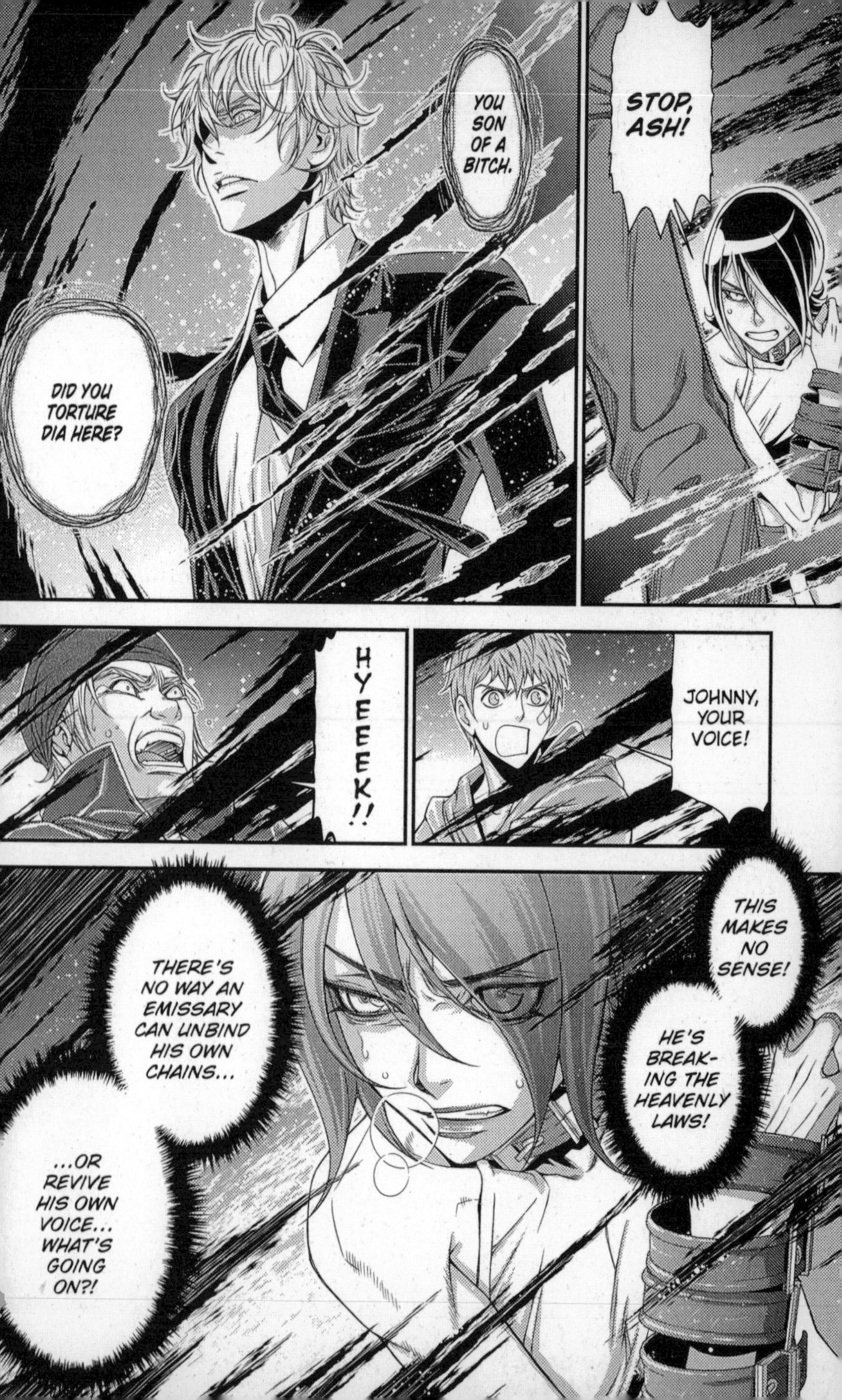
STOP, ASH!
YOU SON OF A BITCH.
DID YOU TORTURE DIA HERE?
JOHNNY, YOUR VOICE!
HYEEEK!!
THIS MAKES NO SENSE!
HE'S BREAK-ING THE HEAVENLY LAWS!
THERE'S NO WAY AN EMISSARY CAN UNBIND HIS OWN CHAINS...
...OR REVIVE HIS OWN VOICE... WHAT'S GOING ON?!

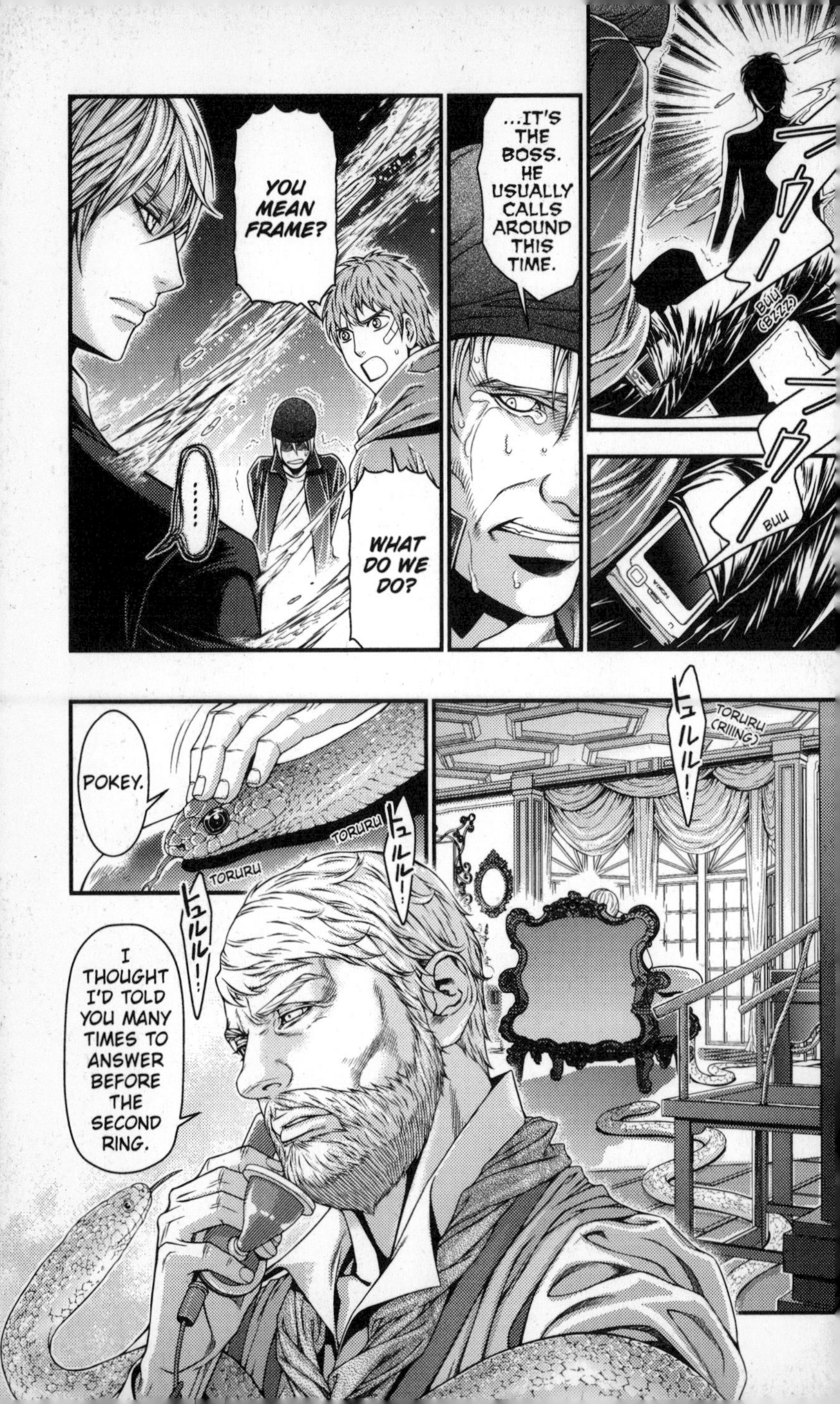
BUU (BZZZ)
BUU
...IT'S THE BOSS. HE USUALLY CALLS AROUND THIS TIME.
YOU MEAN FRAME?
WHAT DO WE DO?
......
TORURU (RIIING)
ヒュルルル!
POKEY.
TORURU
TORURU
ヒュルルル!
ヒュルルル!
I THOUGHT I'D TOLD YOU MANY TIMES TO ANSWER BEFORE THE SECOND RING.

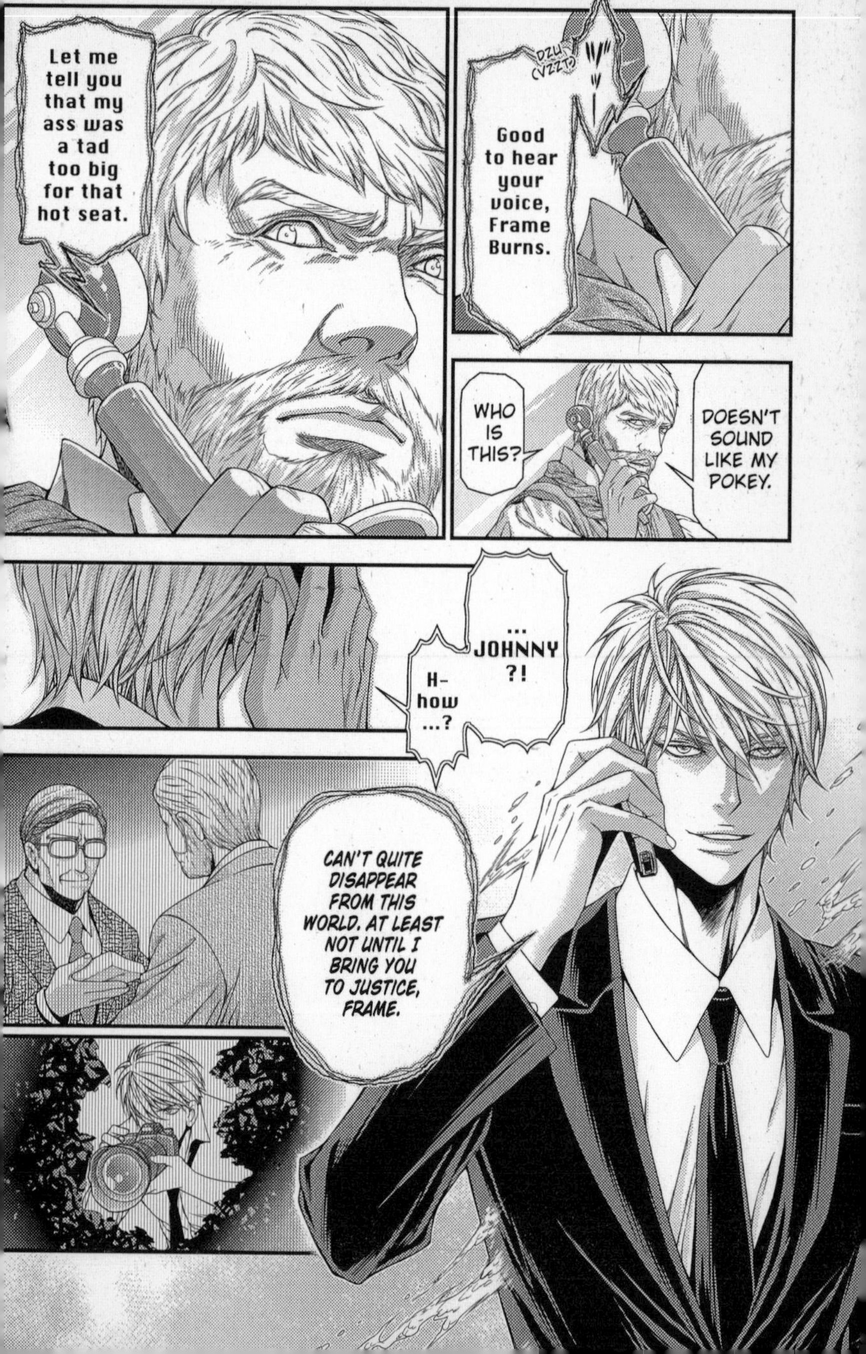
DZU (VZZT)
Good to hear your voice, Frame Burns.
DOESN'T SOUND LIKE MY POKEY.
WHO IS THIS?
Let me tell you that my ass was a tad too big for that hot seat.
... JOHNNY ?!
H- how ...?
CAN'T QUITE DISAPPEAR FROM THIS WORLD. AT LEAST NOT UNTIL I BRING YOU TO JUSTICE, FRAME.

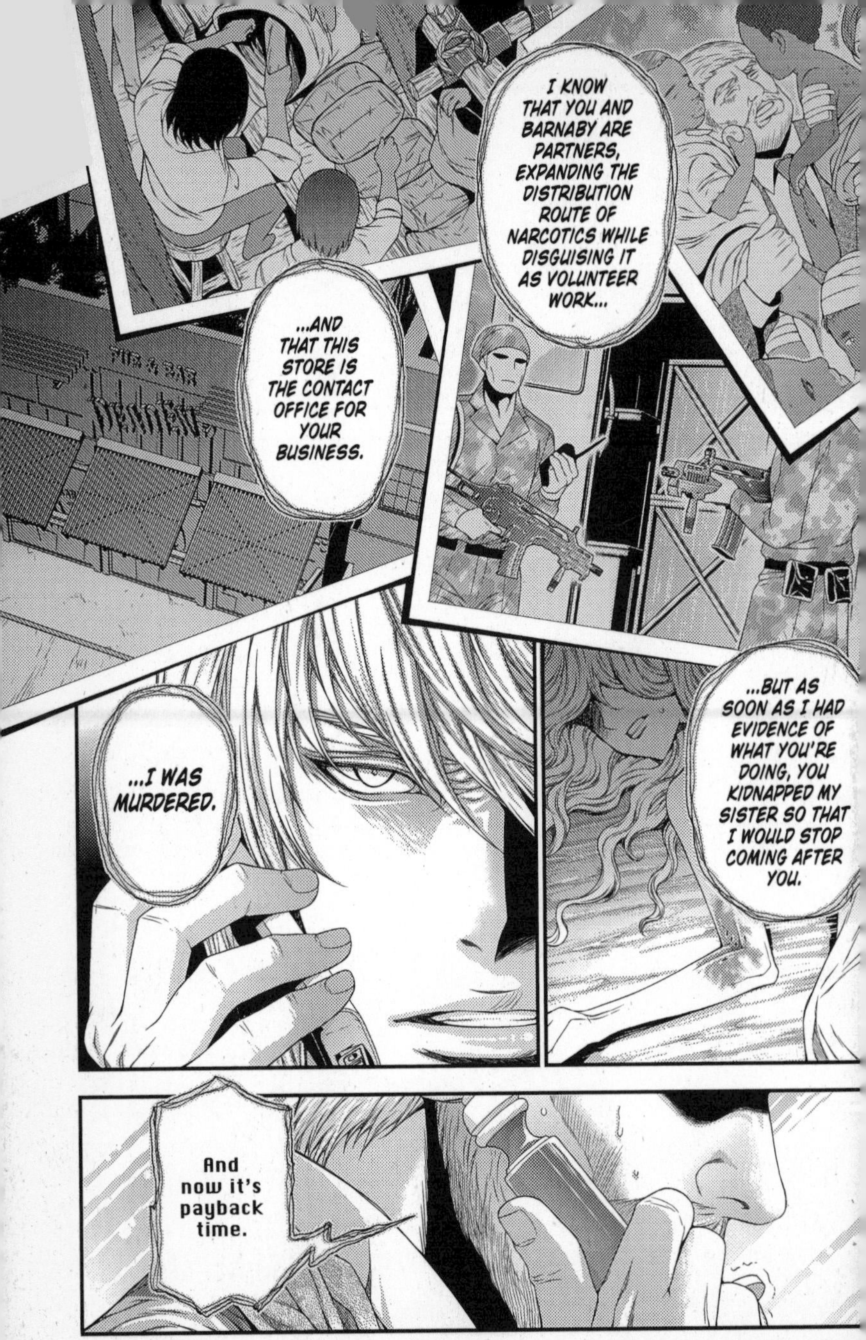
I KNOW THAT YOU AND BARNABY ARE PARTNERS, EXPANDING THE DISTRIBUTION ROUTE OF NARCOTICS WHILE DISGUISING IT AS VOLUNTEER WORK...
...AND THAT THIS STORE IS THE CONTACT OFFICE FOR YOUR BUSINESS.
...BUT AS SOON AS I HAD EVIDENCE OF WHAT YOU'RE DOING, YOU KIDNAPPED MY SISTER SO THAT I WOULD STOP COMING AFTER YOU.
...I WAS MURDERED.
And now it's payback time.

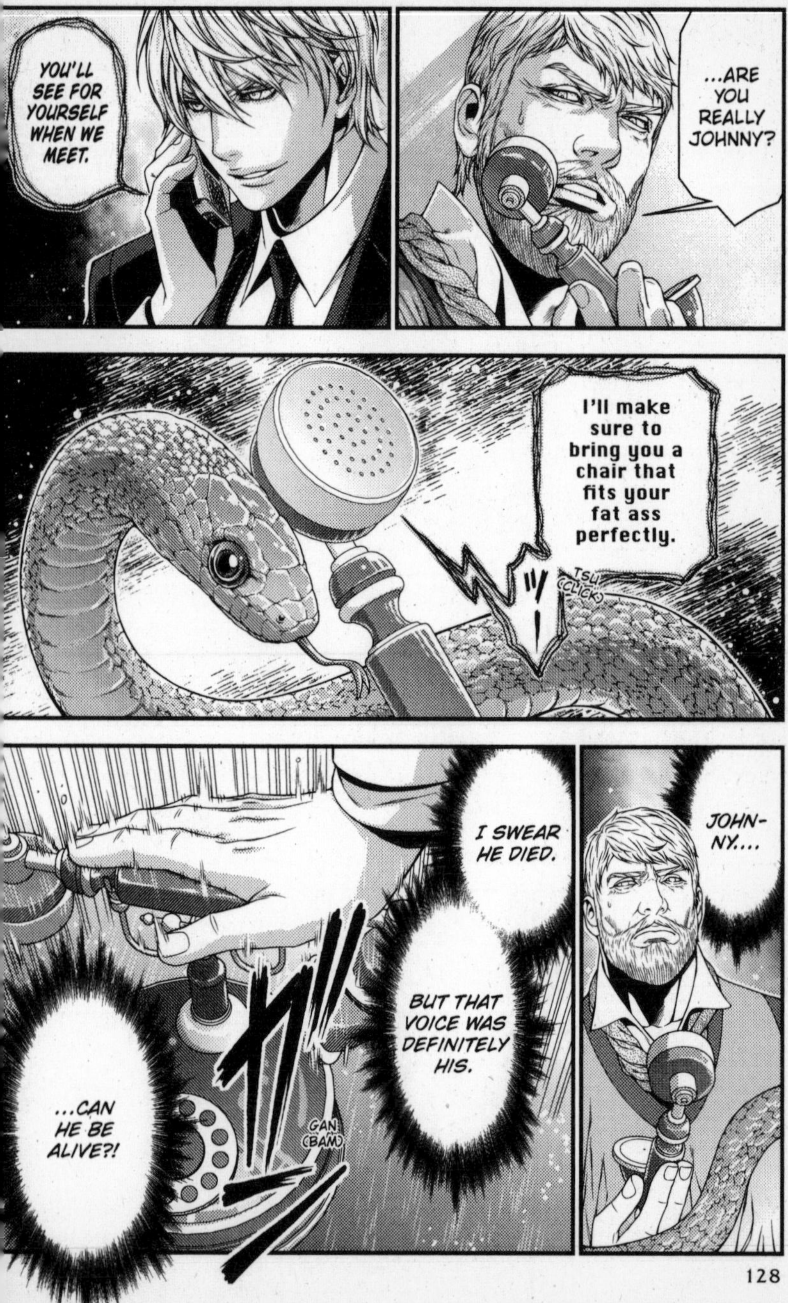
...ARE YOU REALLY JOHNNY?
YOU'LL SEE FOR YOURSELF WHEN WE MEET.
I'll make sure to bring you a chair that fits your fat ass perfectly.
TSU (CLICK)
JOHN-NY....
I SWEAR HE DIED.
BUT THAT VOICE WAS DEFINITELY HIS.
GAN (BAM)
...CAN HE BE ALIVE?!

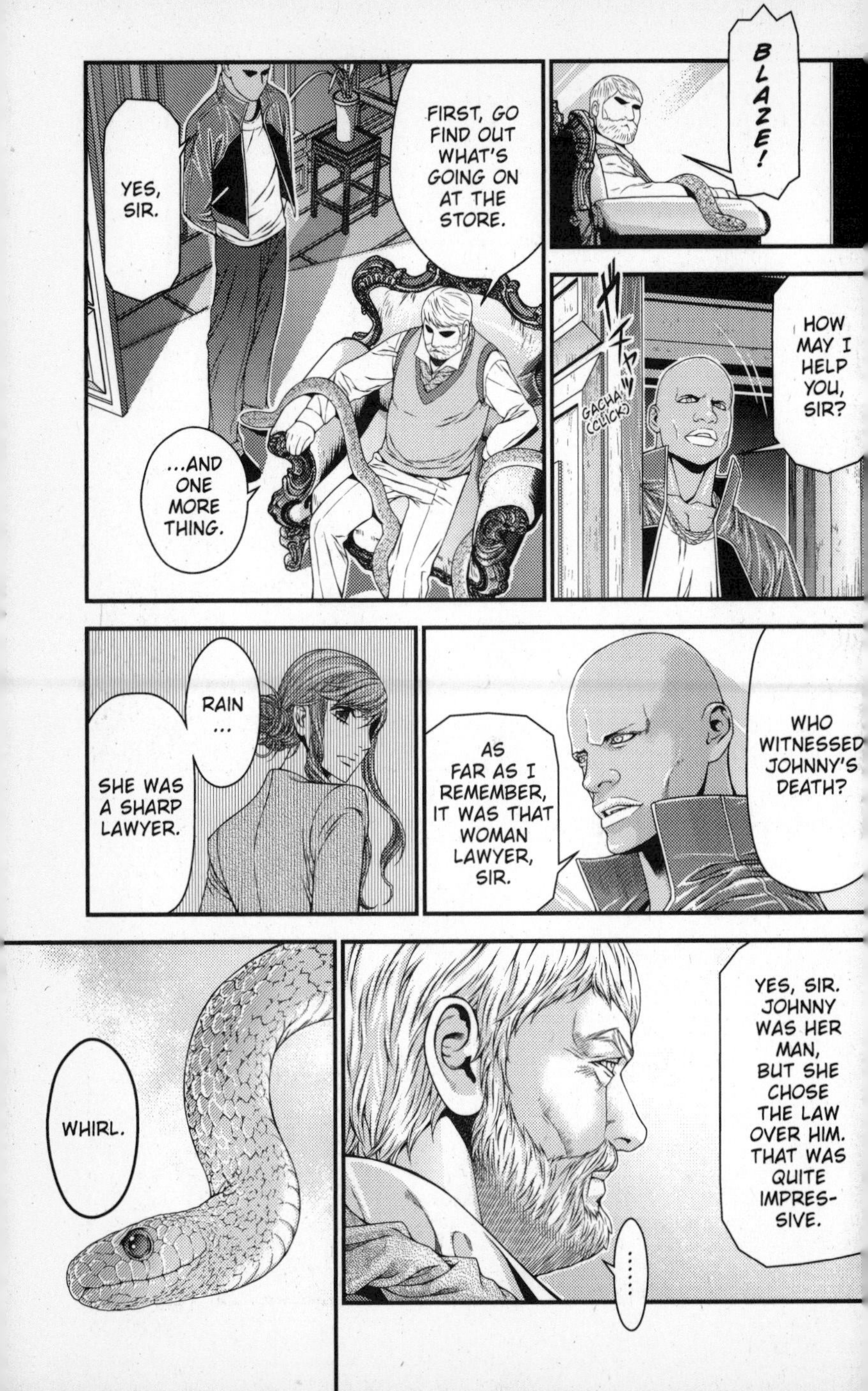
BLAZE!
GACHA (CLICK)
HOW MAY I HELP YOU, SIR?
FIRST, GO FIND OUT WHAT'S GOING ON AT THE STORE.
YES, SIR.
...AND ONE MORE THING.
WHO WITNESSED JOHNNY'S DEATH?
AS FAR AS I REMEMBER, IT WAS THAT WOMAN LAWYER, SIR.
RAIN...
SHE WAS A SHARP LAWYER.
YES, SIR. JOHNNY WAS HER MAN, BUT SHE CHOSE THE LAW OVER HIM. THAT WAS QUITE IMPRES-SIVE.
......
WHIRL.

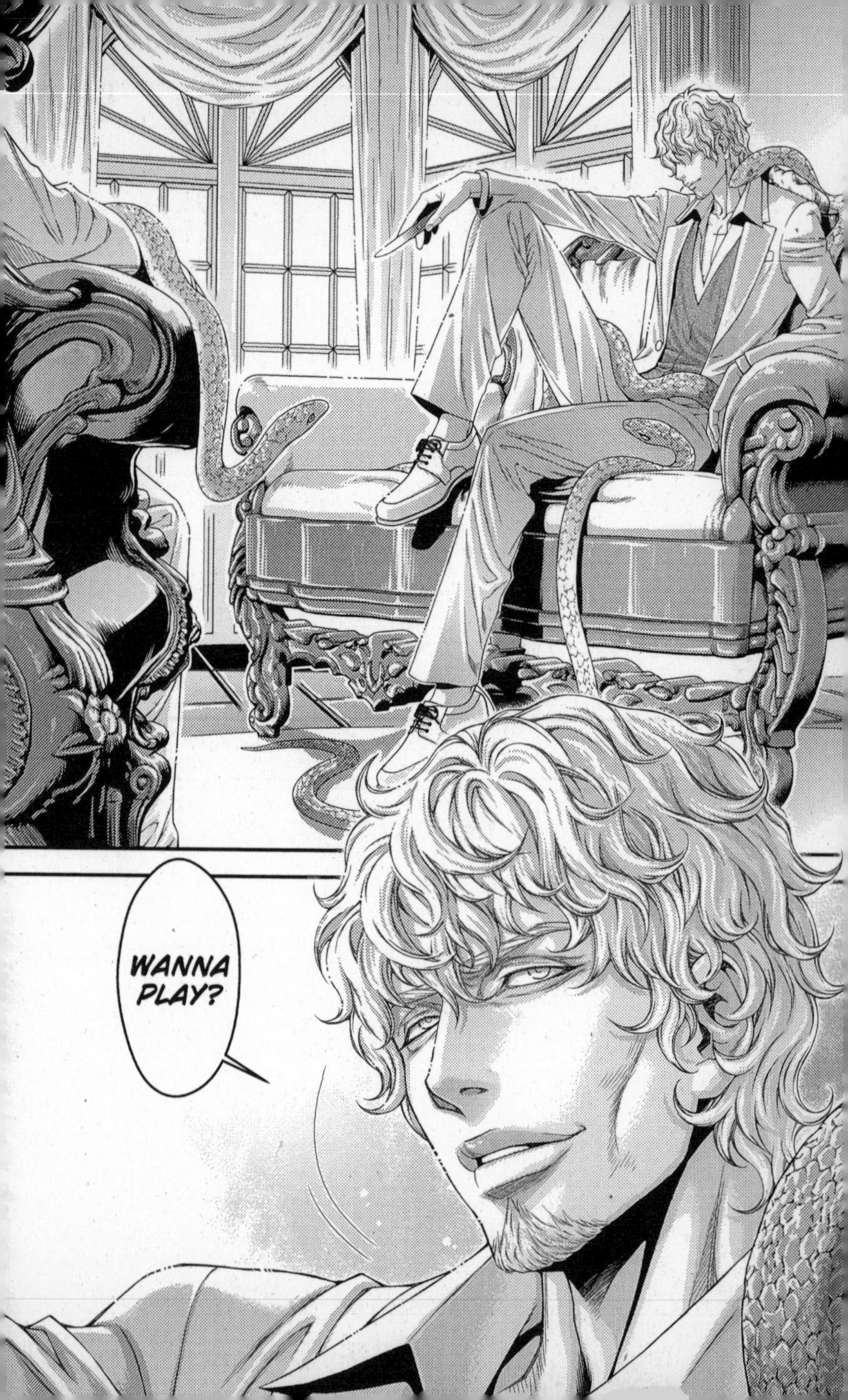
WANNA PLAY?

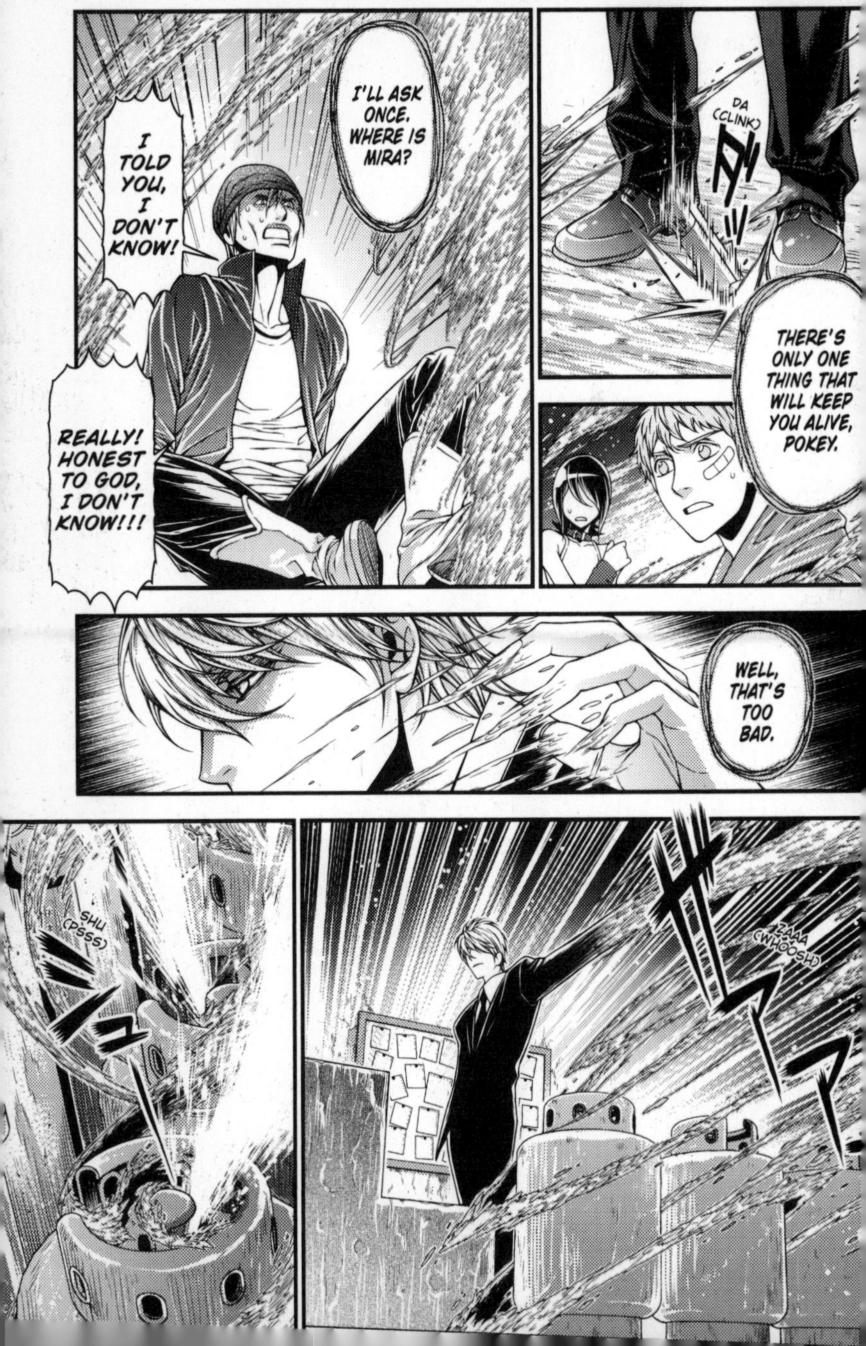
DA (CLINK)
THERE'S ONLY ONE THING THAT WILL KEEP YOU ALIVE, POKEY.
I'LL ASK ONCE. WHERE IS MIRA?
I TOLD YOU, I DON'T KNOW!
REALLY! HONEST TO GOD, I DON'T KNOW!!!
WELL, THAT'S TOO BAD.
ZAAA (WHOOSH)
SHU (PSSS)

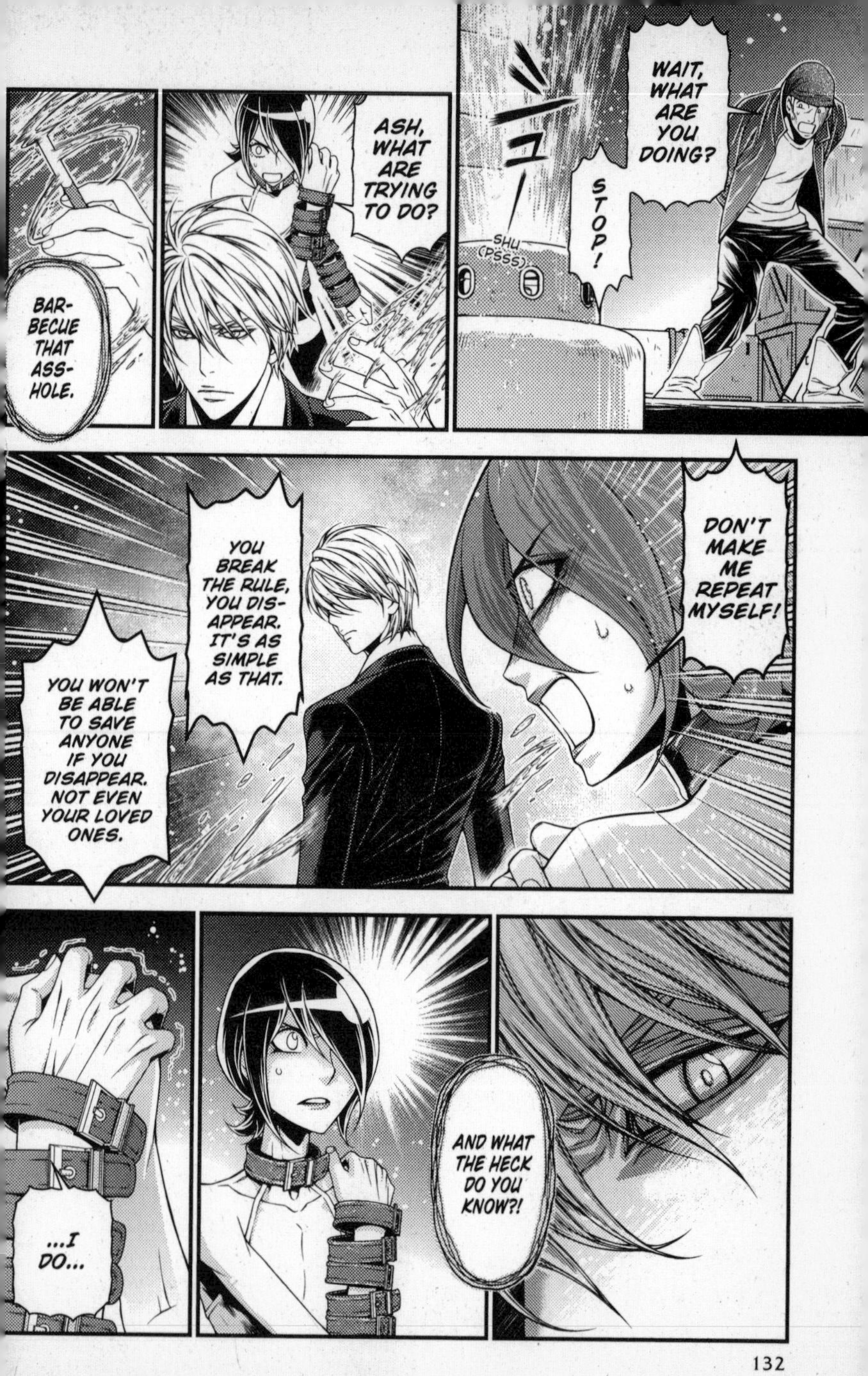
WAIT, WHAT ARE YOU DOING?
STOP!
SHU (PSSS)
ASH, WHAT ARE TRYING TO DO?
BAR-BECUE THAT ASS-HOLE.
DON'T MAKE ME REPEAT MYSELF!
YOU BREAK THE RULE, YOU DIS-APPEAR. IT'S AS SIMPLE AS THAT.
YOU WON'T BE ABLE TO SAVE ANYONE IF YOU DISAPPEAR. NOT EVEN YOUR LOVED ONES.
AND WHAT THE HECK DO YOU KNOW?!
...I DO...

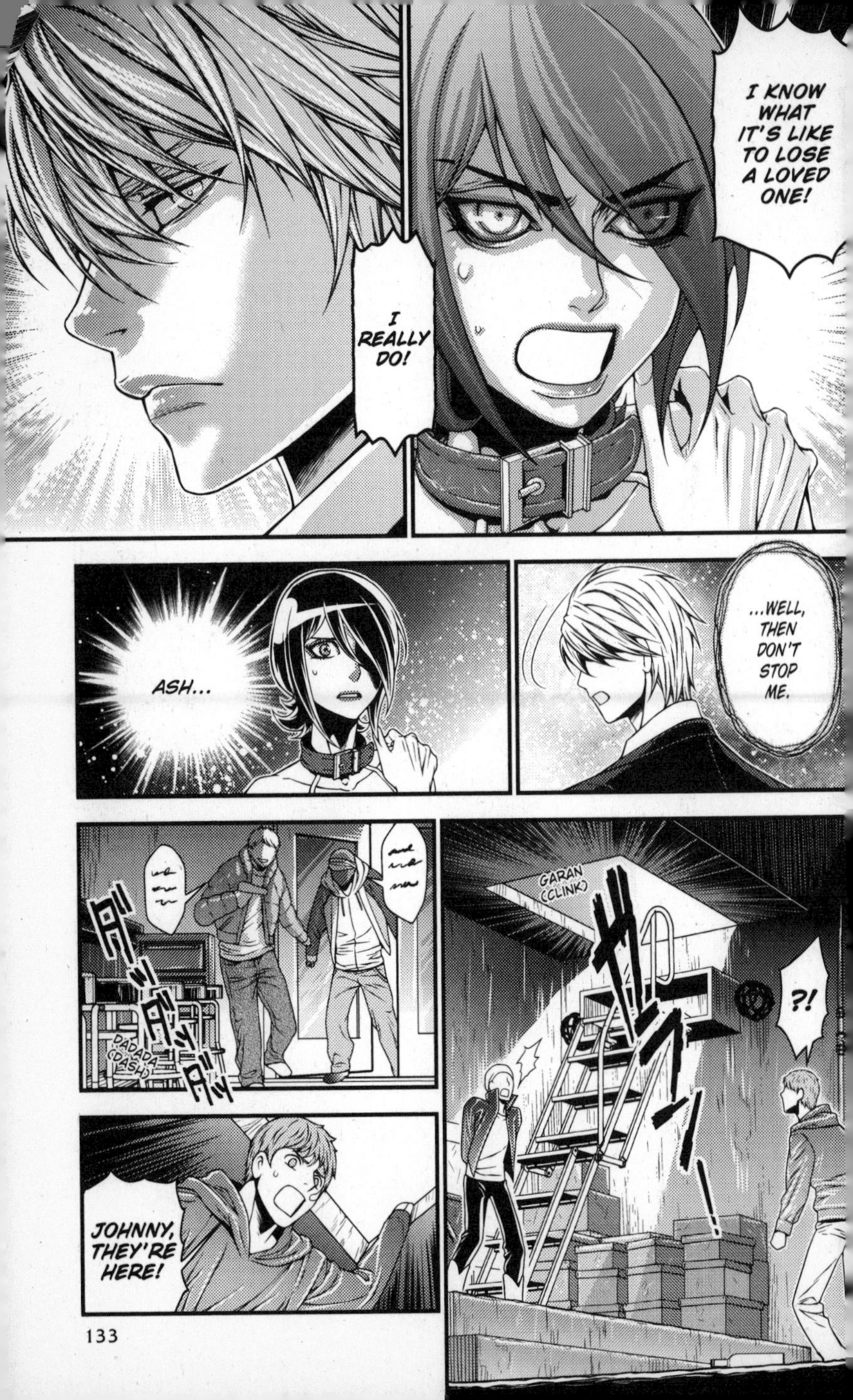
I KNOW WHAT IT'S LIKE TO LOSE A LOVED ONE!
I REALLY DO!
...WELL, THEN DON'T STOP ME.
ASH...
GARAN (CLINK)
?!
DADADA (DASH)
JOHNNY, THEY'RE HERE!

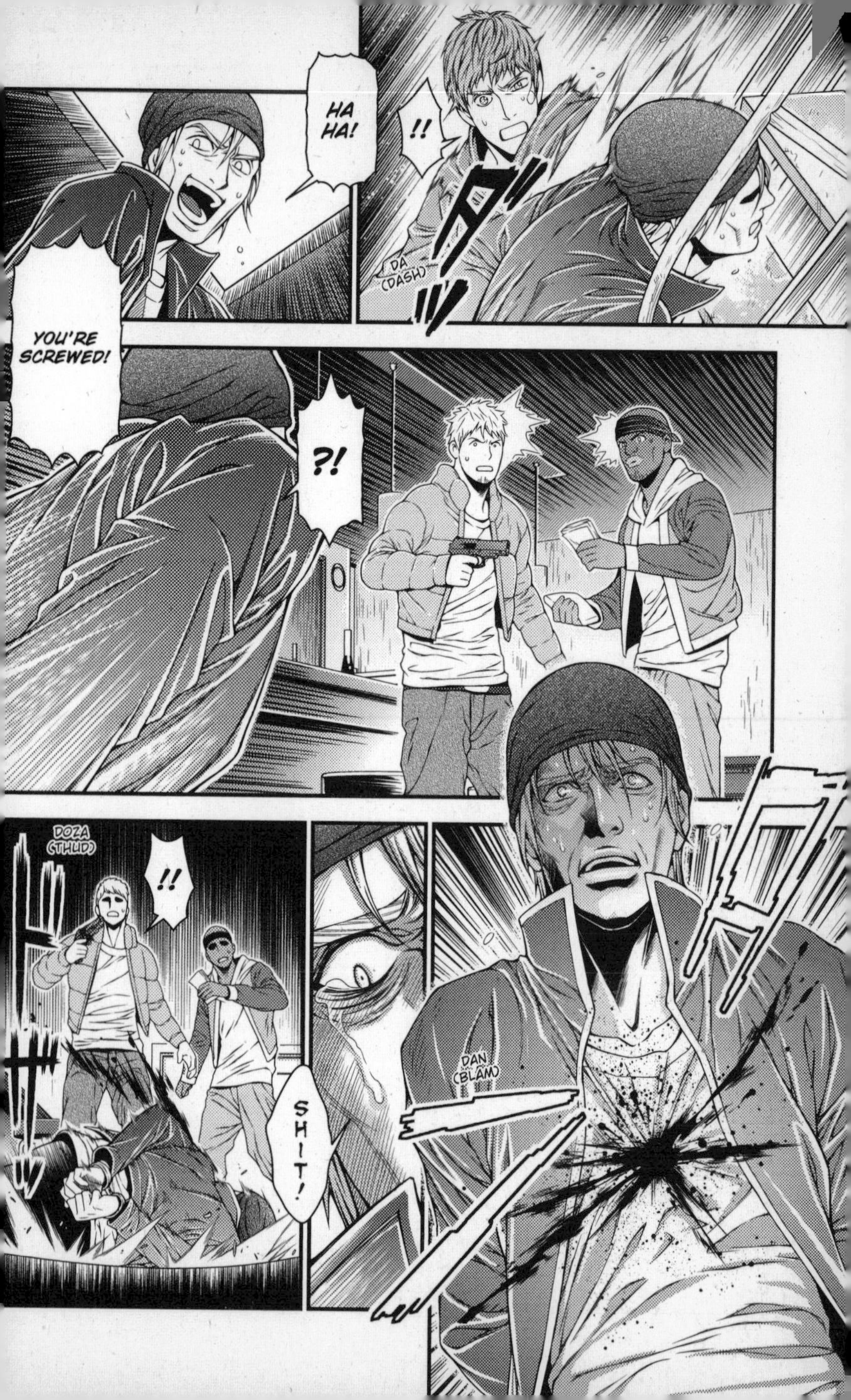
!!
DA (DASH)
HA HA!
YOU'RE SCREWED!
?!
DAN (BLAM)
SHIT!
DOZA (THUD)
!!

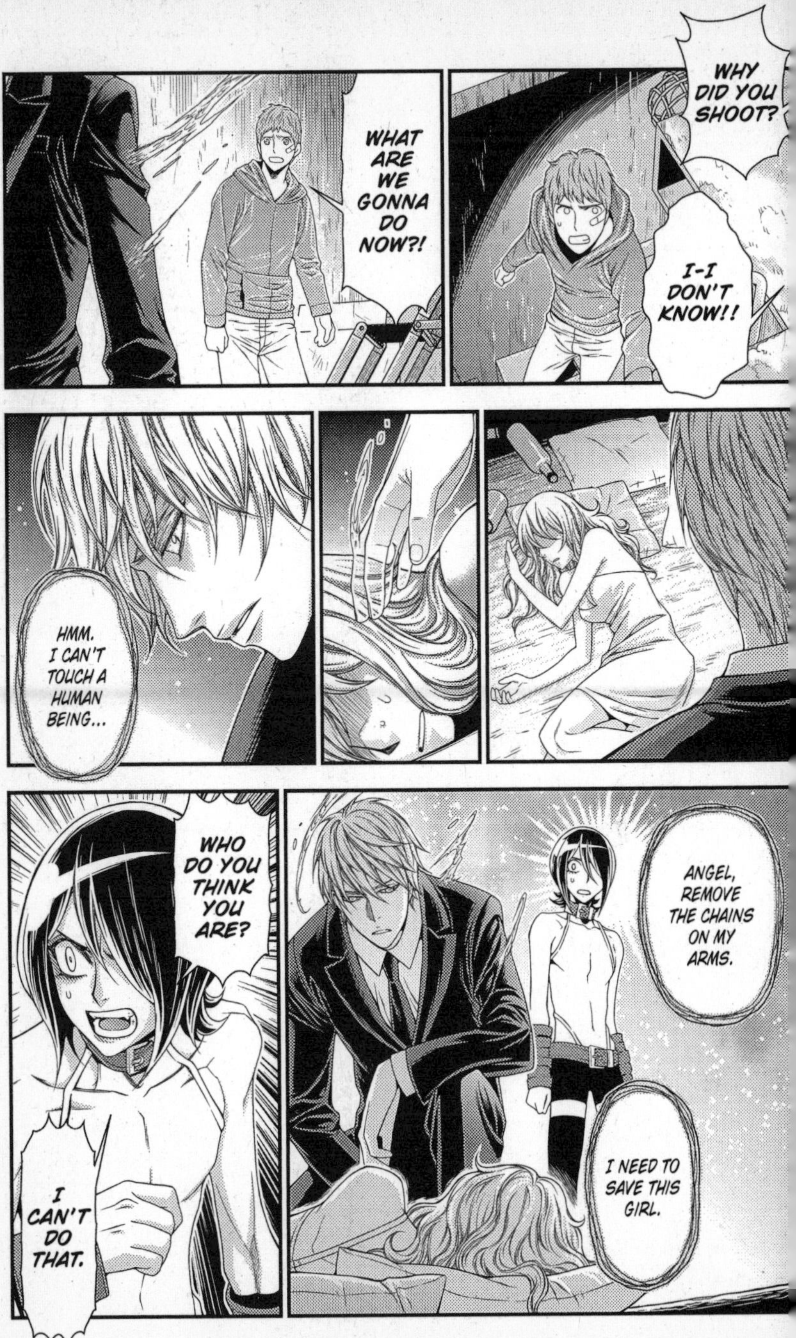
WHY DID YOU SHOOT?
I-I DON'T KNOW!!
WHAT ARE WE GONNA DO NOW?!
HMM. I CAN'T TOUCH A HUMAN BEING...
ANGEL, REMOVE THE CHAINS ON MY ARMS.
I NEED TO SAVE THIS GIRL.
WHO DO YOU THINK YOU ARE?
I CAN'T DO THAT.

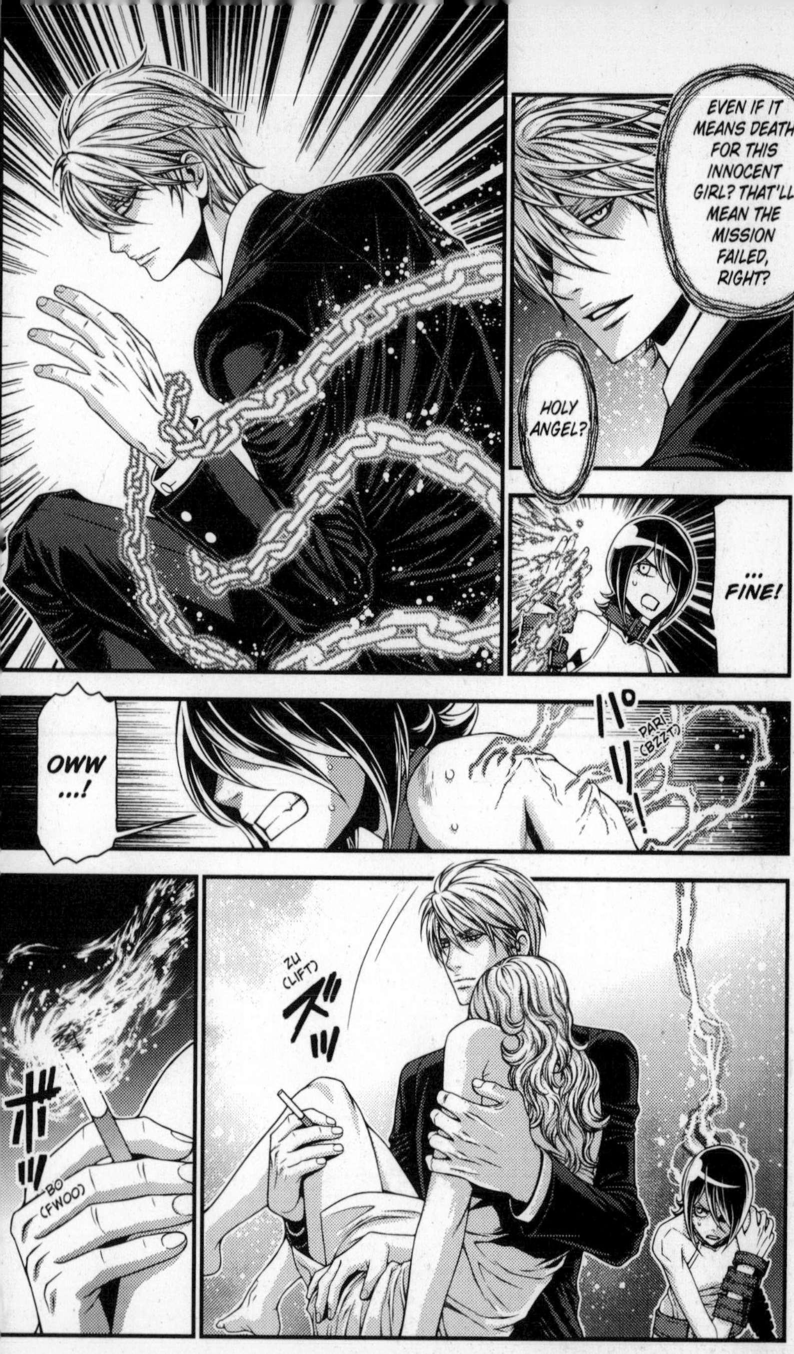
EVEN IF IT MEANS DEATH FOR THIS INNOCENT GIRL? THAT'LL MEAN THE MISSION FAILED, RIGHT?
HOLY ANGEL?
...FINE!
PARI (BZZT)
OWW ...!
ZU (LIFT)
BO (FWOO)

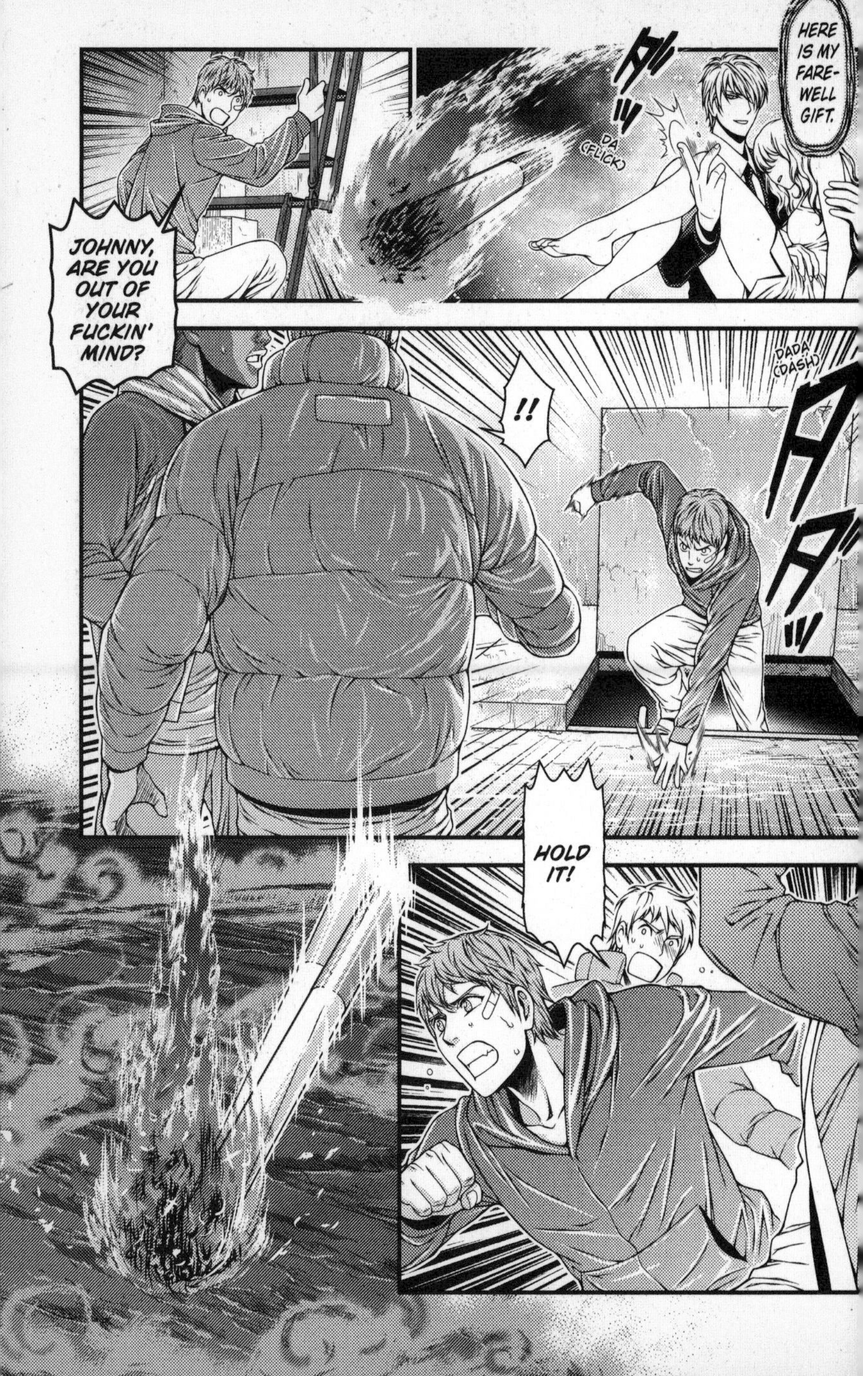
HERE IS MY FARE-WELL GIFT.
DA (FLICK)
JOHNNY, ARE YOU OUT OF YOUR FUCKIN' MIND?
DADA (DASH)
!!
HOLD IT!

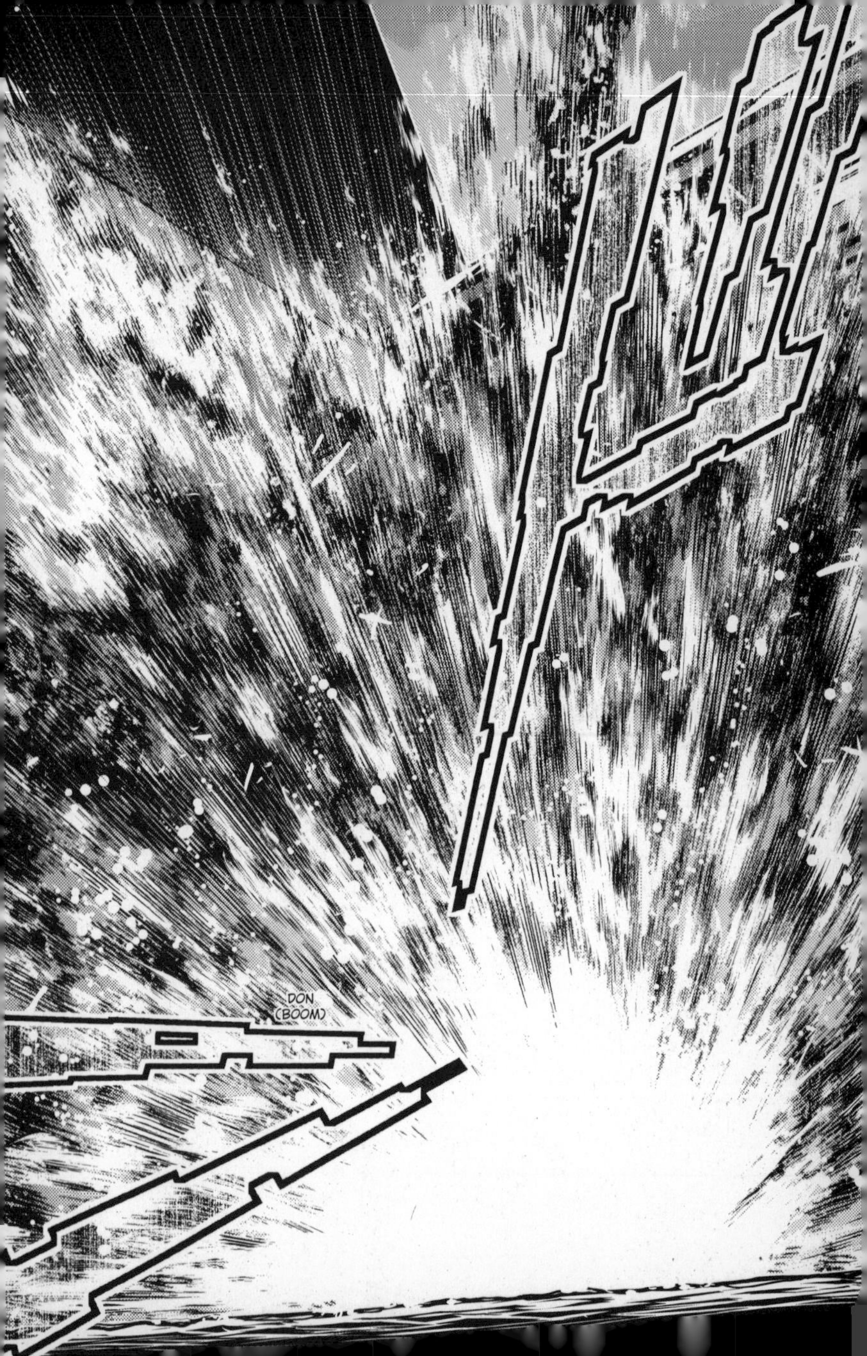
DON
(BOOM)

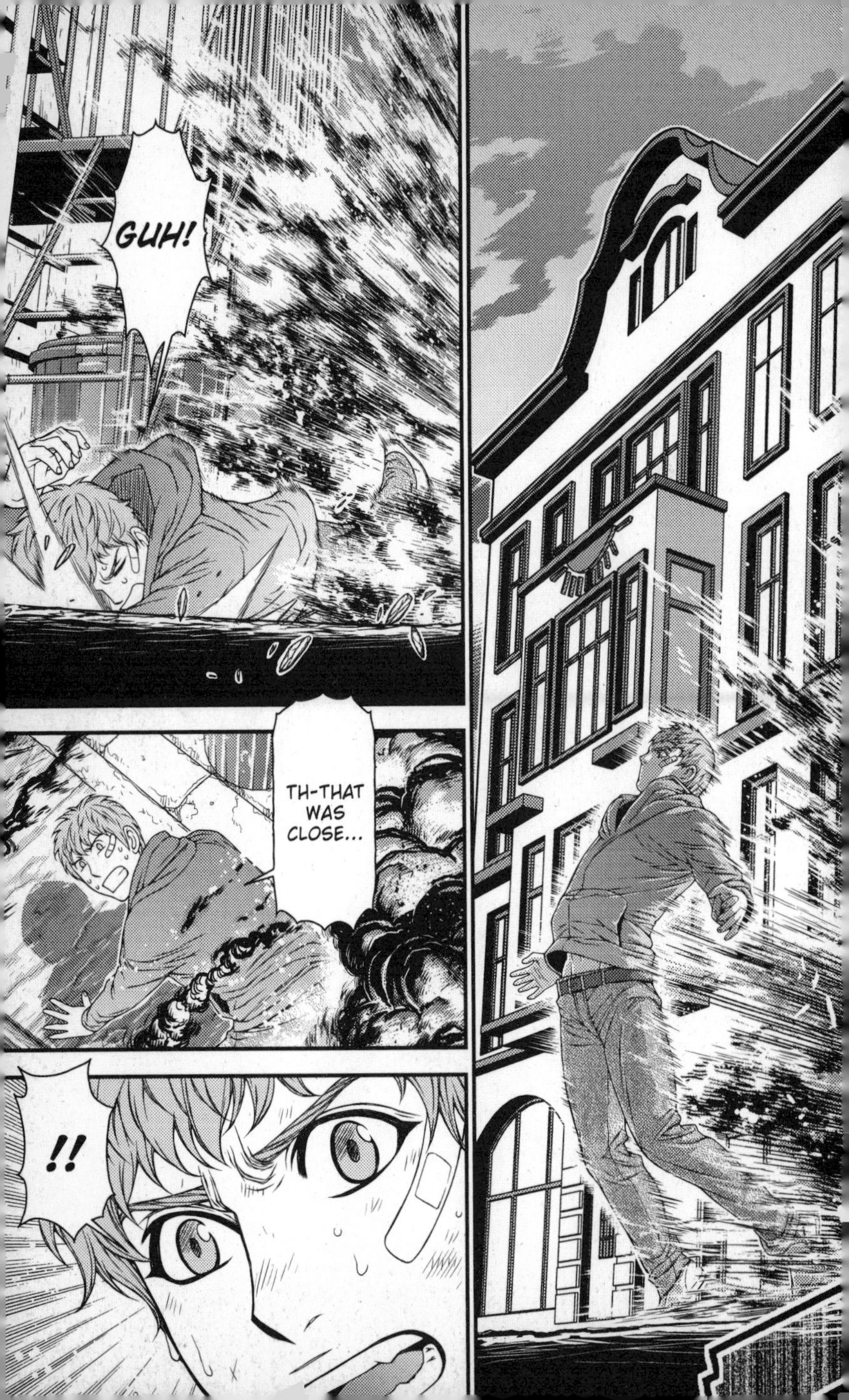
GUH!
TH-THAT WAS CLOSE...
!!

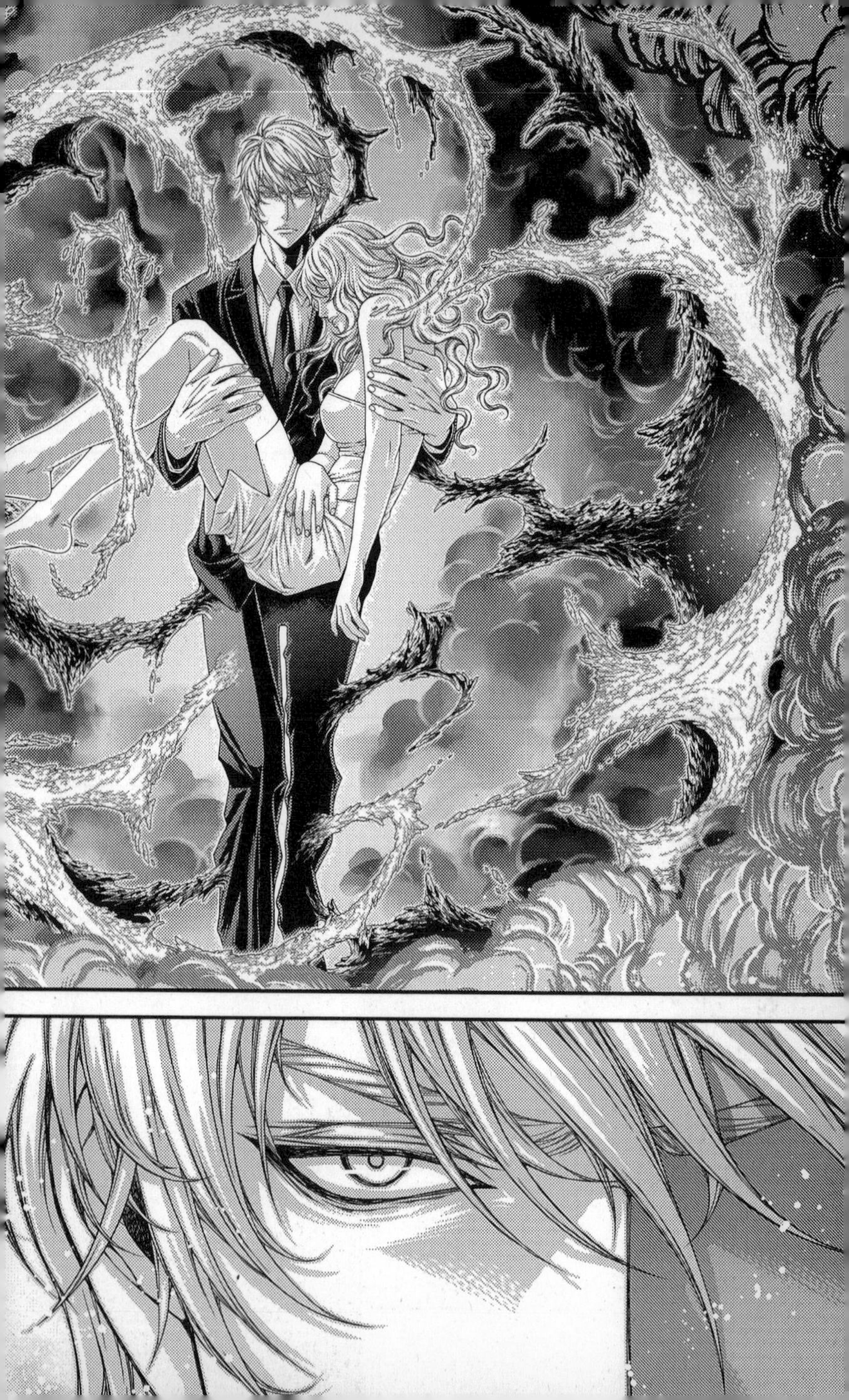

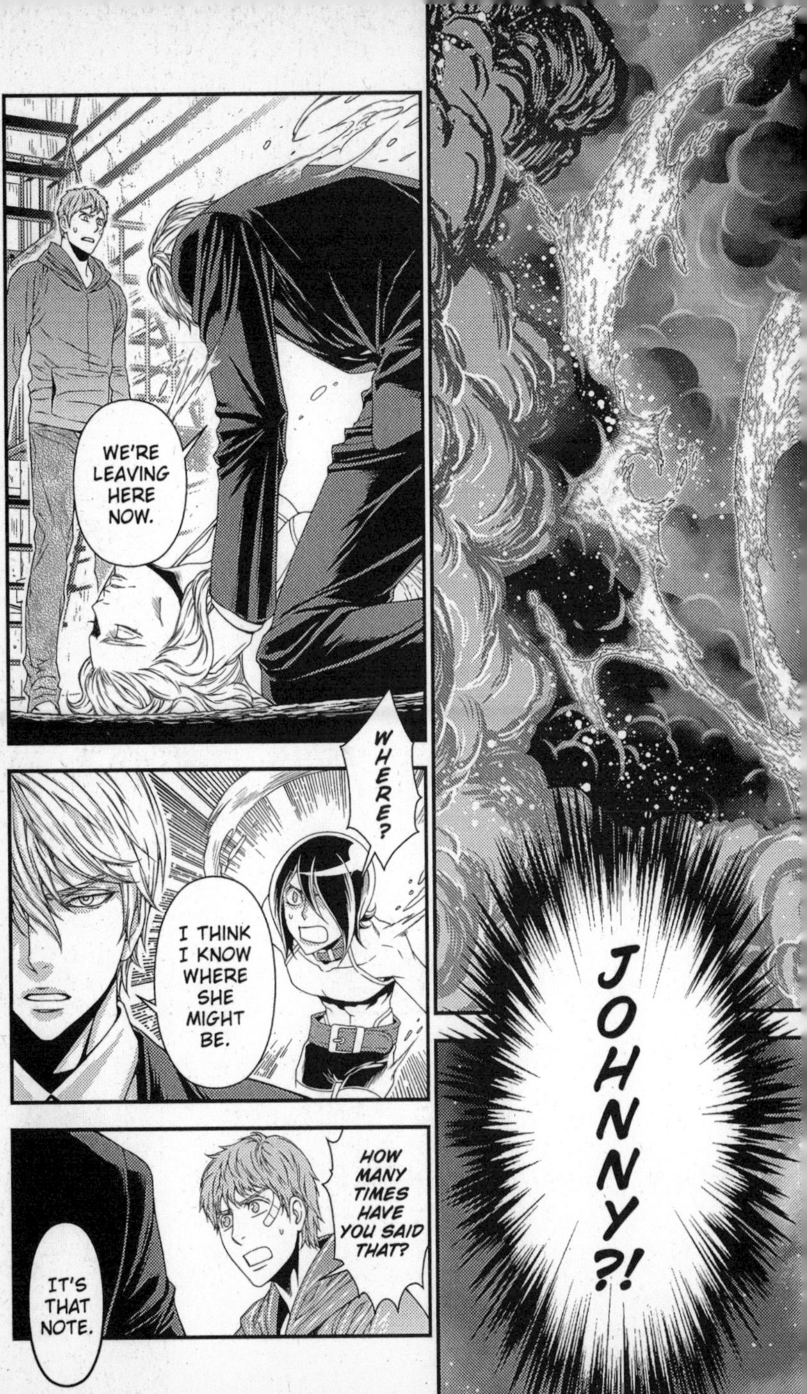
JOHNNY?!
WE'RE LEAVING HERE NOW.
WHERE?
I THINK I KNOW WHERE SHE MIGHT BE.
HOW MANY TIMES HAVE YOU SAID THAT?
IT'S THAT NOTE.

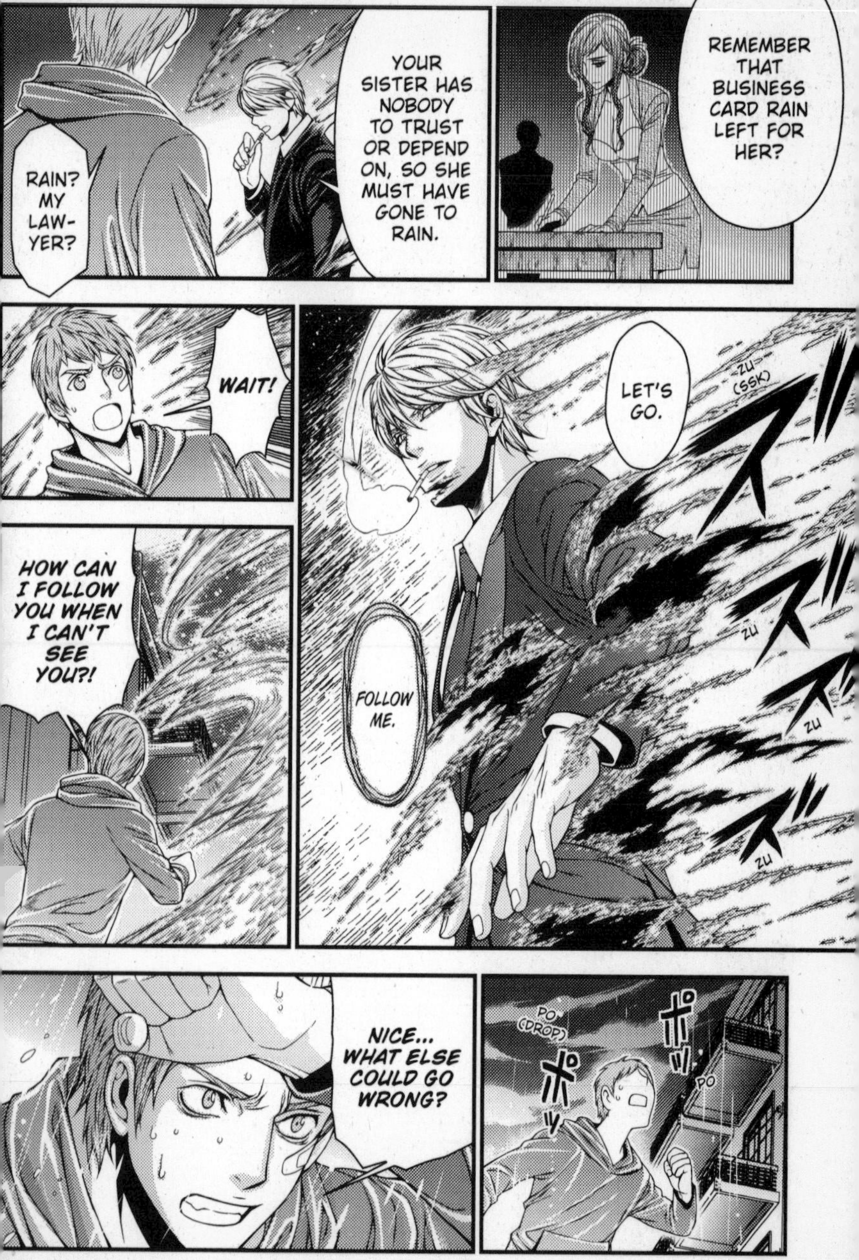
REMEMBER THAT BUSINESS CARD RAIN LEFT FOR HER?
YOUR SISTER HAS NOBODY TO TRUST OR DEPEND ON, SO SHE MUST HAVE GONE TO RAIN.
RAIN? MY LAWYER?
LET'S GO.
ZU (SSK)
FOLLOW ME.
ZU
ZU
ZU
WAIT!
HOW CAN I FOLLOW YOU WHEN I CAN'T SEE YOU?!
PO (DROP)
PO
NICE... WHAT ELSE COULD GO WRONG?

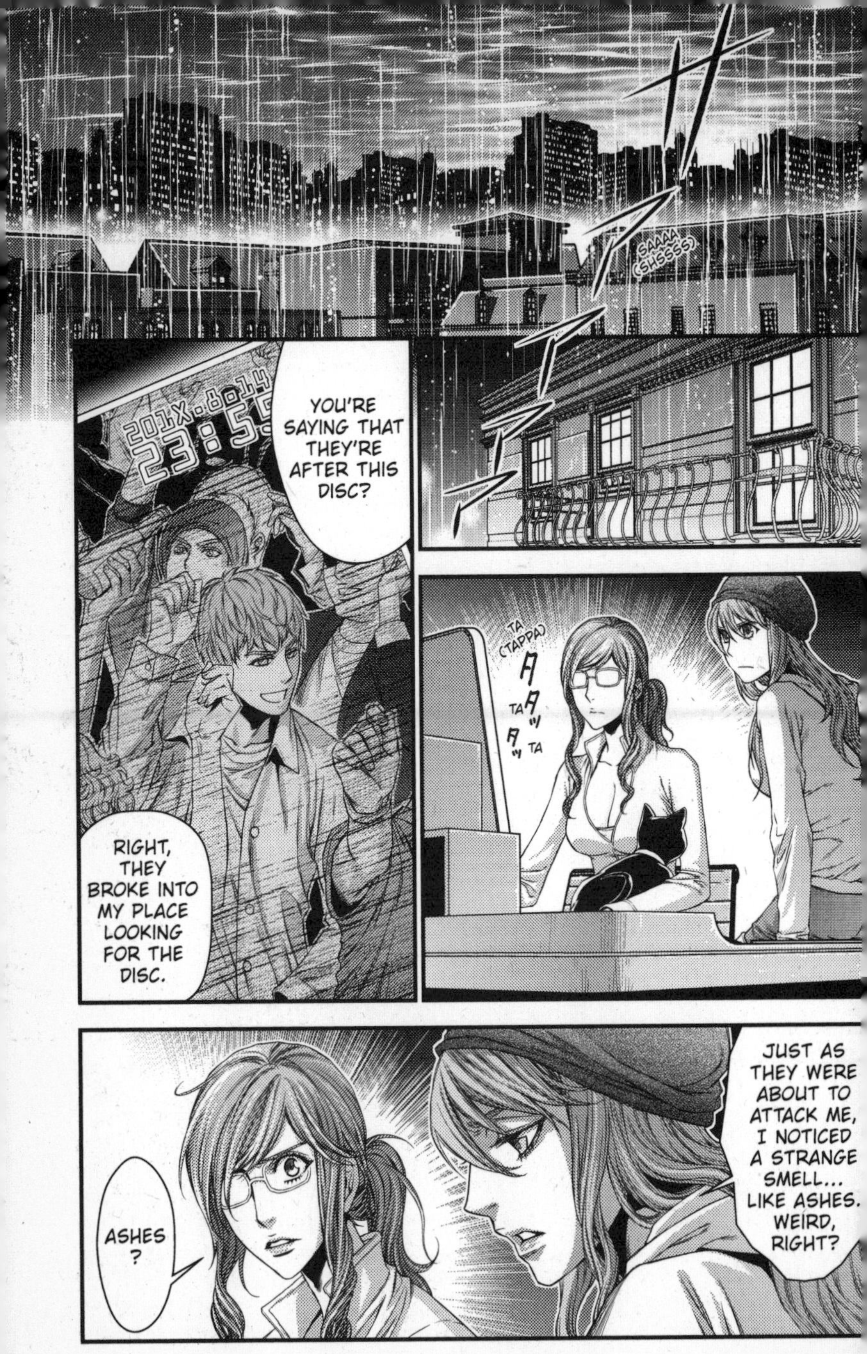
SAAAA (SHSSSS)
TA (TAPPA)
TA
TA
201X.8.14
23:55
YOU'RE SAYING THAT THEY'RE AFTER THIS DISC?
RIGHT, THEY BROKE INTO MY PLACE LOOKING FOR THE DISC.
JUST AS THEY WERE ABOUT TO ATTACK ME, I NOTICED A STRANGE SMELL... LIKE ASHES. WEIRD, RIGHT?
ASHES?

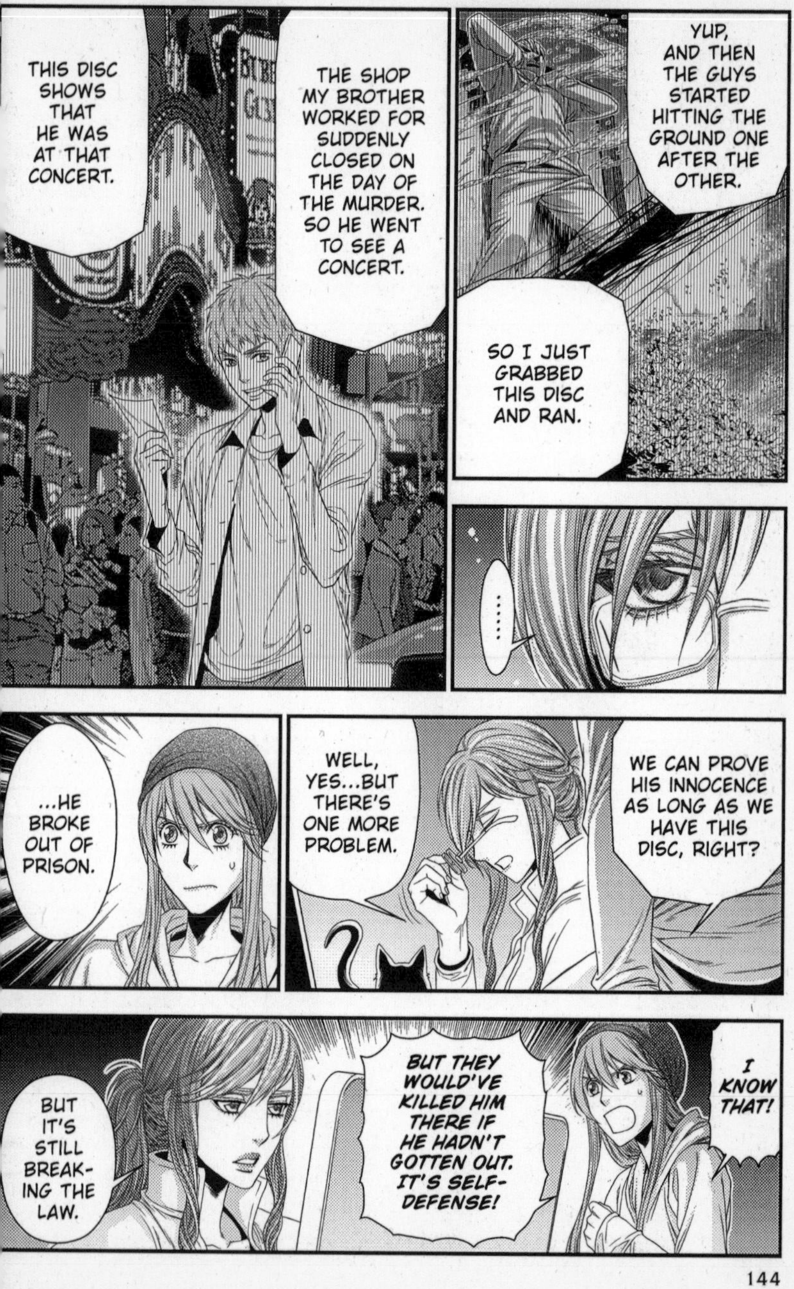
YUP, AND THEN THE GUYS STARTED HITTING THE GROUND ONE AFTER THE OTHER.
SO I JUST GRABBED THIS DISC AND RAN.
......
THE SHOP MY BROTHER WORKED FOR SUDDENLY CLOSED ON THE DAY OF THE MURDER. SO HE WENT TO SEE A CONCERT.
THIS DISC SHOWS THAT HE WAS AT THAT CONCERT.
WE CAN PROVE HIS INNOCENCE AS LONG AS WE HAVE THIS DISC, RIGHT?
WELL, YES...BUT THERE'S ONE MORE PROBLEM.
...HE BROKE OUT OF PRISON.
I KNOW THAT!
BUT THEY WOULD'VE KILLED HIM THERE IF HE HADN'T GOTTEN OUT. IT'S SELF-DEFENSE!
BUT IT'S STILL BREAKING THE LAW.

THERE YOU GO AGAIN!

LAW'S THE ONLY THING YOU CARE ABOUT, JUST LIKE WHAT YOU DID TO JOHNNY, RIGHT?!

!!

!

?!

コン

KON (KNOCK)

KON

JOSH?!

DADA (DASH)

ダッ

ダッ

WAIT, MIRA!!

...?

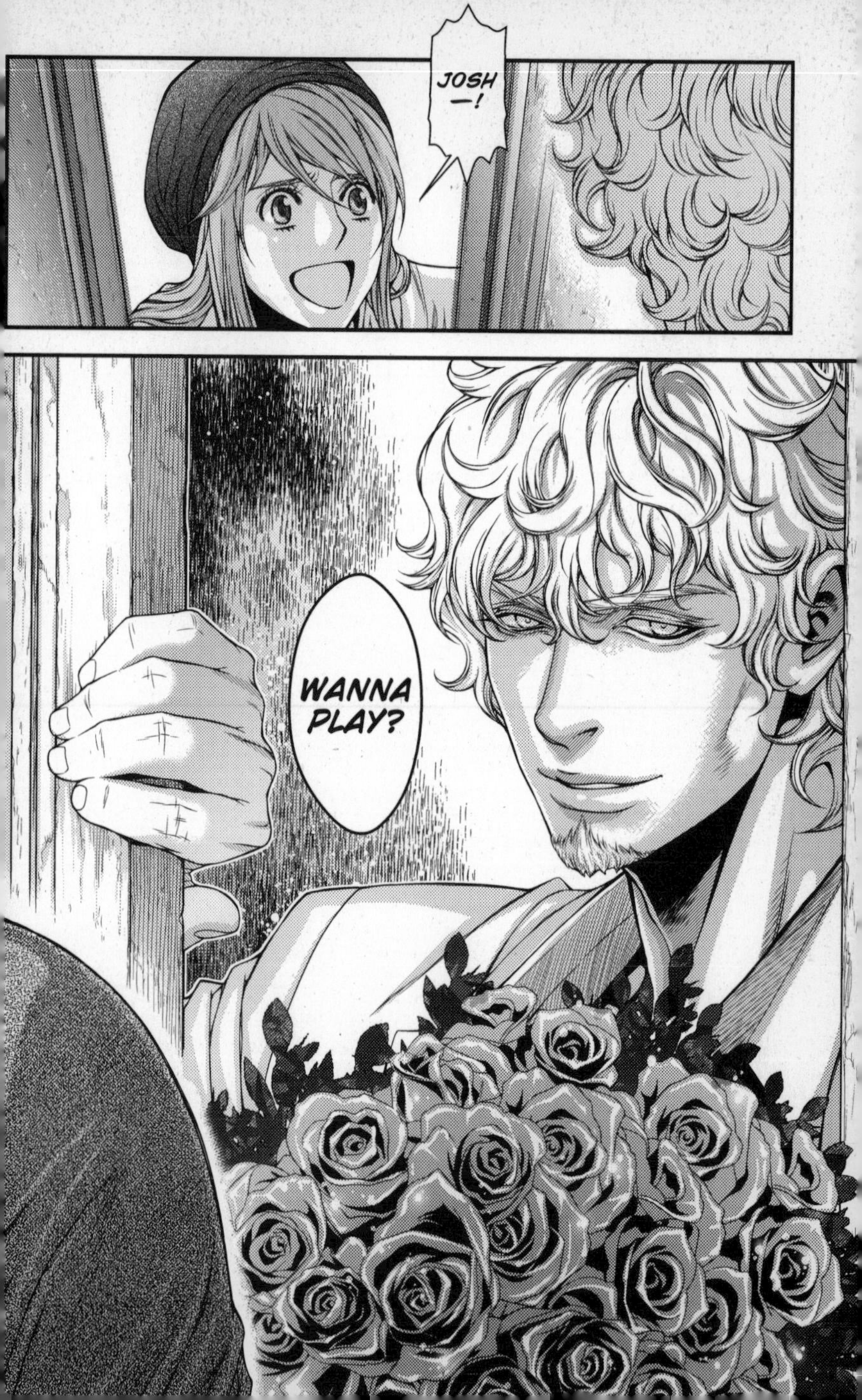
JOSH—!
WANNA PLAY?

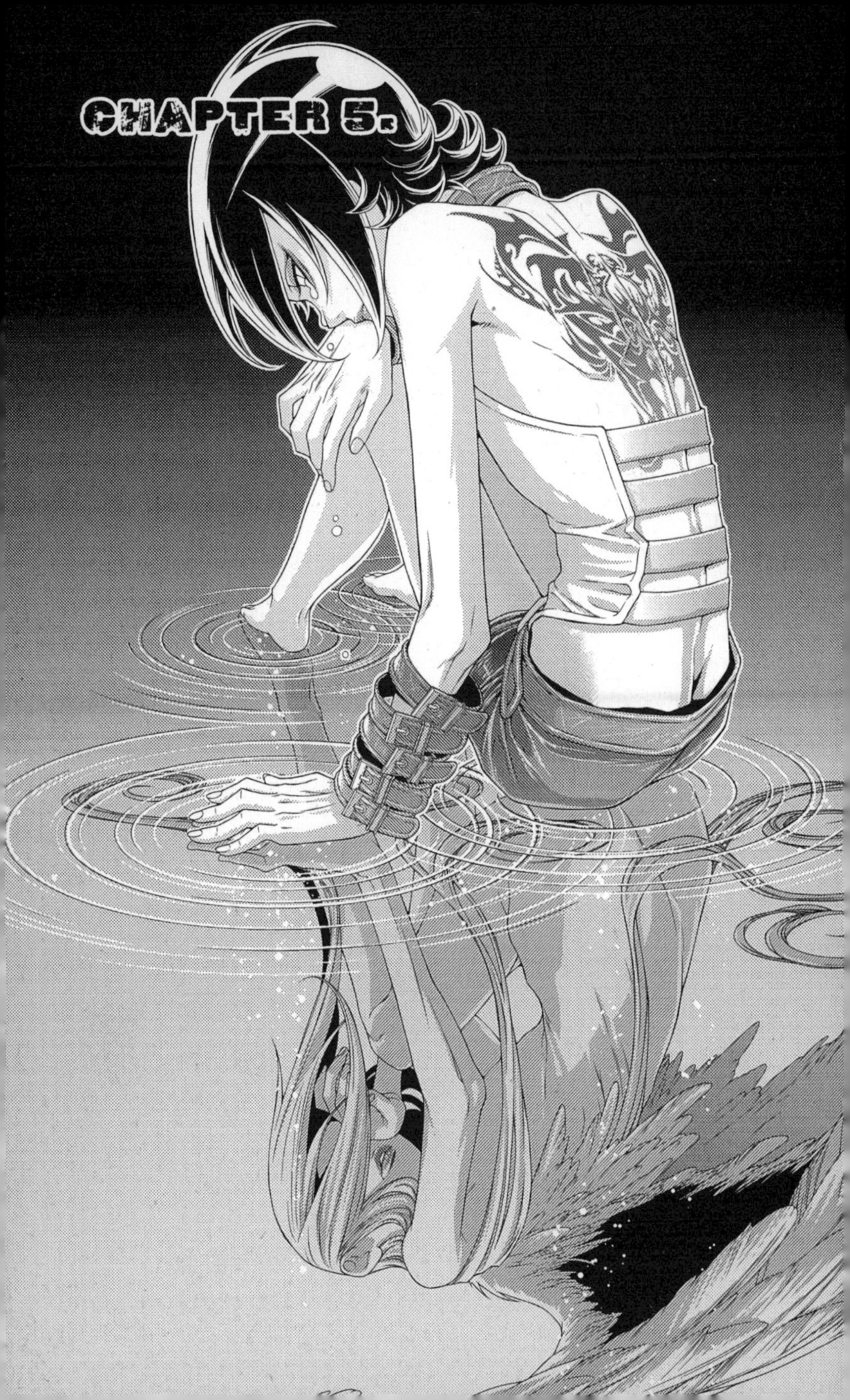
CHAPTER 5.

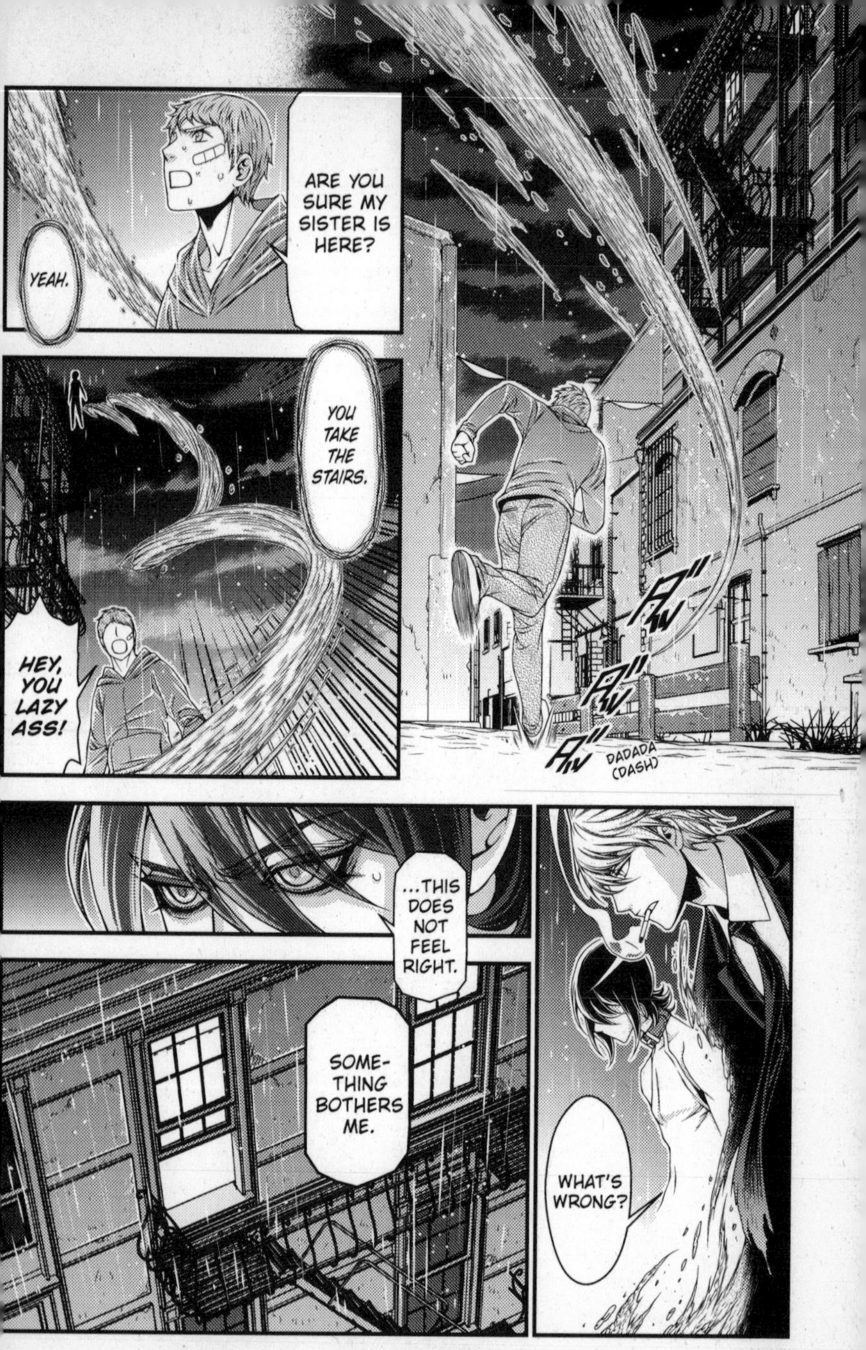
DADADA (DASH)
ARE YOU SURE MY SISTER IS HERE?
YEAH.
YOU TAKE THE STAIRS.
HEY, YOU LAZY ASS!
WHAT'S WRONG?
...THIS DOES NOT FEEL RIGHT.
SOME-THING BOTHERS ME.

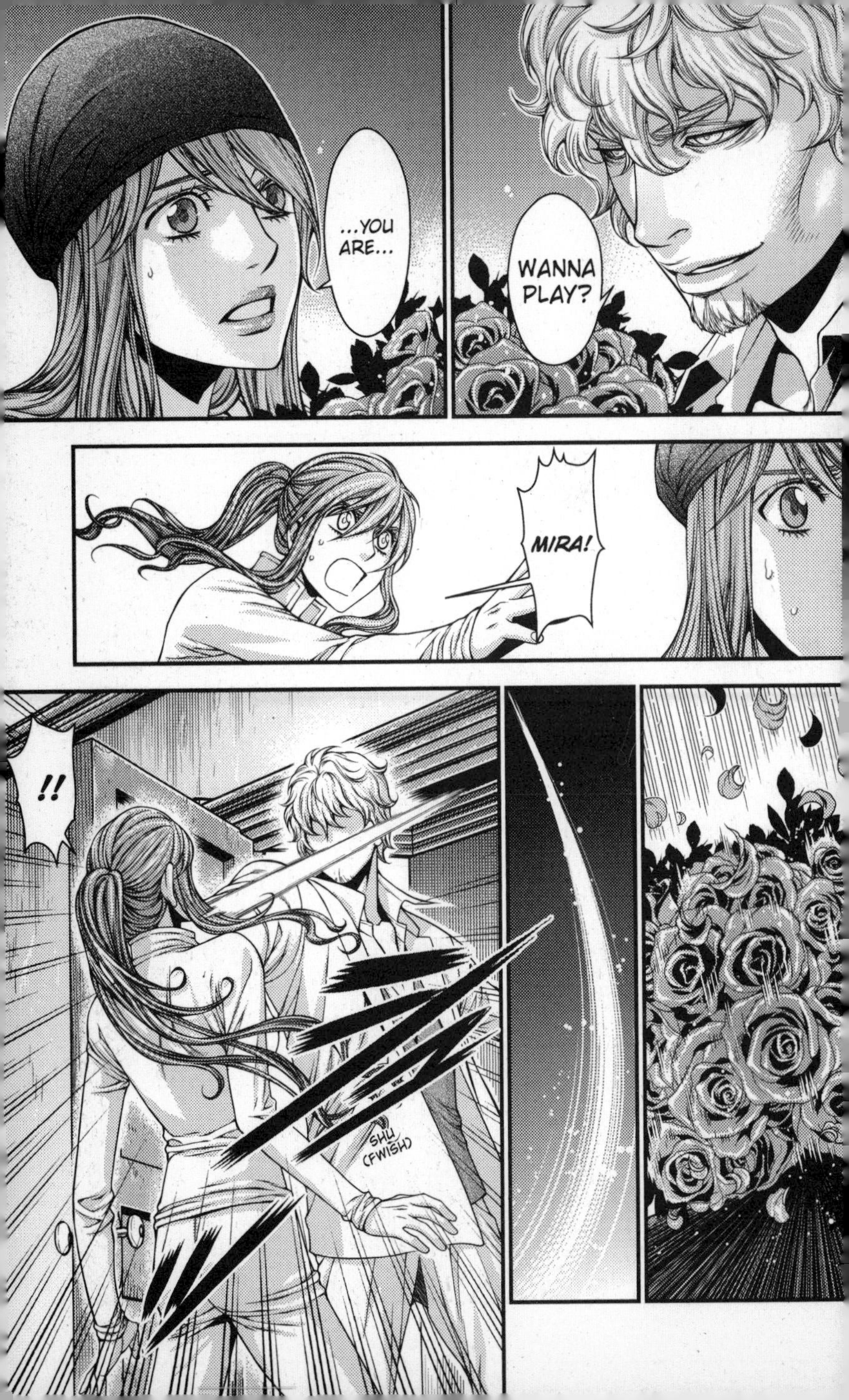
WANNA PLAY?
...YOU ARE...
MIRA!
!!
SHU (FWISH)

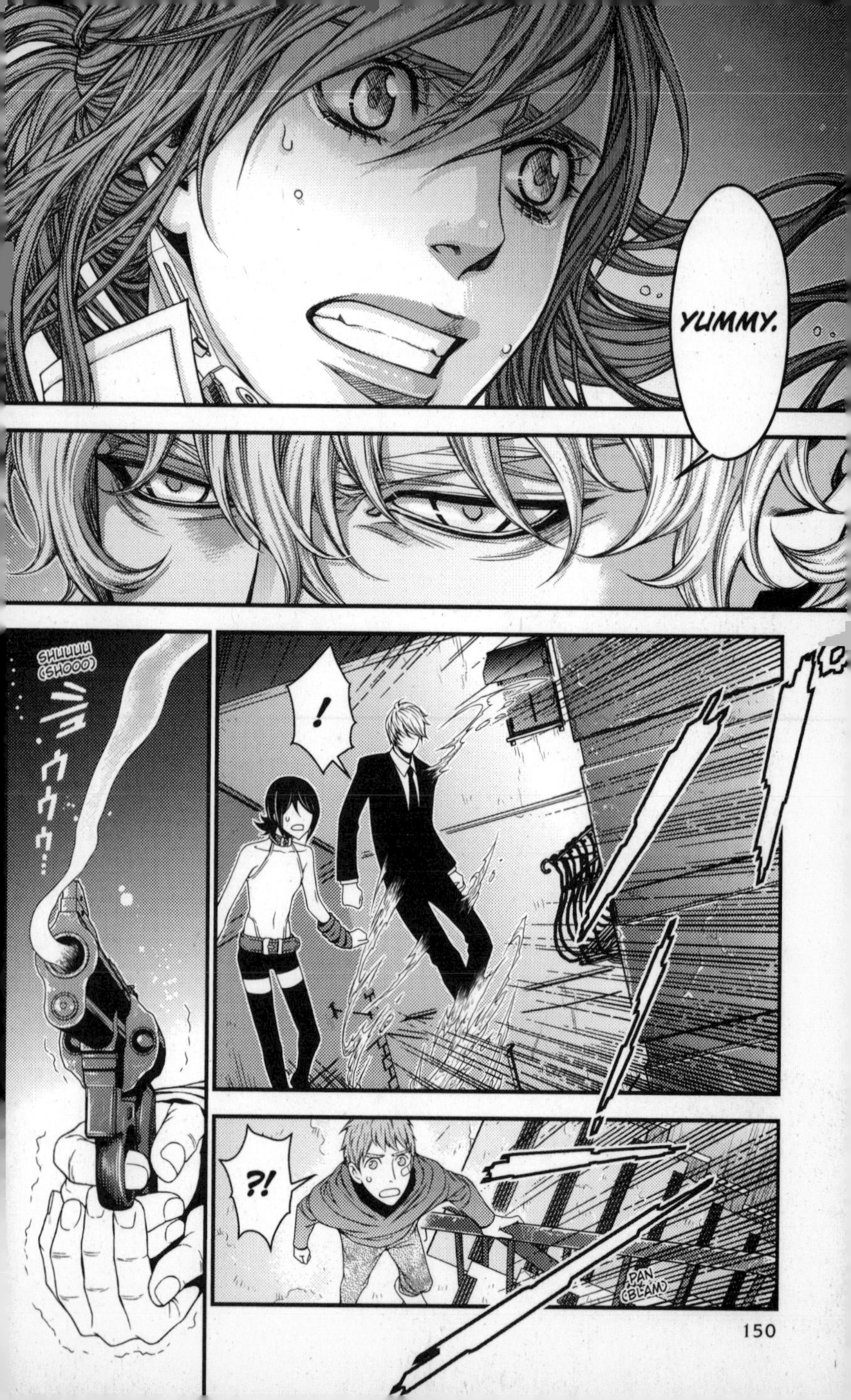
YUMMY.
!
?!
PAN
(BLAM)
SHUUUU
(SHOOO)
シュウウウ…

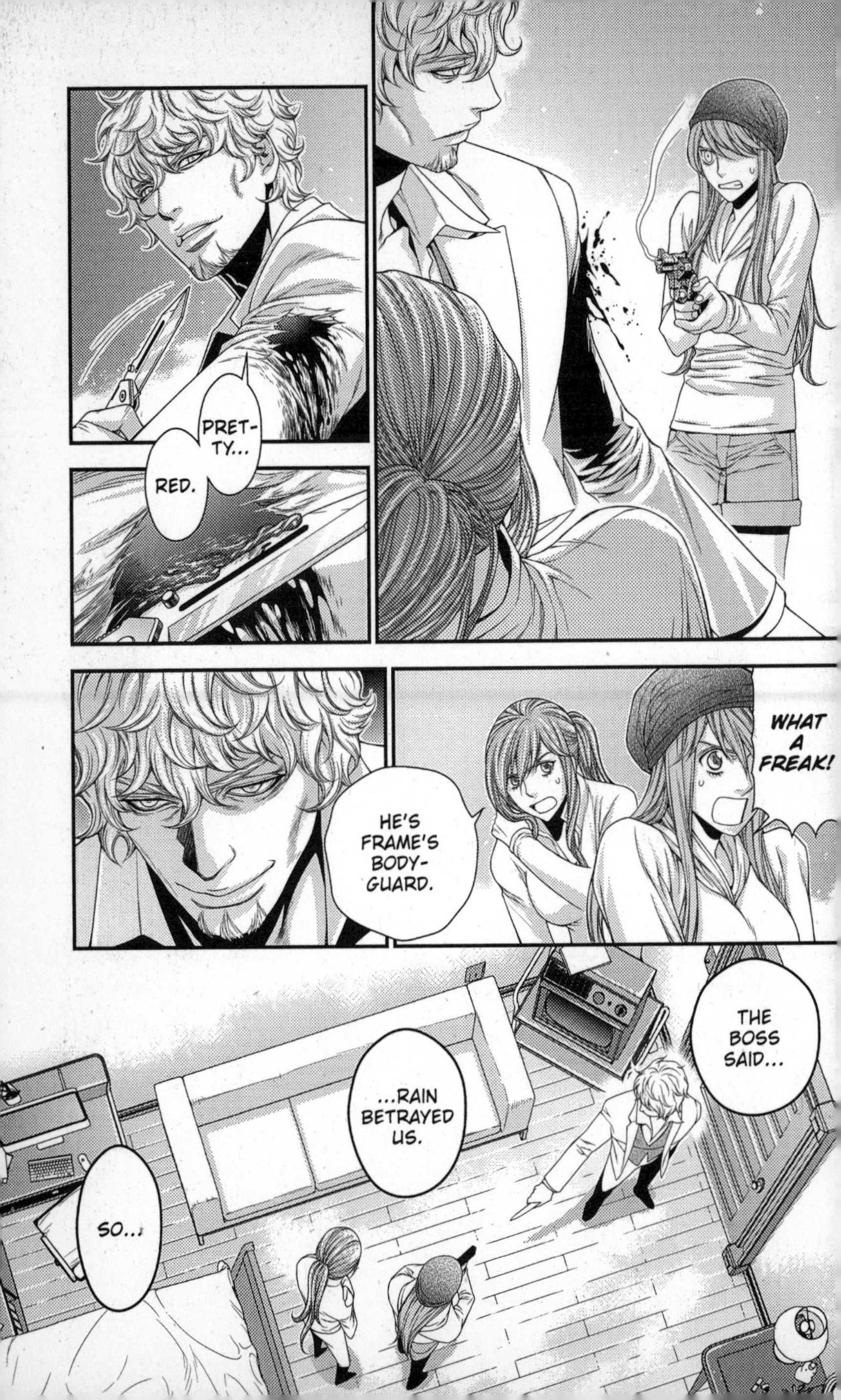
PRET-TY...
RED.
WHAT A FREAK!
HE'S FRAME'S BODY-GUARD.
THE BOSS SAID...
...RAIN BETRAYED US.
SO...

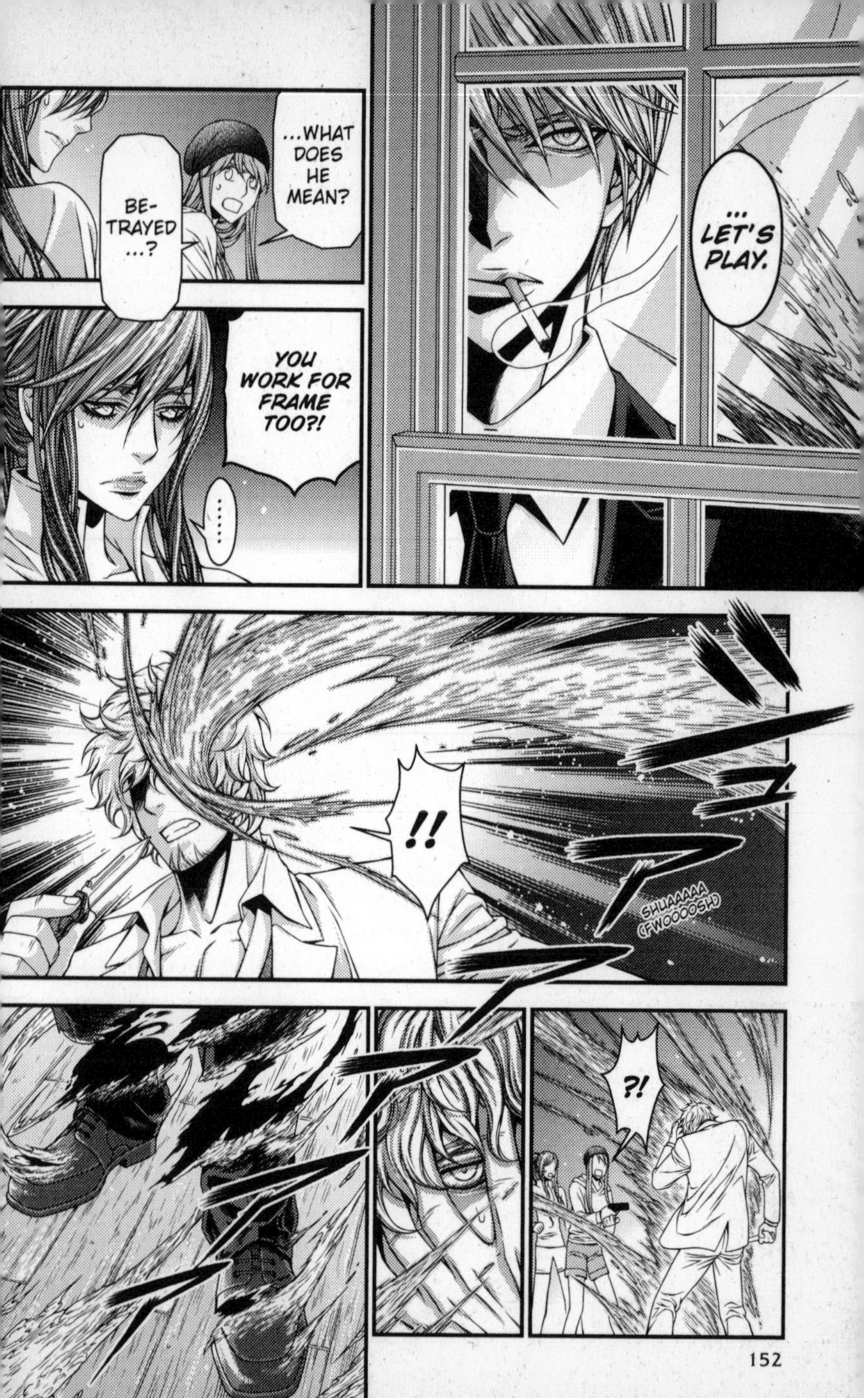

... LET'S PLAY.
...WHAT DOES HE MEAN?
BE-TRAYED ...?
YOU WORK FOR FRAME TOO?!
......
!!
SHUAAAAA (FWOOOOSH)
?!

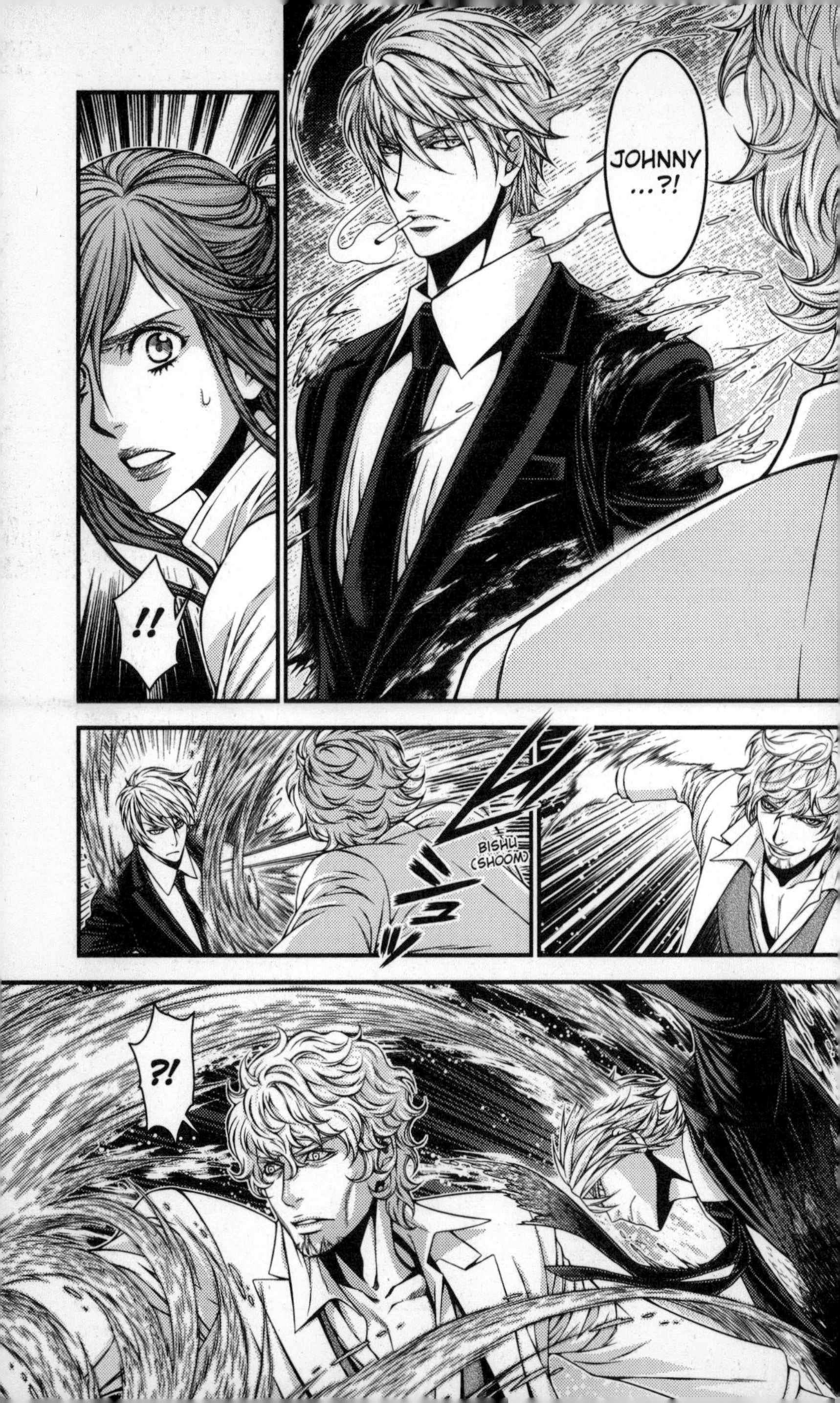
JOHNNY ...?!
!!
BISHU (SHOOM)
?!

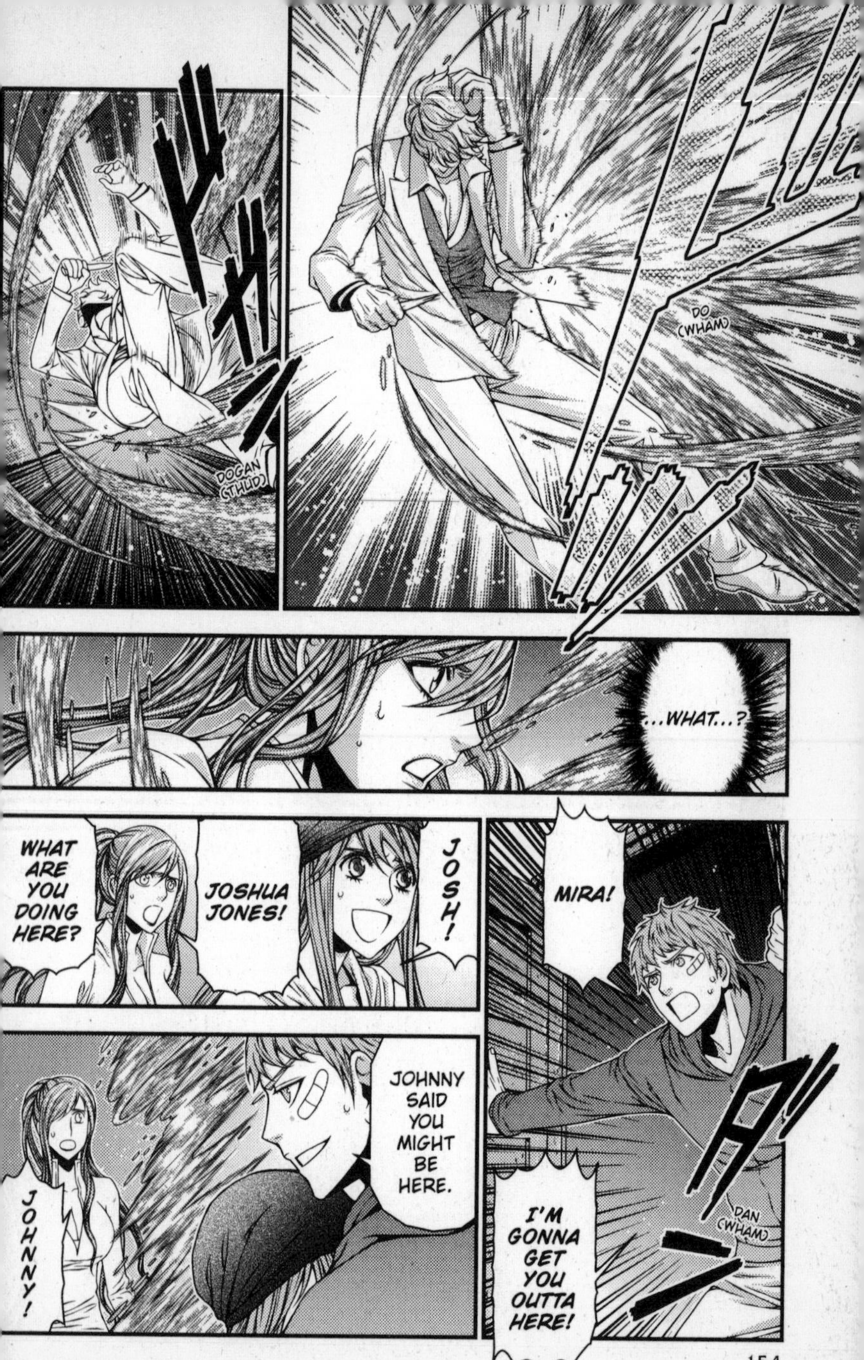
DO (WHAM)
DOGAN (THUD)
...WHAT...?
MIRA!
DAN (WHAM)
I'M GONNA GET YOU OUTTA HERE!
JOSH!
JOSHUA JONES!
WHAT ARE YOU DOING HERE?
JOHNNY SAID YOU MIGHT BE HERE.
JOHNNY!

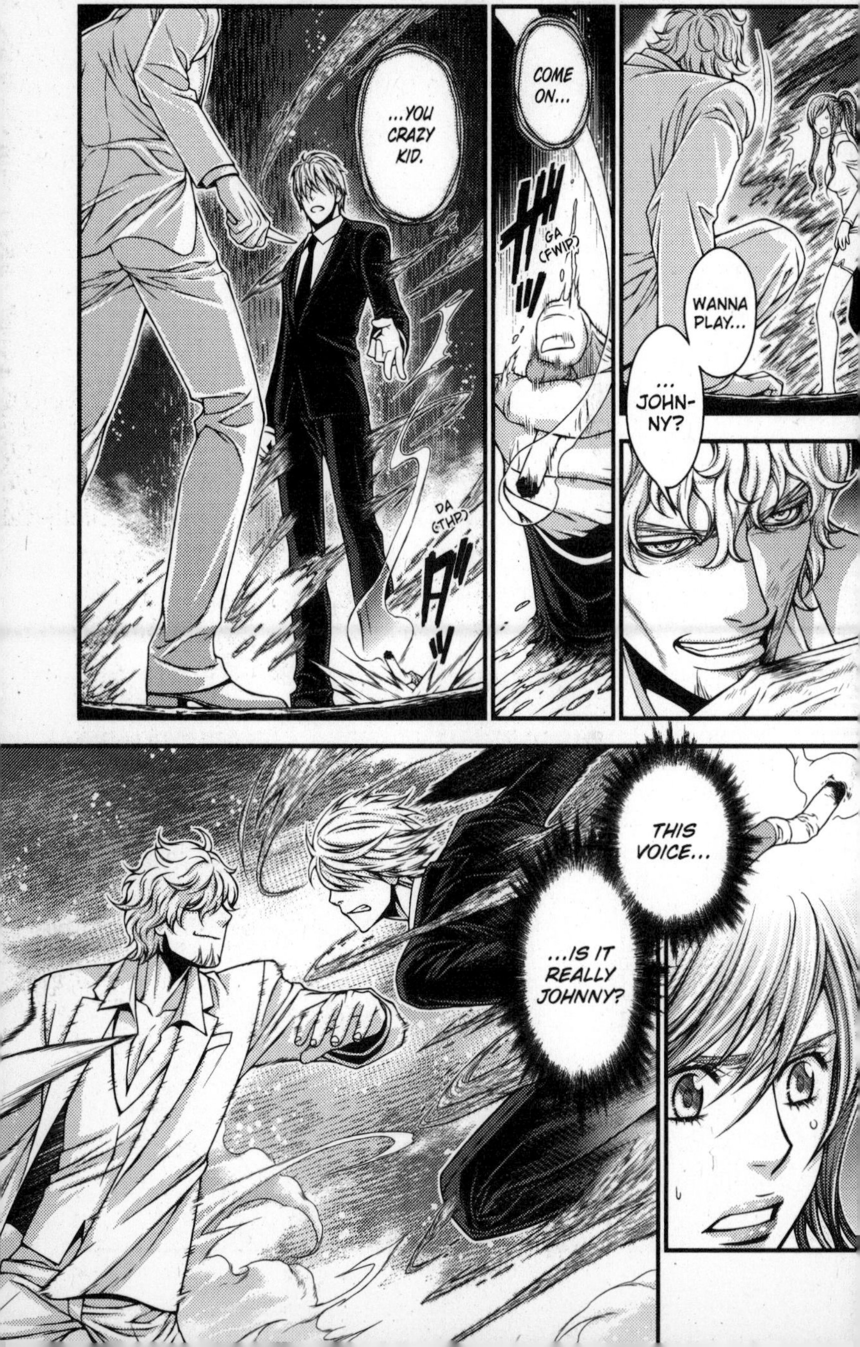
WANNA PLAY...
... JOHN-NY?
COME ON...
GA (FWIP)
...YOU CRAZY KID.
DA (THP)
THIS VOICE...
...IS IT REALLY JOHNNY?

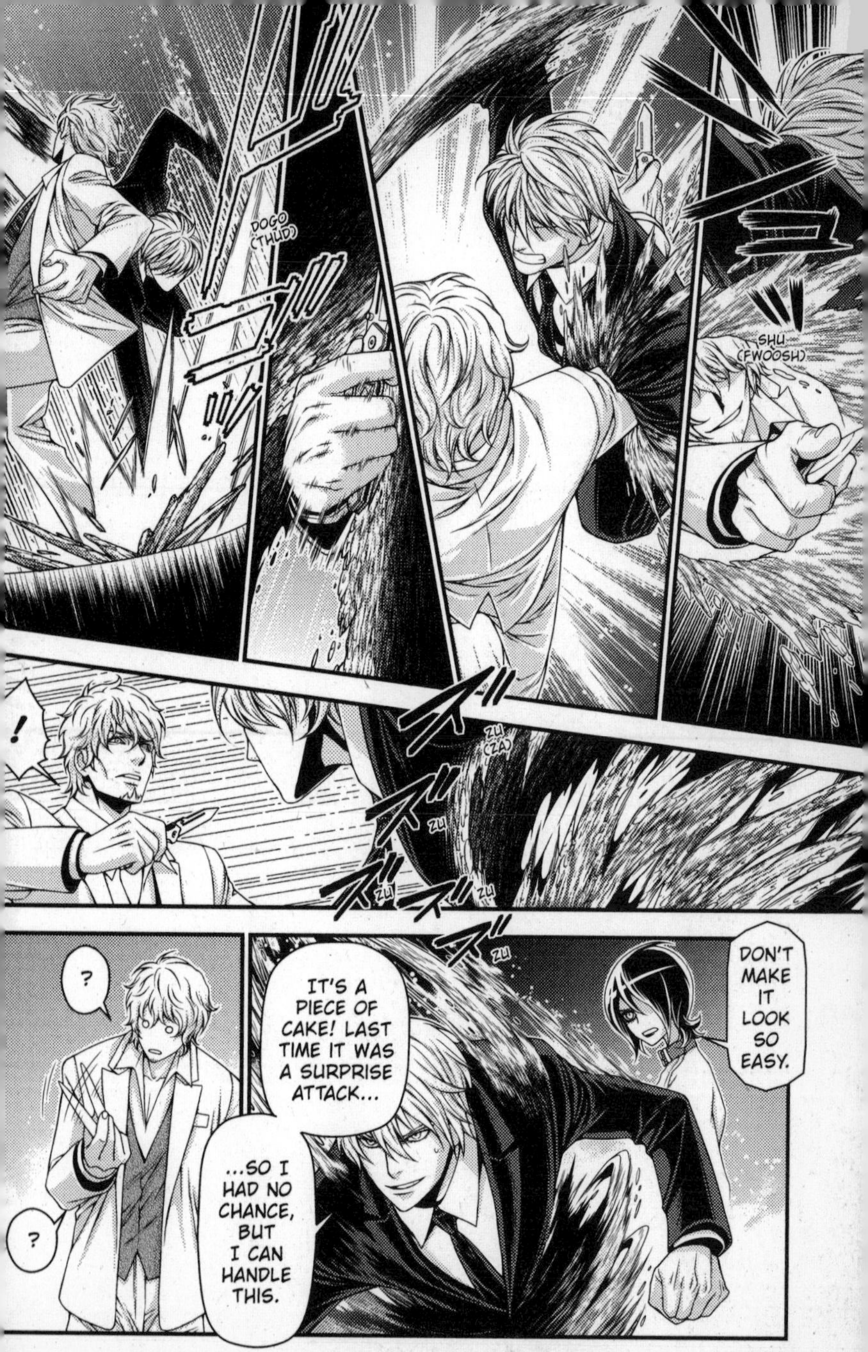
SHU (FWOOSH)
DOGO (THUD)
ZU (ZA)
ZU
ZU
ZU
!
DON'T MAKE IT LOOK SO EASY.
ZU
IT'S A PIECE OF CAKE! LAST TIME IT WAS A SURPRISE ATTACK...
...SO I HAD NO CHANCE, BUT I CAN HANDLE THIS.
?
?

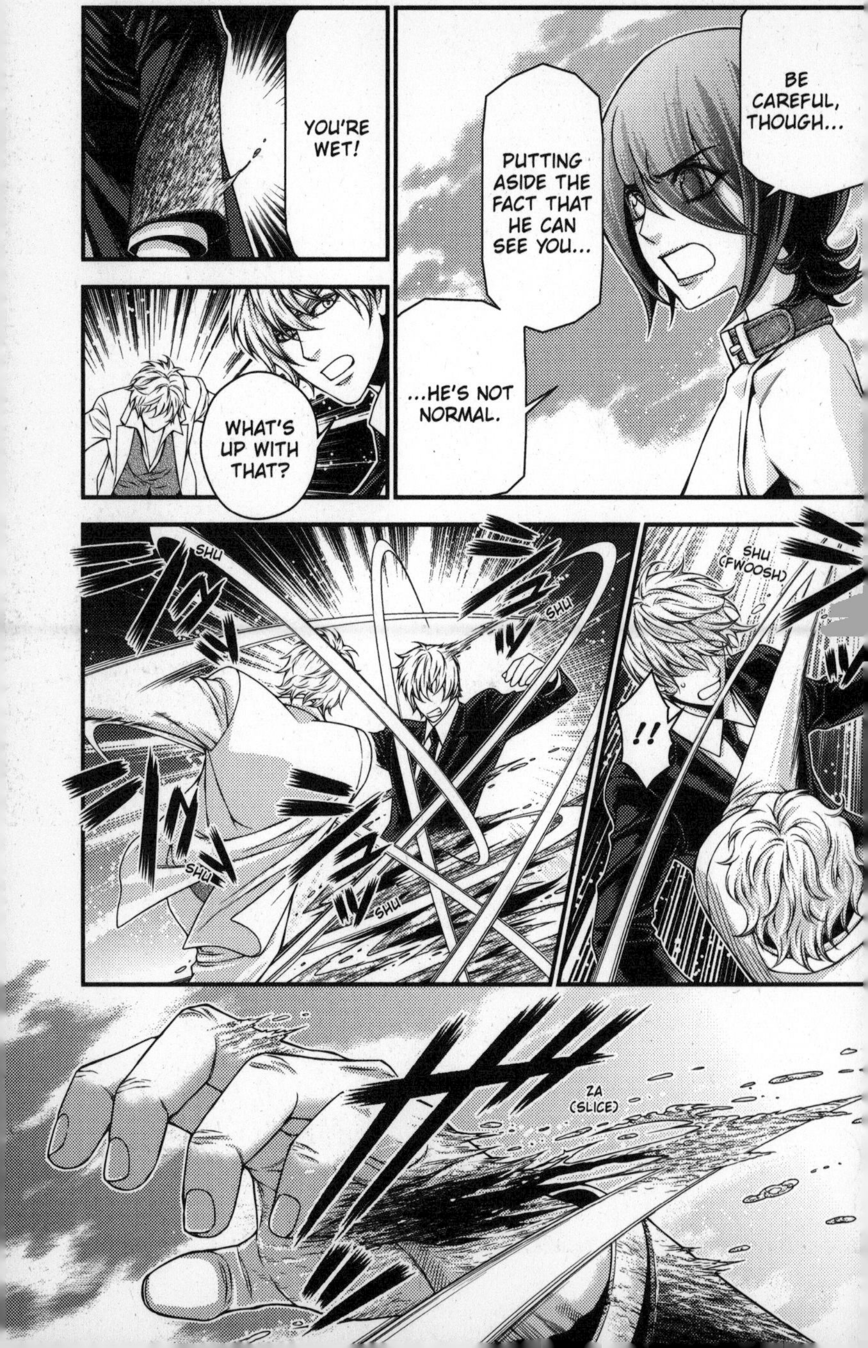
BE CAREFUL, THOUGH...
PUTTING ASIDE THE FACT THAT HE CAN SEE YOU...
...HE'S NOT NORMAL.
YOU'RE WET!
WHAT'S UP WITH THAT?
SHU (FWOOSH)
!!
SHU
SHU
SHU
SHU
ZA (SLICE)

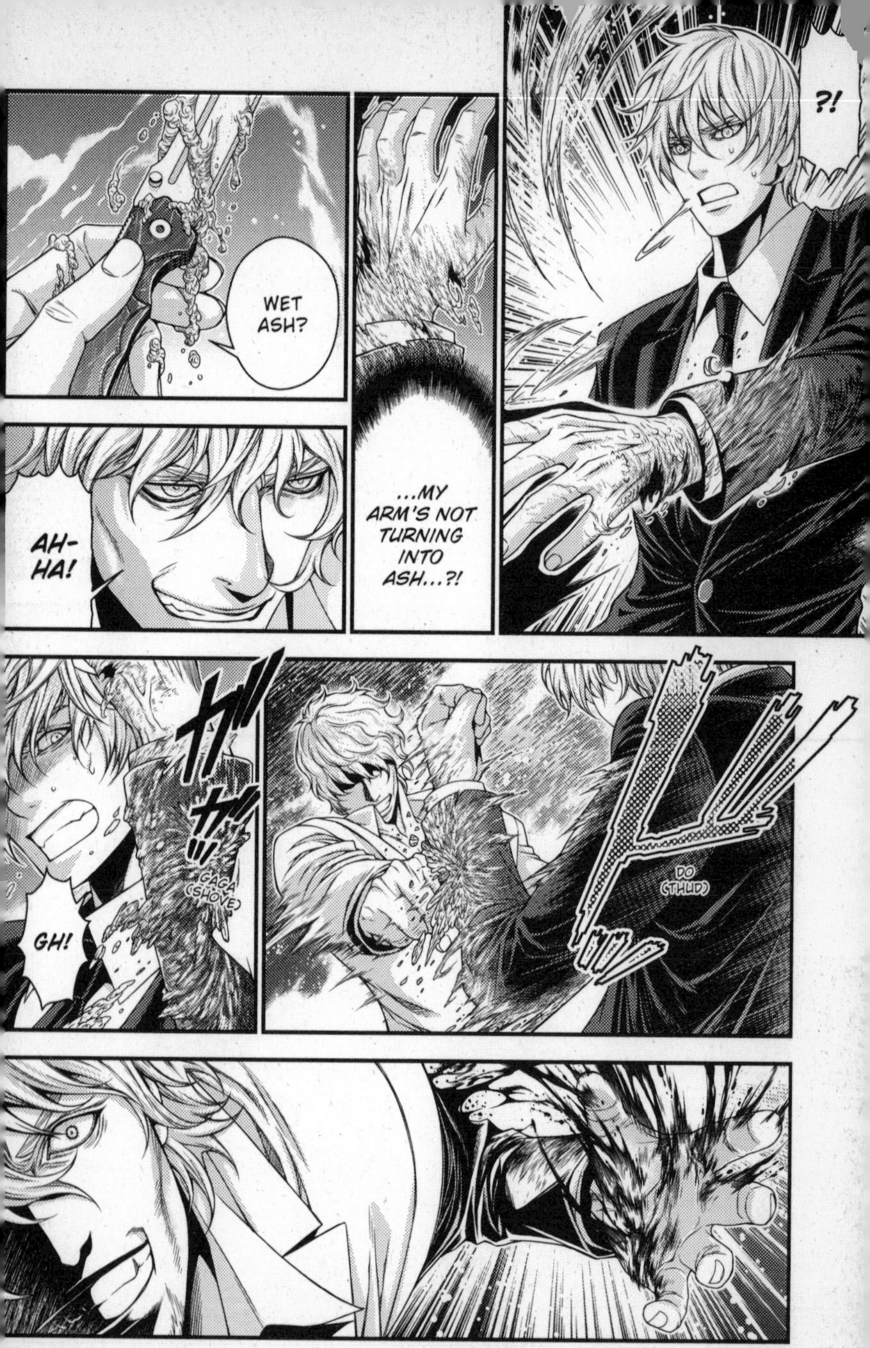
?!
...MY ARM'S NOT TURNING INTO ASH...?!
WET ASH?
AH-HA!
DO (THUD)
GAGA (SHOVE)
GH!

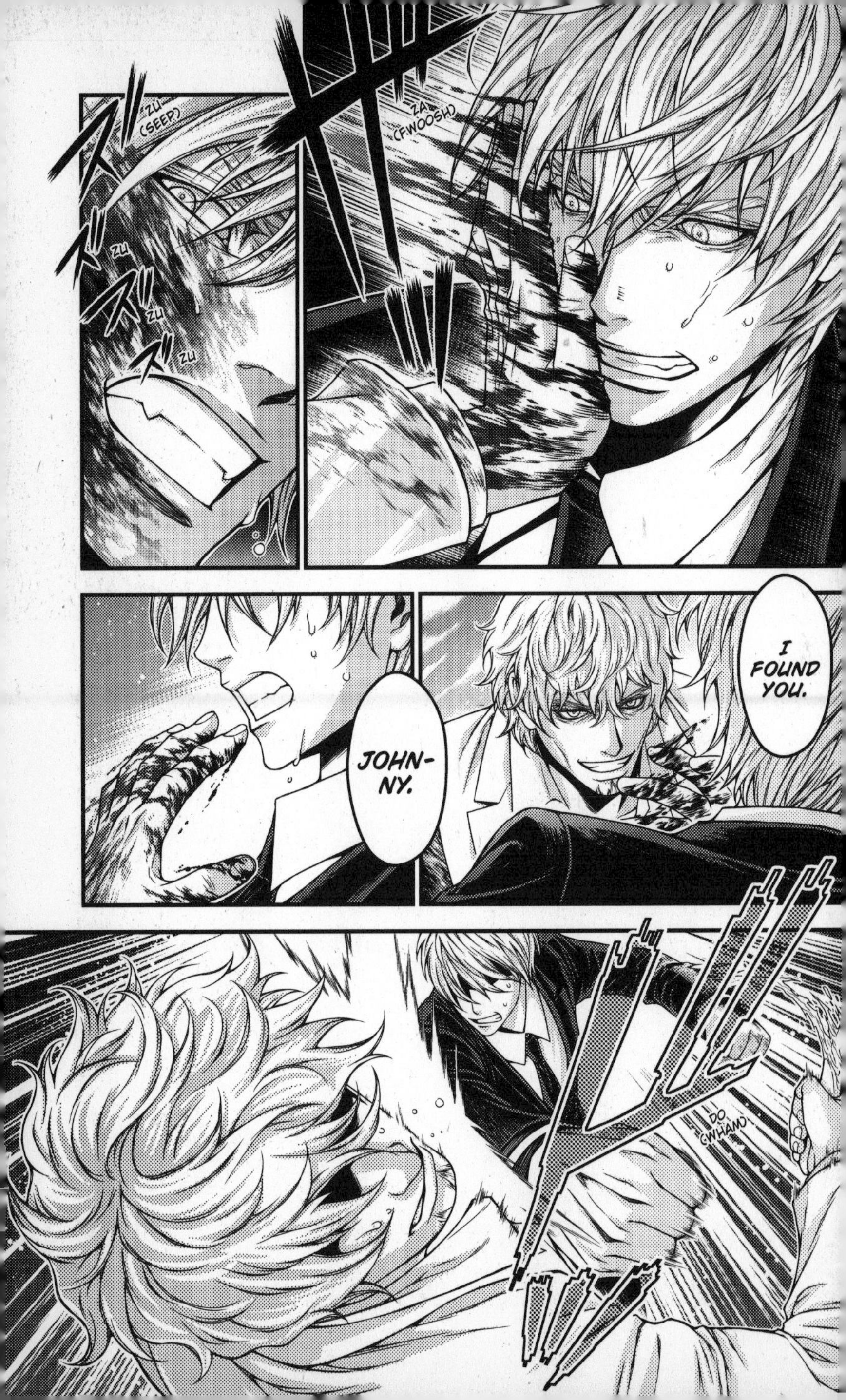
ZA (FWOOSH)
ZU (SEEP)
ZU
ZU
ZU
I FOUND YOU.
JOHN-NY.
DO (WHAM)

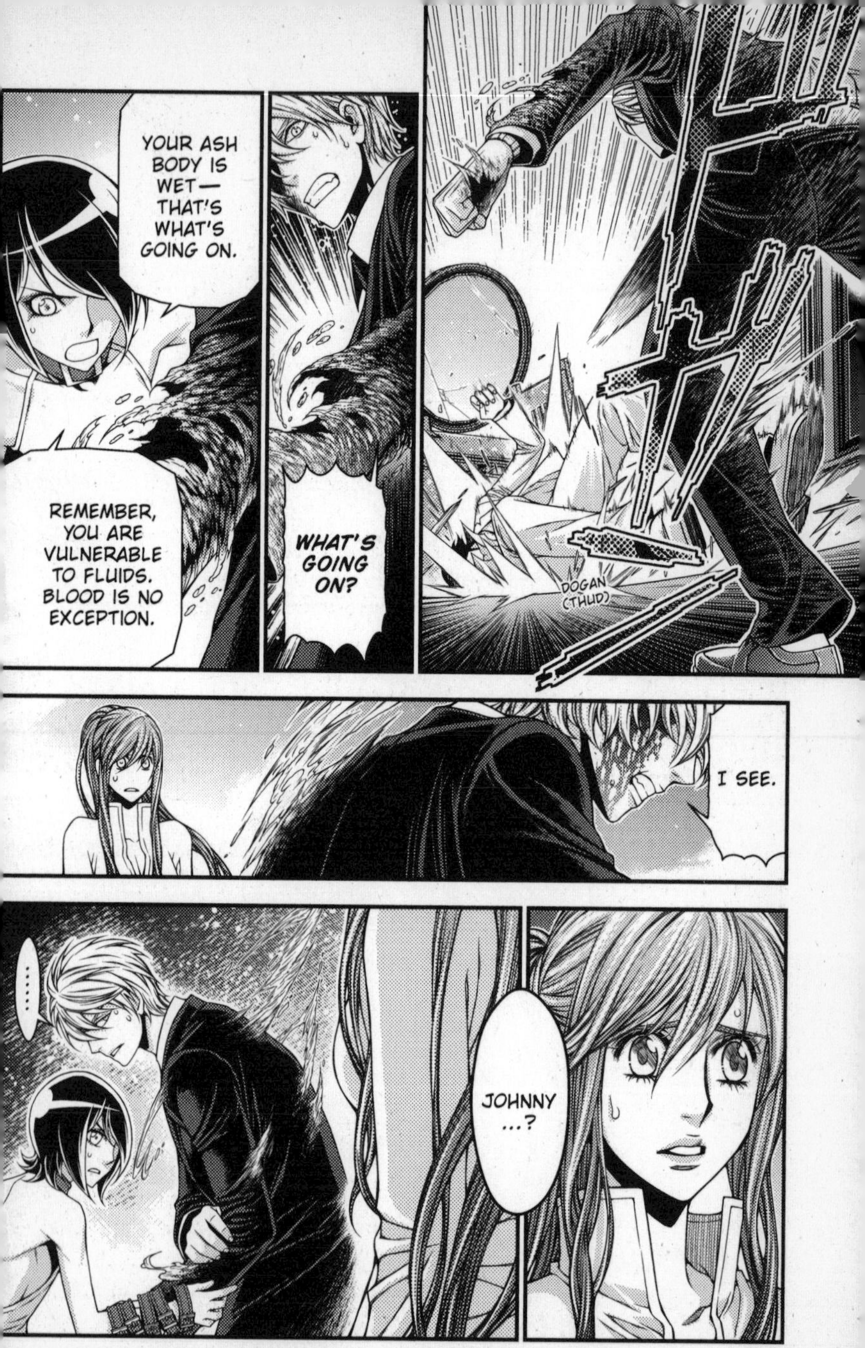
DOGAN (THUD)
WHAT'S GOING ON?
YOUR ASH BODY IS WET— THAT'S WHAT'S GOING ON.
REMEMBER, YOU ARE VULNERABLE TO FLUIDS. BLOOD IS NO EXCEPTION.
I SEE.
JOHNNY ...?
......

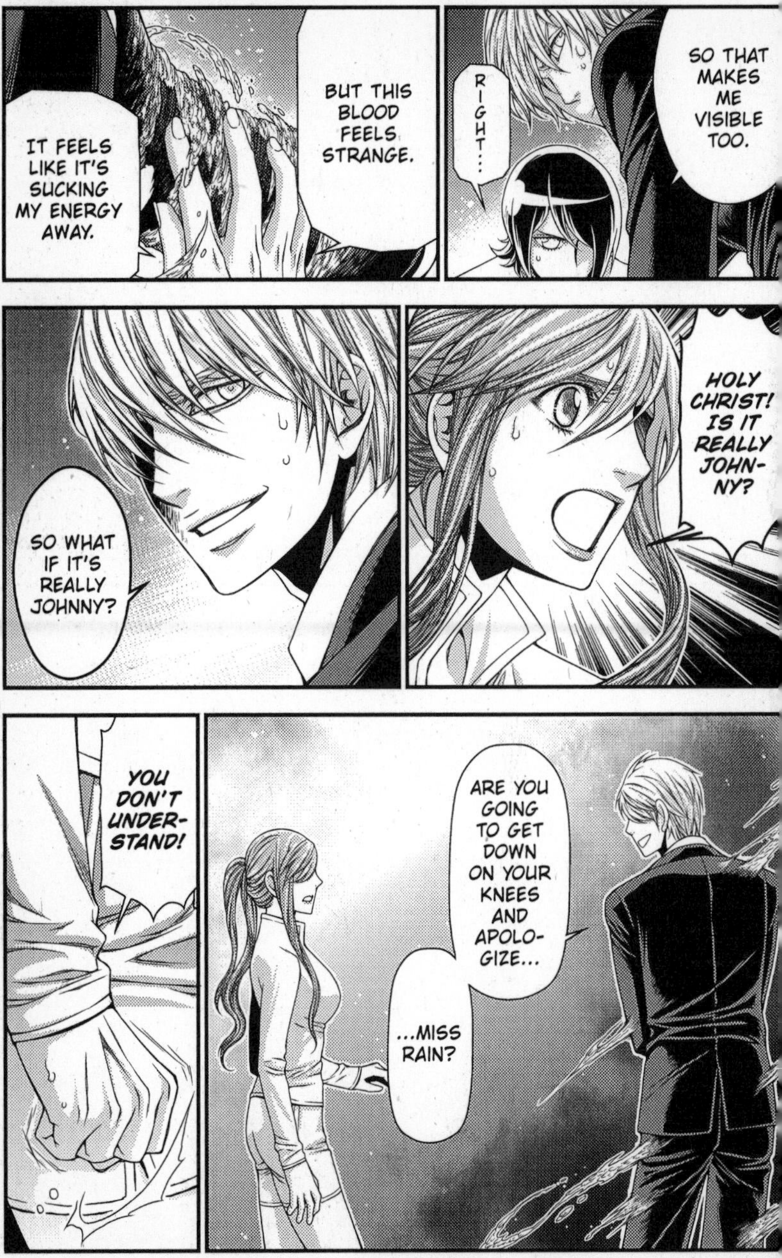
SO THAT MAKES ME VISIBLE TOO.
RIGHT...
BUT THIS BLOOD FEELS STRANGE.
IT FEELS LIKE IT'S SUCKING MY ENERGY AWAY.
HOLY CHRIST! IS IT REALLY JOHNNY?
SO WHAT IF IT'S REALLY JOHNNY?
ARE YOU GOING TO GET DOWN ON YOUR KNEES AND APOLOGIZE...
...MISS RAIN?
YOU DON'T UNDERSTAND!

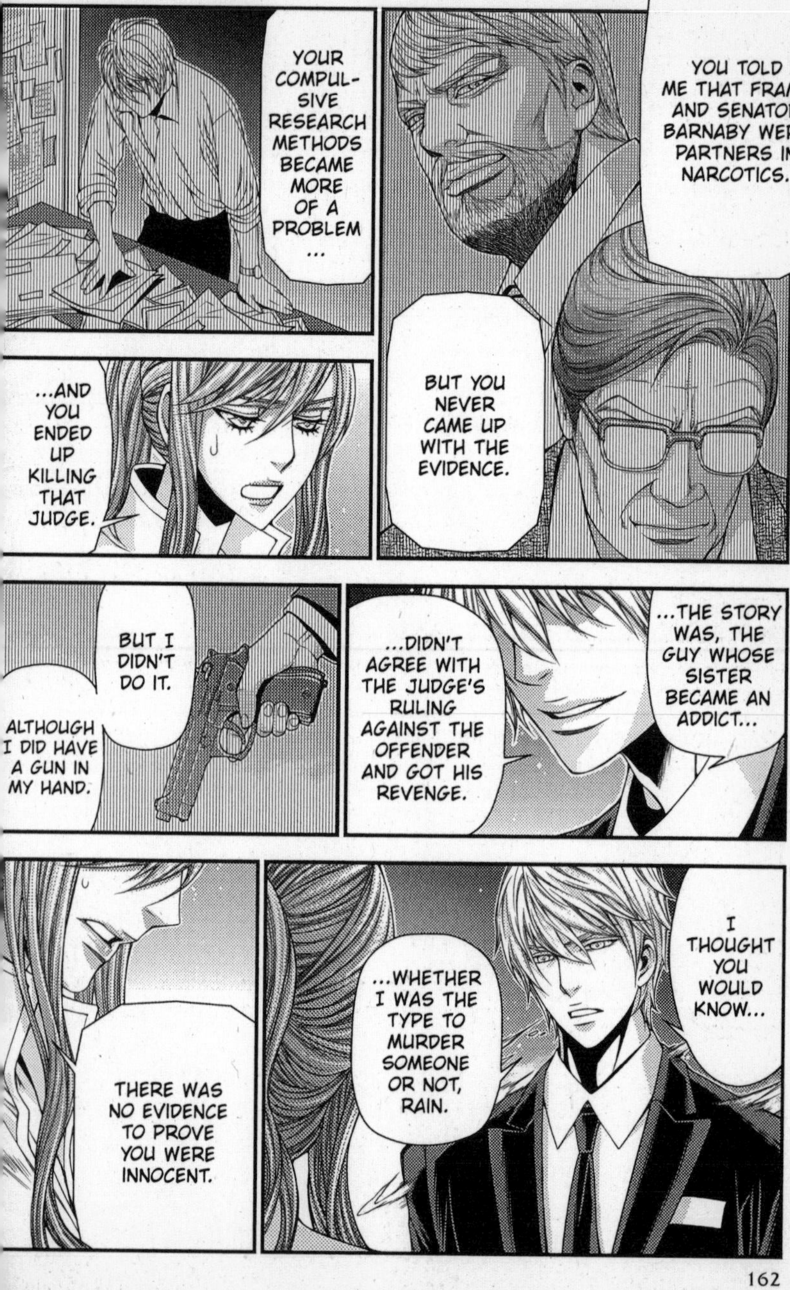
YOU TOLD ME THAT FRAME AND SENATOR BARNABY WERE PARTNERS IN NARCOTICS.
BUT YOU NEVER CAME UP WITH THE EVIDENCE.
YOUR COMPUL-SIVE RESEARCH METHODS BECAME MORE OF A PROBLEM ...
...AND YOU ENDED UP KILLING THAT JUDGE.
...THE STORY WAS, THE GUY WHOSE SISTER BECAME AN ADDICT...
...DIDN'T AGREE WITH THE JUDGE'S RULING AGAINST THE OFFENDER AND GOT HIS REVENGE.
BUT I DIDN'T DO IT.
ALTHOUGH I DID HAVE A GUN IN MY HAND.
I THOUGHT YOU WOULD KNOW...
...WHETHER I WAS THE TYPE TO MURDER SOMEONE OR NOT, RAIN.
THERE WAS NO EVIDENCE TO PROVE YOU WERE INNOCENT.

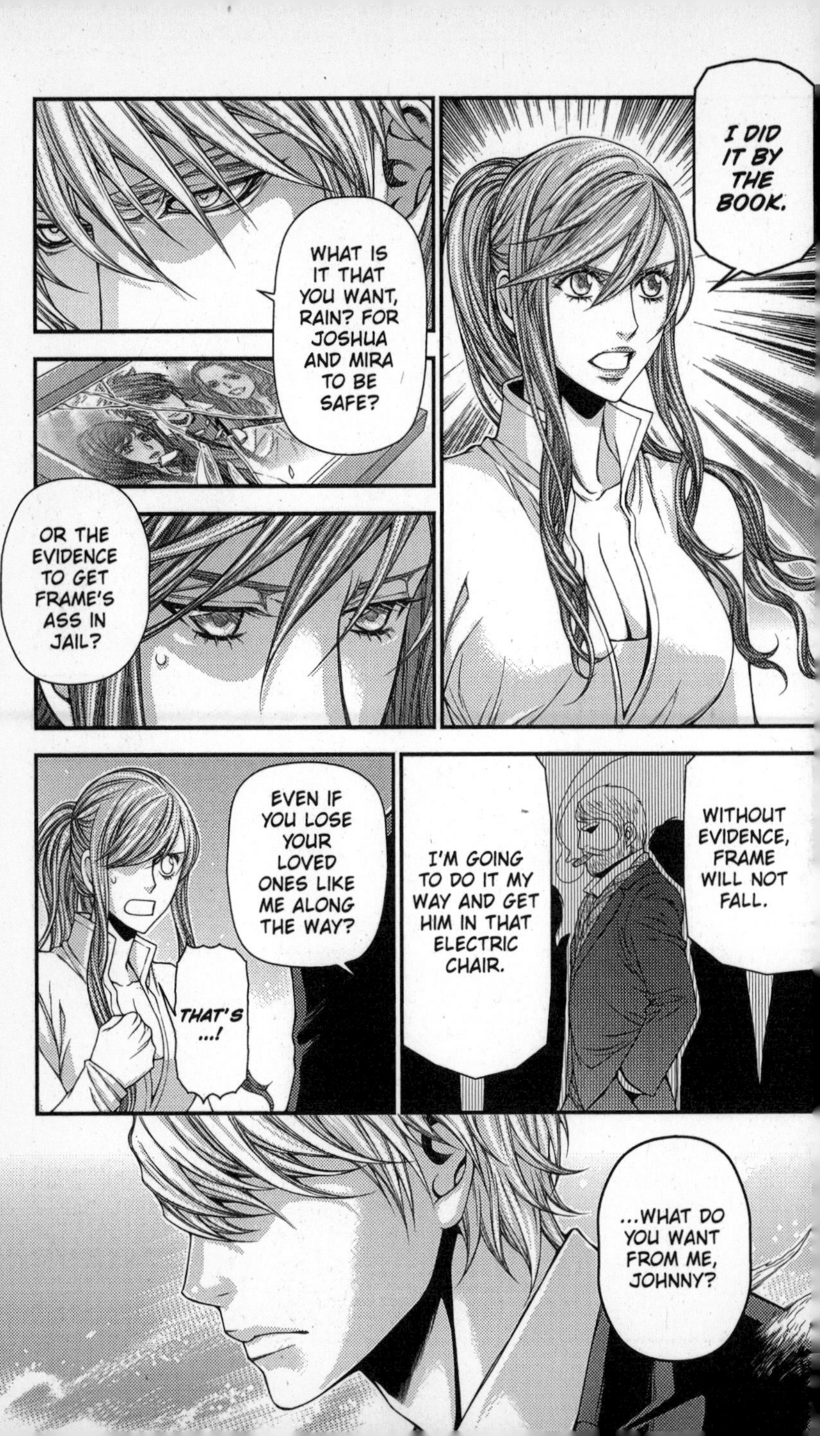
I DID IT BY THE BOOK.
WHAT IS IT THAT YOU WANT, RAIN? FOR JOSHUA AND MIRA TO BE SAFE?
OR THE EVIDENCE TO GET FRAME'S ASS IN JAIL?
WITHOUT EVIDENCE, FRAME WILL NOT FALL.
I'M GOING TO DO IT MY WAY AND GET HIM IN THAT ELECTRIC CHAIR.
EVEN IF YOU LOSE YOUR LOVED ONES LIKE ME ALONG THE WAY?
THAT'S ...!
...WHAT DO YOU WANT FROM ME, JOHNNY?

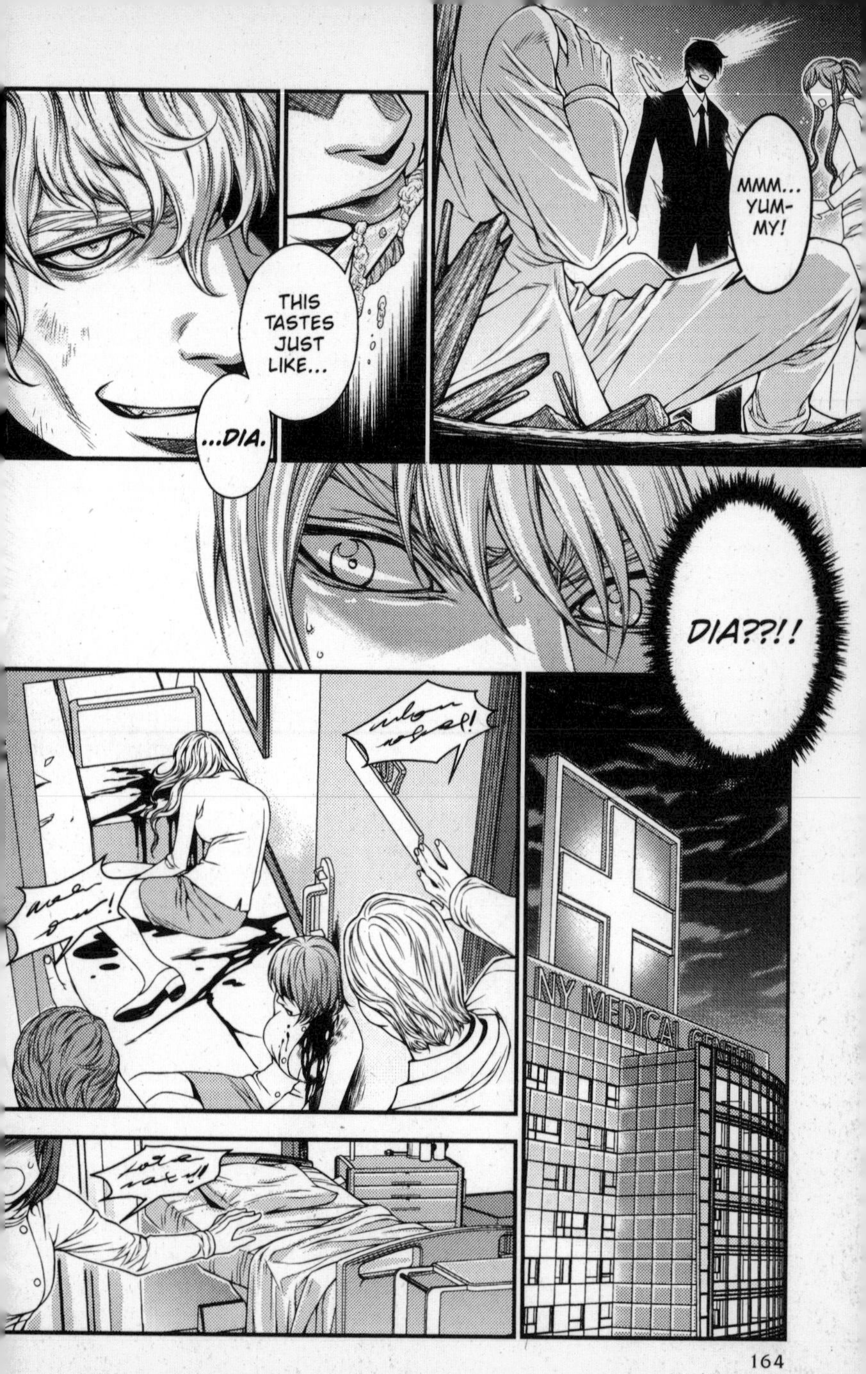
MMM... YUM-MY!
THIS TASTES JUST LIKE...
...DIA.
DIA??!!
NY MEDICAL CENTER

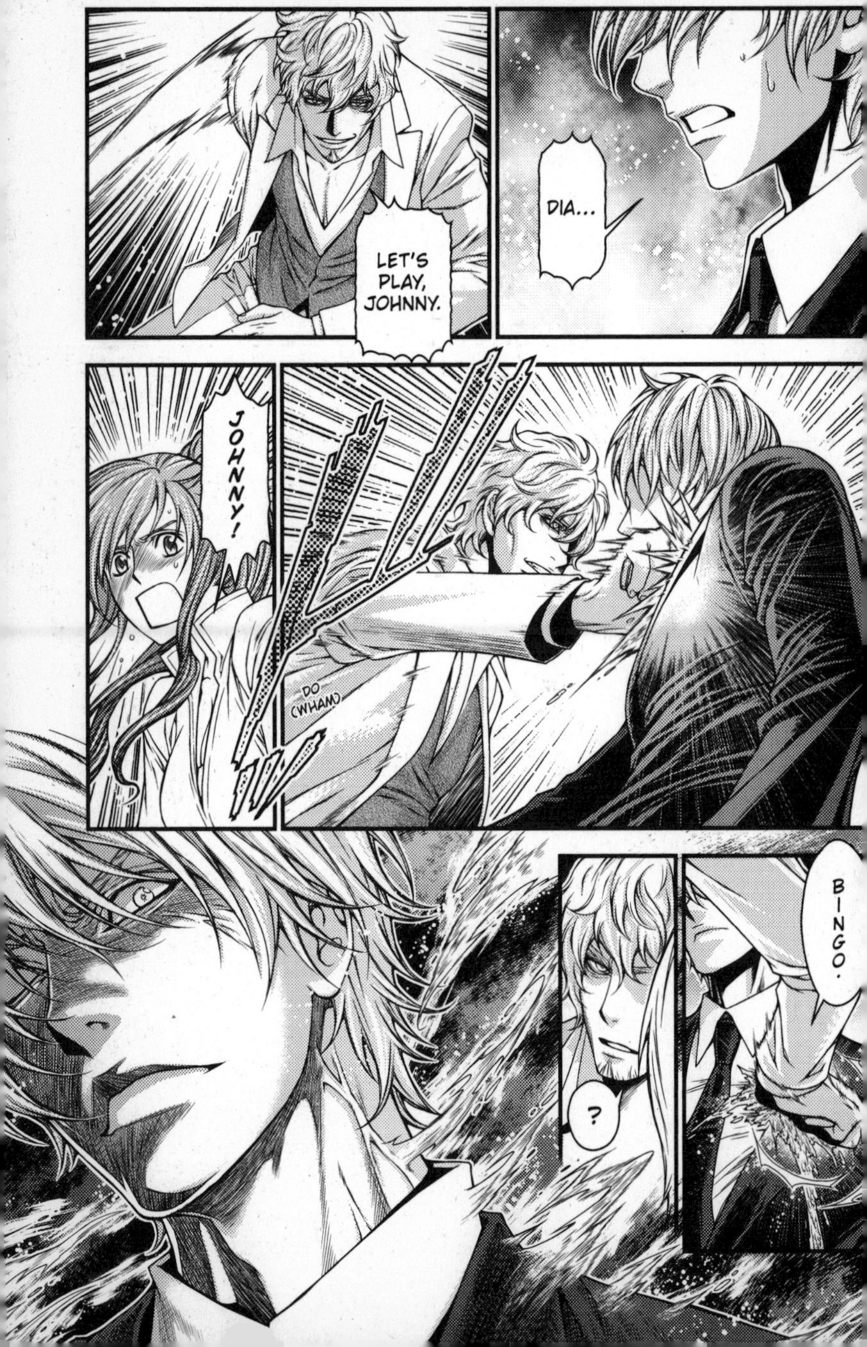
DIA...
LET'S PLAY, JOHNNY.
DO (WHAM)
JOHNNY!
BINGO.
?

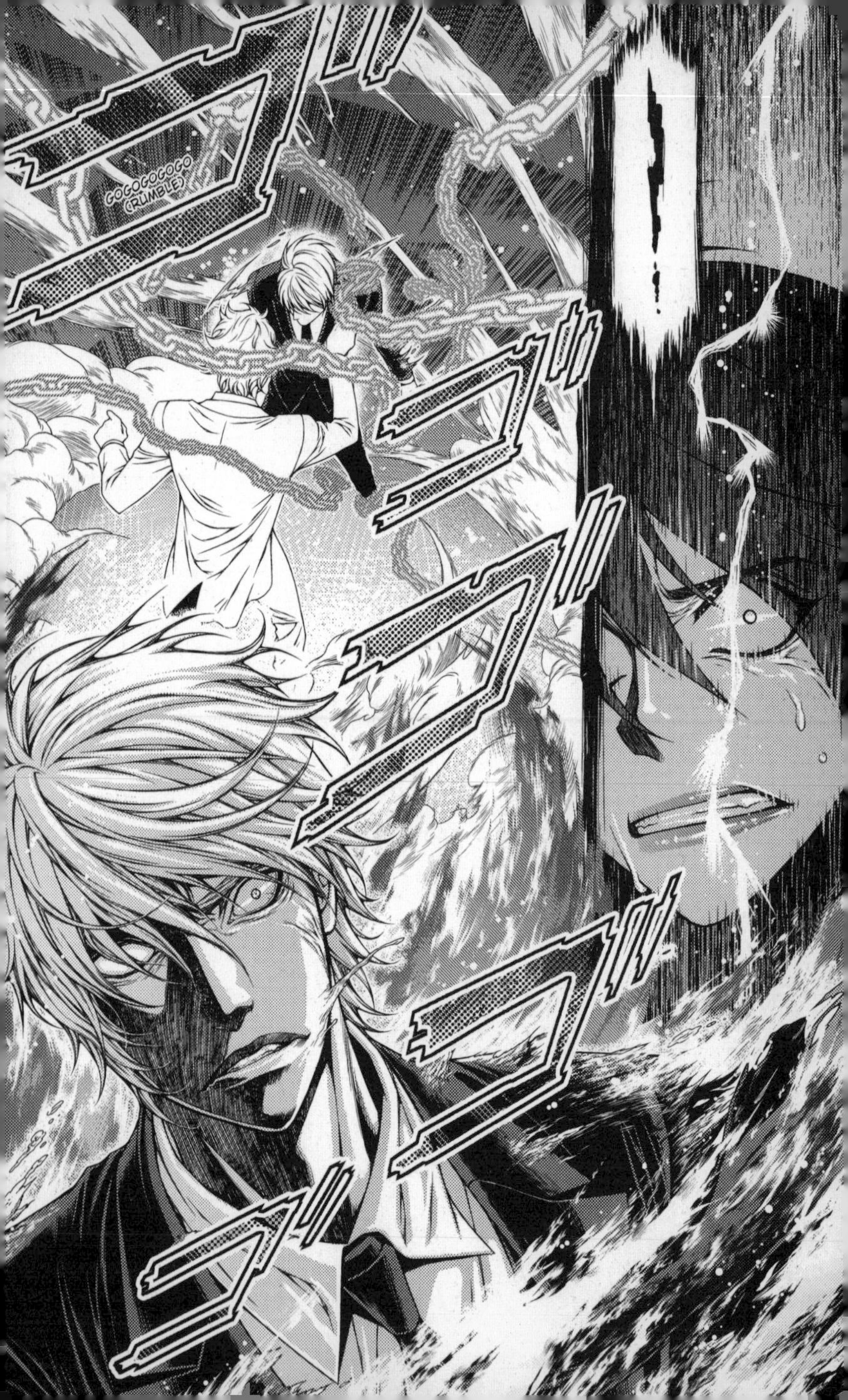
GOGOGOGOGO
(RUMBLE)

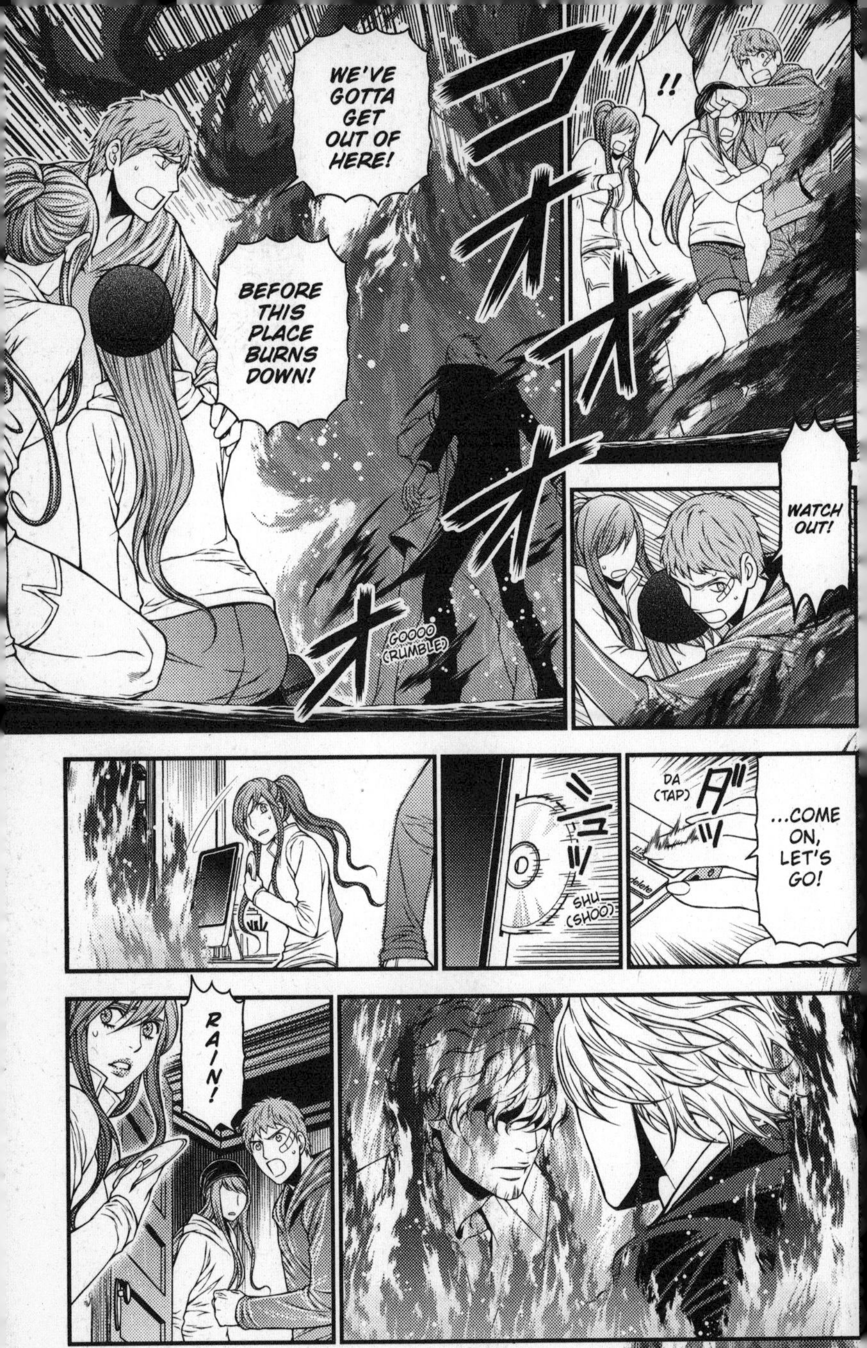
!!
WATCH OUT!
WE'VE GOTTA GET OUT OF HERE!
BEFORE THIS PLACE BURNS DOWN!
GOOOO (RUMBLE)
DA (TAP)
...COME ON, LET'S GO!
SHU (SHOO)
RAIN!

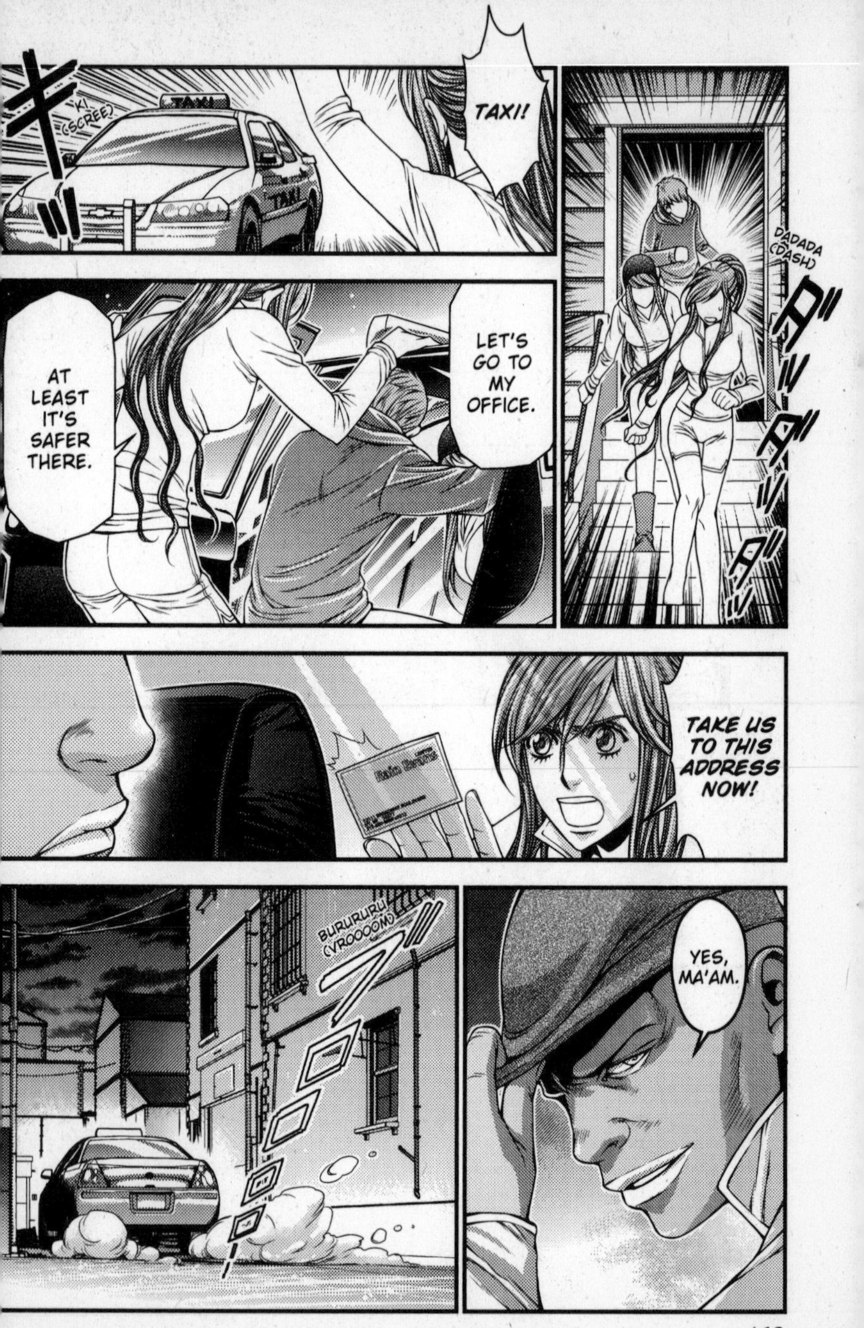
DADADA (DASH)
TAXI!
KI (SCREE)
LET'S GO TO MY OFFICE.
AT LEAST IT'S SAFER THERE.
TAKE US TO THIS ADDRESS NOW!
YES, MA'AM.
BURURURU (VROOOOM)

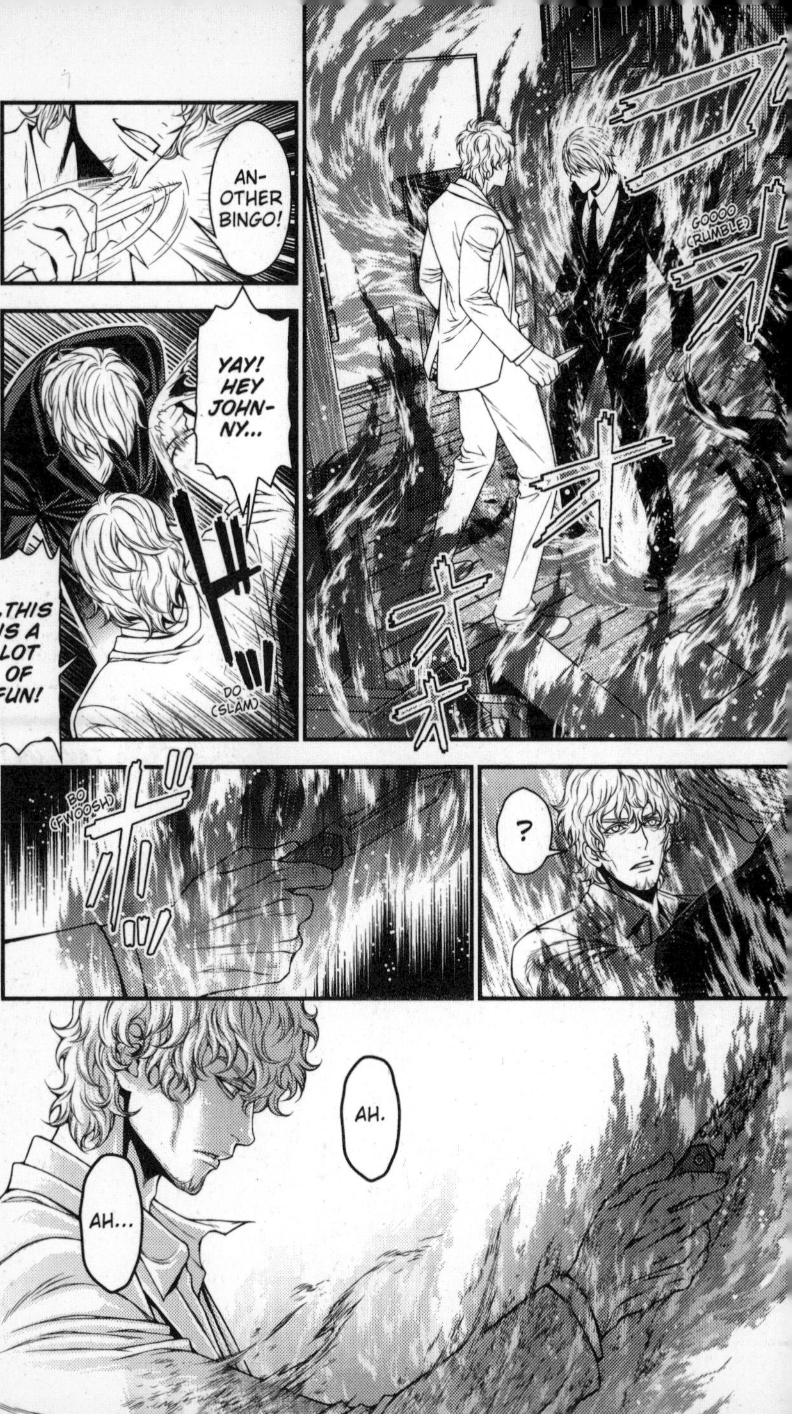
GOOOO (RUMBLE)
AN-OTHER BINGO!
YAY! HEY JOHN-NY...
...THIS IS A LOT OF FUN!
DO (SLAM)
?
BO (FWOOSH)
AH.
AH...

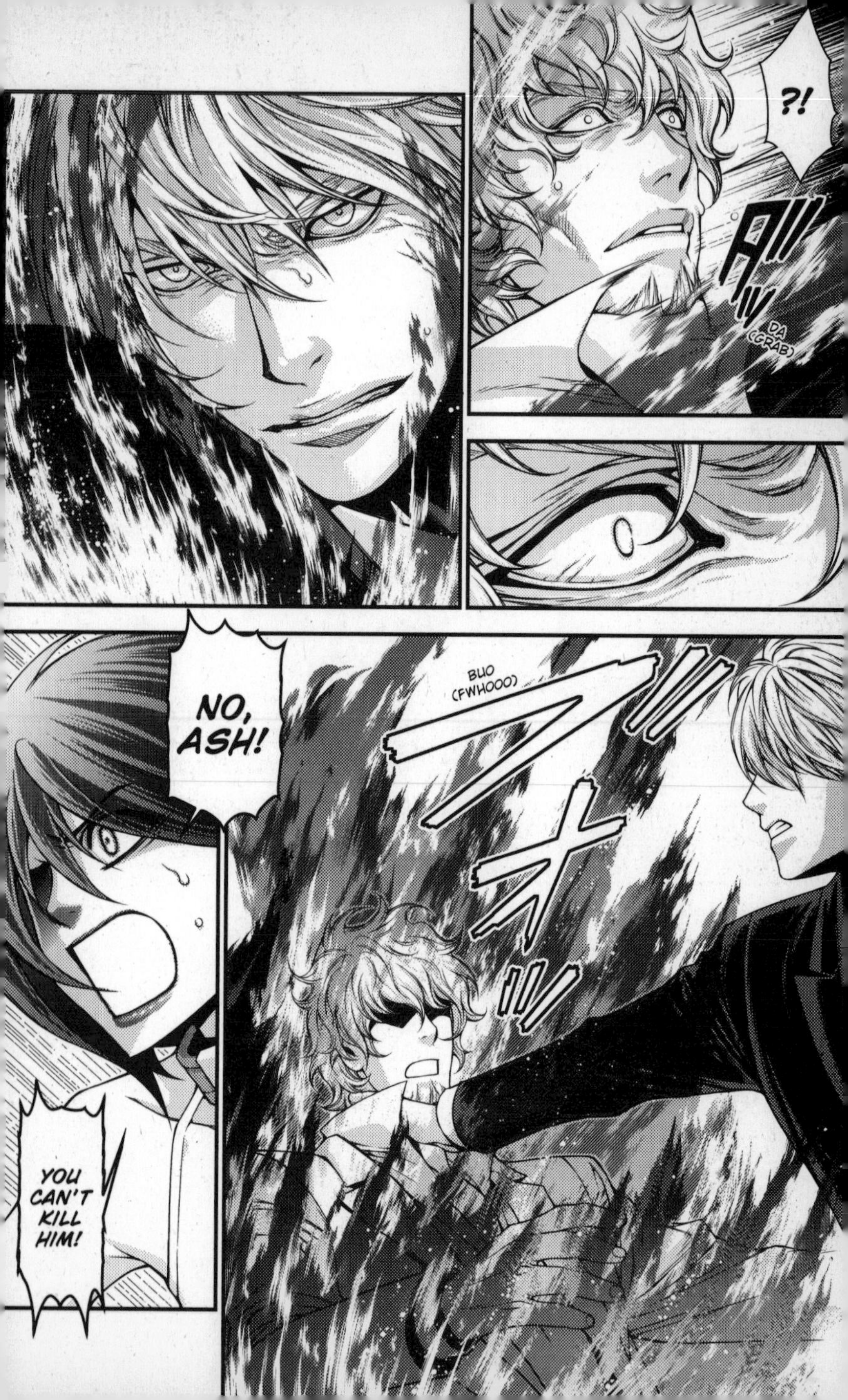
?!
DA (GRAB)
BUO (FWHOOO)
NO, ASH!
YOU CAN'T KILL HIM!

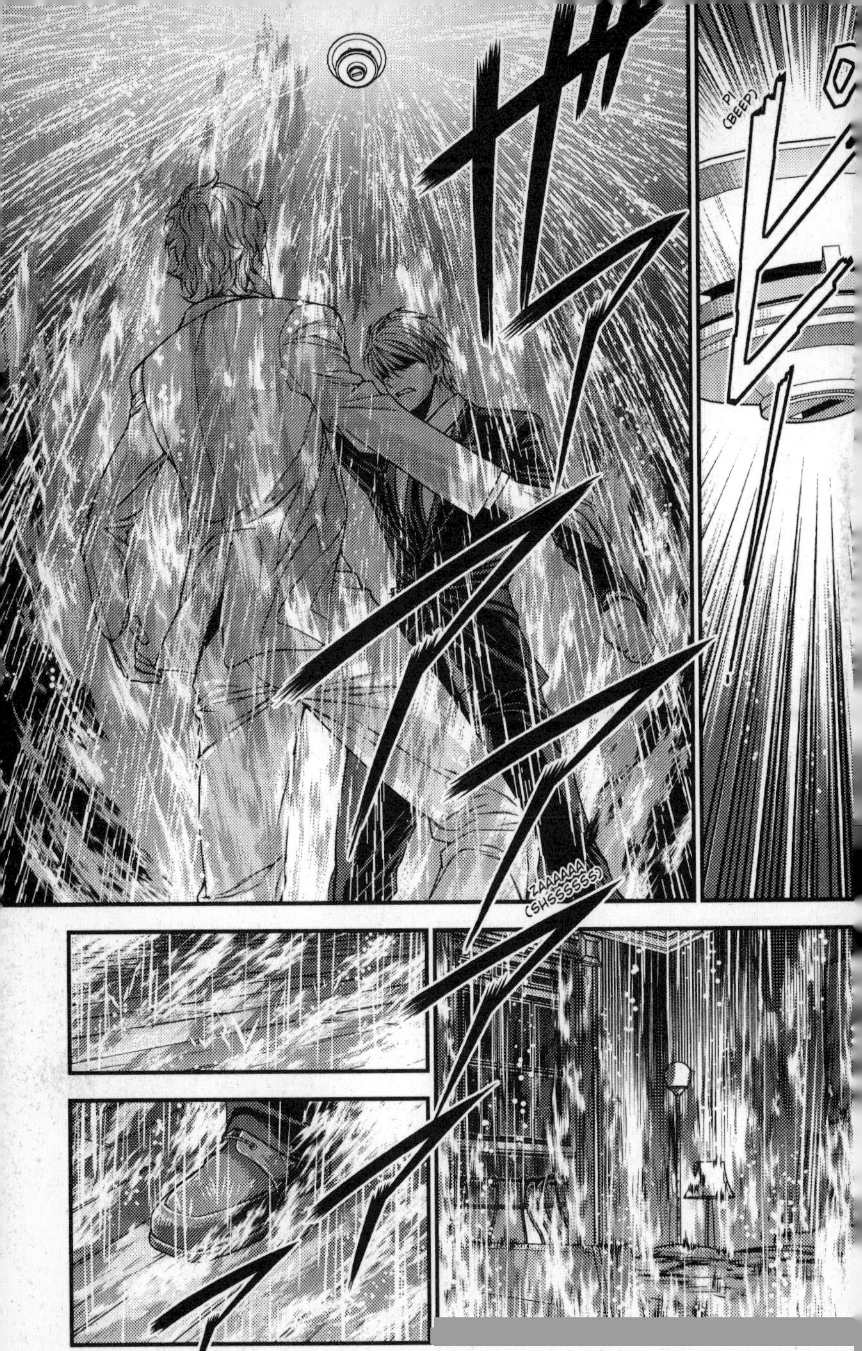
PI (BEEP)
ZAAAAAA (SHSSSSSSS)

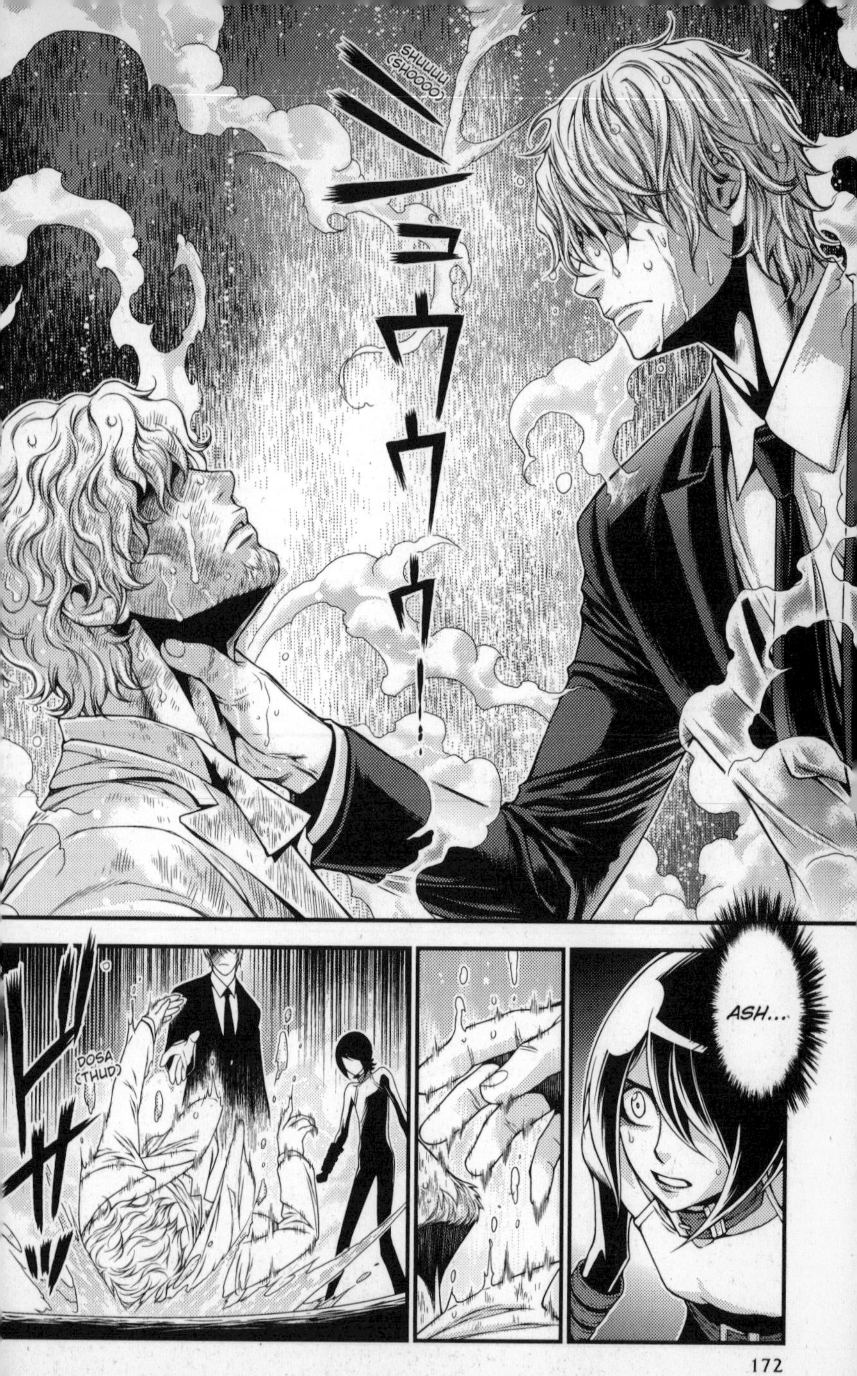
SHUUUNN (SHOOOO)
DOSA (THUD)
ASH...

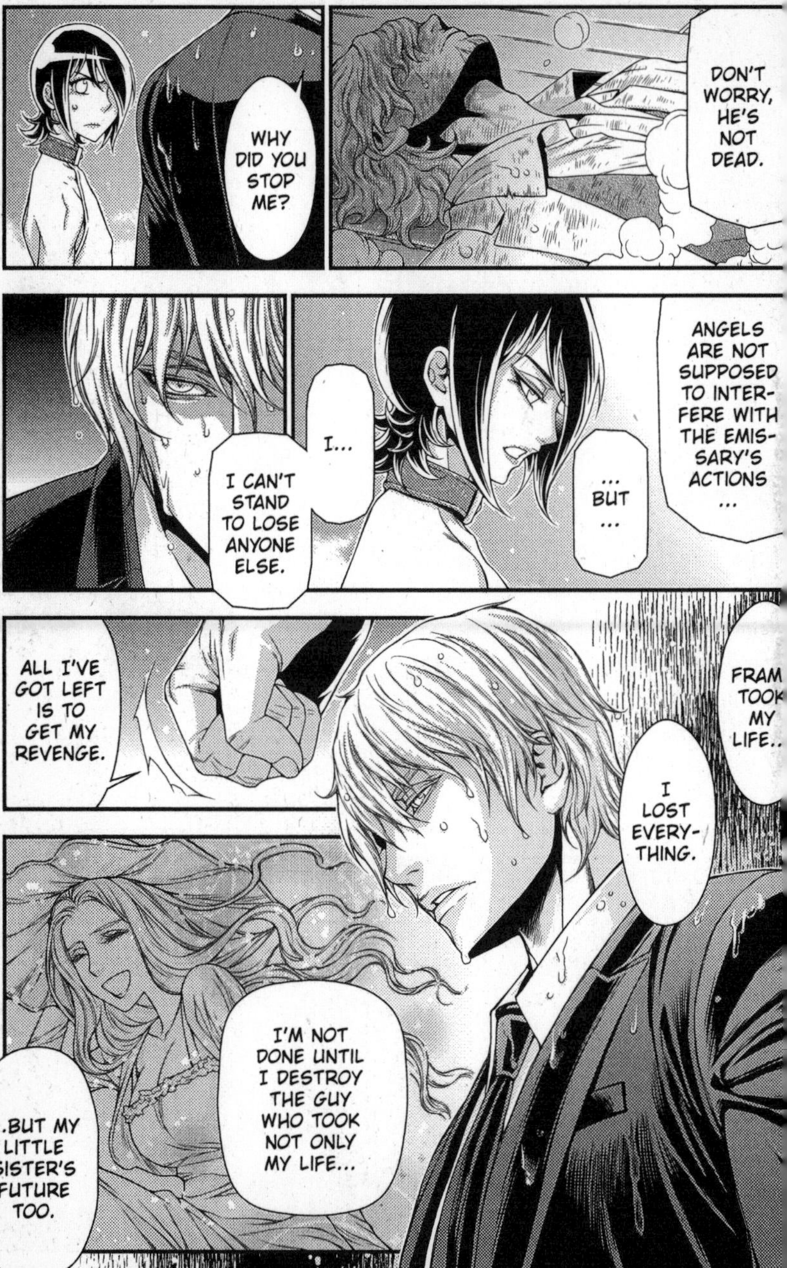
DON'T WORRY, HE'S NOT DEAD.
WHY DID YOU STOP ME?
ANGELS ARE NOT SUPPOSED TO INTER-FERE WITH THE EMIS-SARY'S ACTIONS ...
... BUT ...
I...
I CAN'T STAND TO LOSE ANYONE ELSE.
FRAM TOOK MY LIFE...
I LOST EVERY-THING.
ALL I'VE GOT LEFT IS TO GET MY REVENGE.
I'M NOT DONE UNTIL I DESTROY THE GUY WHO TOOK NOT ONLY MY LIFE...
...BUT MY LITTLE SISTER'S FUTURE TOO.

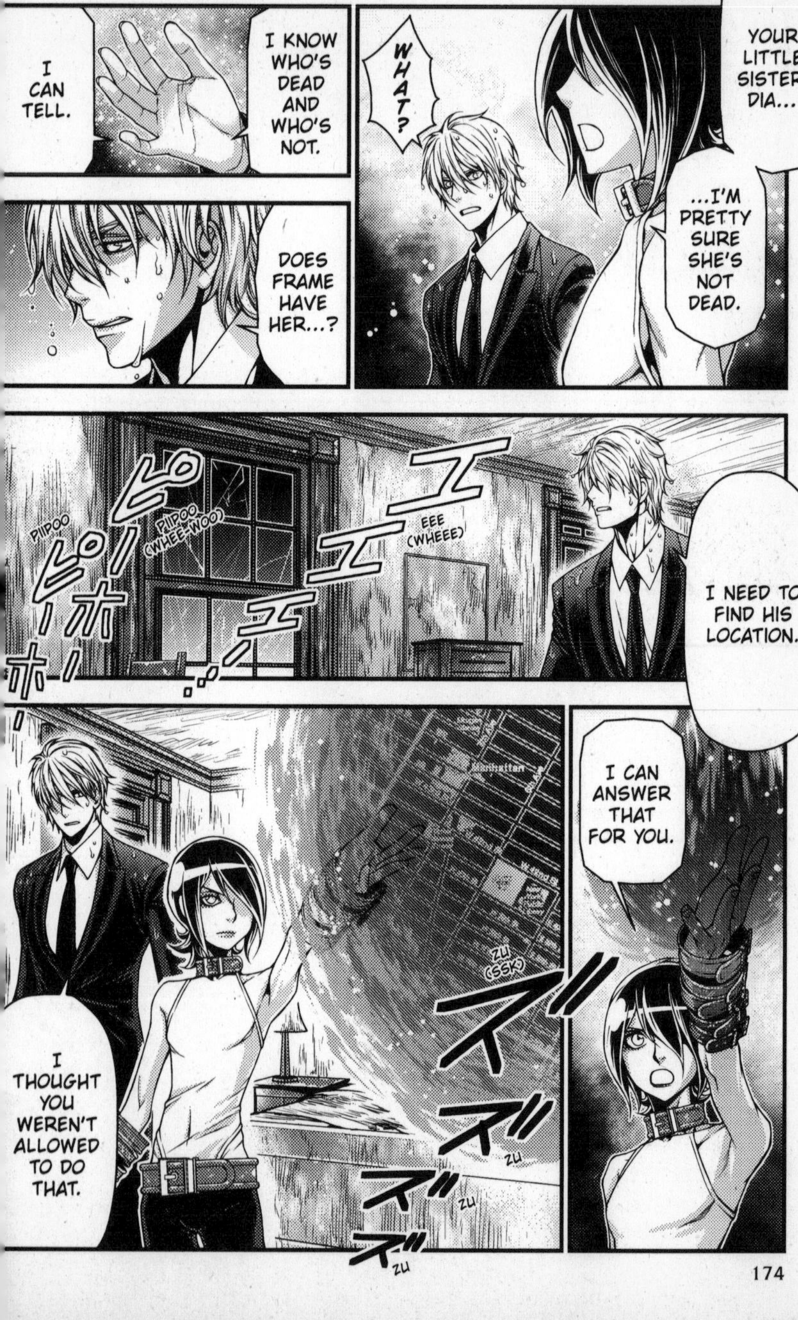
YOUR LITTLE SISTER, DIA...
WHAT?
...I'M PRETTY SURE SHE'S NOT DEAD.
I KNOW WHO'S DEAD AND WHO'S NOT.
I CAN TELL.
DOES FRAME HAVE HER...?
I NEED TO FIND HIS LOCATION.
EEE (WHEEE)
PIIPOO (WHEE-WOO)
PIIPOO
I CAN ANSWER THAT FOR YOU.
ZU (SSK)
ZU
ZU
ZU
I THOUGHT YOU WEREN'T ALLOWED TO DO THAT.

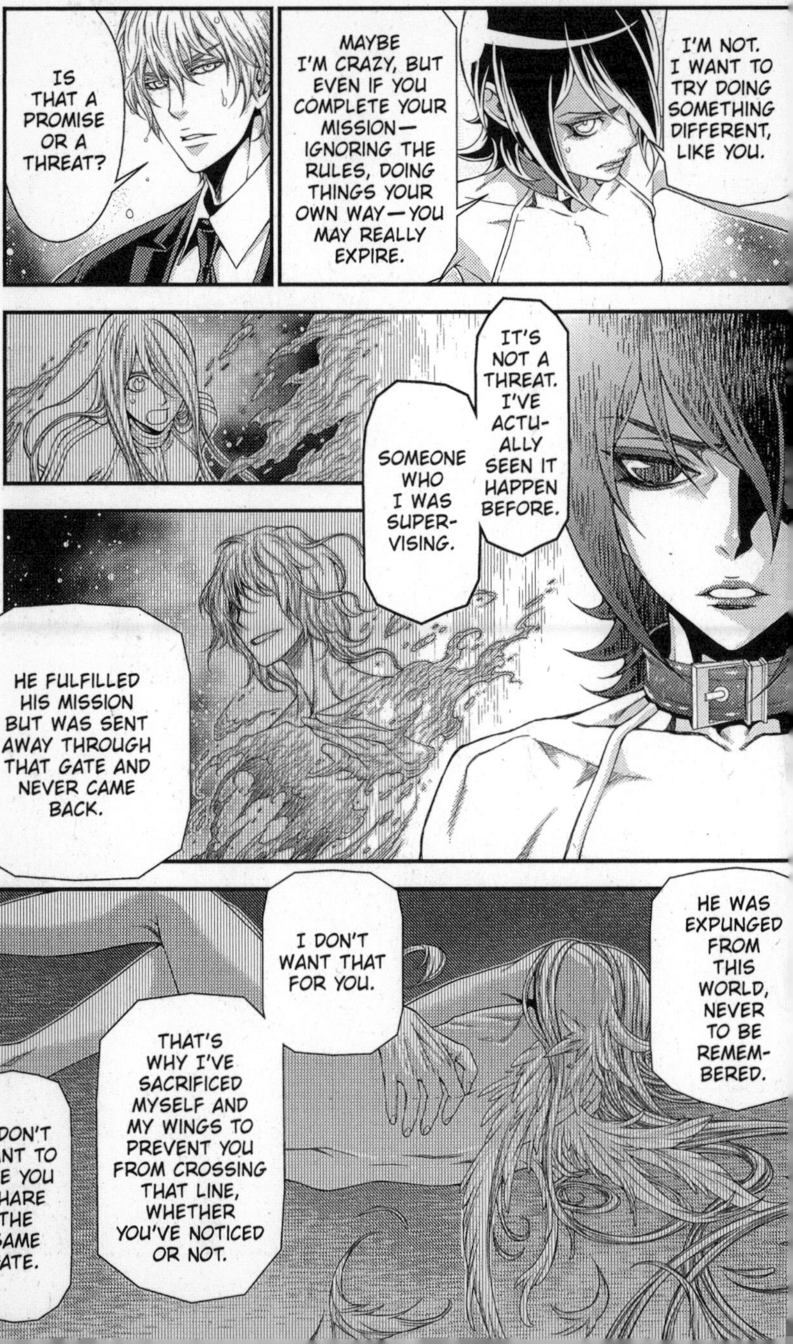
I'M NOT. I WANT TO TRY DOING SOMETHING DIFFERENT, LIKE YOU.
MAYBE I'M CRAZY, BUT EVEN IF YOU COMPLETE YOUR MISSION—IGNORING THE RULES, DOING THINGS YOUR OWN WAY—YOU MAY REALLY EXPIRE.
IS THAT A PROMISE OR A THREAT?
IT'S NOT A THREAT. I'VE ACTU-ALLY SEEN IT HAPPEN BEFORE.
SOMEONE WHO I WAS SUPER-VISING.
HE FULFILLED HIS MISSION BUT WAS SENT AWAY THROUGH THAT GATE AND NEVER CAME BACK.
HE WAS EXPUNGED FROM THIS WORLD, NEVER TO BE REMEM-BERED.
I DON'T WANT THAT FOR YOU.
THAT'S WHY I'VE SACRIFICED MYSELF AND MY WINGS TO PREVENT YOU FROM CROSSING THAT LINE, WHETHER YOU'VE NOTICED OR NOT.
I DON'T WANT TO SEE YOU SHARE THE SAME FATE.

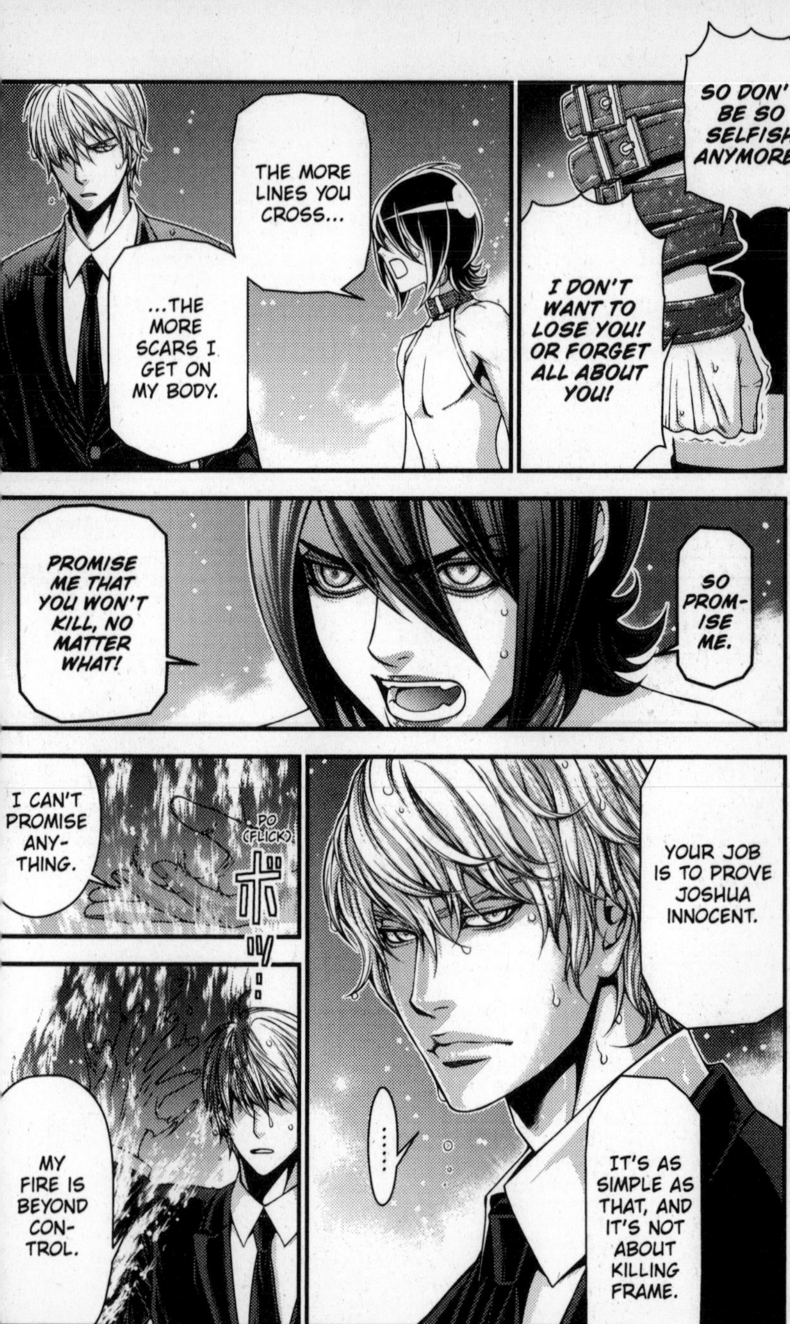
SO DON'T BE SO SELFISH ANYMORE!
I DON'T WANT TO LOSE YOU! OR FORGET ALL ABOUT YOU!
THE MORE LINES YOU CROSS...
...THE MORE SCARS I GET ON MY BODY.
SO PROMISE ME.
PROMISE ME THAT YOU WON'T KILL, NO MATTER WHAT!
YOUR JOB IS TO PROVE JOSHUA INNOCENT.
IT'S AS SIMPLE AS THAT, AND IT'S NOT ABOUT KILLING FRAME.
......
I CAN'T PROMISE ANYTHING.
PO (FLICK)
MY FIRE IS BEYOND CONTROL.

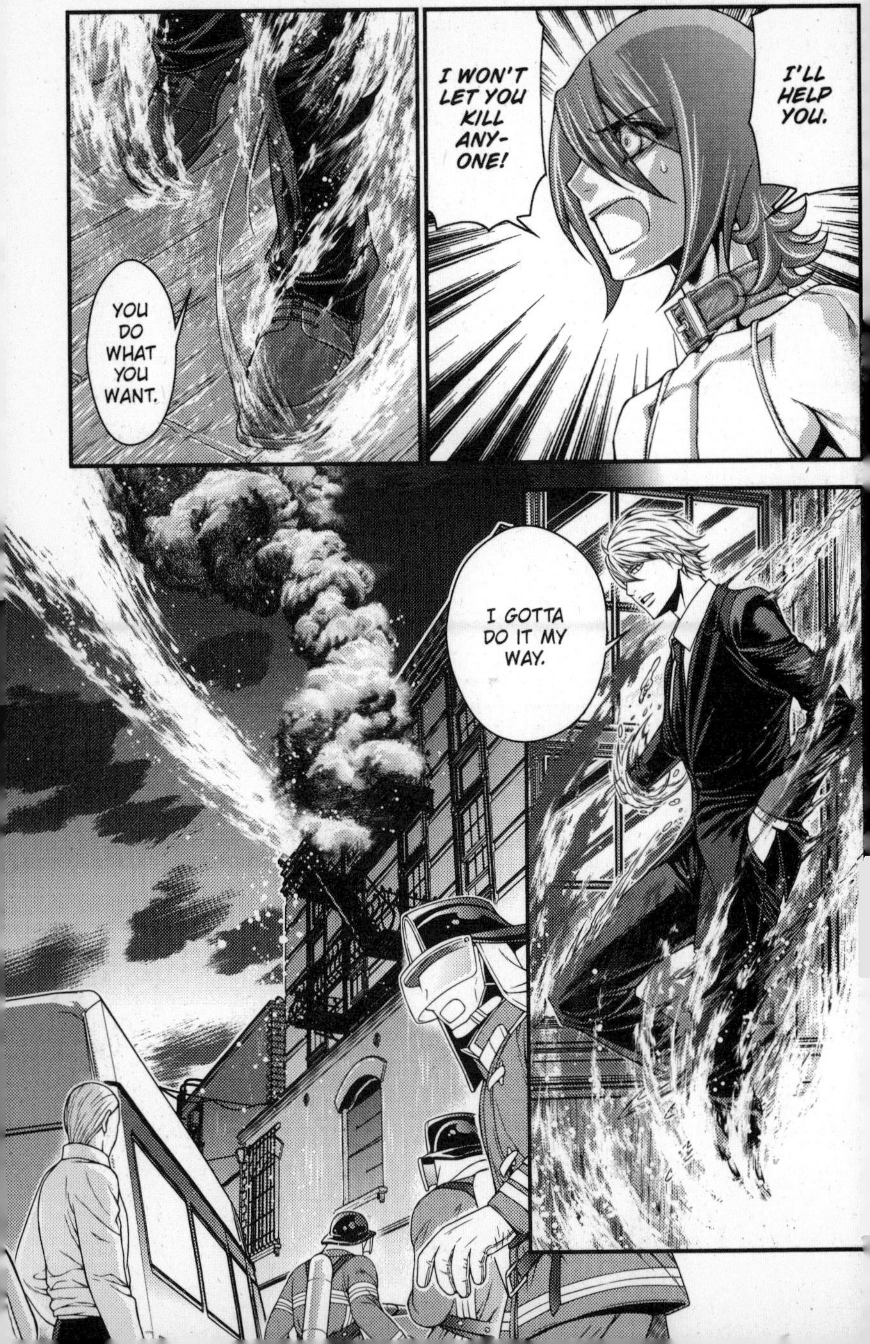
I'LL HELP YOU.
I WON'T LET YOU KILL ANY-ONE!
YOU DO WHAT YOU WANT.
I GOTTA DO IT MY WAY.

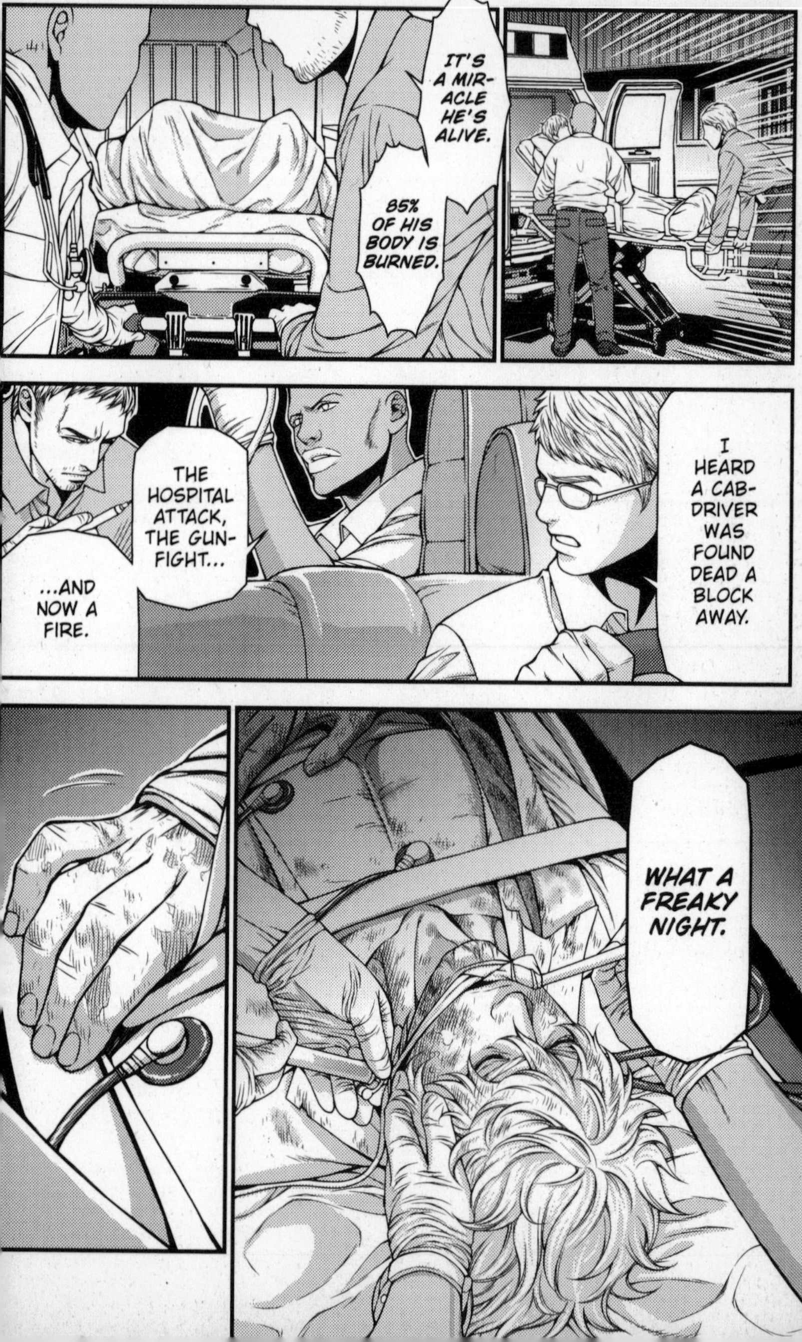
IT'S A MIRACLE HE'S ALIVE.
85% OF HIS BODY IS BURNED.
I HEARD A CAB-DRIVER WAS FOUND DEAD A BLOCK AWAY.
THE HOSPITAL ATTACK, THE GUNFIGHT...
...AND NOW A FIRE.
WHAT A FREAKY NIGHT.

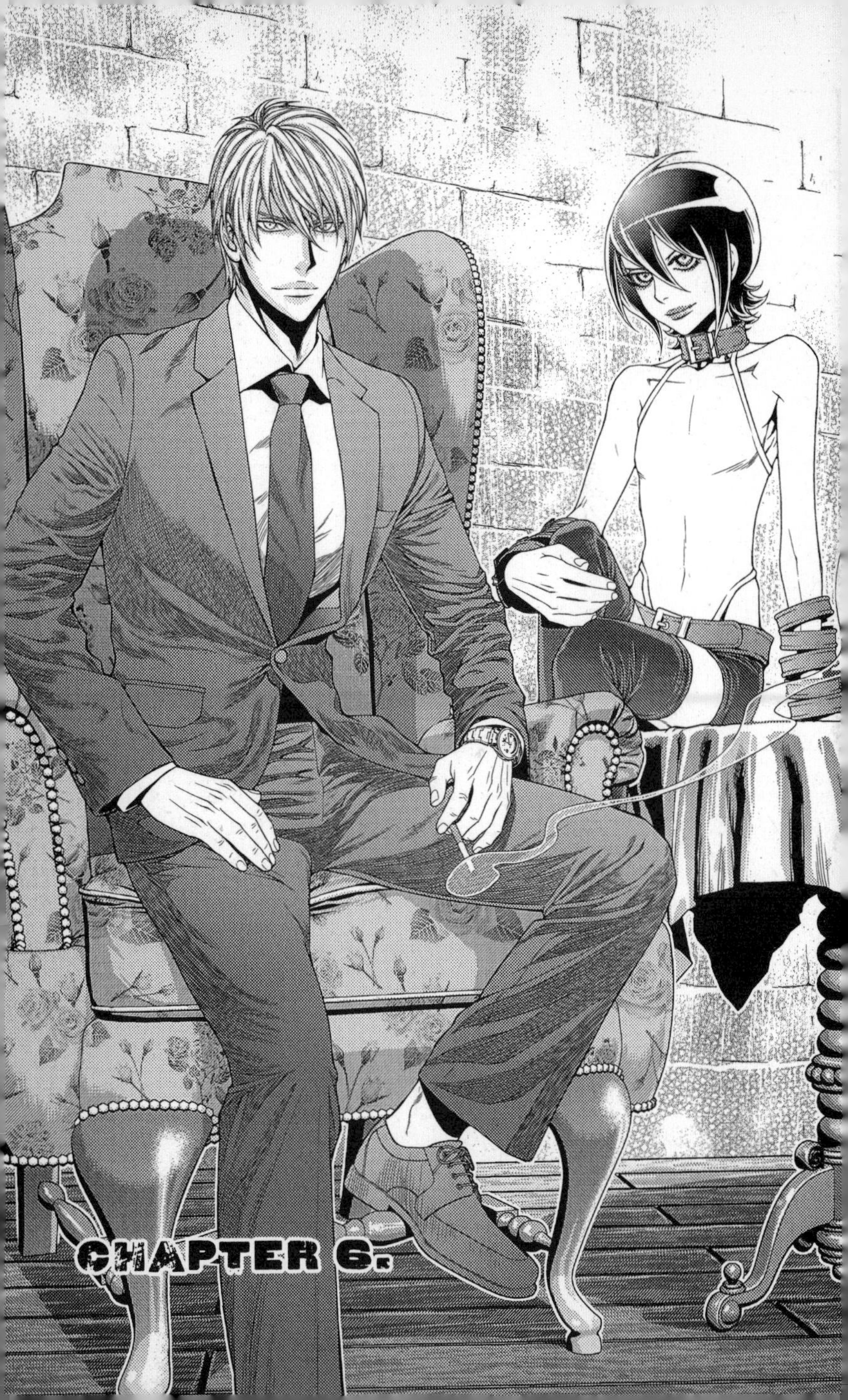
CHAPTER 6.

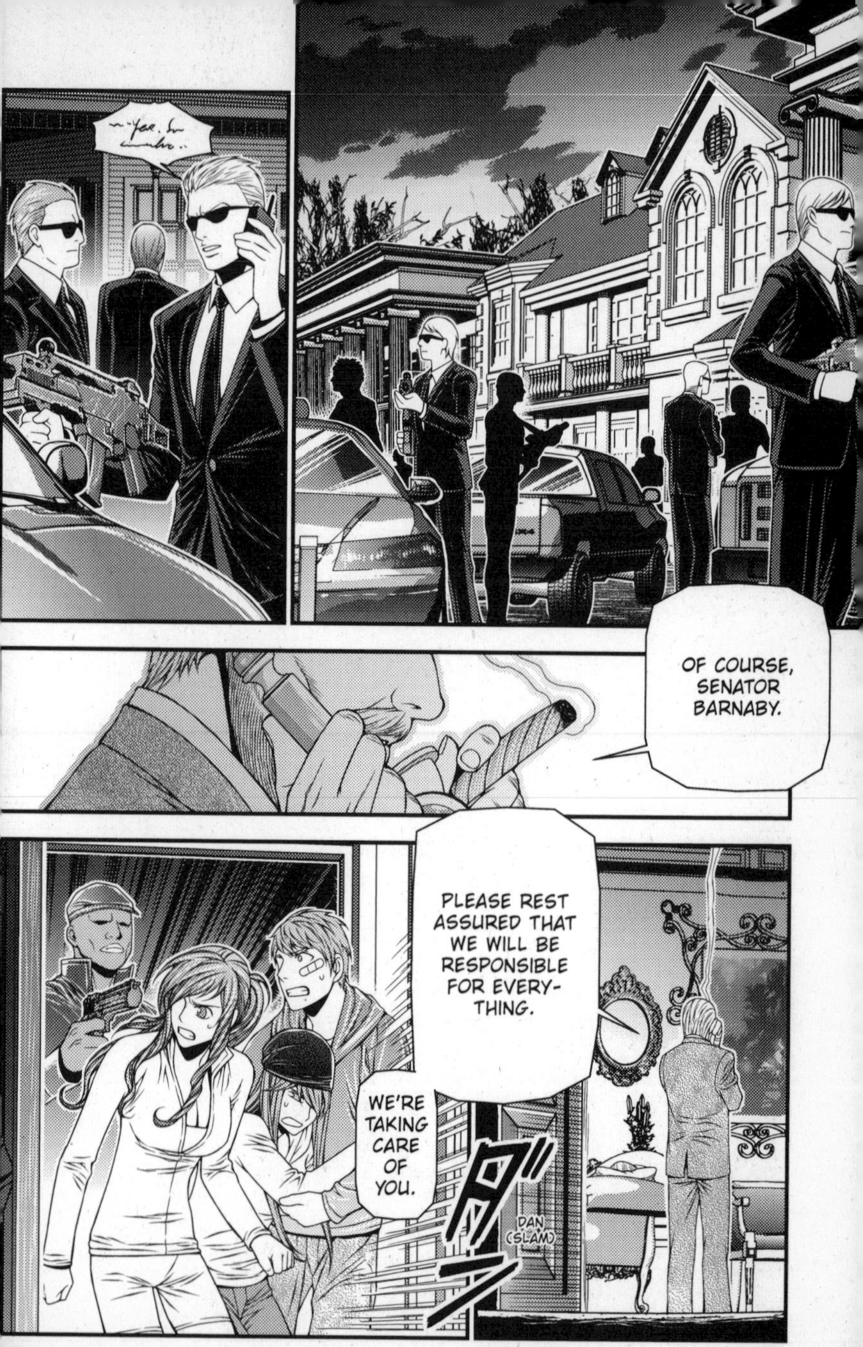
OF COURSE, SENATOR BARNABY.
PLEASE REST ASSURED THAT WE WILL BE RESPONSIBLE FOR EVERY-THING.
DAN (SLAM)
WE'RE TAKING CARE OF YOU.

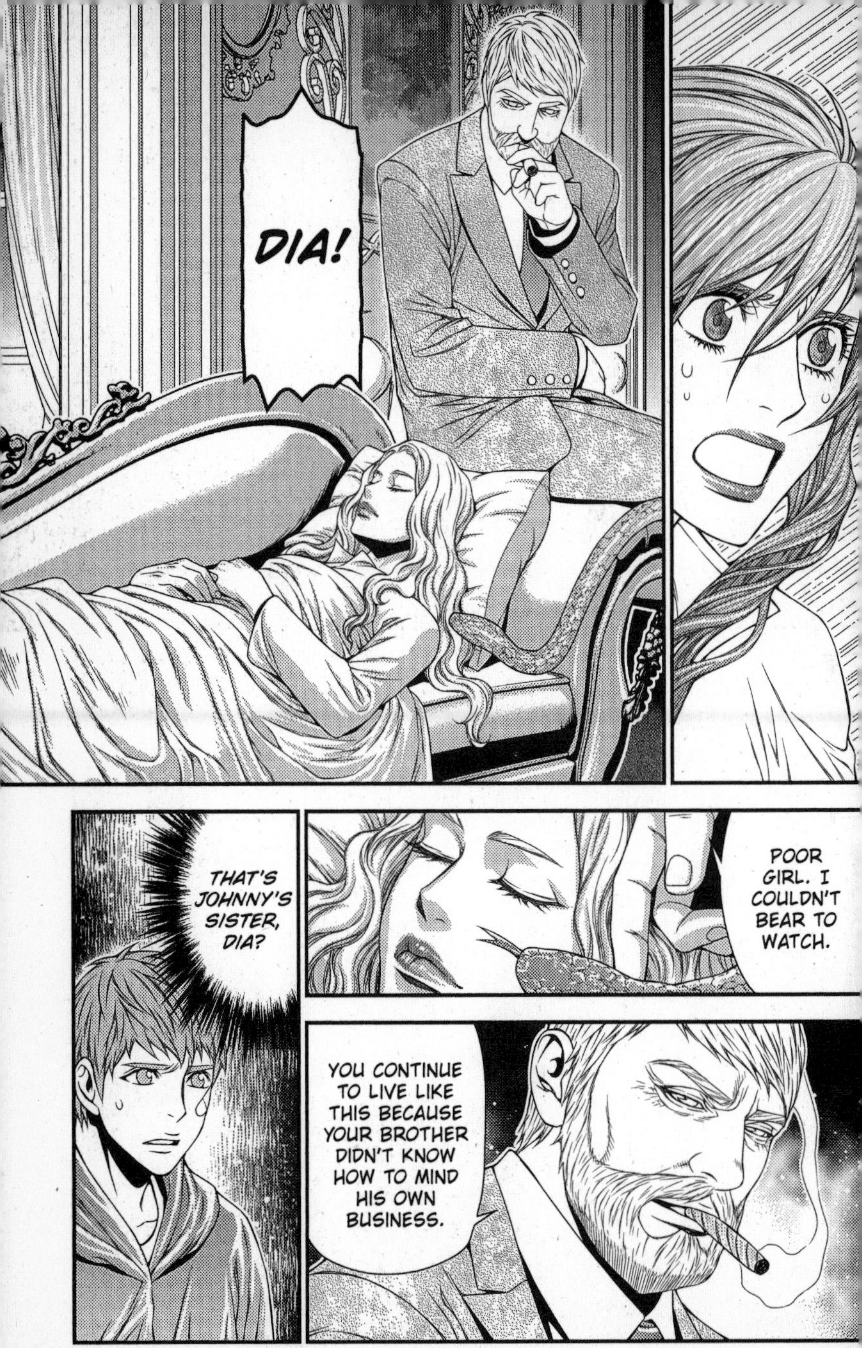
DIA!
POOR GIRL. I COULDN'T BEAR TO WATCH.
YOU CONTINUE TO LIVE LIKE THIS BECAUSE YOUR BROTHER DIDN'T KNOW HOW TO MIND HIS OWN BUSINESS.
THAT'S JOHNNY'S SISTER, DIA?

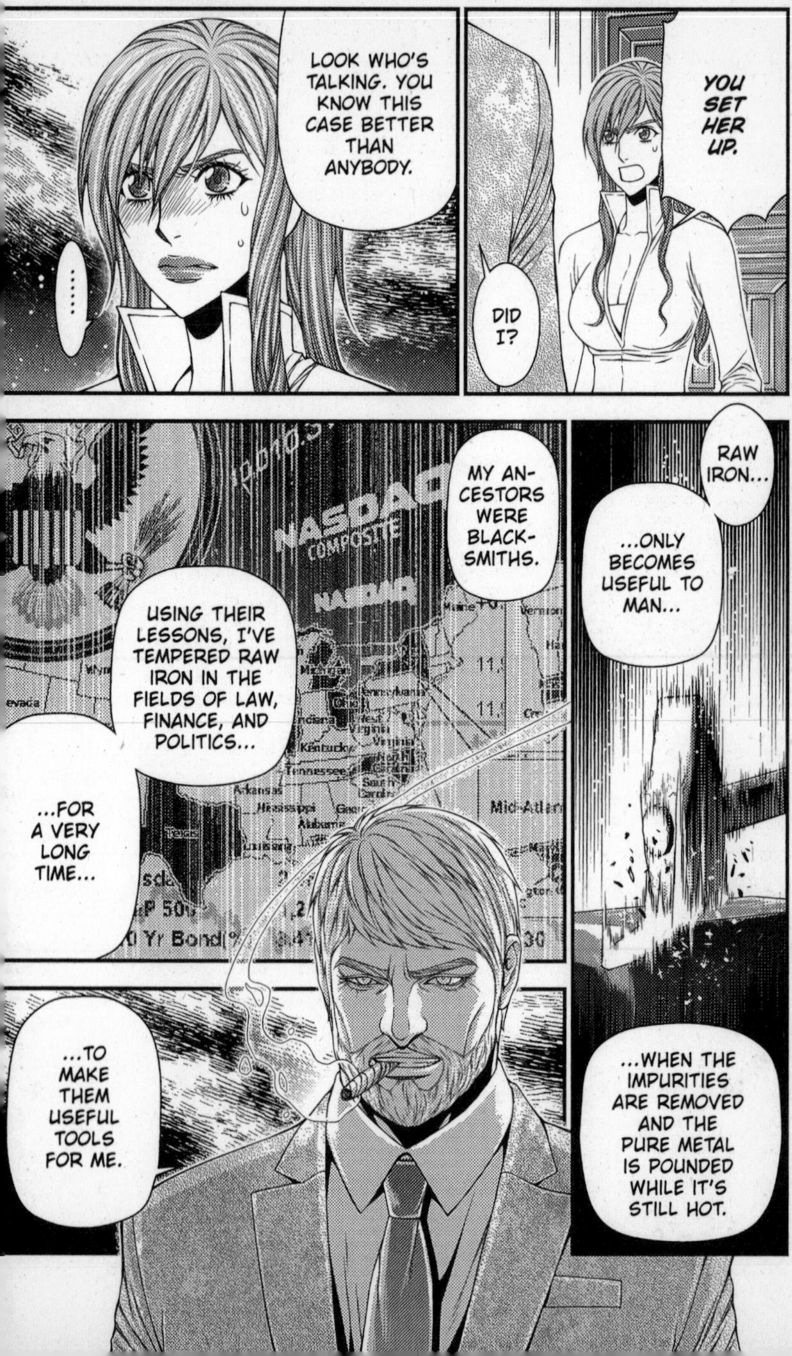
YOU SET HER UP.
DID I?
LOOK WHO'S TALKING. YOU KNOW THIS CASE BETTER THAN ANYBODY.
......
RAW IRON...
...ONLY BECOMES USEFUL TO MAN...
...WHEN THE IMPURITIES ARE REMOVED AND THE PURE METAL IS POUNDED WHILE IT'S STILL HOT.
MY ANCESTORS WERE BLACKSMITHS.
USING THEIR LESSONS, I'VE TEMPERED RAW IRON IN THE FIELDS OF LAW, FINANCE, AND POLITICS...
...FOR A VERY LONG TIME...
...TO MAKE THEM USEFUL TOOLS FOR ME.

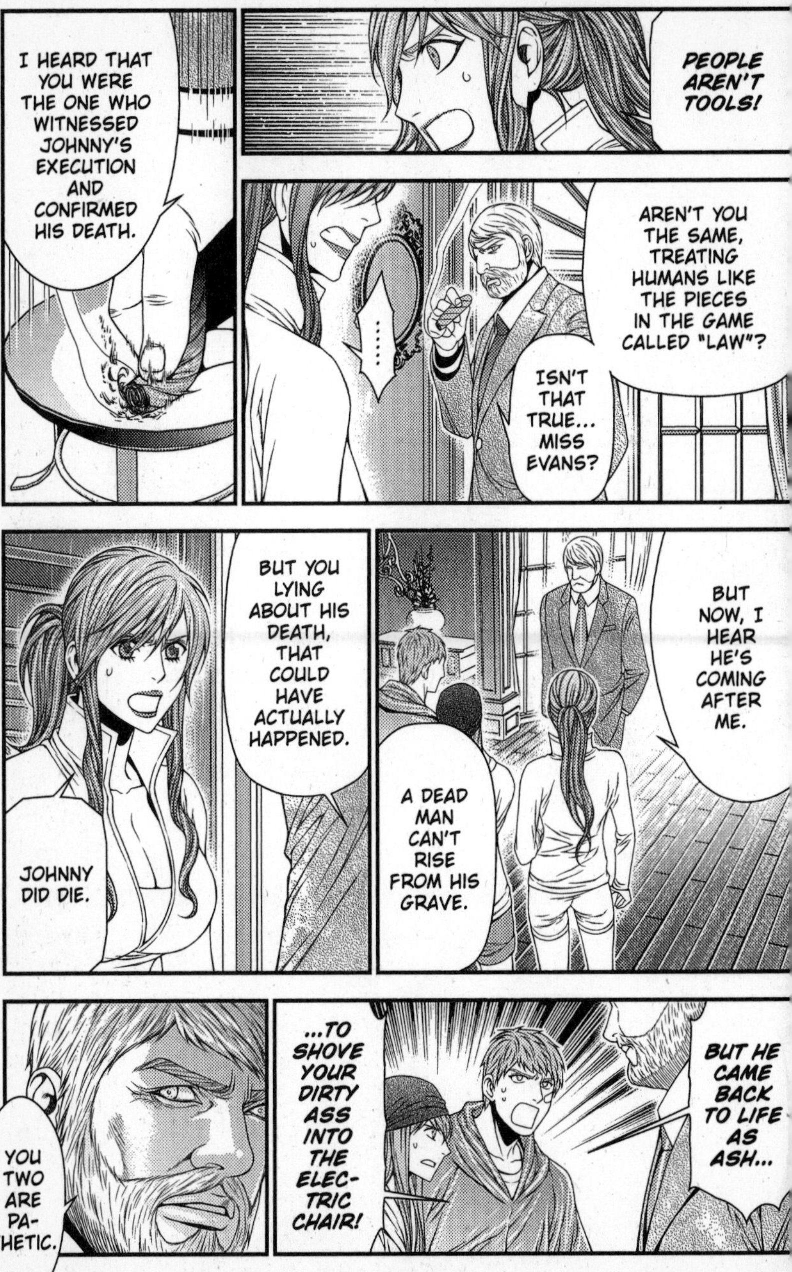
PEOPLE AREN'T TOOLS!
......
AREN'T YOU THE SAME, TREATING HUMANS LIKE THE PIECES IN THE GAME CALLED "LAW"?
ISN'T THAT TRUE... MISS EVANS?
I HEARD THAT YOU WERE THE ONE WHO WITNESSED JOHNNY'S EXECUTION AND CONFIRMED HIS DEATH.
BUT NOW, I HEAR HE'S COMING AFTER ME.
A DEAD MAN CAN'T RISE FROM HIS GRAVE.
BUT YOU LYING ABOUT HIS DEATH, THAT COULD HAVE ACTUALLY HAPPENED.
JOHNNY DID DIE.
BUT HE CAME BACK TO LIFE AS ASH...
...TO SHOVE YOUR DIRTY ASS INTO THE ELEC-TRIC CHAIR!
YOU TWO ARE PA-THETIC.

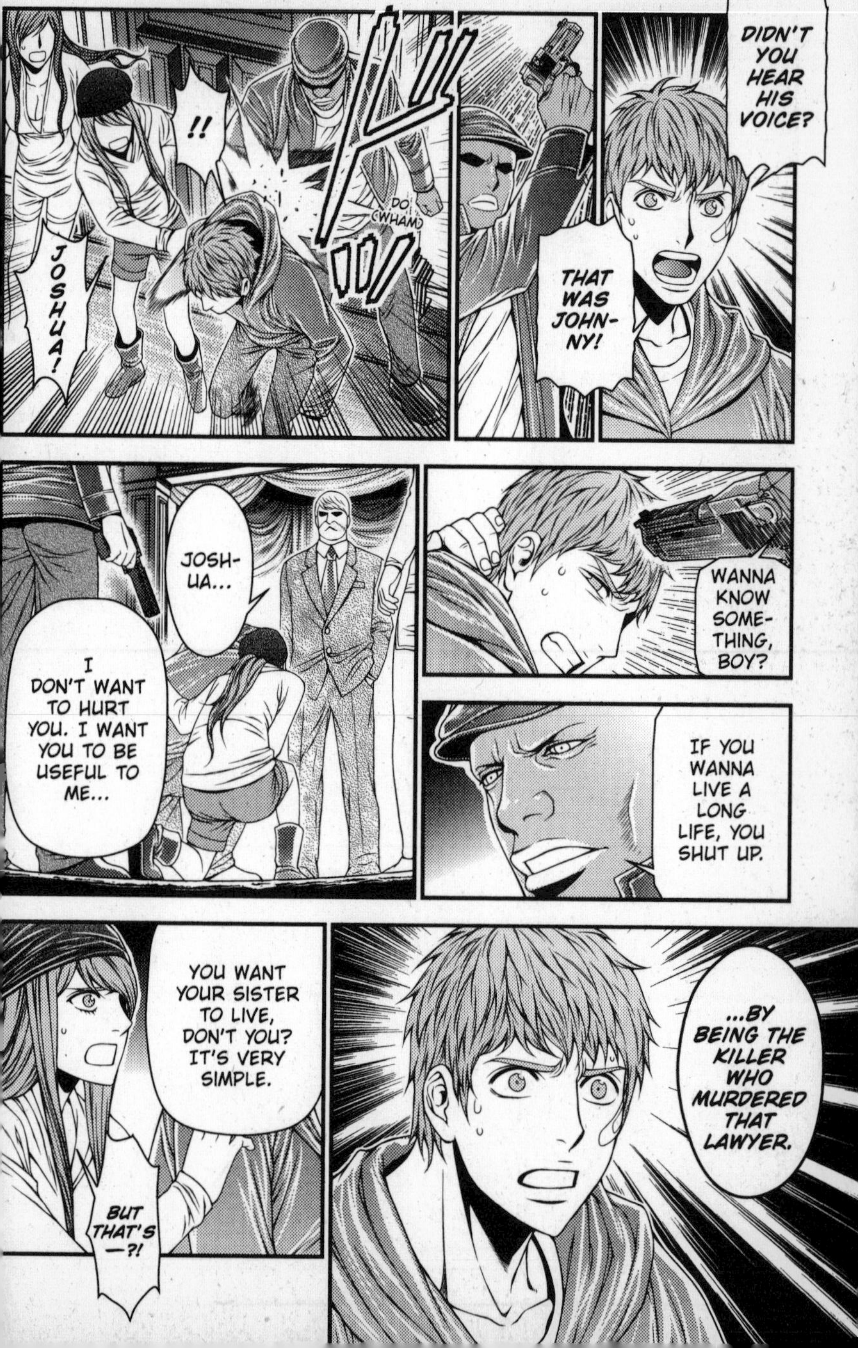

!!
DO (WHAM)
JOSHUA!
DIDN'T YOU HEAR HIS VOICE?
THAT WAS JOHNNY!
JOSH-UA...
I DON'T WANT TO HURT YOU. I WANT YOU TO BE USEFUL TO ME...
WANNA KNOW SOMETHING, BOY?
IF YOU WANNA LIVE A LONG LIFE, YOU SHUT UP.
YOU WANT YOUR SISTER TO LIVE, DON'T YOU? IT'S VERY SIMPLE.
BUT THAT'S—?!
...BY BEING THE KILLER WHO MURDERED THAT LAWYER.

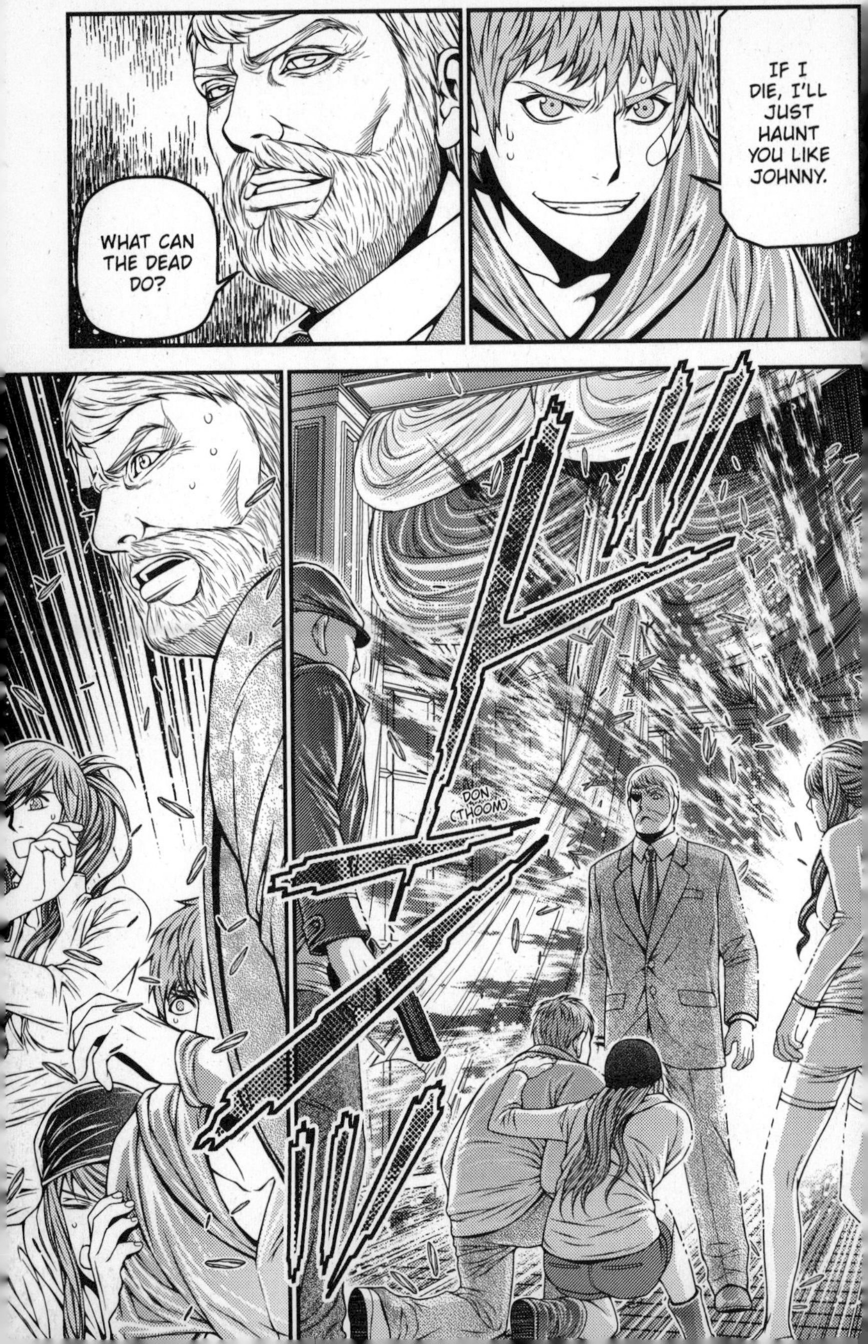
IF I DIE, I'LL JUST HAUNT YOU LIKE JOHNNY.
WHAT CAN THE DEAD DO?
DON (THOOM)

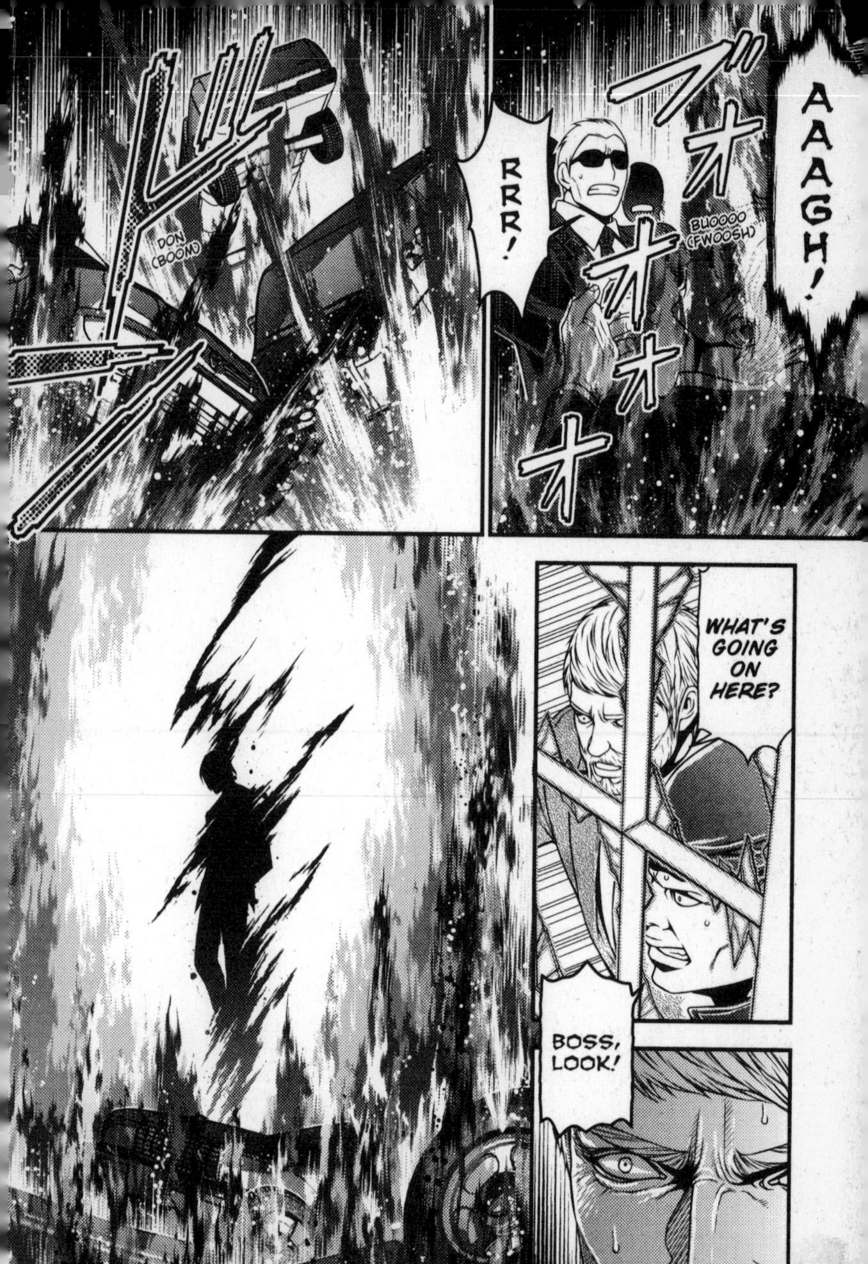
AAAGH!
BUOOOO (FWOOSH)
RRR!
DON (BOOM)
WHAT'S GOING ON HERE?
BOSS, LOOK!

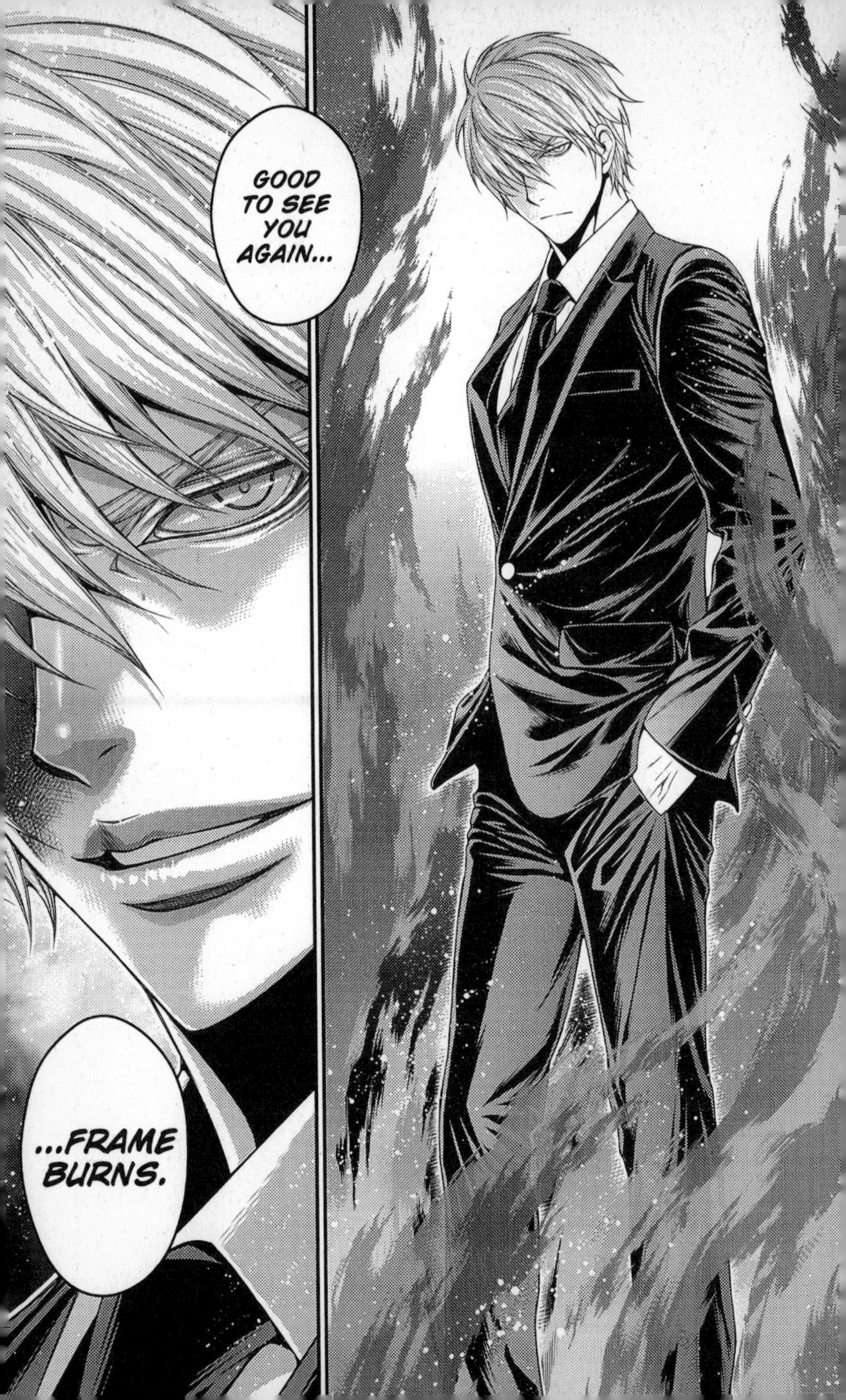
GOOD TO SEE YOU AGAIN...
...FRAME BURNS.

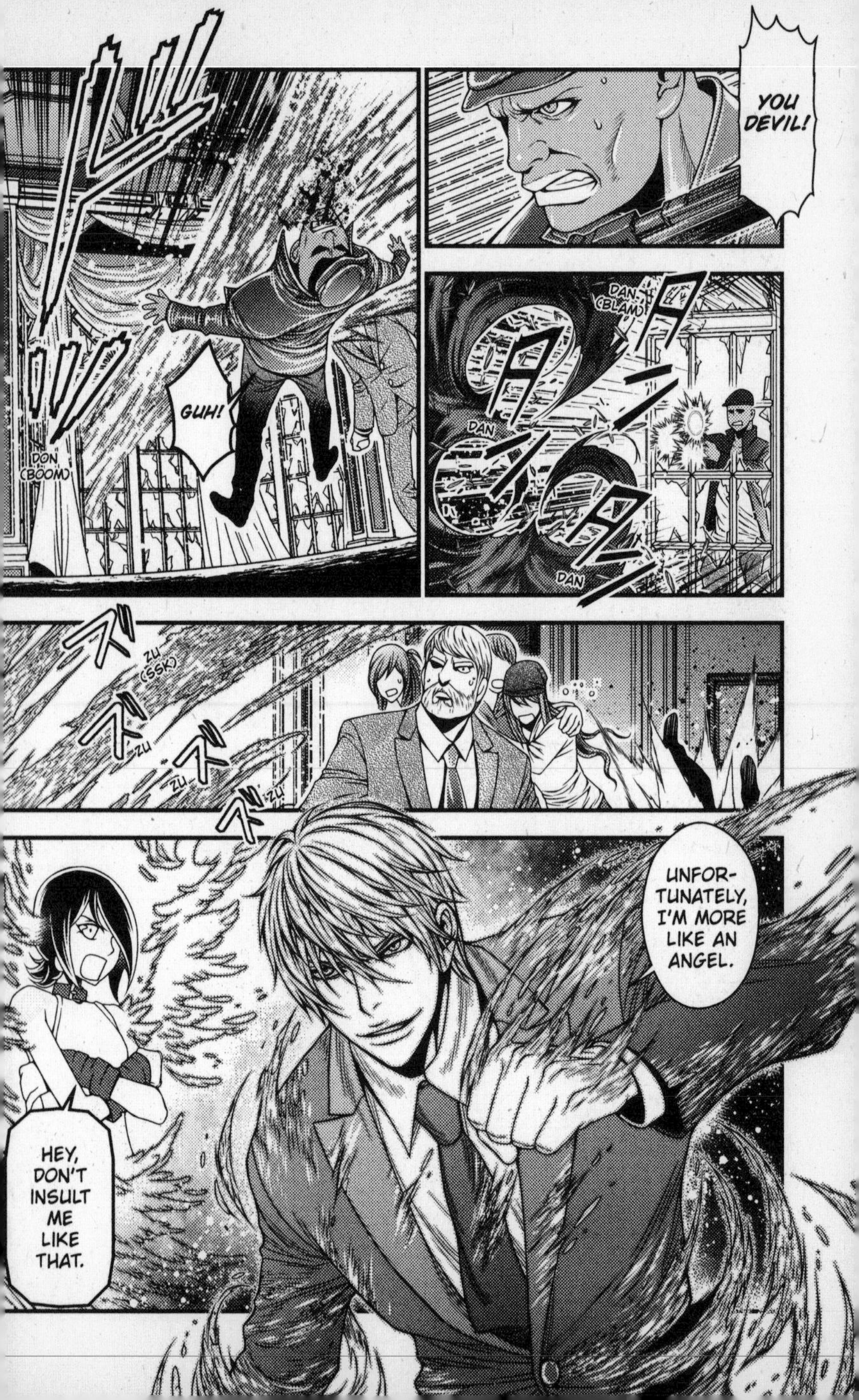
YOU DEVIL!
DAN (BLAM)
DAN
DAN
GUH!
DON (BOOM)
ZU (SSK)
ZU
ZU
ZU
UNFORTUNATELY, I'M MORE LIKE AN ANGEL.
HEY, DON'T INSULT ME LIKE THAT.

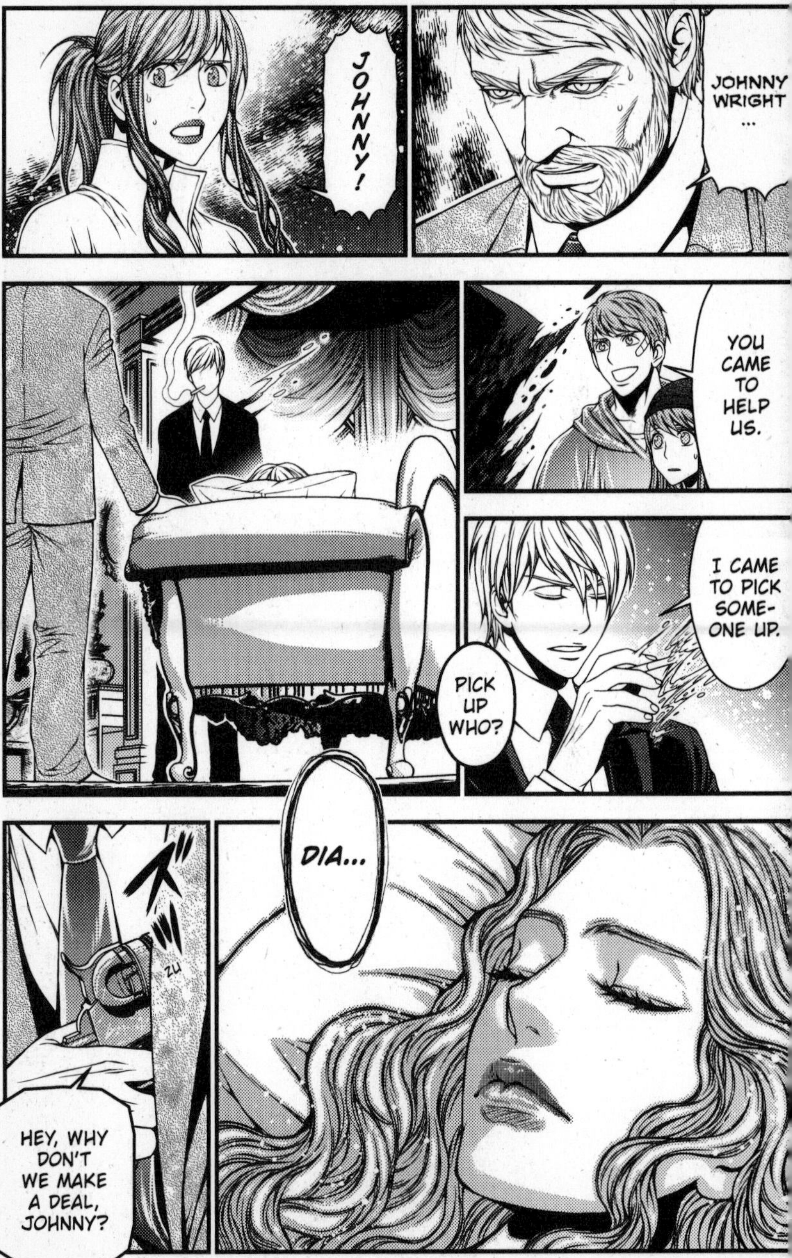
JOHNNY WRIGHT ...
JOHNNY!
YOU CAME TO HELP US.
I CAME TO PICK SOME-ONE UP.
PICK UP WHO?
DIA...
ズ
ZU
HEY, WHY DON'T WE MAKE A DEAL, JOHNNY?

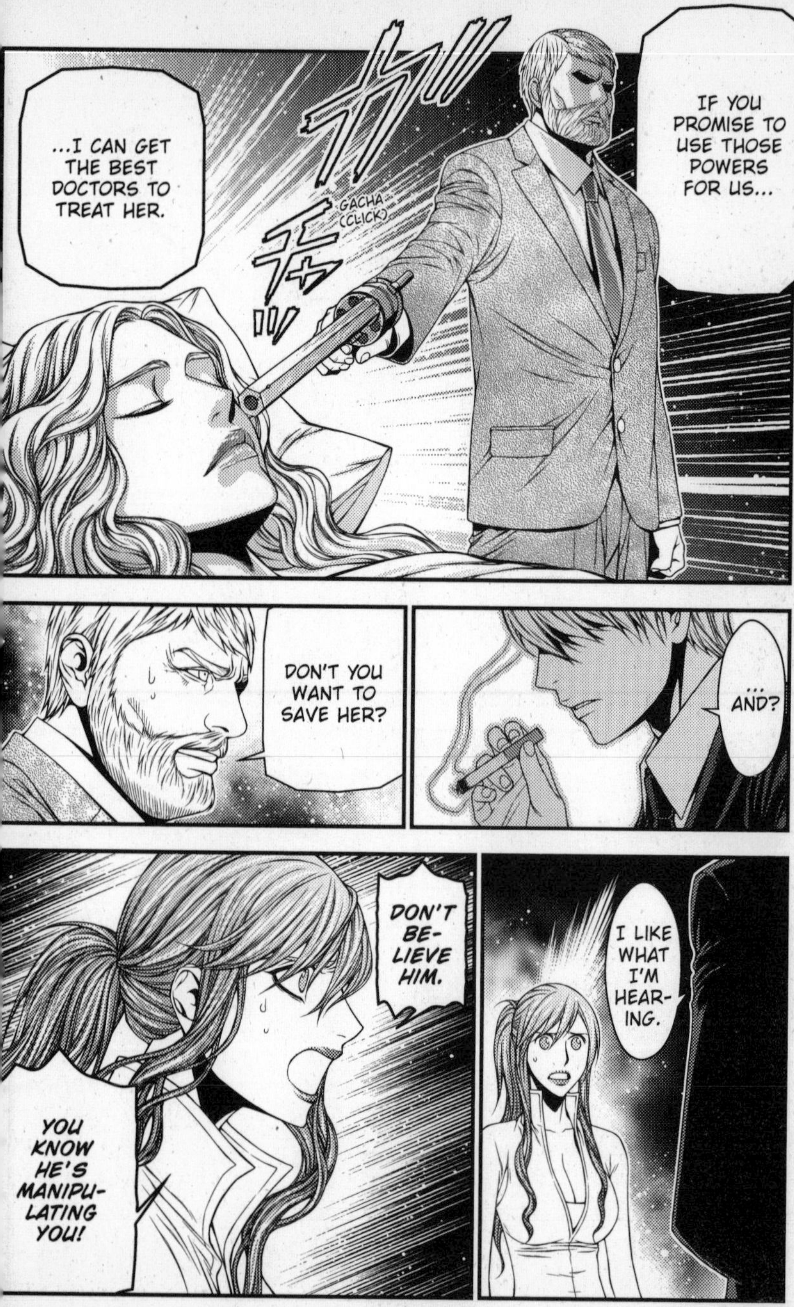
IF YOU PROMISE TO USE THOSE POWERS FOR US...
...I CAN GET THE BEST DOCTORS TO TREAT HER.
GACHA (CLICK)
... AND?
DON'T YOU WANT TO SAVE HER?
I LIKE WHAT I'M HEAR-ING.
DON'T BE-LIEVE HIM.
YOU KNOW HE'S MANIPU-LATING YOU!

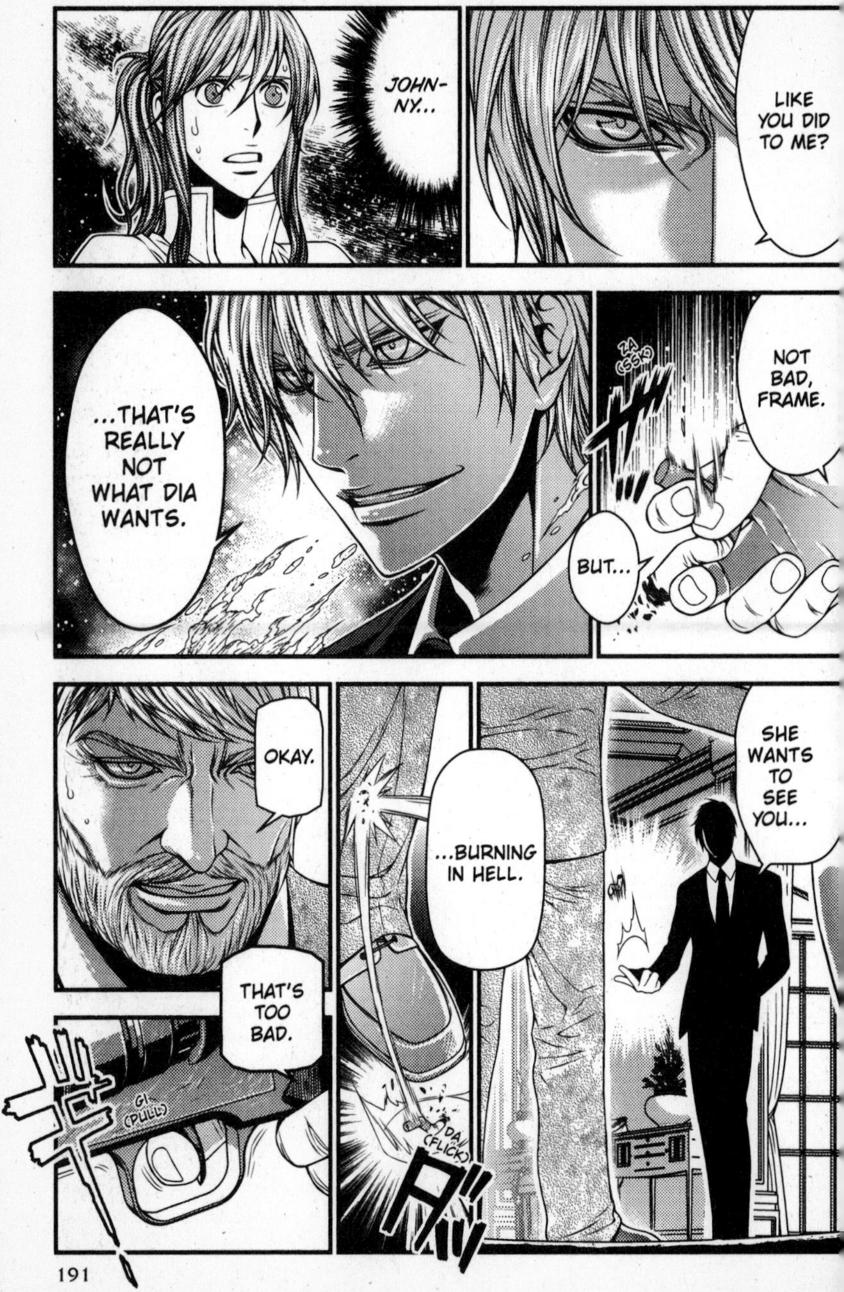
LIKE YOU DID TO ME?
JOHN-NY...
ZA (SSK)
NOT BAD, FRAME.
BUT...
...THAT'S REALLY NOT WHAT DIA WANTS.
SHE WANTS TO SEE YOU...
...BURNING IN HELL.
DA (FLICK)
OKAY.
THAT'S TOO BAD.
GI (PULL)

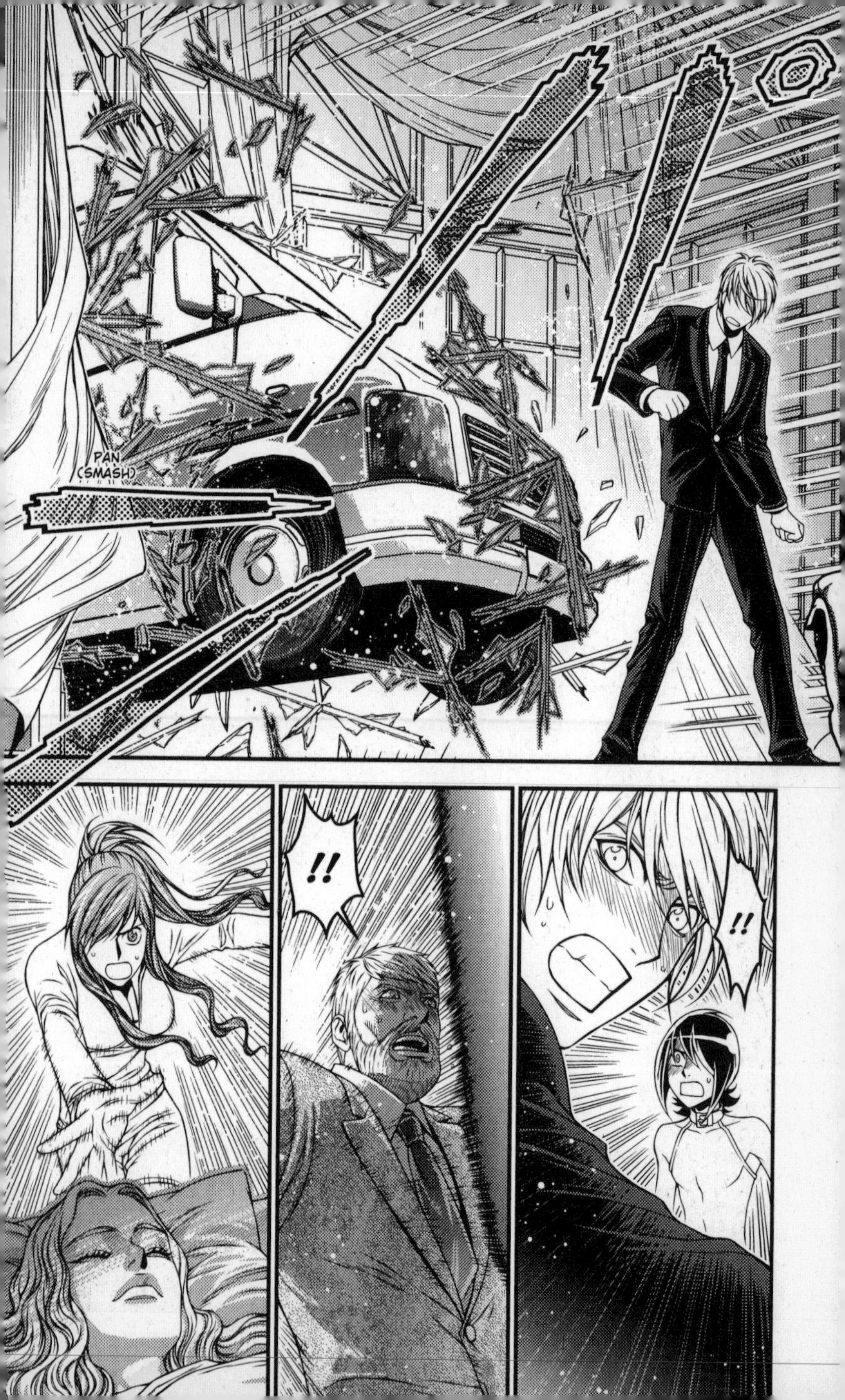
PAN
(SMASH)
!!
!!

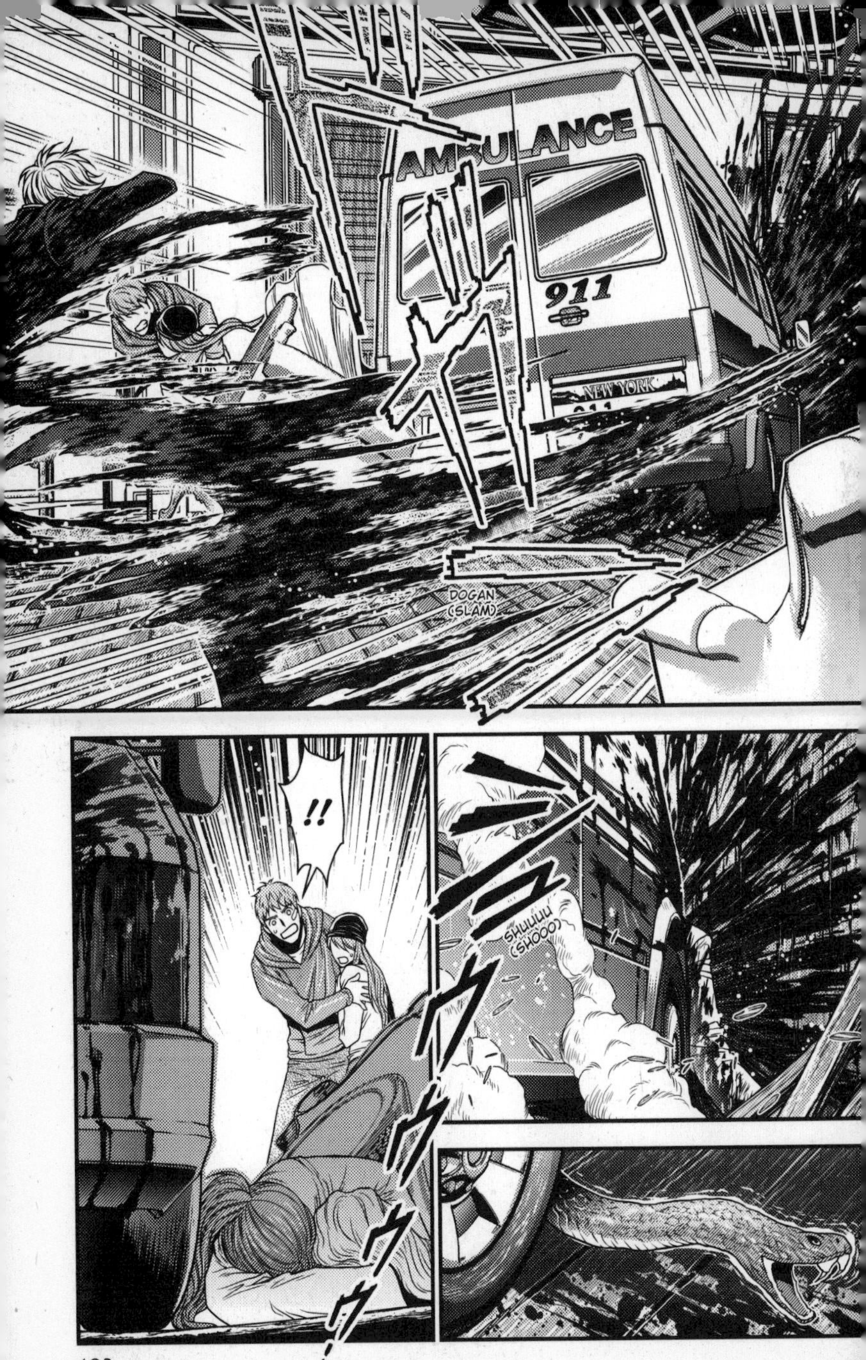
AMBULANCE
911
NEW YORK
DOGAN
(SLAM)
SHUUUUN
(SHOOO)
!!

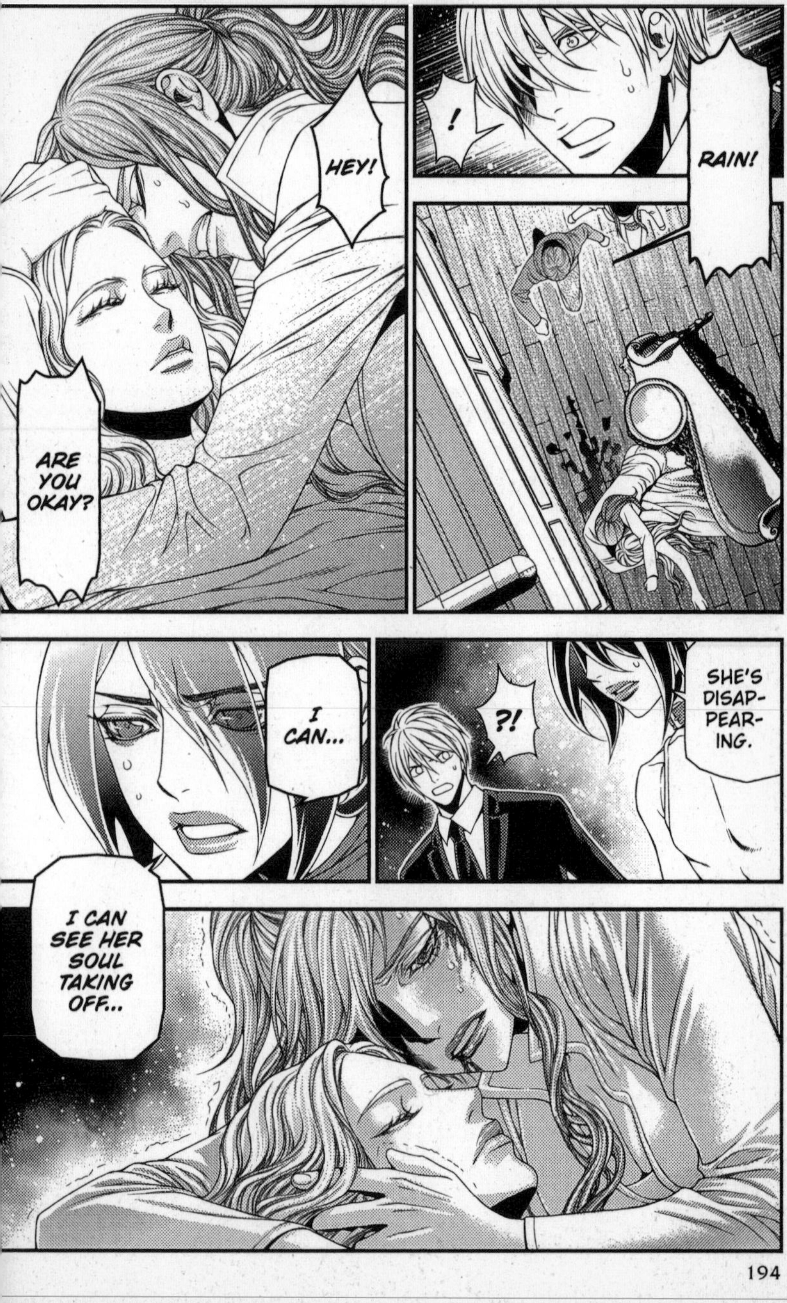
RAIN!
!
HEY!
ARE YOU OKAY?
SHE'S DISAP-PEARING.
?!
I CAN...
I CAN SEE HER SOUL TAKING OFF...

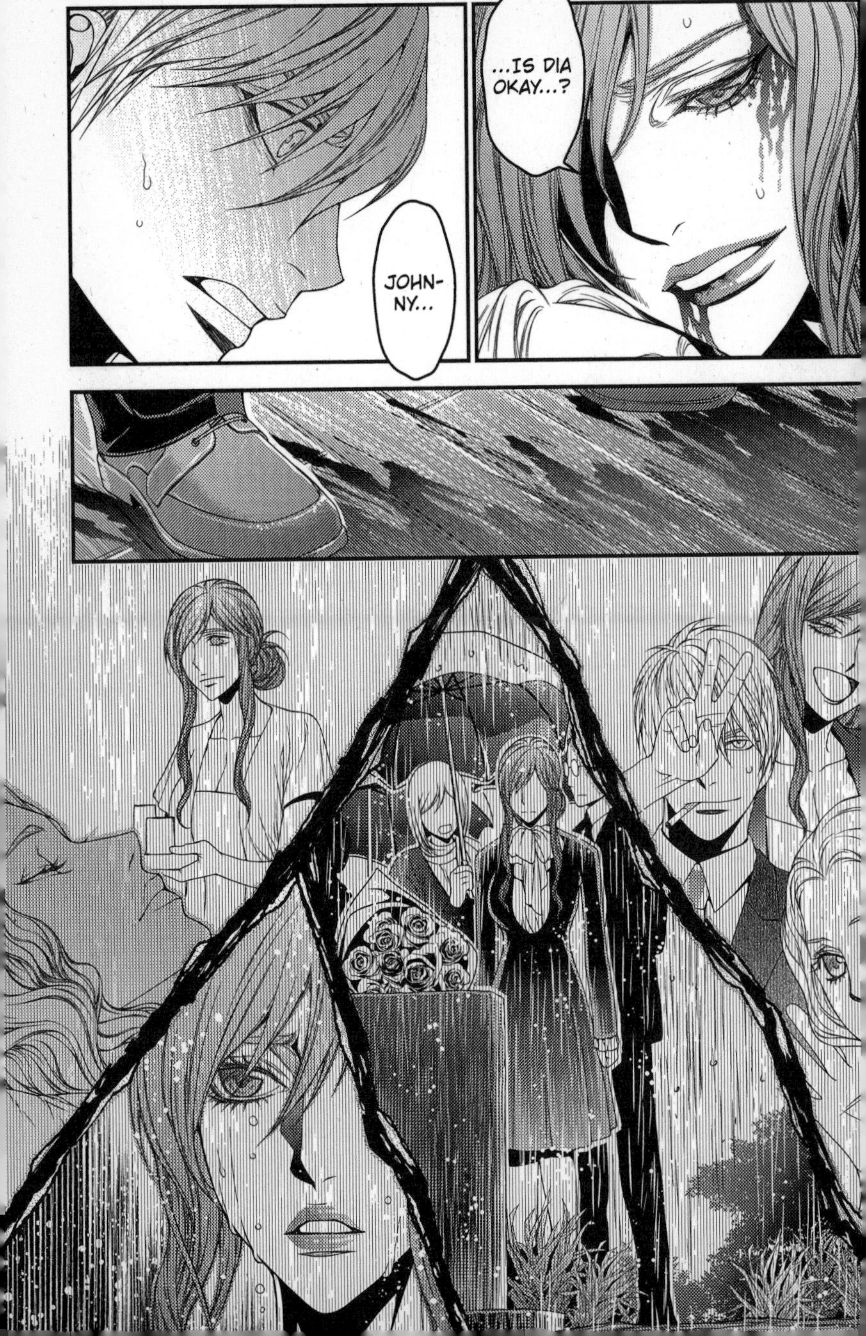
...IS DIA OKAY...?
JOHN-NY...

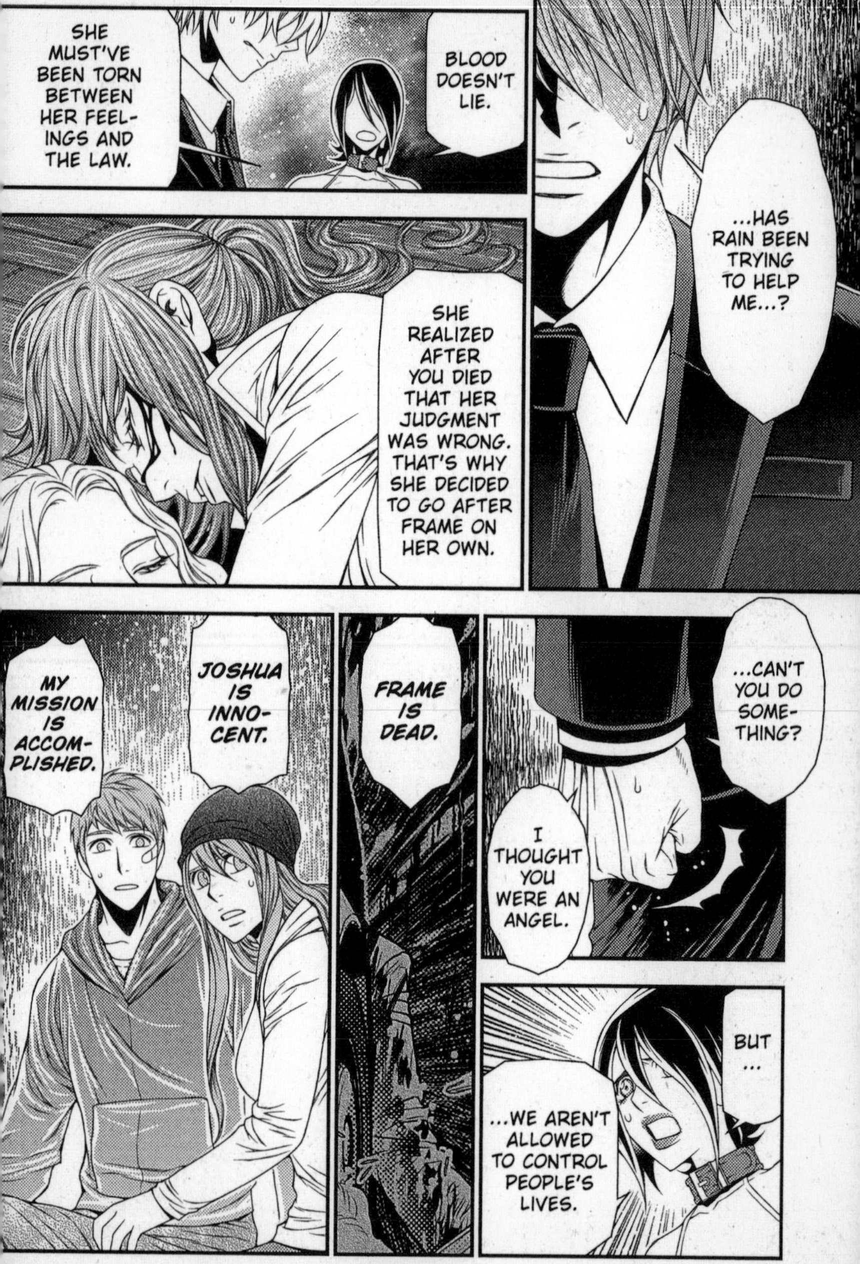
...HAS RAIN BEEN TRYING TO HELP ME...?
BLOOD DOESN'T LIE.
SHE MUST'VE BEEN TORN BETWEEN HER FEEL-INGS AND THE LAW.
SHE REALIZED AFTER YOU DIED THAT HER JUDGMENT WAS WRONG. THAT'S WHY SHE DECIDED TO GO AFTER FRAME ON HER OWN.
...CAN'T YOU DO SOME-THING?
I THOUGHT YOU WERE AN ANGEL.
BUT ...
...WE AREN'T ALLOWED TO CONTROL PEOPLE'S LIVES.
FRAME IS DEAD.
JOSHUA IS INNO-CENT.
MY MISSION IS ACCOM-PLISHED.

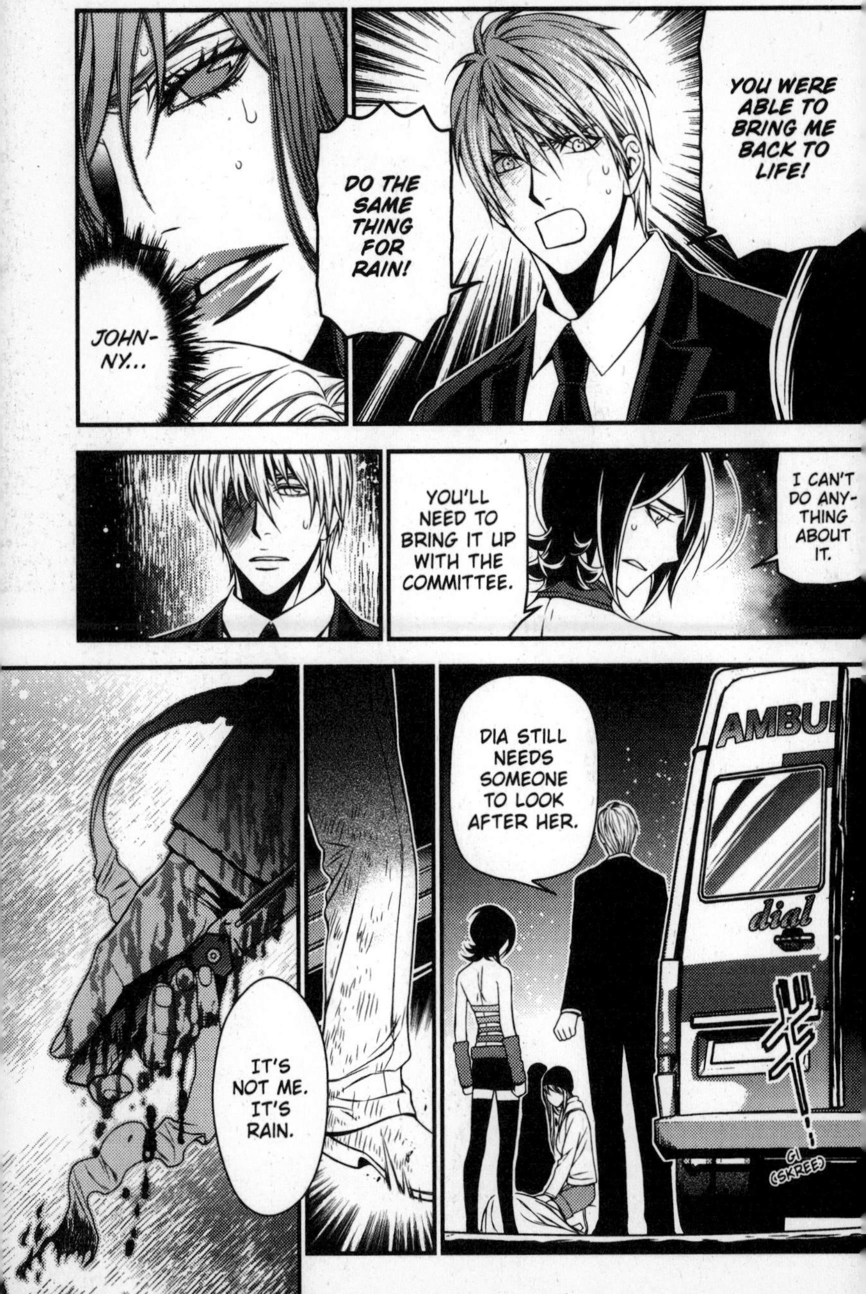
YOU WERE ABLE TO BRING ME BACK TO LIFE!
DO THE SAME THING FOR RAIN!
JOHN-NY...
I CAN'T DO ANY-THING ABOUT IT.
YOU'LL NEED TO BRING IT UP WITH THE COMMITTEE.
DIA STILL NEEDS SOMEONE TO LOOK AFTER HER.
GI (SKREE)
IT'S NOT ME. IT'S RAIN.

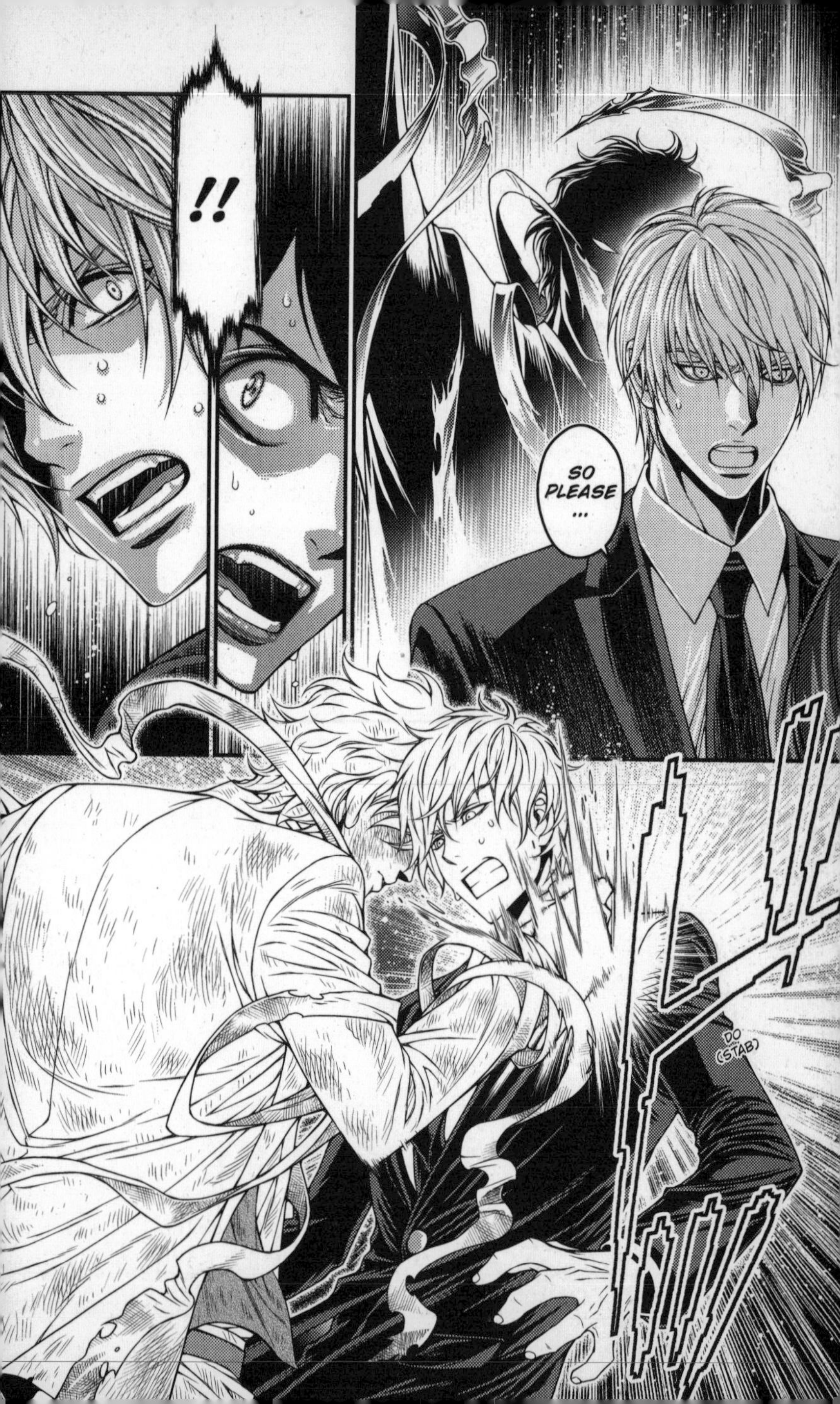
SO PLEASE ...
!!
DO (STAB)

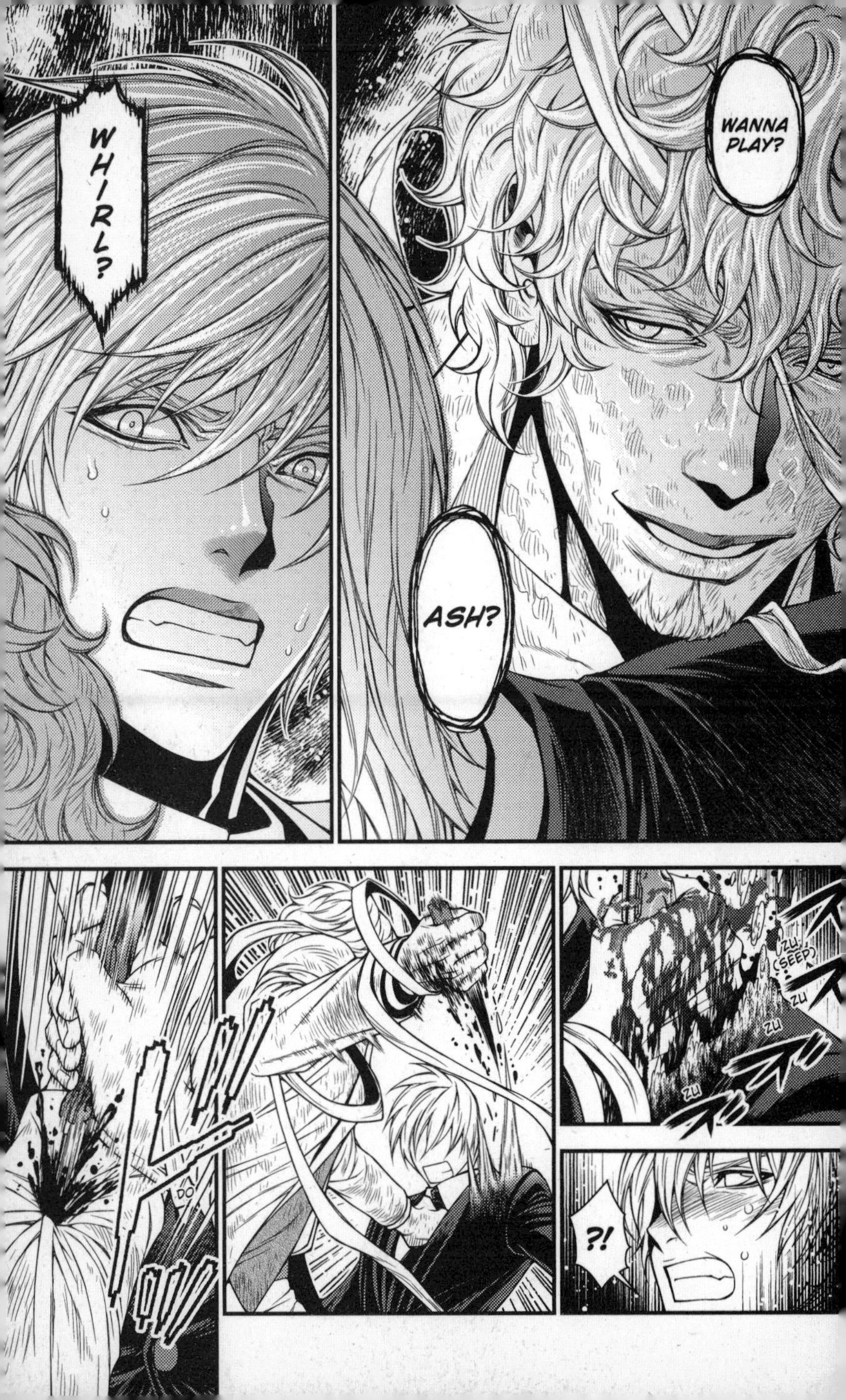
WANNA PLAY?
ASH?
WHIRL?
ZU (SEEP)
ZU
ZU
ZU
?!
DO

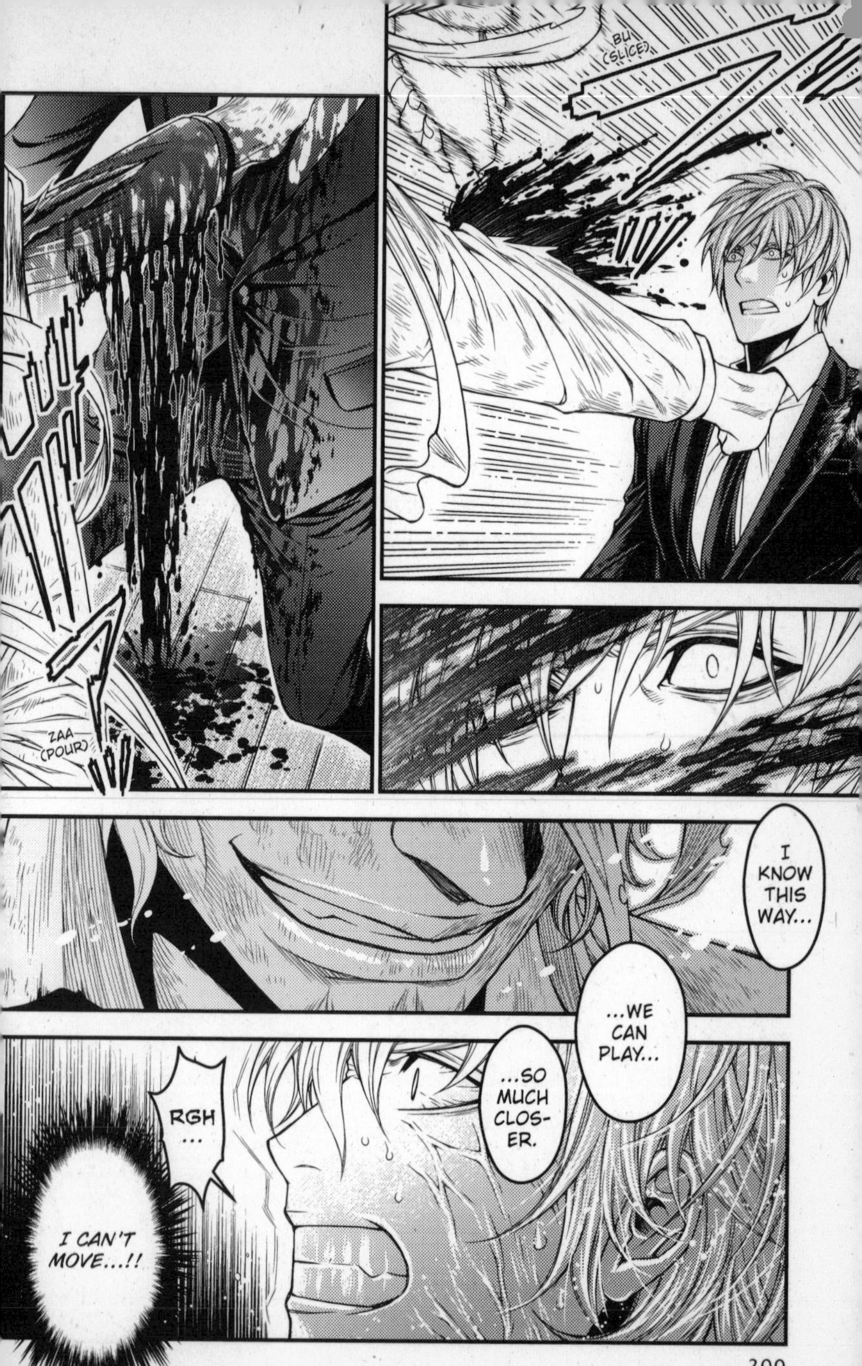
BU (SLICE)
ZAA (POUR)
I KNOW THIS WAY...
...WE CAN PLAY...
...SO MUCH CLOS-ER.
RGH...
I CAN'T MOVE...!!

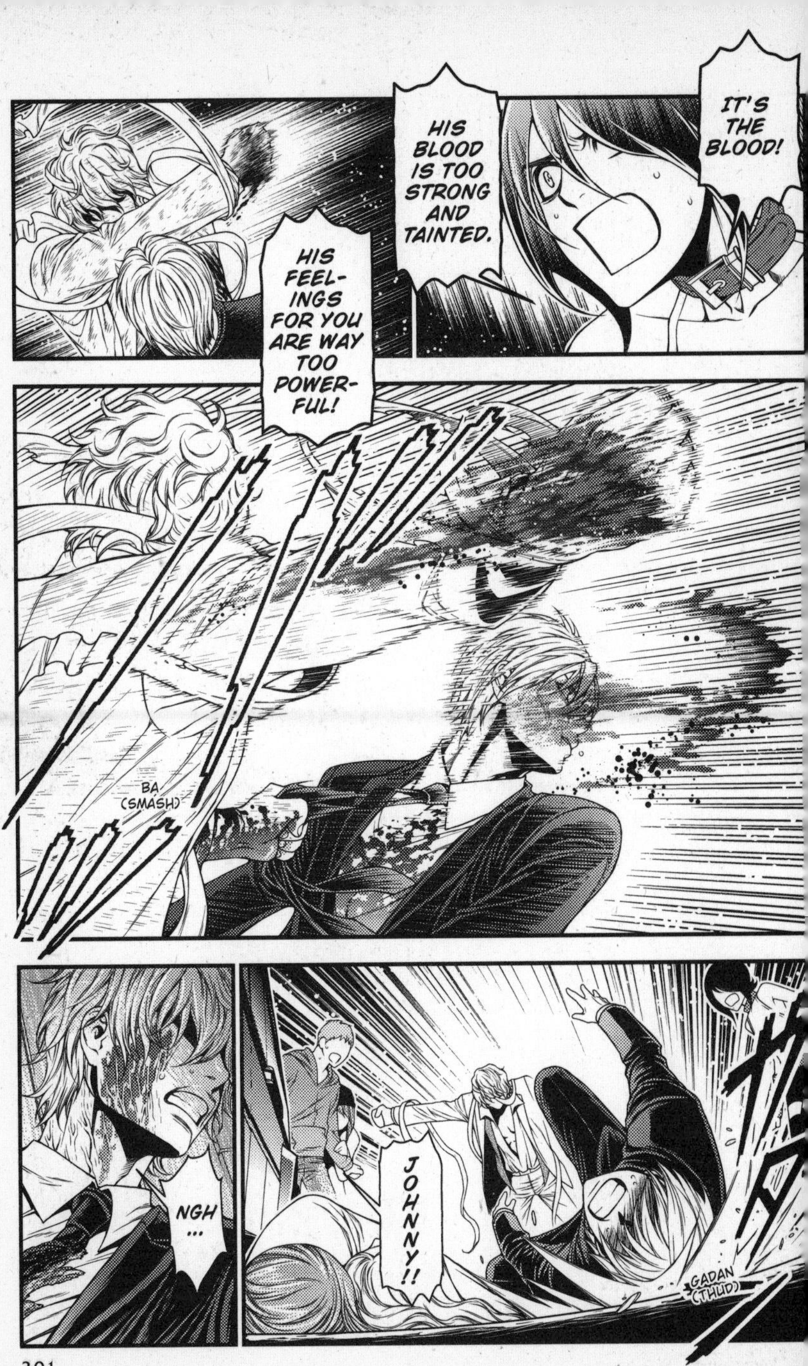

IT'S THE BLOOD!
HIS BLOOD IS TOO STRONG AND TAINTED.
HIS FEEL-INGS FOR YOU ARE WAY TOO POWER-FUL!
BA (SMASH)
JOHNNY!!
GADAN (THUD)
NGH ...

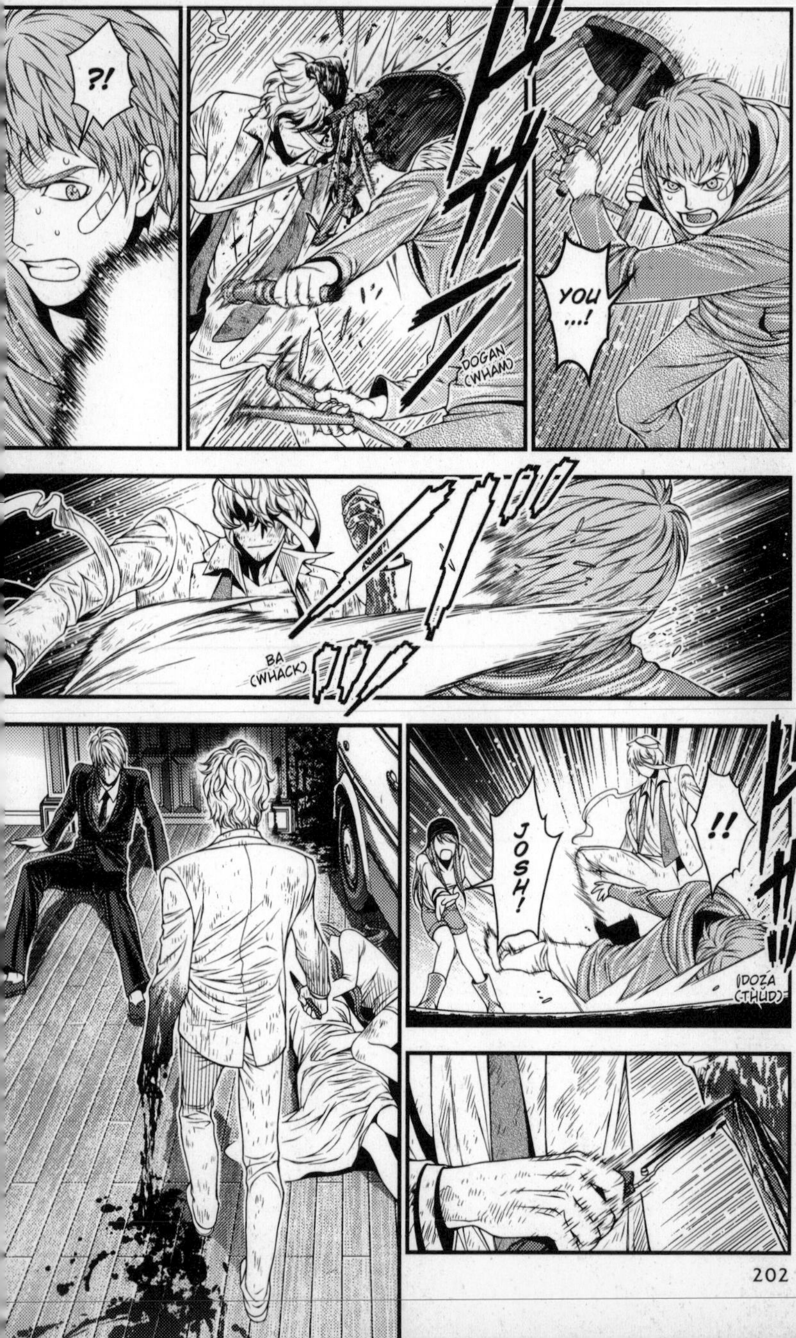
YOU ...!
DOGAN (WHAM)
?!
BA (WHACK)
!!
JOSH!
DOZA (THUD)

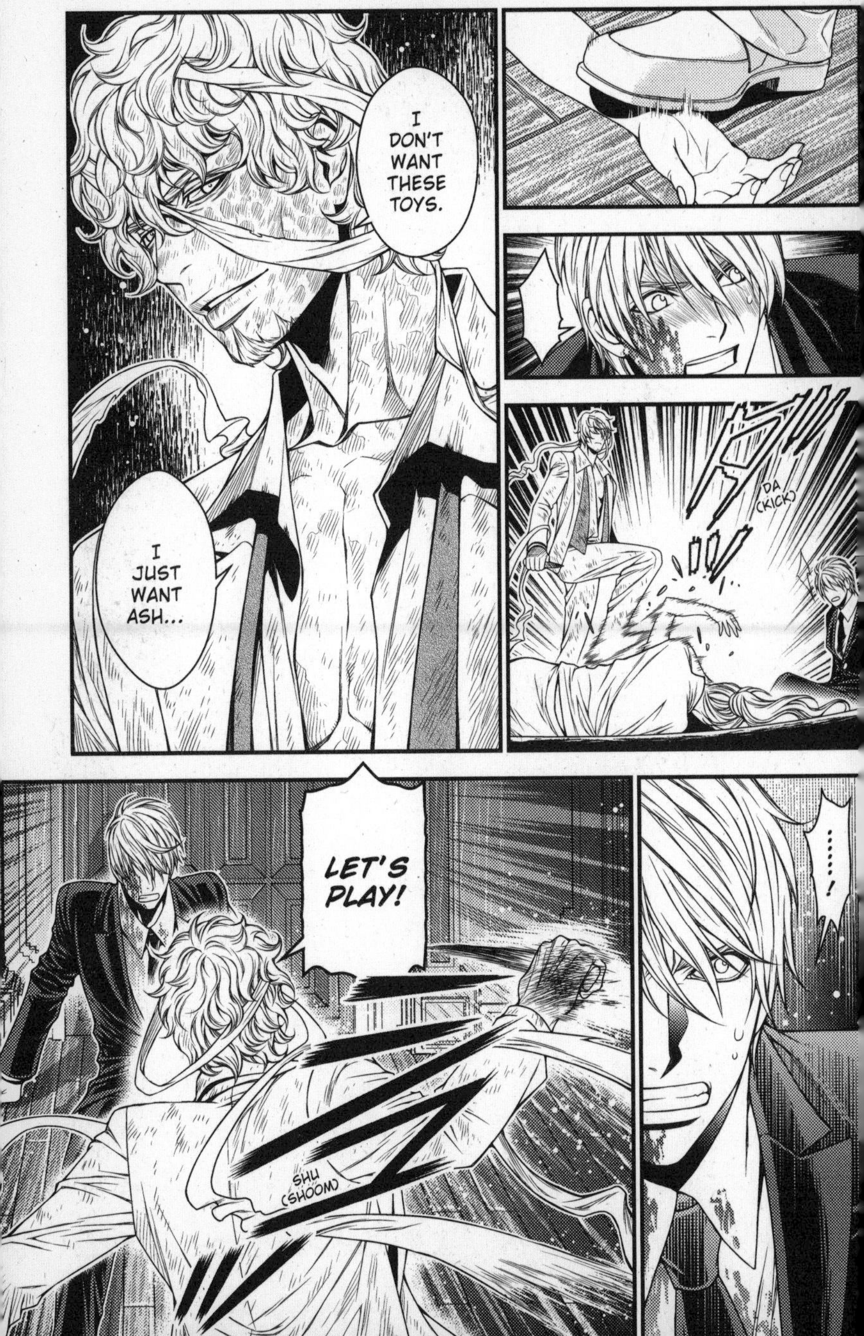
DA (KICK)
I DON'T WANT THESE TOYS.
I JUST WANT ASH...
......!
LET'S PLAY!
SHU (SHOOM)

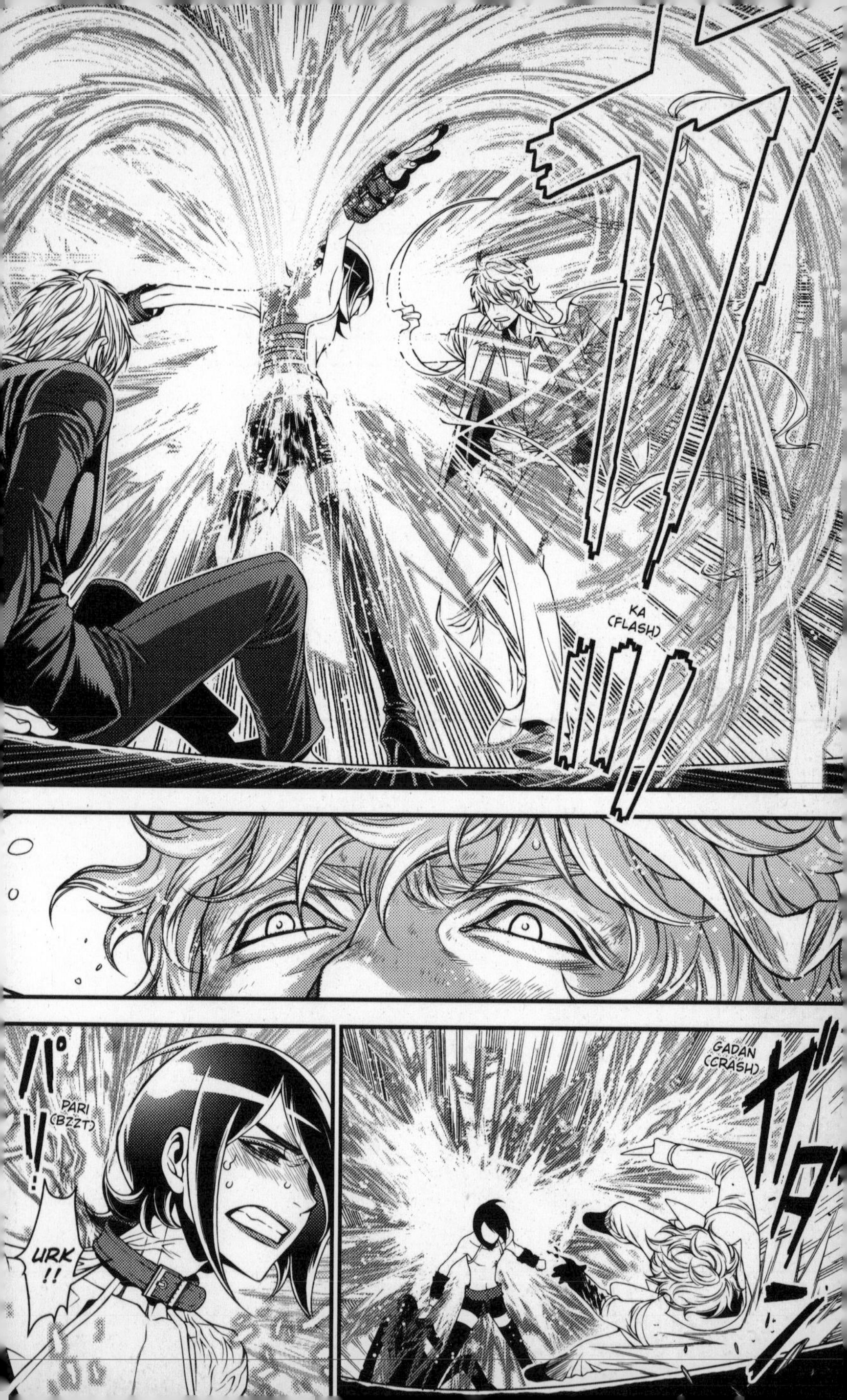
KA
(FLASH)
GADAN
(CRASH)
PARI
(BZZT)
URK
!!

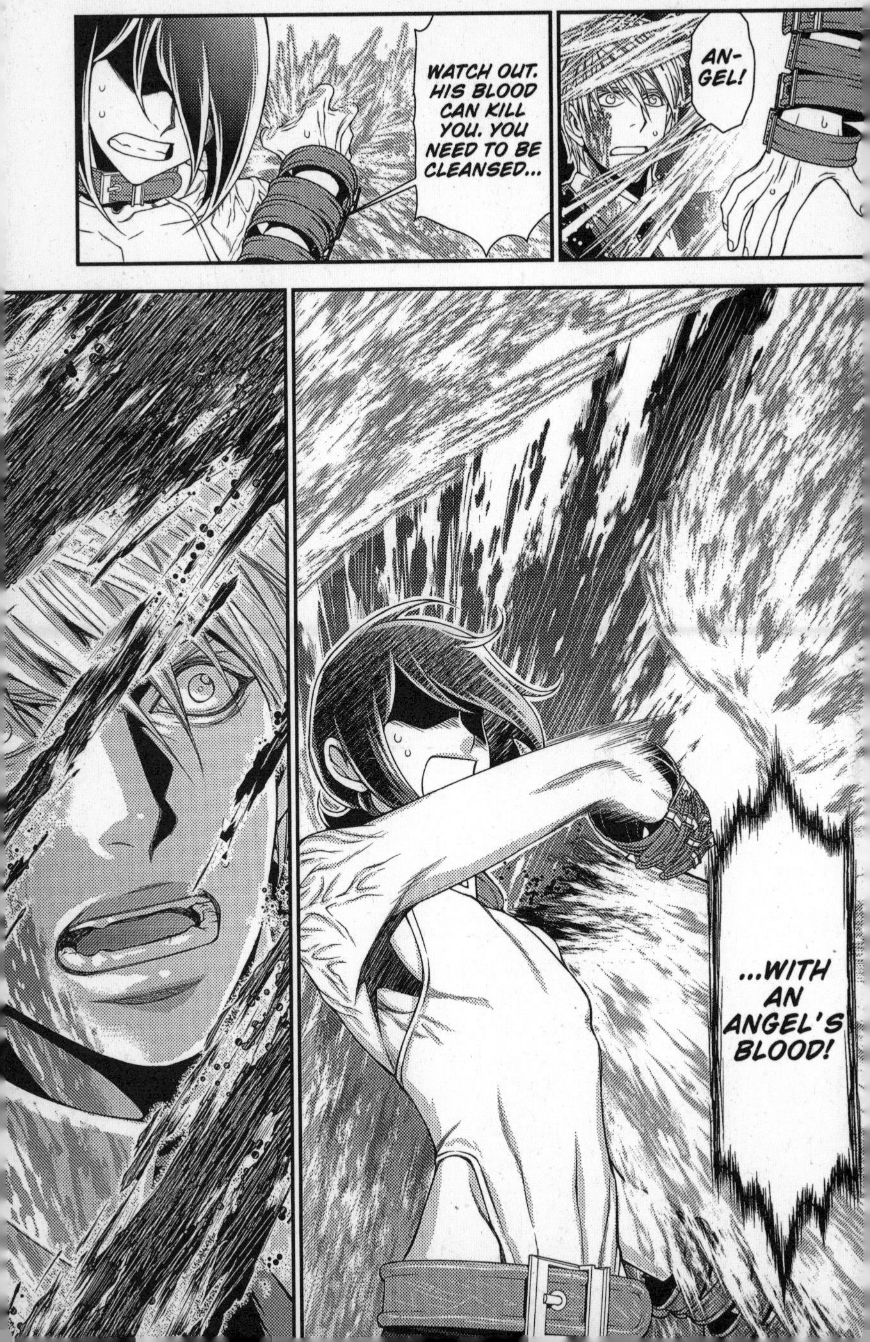
AN-GEL!
WATCH OUT. HIS BLOOD CAN KILL YOU. YOU NEED TO BE CLEANSED...
...WITH AN ANGEL'S BLOOD!

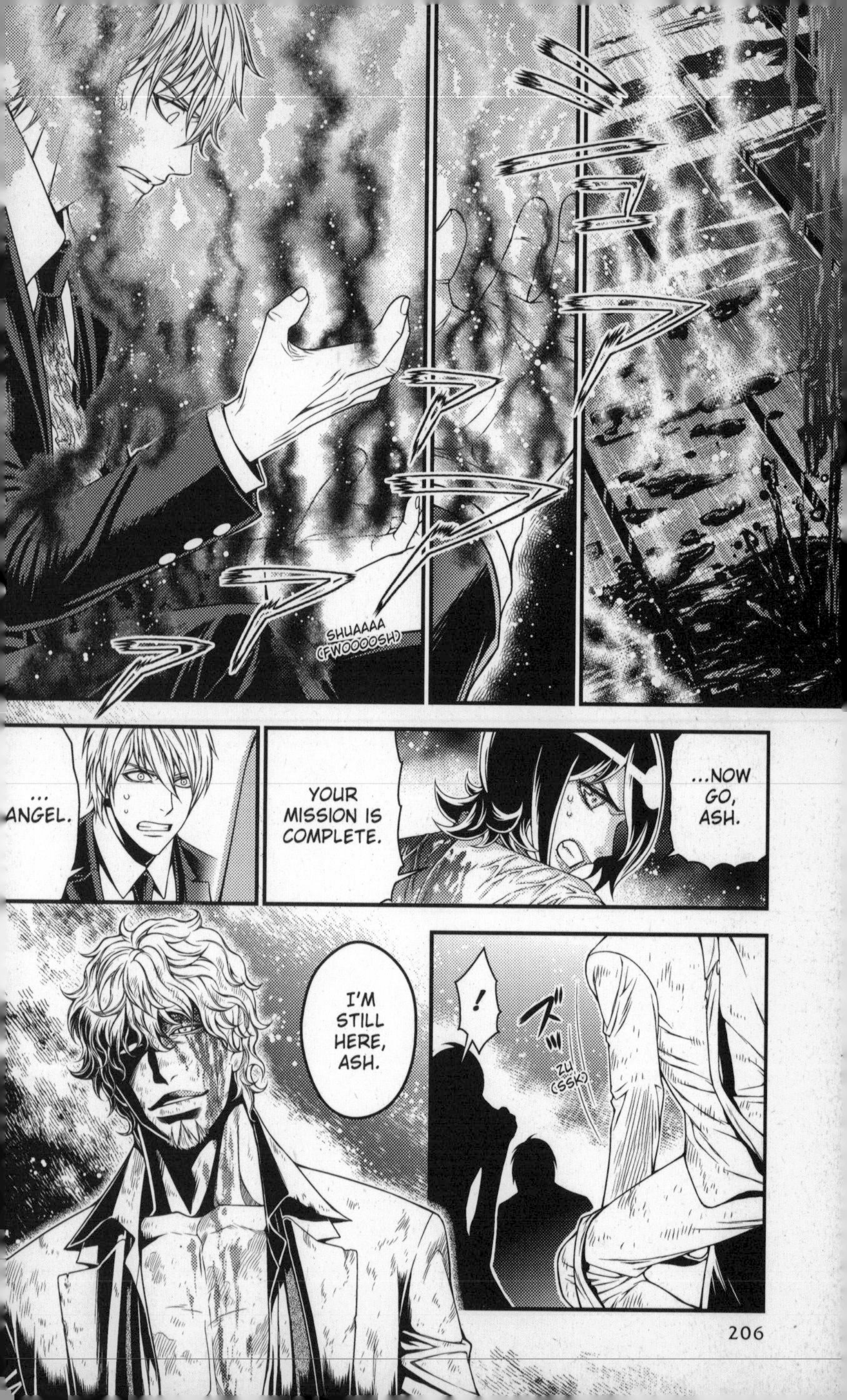
SHUAAAA (FWOOOOSH)
...NOW GO, ASH.
YOUR MISSION IS COMPLETE.
... ANGEL.
!
ZU (SSK)
I'M STILL HERE, ASH.

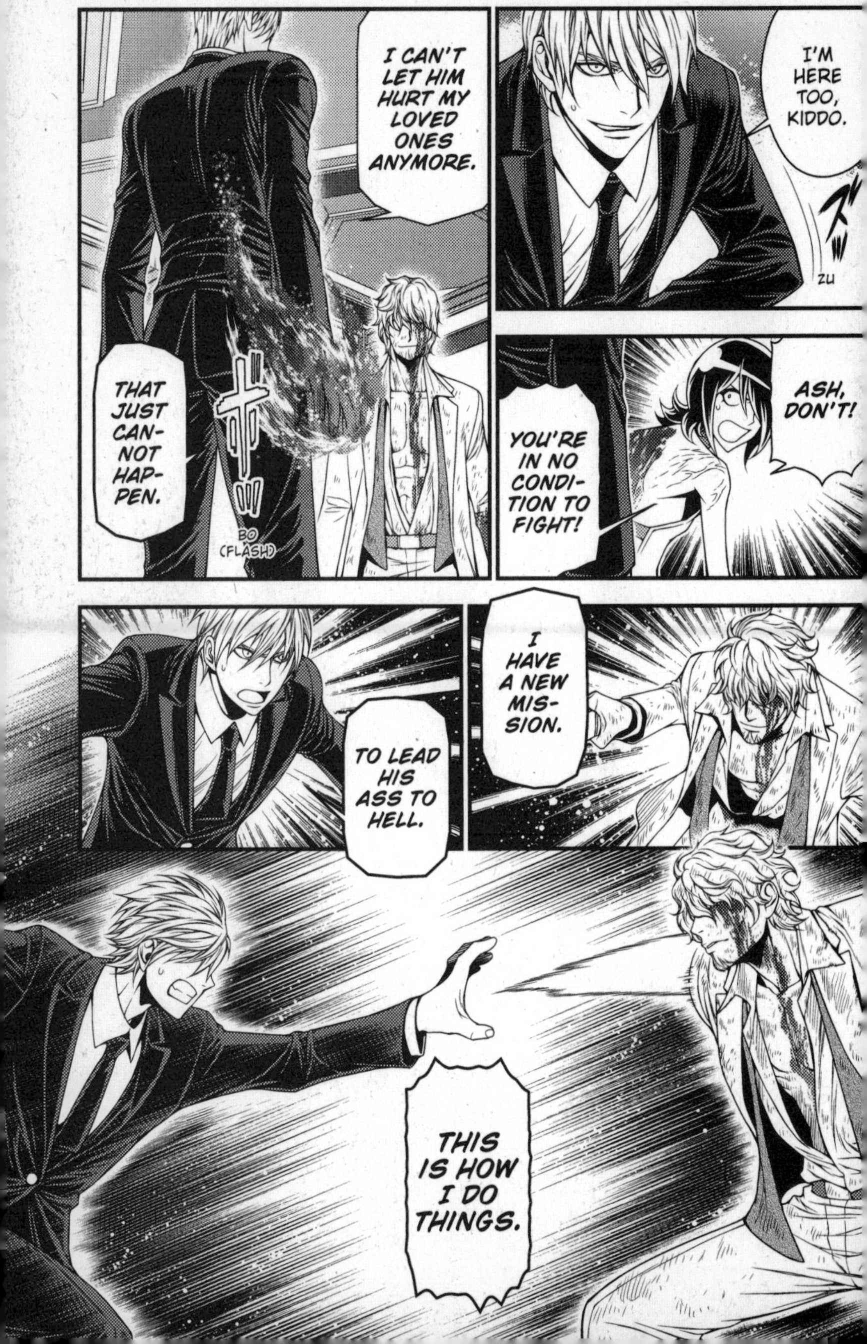
I'M HERE TOO, KIDDO.
ZU
ASH, DON'T!
YOU'RE IN NO CONDITION TO FIGHT!
I CAN'T LET HIM HURT MY LOVED ONES ANYMORE.
THAT JUST CAN-NOT HAP-PEN.
BO (FLASH)
I HAVE A NEW MIS-SION.
TO LEAD HIS ASS TO HELL.
THIS IS HOW I DO THINGS.

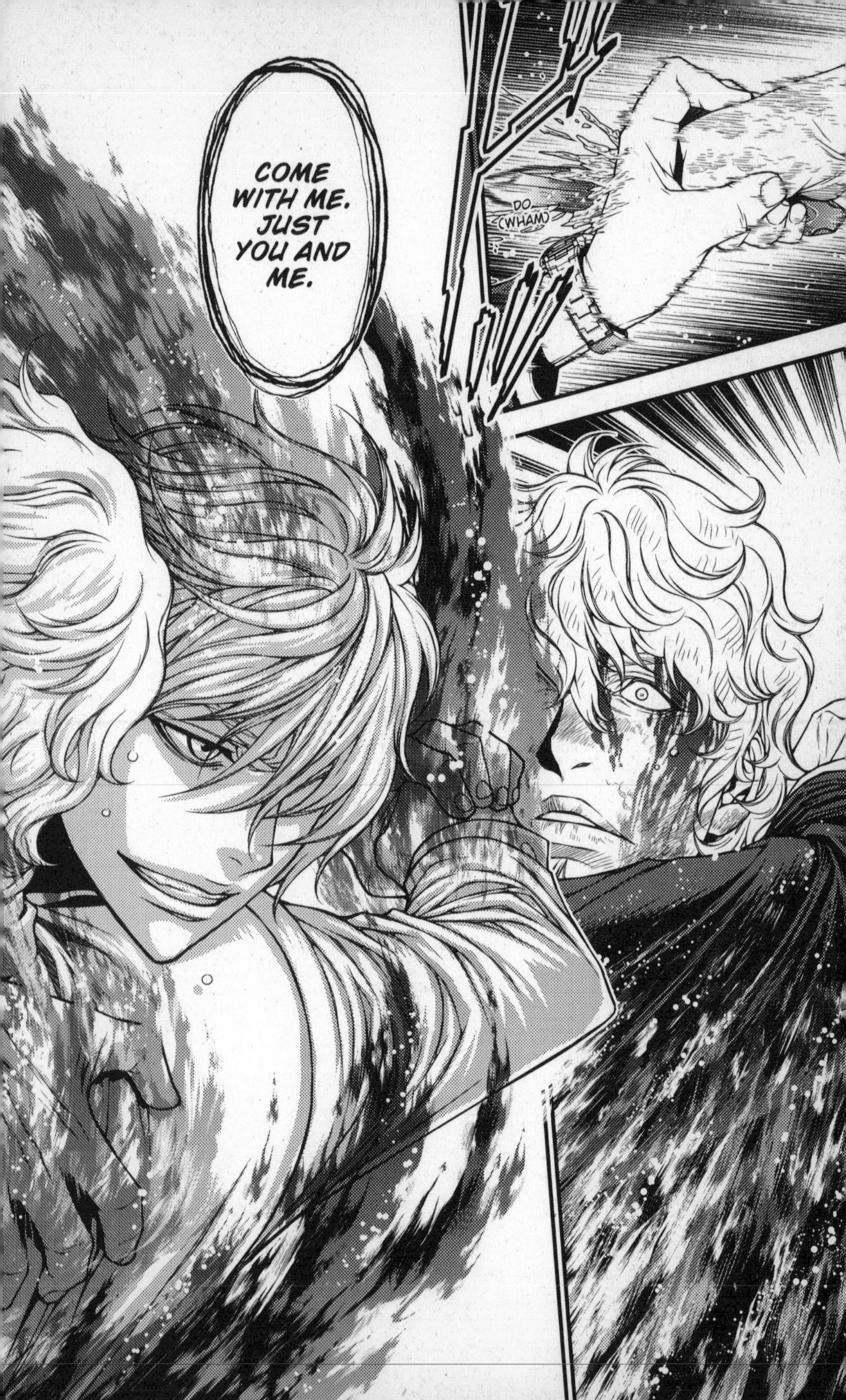
DO
(WHAM)
COME WITH ME. JUST YOU AND ME.

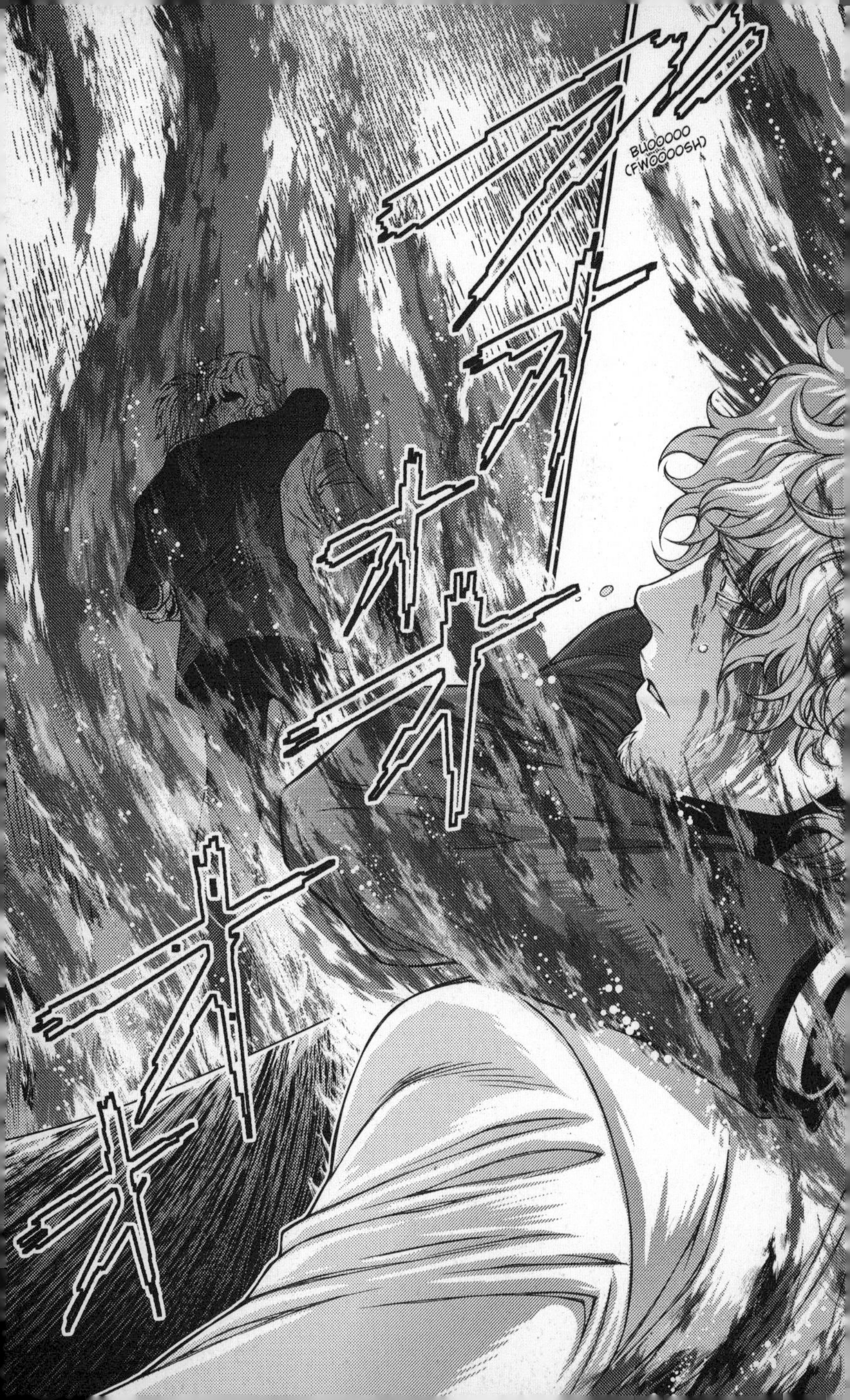
BUOOOOO
(FWOOOOSH)

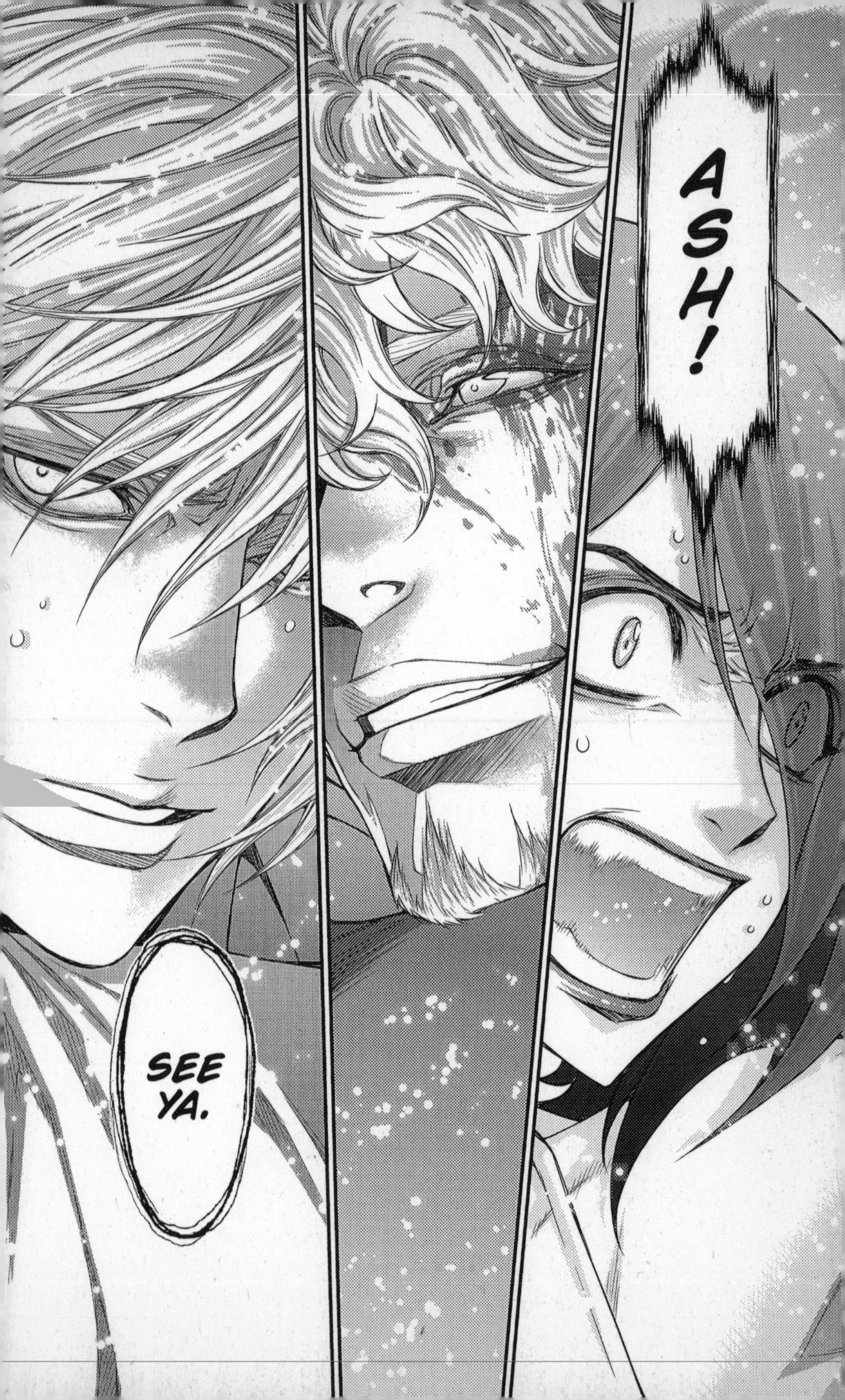
ASH!
SEE YA.

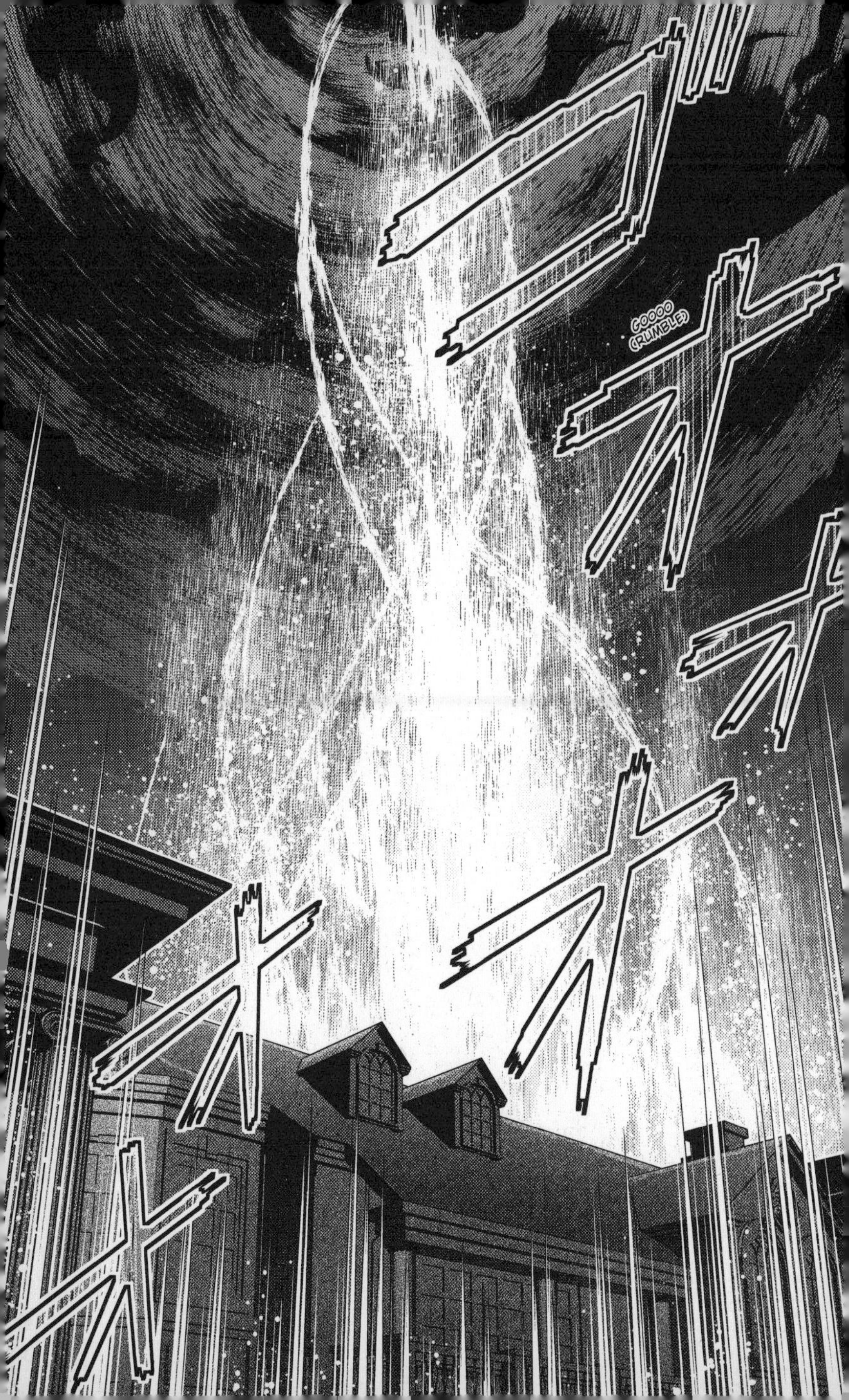
GOOOO
(RUMBLE)

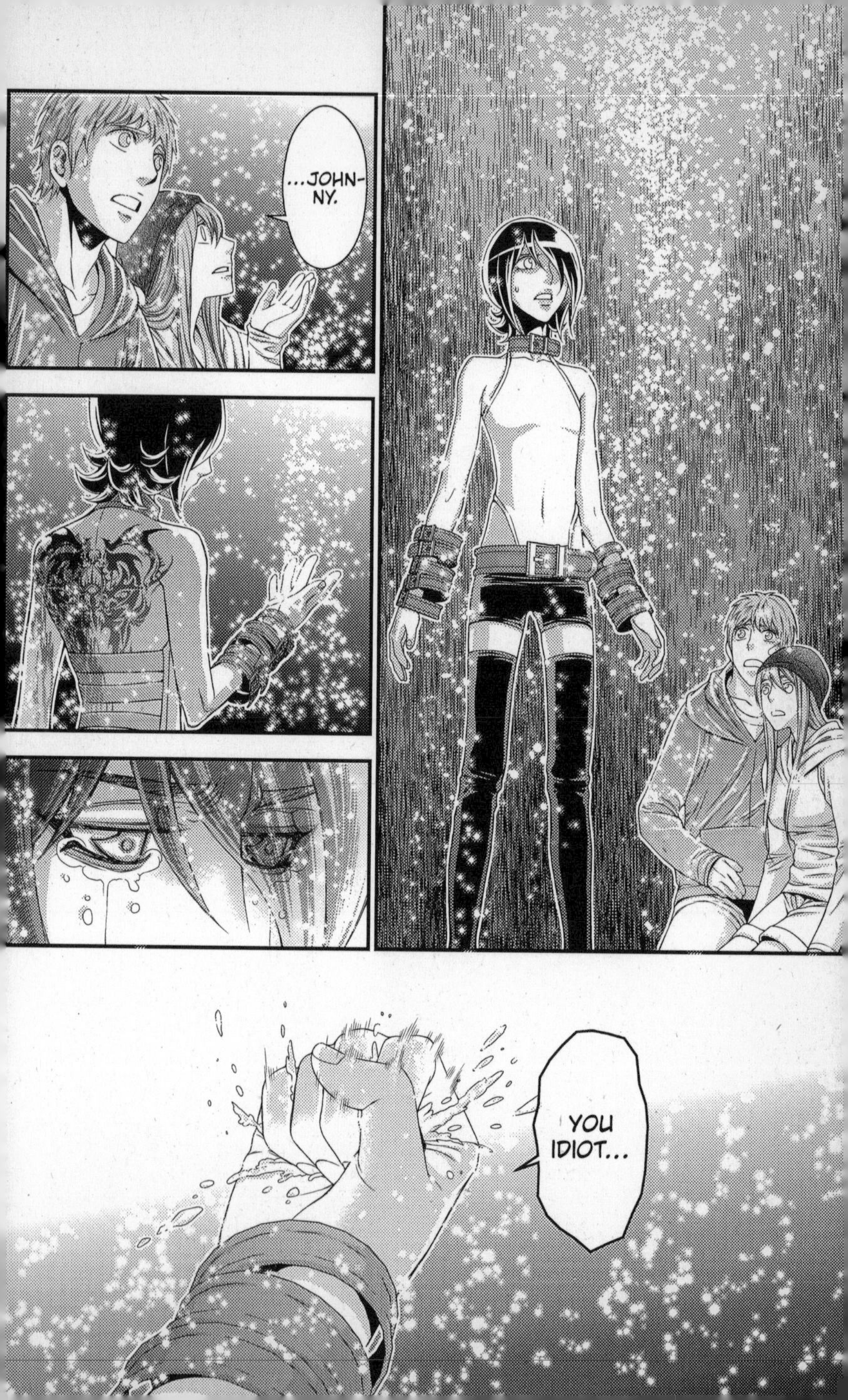
...JOHN-
NY.
YOU IDIOT...

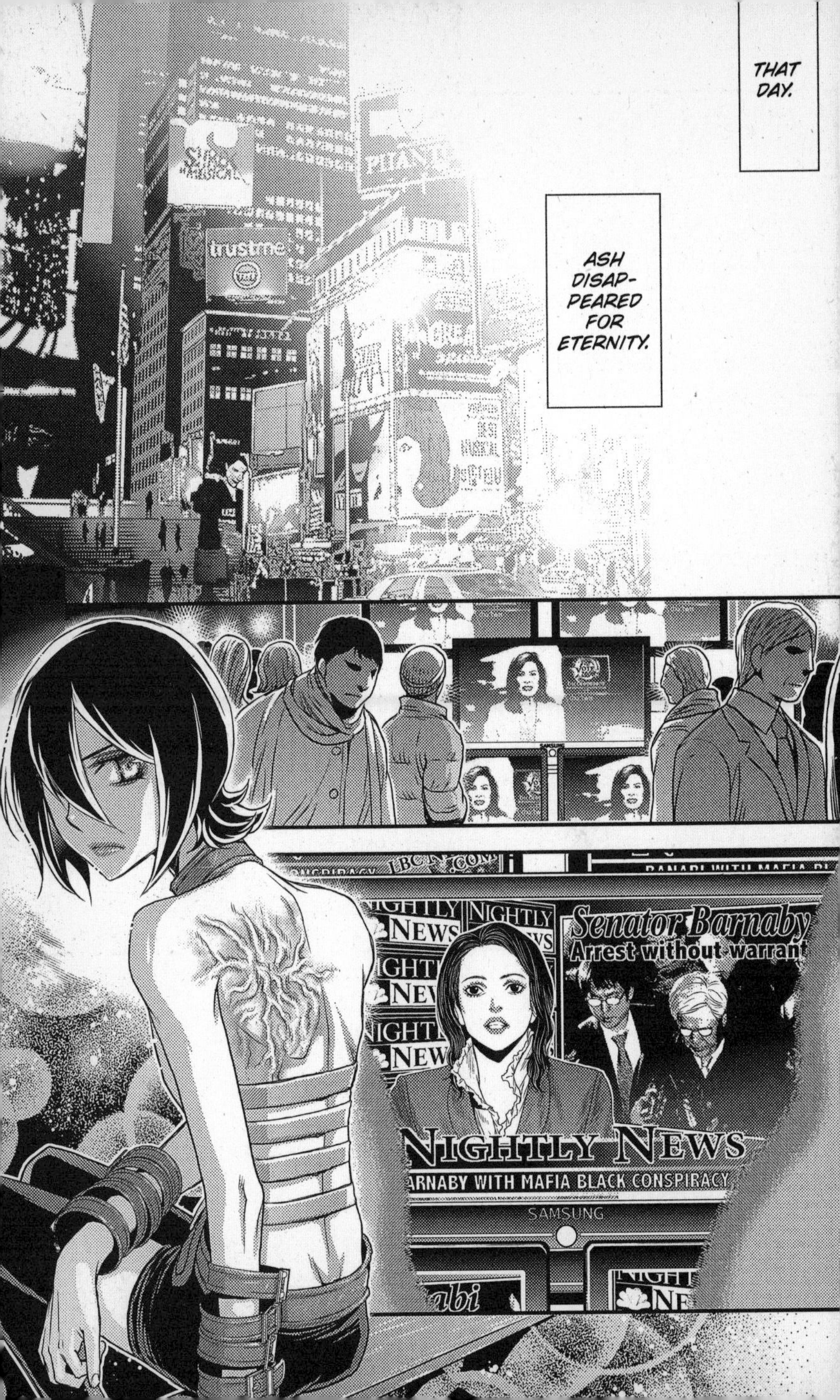
THAT DAY.
ASH DISAP-PEARED FOR ETERNITY.
trustme
Senator Barnaby
Arrest without warrant
NIGHTLY NEWS
ARNABY WITH MAFIA BLACK CONSPIRACY
SAMSUNG

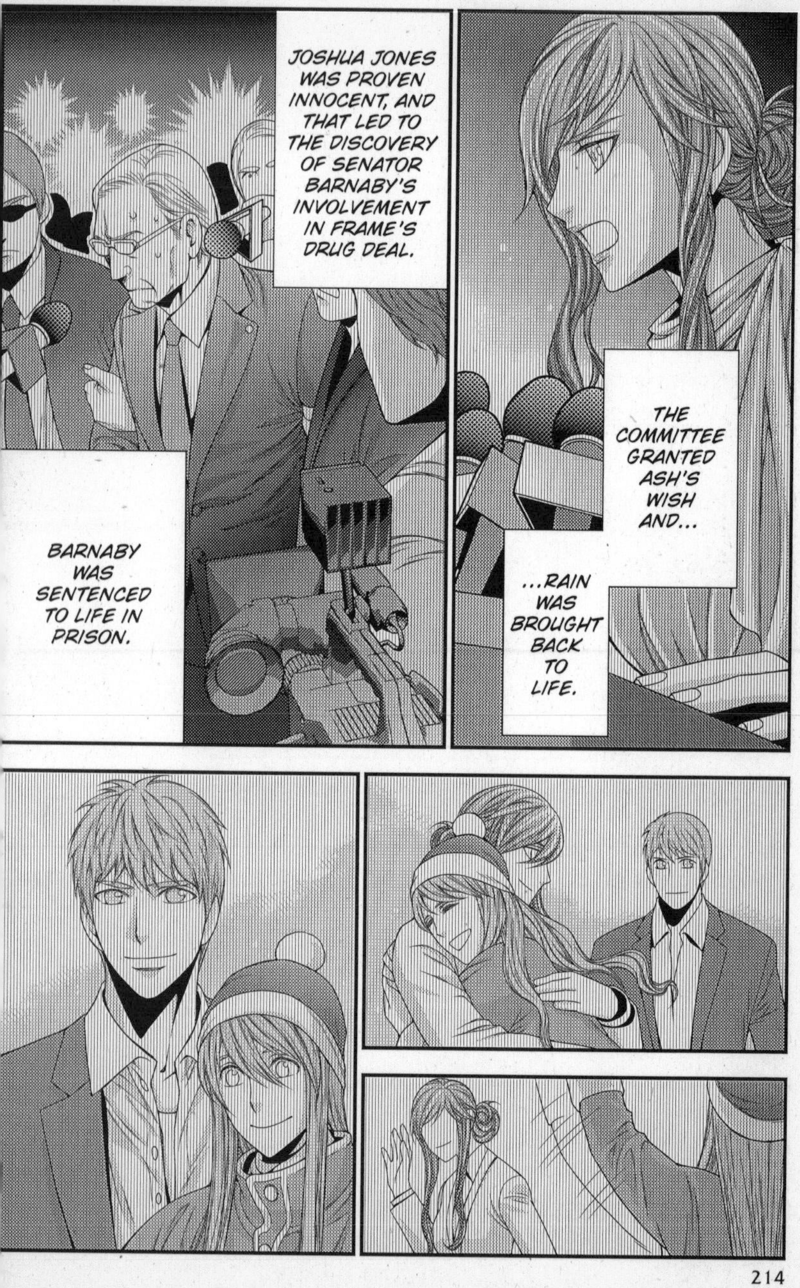
THE COMMITTEE GRANTED ASH'S WISH AND...
...RAIN WAS BROUGHT BACK TO LIFE.
JOSHUA JONES WAS PROVEN INNOCENT, AND THAT LED TO THE DISCOVERY OF SENATOR BARNABY'S INVOLVEMENT IN FRAME'S DRUG DEAL.
BARNABY WAS SENTENCED TO LIFE IN PRISON.

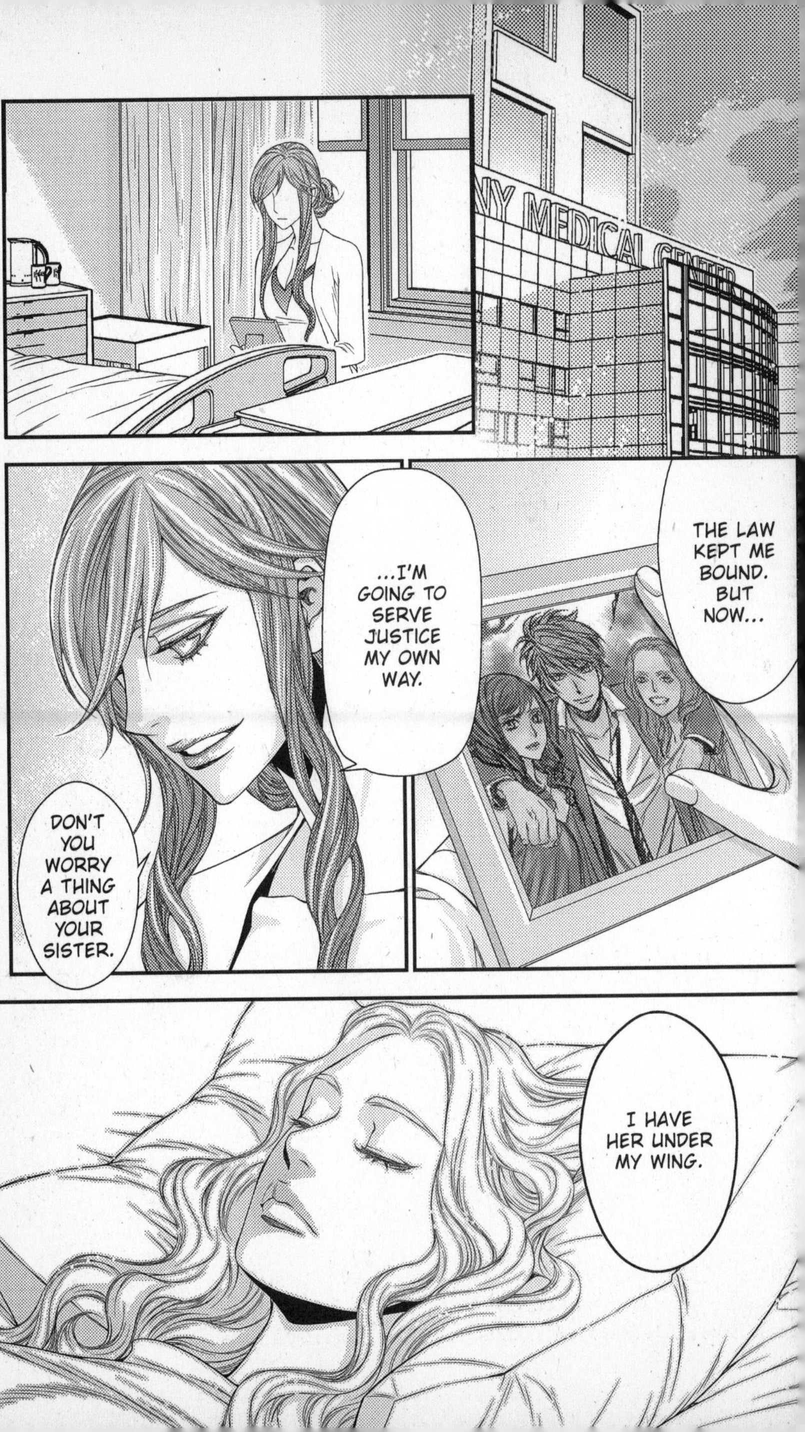
NY MEDICAL
THE LAW KEPT ME BOUND. BUT NOW...
...I'M GOING TO SERVE JUSTICE MY OWN WAY.
DON'T YOU WORRY A THING ABOUT YOUR SISTER.
I HAVE HER UNDER MY WING.

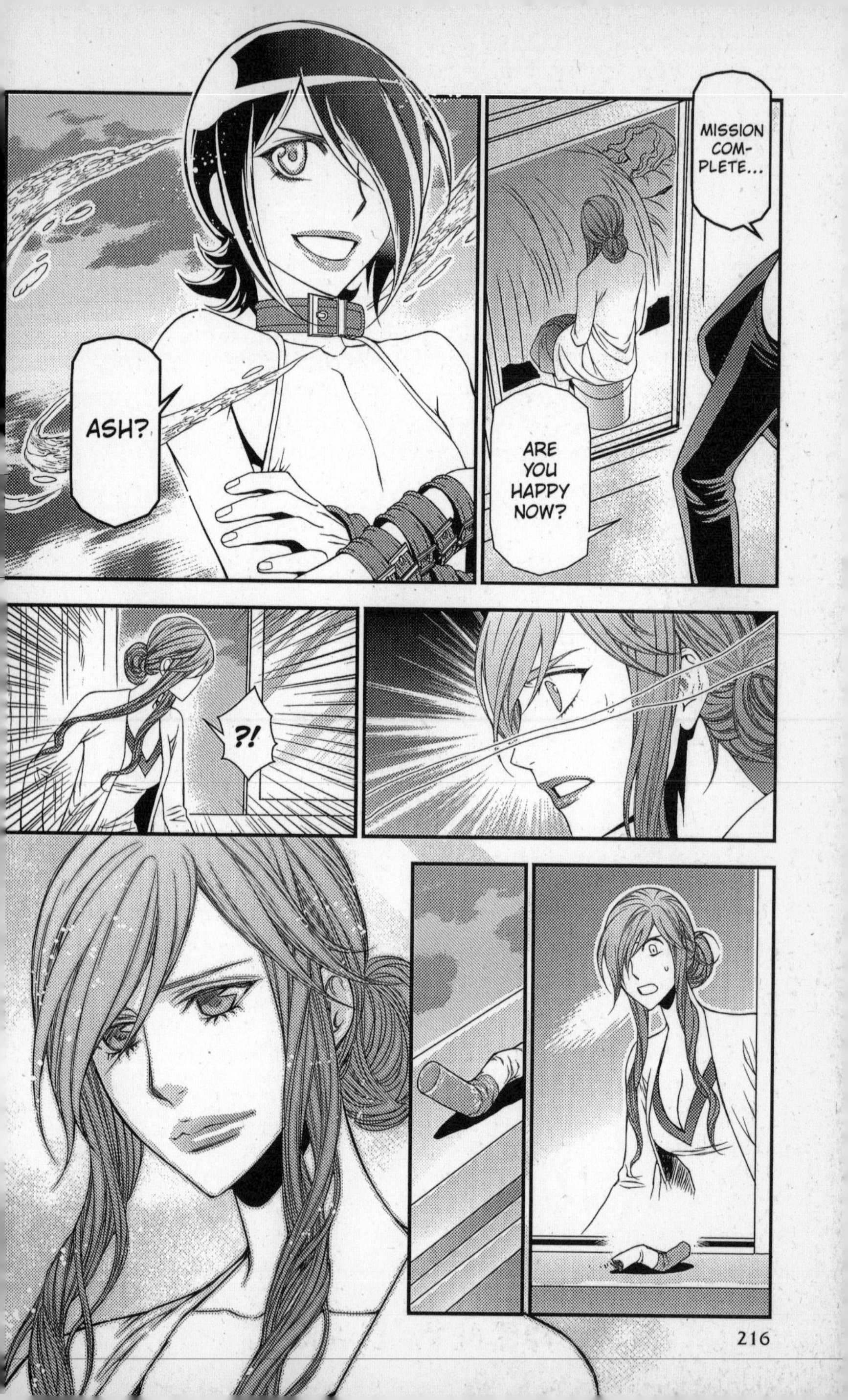
MISSION COM-PLETE...
ARE YOU HAPPY NOW?
ASH?
?!

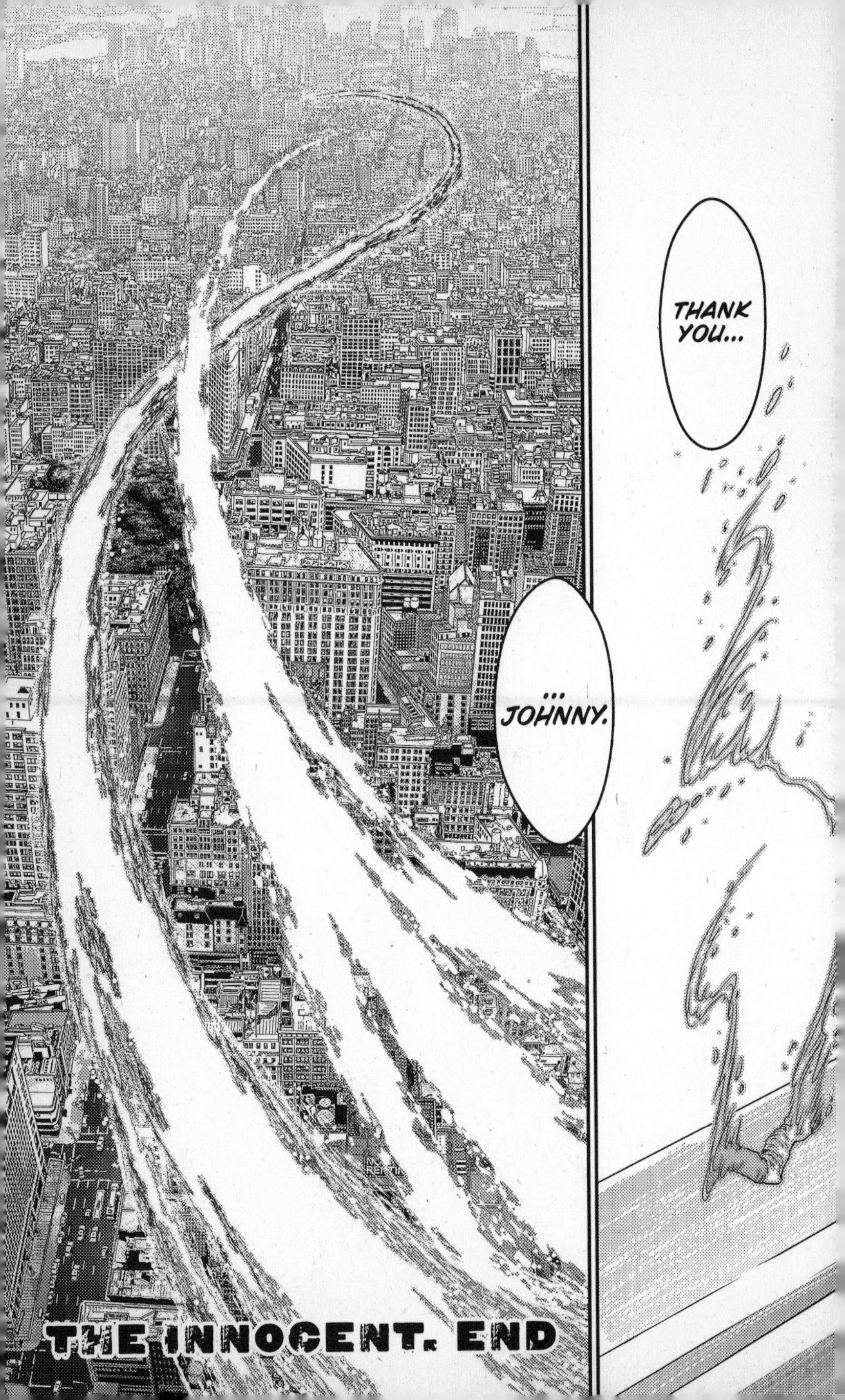
THANK YOU...
...JOHNNY.
THE INNOCENT. END

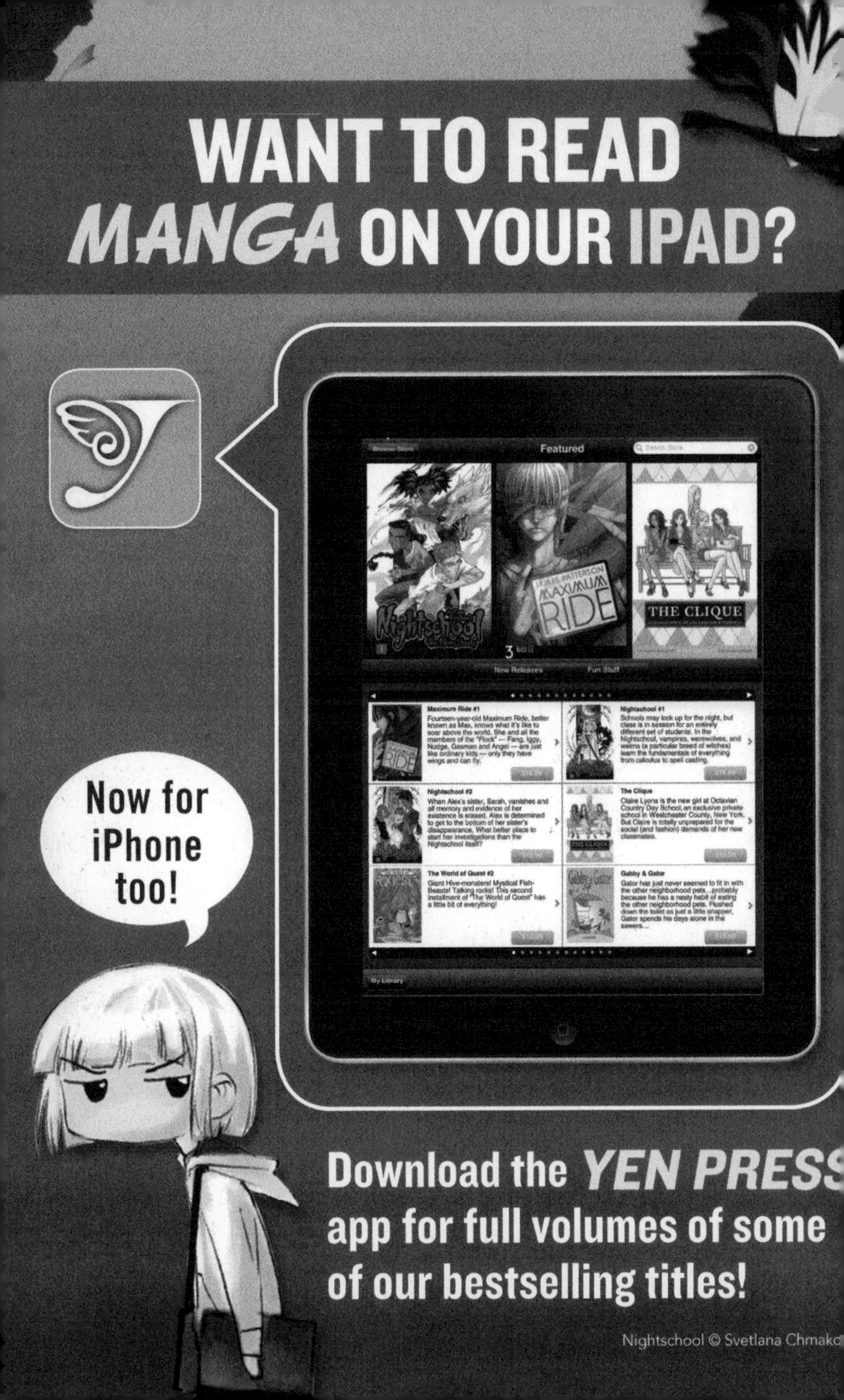
WANT TO READ MANGA ON YOUR IPAD?
Now for iPhone too!
Featured
JAMES PATTERSON MAXIMUM RIDE
THE CLIQUE
Download the YEN PRESS app for full volumes of some of our bestselling titles!
Nightschool © Svetlana Chmakova

MAXIMUM RIDE

LIKE YOU'VE NEVER SEEN HER BEFORE

ON SALE NOW.

THE NEW MANGA SERIES BY
JAMES PATTERSON & NARAE LEE

Yen Press
www.yenpress.com

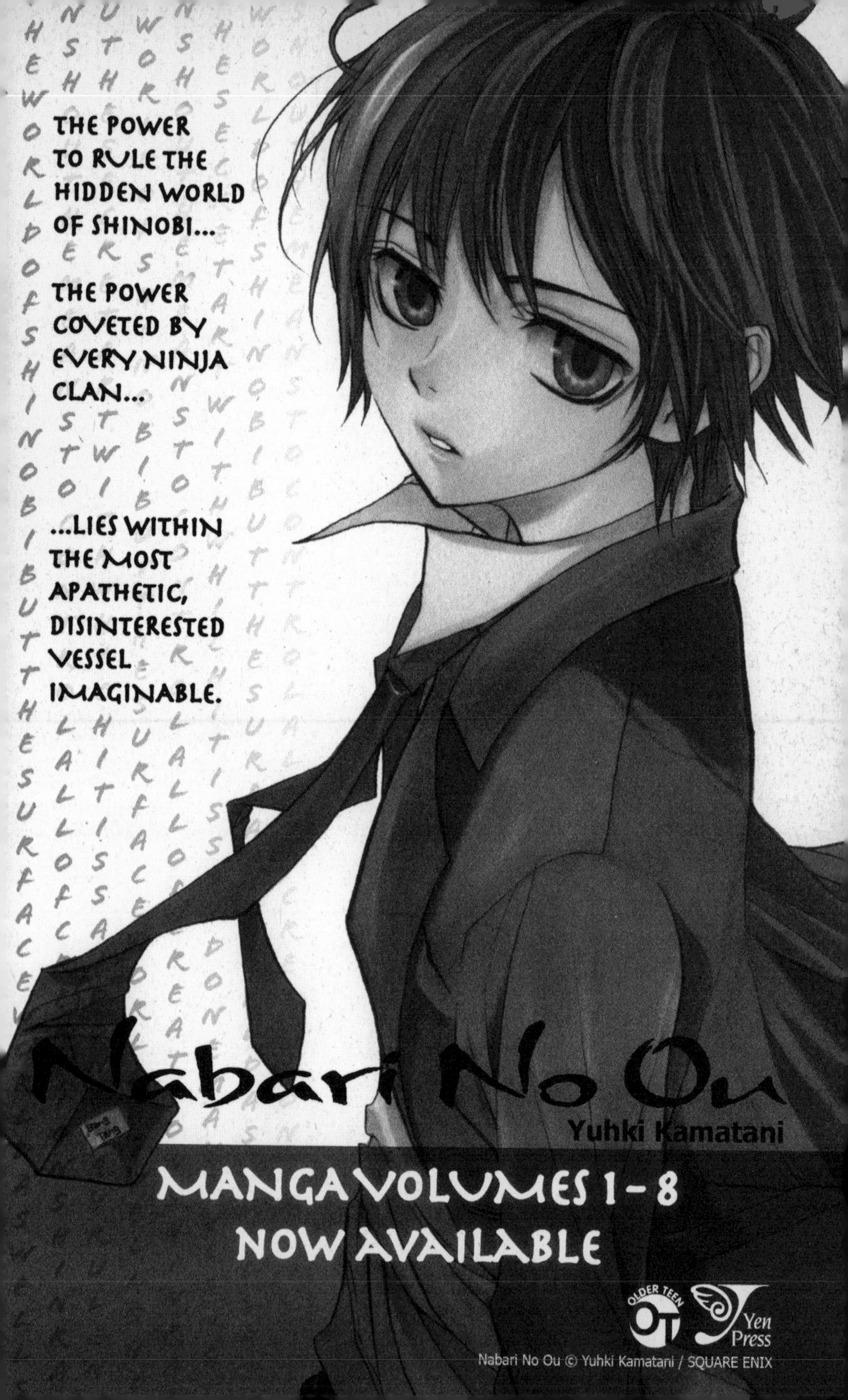
THE POWER TO RULE THE HIDDEN WORLD OF SHINOBI...
THE POWER COVETED BY EVERY NINJA CLAN...
...LIES WITHIN THE MOST APATHETIC, DISINTERESTED VESSEL IMAGINABLE.
Nabari No Ou
Yuhki Kamatani
MANGA VOLUMES 1 - 8
NOW AVAILABLE
OLDER TEEN
OT
Yen Press
Nabari No Ou © Yuhki Kamatani / SQUARE ENIX

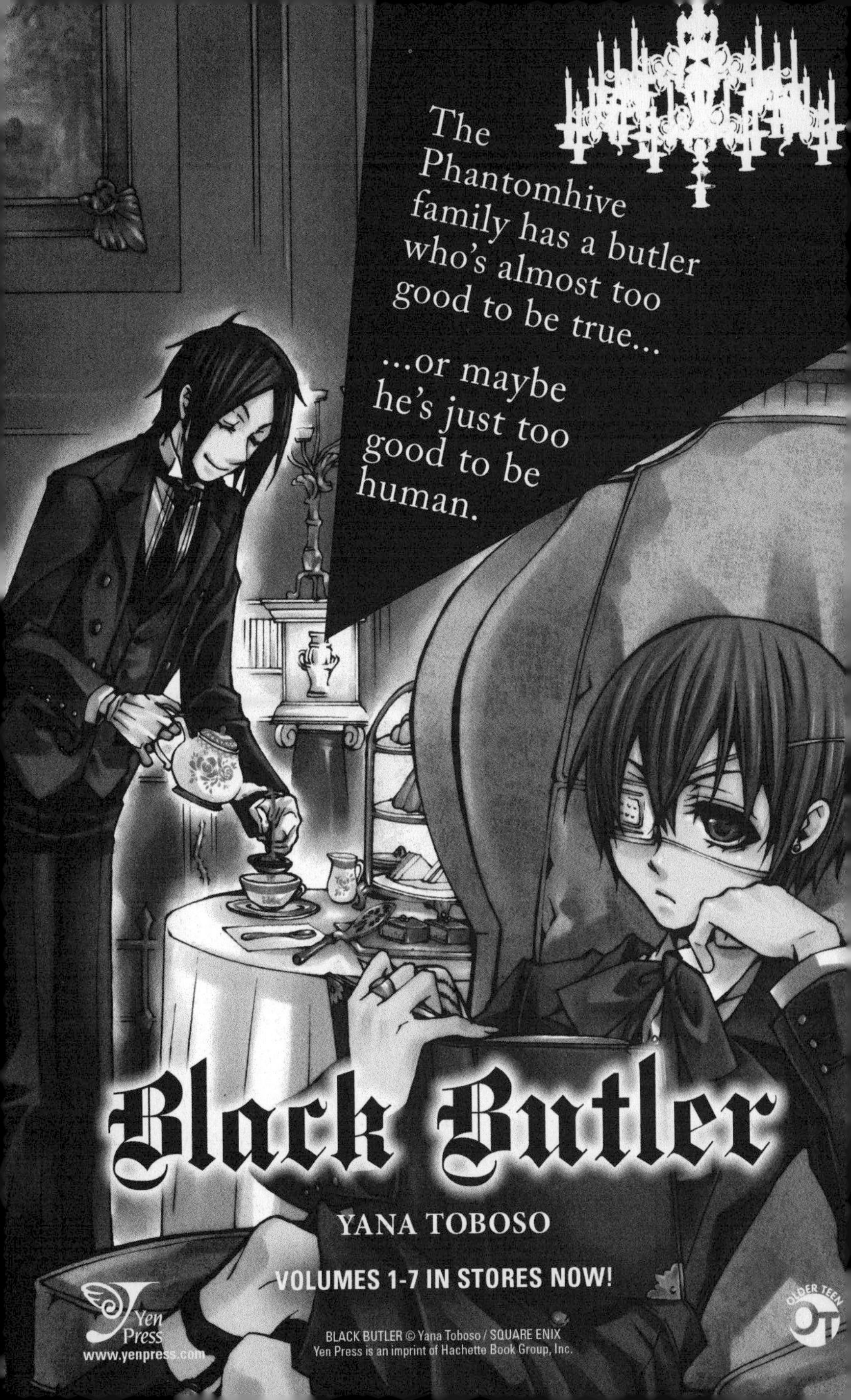
The Phantomhive family has a butler who's almost too good to be true...
...or maybe he's just too good to be human.
Black Butler
YANA TOBOSO
VOLUMES 1-7 IN STORES NOW!
Yen Press
www.yenpress.com
BLACK BUTLER © Yana Toboso / SQUARE ENIX
Yen Press is an imprint of Hachette Book Group, Inc.
OLDER TEEN
OT

Kieli sees ghosts.
Harvey cannot die.
He will throw
her world into
chaos...
...and become her
one true friend.

STORY BY **Yukako Kabei**
ART BY **Shiori Teshirogi**

KIELI

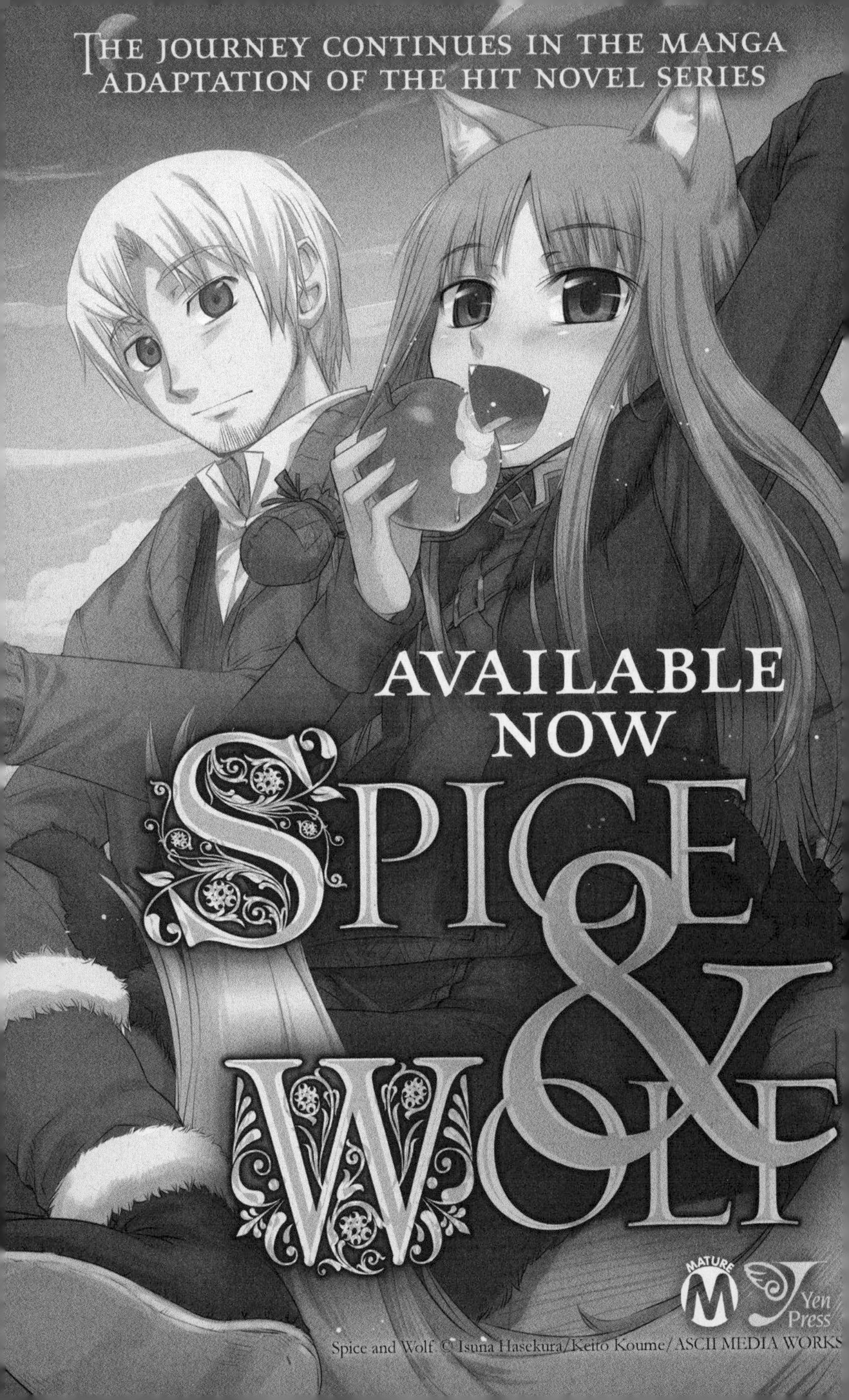
THE JOURNEY CONTINUES IN THE MANGA
ADAPTATION OF THE HIT NOVEL SERIES
AVAILABLE
NOW
SPICE & WOLF
MATURE
Yen Press
Spice and Wolf © Isuna Hasekura/Keito Koume/ASCII MEDIA WORKS

THE INNOCENT

MADRONA

BY AVI ARAD & JUNICHI FUJISAKU
ART BY YASUNG KO

Lettering: Chris Counasse

THE INNOCENT © AVI ARAD • Production I.G © Ko Yasung/MAG Garden 2011. All rights reserved. First published in Japan in 2011 by MAG Garden Corporation. English translation rights arranged with MAG Garden Corporation through Tuttle-Mori Agency, Inc., Tokyo.

English translation © 2011 Hachette Book Group, Inc.

Yen Press
Hachette Book Group
237 Park Avenue, New York, NY 10017

www.HachetteBookGroup.com
www.YenPress.com

Yen Press is an imprint of Hachette Book Group, Inc. The Yen Press name and logo are trademarks of Hachette Book Group, Inc.

First Yen Press Edition: November 2011

ISBN: 978-0-316-20103-2

10 9 8 7 6 5 4 3

BVG

Printed in the United States of America

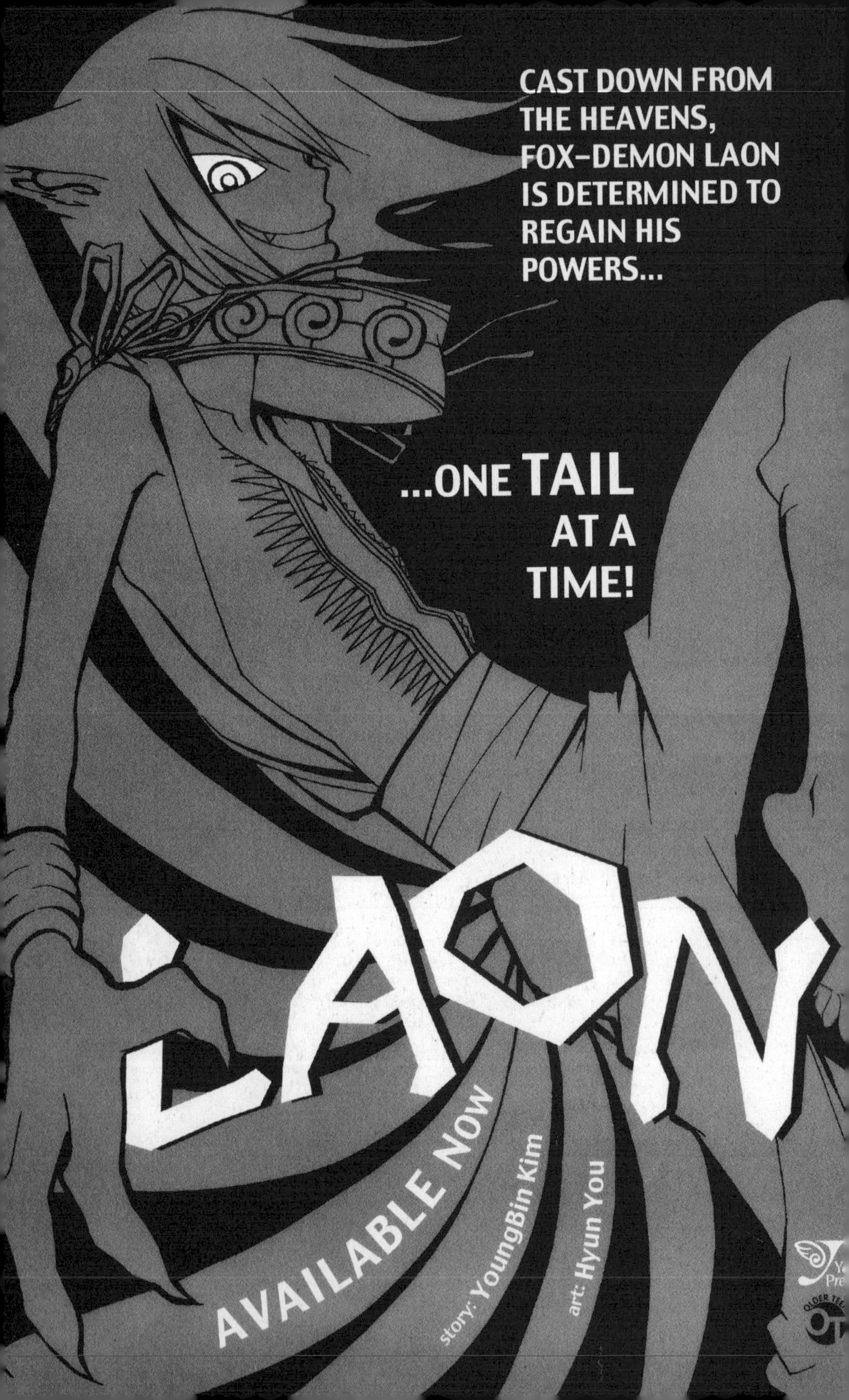
CAST DOWN FROM THE HEAVENS, FOX-DEMON LAON IS DETERMINED TO REGAIN HIS POWERS...
...ONE TAIL AT A TIME!
LAON
AVAILABLE NOW
story: YoungBin Kim
art: Hyun You

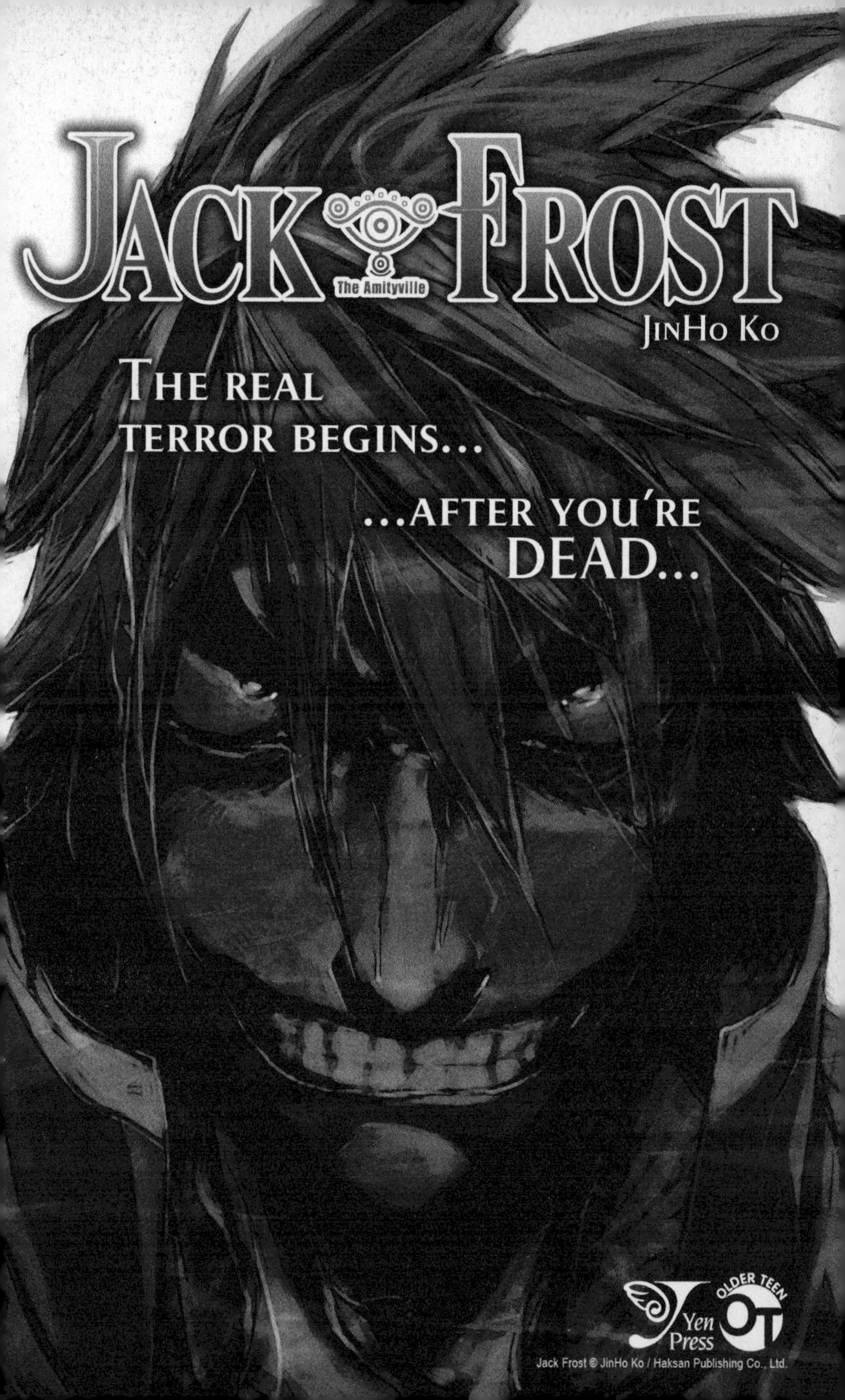
JACK FROST
The Amityville
JINHO KO
THE REAL TERROR BEGINS...
...AFTER YOU'RE DEAD...
Yen Press
OLDER TEEN
OT
Jack Frost © JinHo Ko / Haksan Publishing Co., Ltd.

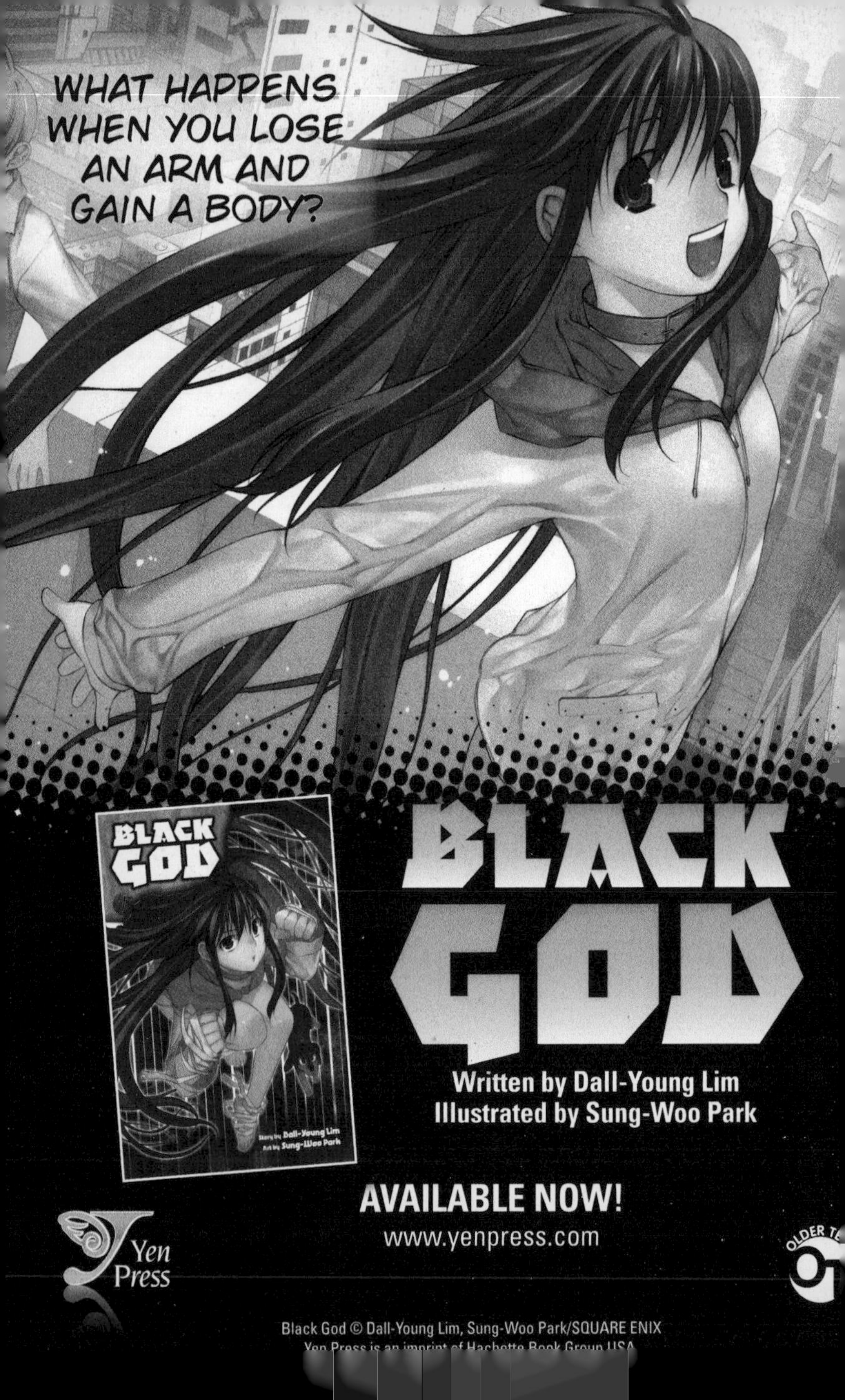
WHAT HAPPENS WHEN YOU LOSE AN ARM AND GAIN A BODY?
BLACK GOD
Story by Dall-Young Lim
Art by Sung-Woo Park
BLACK GOD
Written by Dall-Young Lim
Illustrated by Sung-Woo Park
AVAILABLE NOW!
www.yenpress.com
Yen Press
Black God © Dall-Young Lim, Sung-Woo Park/SQUARE ENIX